Clinical Epidemiology:

Principles, Methods, and Applications for Clinical Research

Diederick E. Grobbee, MD, PhD

Professor of Clinical Epidemiology
Julius Center for Health Sciences and Primary Care
University Medical Center Utrecht

Utrecht, Netherlands

Arno W. Hoes, MD, PhD

Professor of Clinical Epidemiology
Julius Center for Health Sciences and Primary Care
University Medical Center Utrecht

Utrecht, Netherlands

JONES AND BARTLETT PUBLISHERS

Sudbury, Massachusetts

BOSTON   TORONTO   LONDON   SINGAPORE

World Headquarters

Jones and Bartlett Publishers	Jones and Bartlett Publishers	Jones and Bartlett Publishers
40 Tall Pine Drive	Canada	International
Sudbury, MA 01776	6339 Ormindale Way	Barb House, Barb Mews
978-443-5000	Mississauga, Ontario L5V 1J2	London W6 7PA
info@jbpub.com	Canada	UK
www.jbpub.com		

Jones and Bartlett's books and products are available through most bookstores and online booksellers. To contact Jones and Bartlett Publishers directly, call 800-832-0034, fax 978-443-8000, or visit our website www.jbpub.com.

Substantial discounts on bulk quantities of Jones and Bartlett's publications are available to corporations, professional associations, and other qualified organizations. For details and specific discount information, contact the special sales department at Jones and Bartlett via the above contact information or send an email to specialsales@jbpub.com.

This publication is designed to provide accurate and authoritative information in regard to the Subject Matter covered. It is sold with the understanding that the publisher is not engaged in rendering legal, accounting, or other professional service. If legal advice or other expert assistance is required, the service of a competent professional person should be sought.

Production Credits

Publisher: Michael Brown
Production Director: Amy Rose
Associate Production Editor: Rachel Rossi
Associate Editor: Katey Birtcher
Marketing Manager: Sophie H. Fleck
Manufacturing and Inventory Control
   Supervisor: Amy Bacus

Composition: Publishers' Design and
   Production Services, Inc.
Cover Design: Timothy Dziewit
Printing and Binding: Malloy, Inc.
Cover Printing: Malloy, Inc.

Library of Congress Cataloging-in-Publication Data
Grobbee, D. E.
   Clinical epidemiology : principles, methods, and applications for clinical research / Diederick E. Grobbee, Arno W. Hoes.
     p. ; cm.
   Includes bibliographical references and index.
   ISBN-13: 978-0-7637-5315-3
   ISBN-10: 0-7637-5315-7
   1. Clinical epidemiology. I. Hoes, Arno W. II. Title.
  [DNLM: 1. Epidemiologic Methods. 2. Epidemiologic Factors. 3. Prognosis. WA 950 G873p 2008]
RA652.2.C55G76 2008
614.4—dc22

                                    2007050241

6048
Printed in the United States of America
12 11 10 09 08   10 9 8 7 6 5 4 3 2

Clinical Epidemiology

With contributions by:

Ale Algra, MD, PhD, Professor of Clinical Epidemiology
Huibert Burger, MD, PhD, Associate Professor of Clinical Epidemiology
Yolanda van der Graaf, MD, PhD, Professor of Clinical Epidemiology
Geert JMG. van der Heijden, PhD, Associate Professor of Clinical
    Epidemiology
Jacobus Lubsen, PhD, Professor of Clinical Epidemiology
Karel GM Moons, PhD, Professor of Clinical Epidemiology
Yvonne T. van der Schouw, PhD, Associate Professor of Epidemiology

To Sjoukje and Carin

Contents

PART 2 PRINCIPLES OF CLINICAL RESEARCH

12   Clinical Epidemiologic Data Analysis   325

Preface

In our current era of evidence-based medicine, with an abundance of published information and a clear need for relevant applied clinical research, clinical epidemiology is increasingly being recognized as an important tool in the critical appraisal of available evidence and the design of new studies.

This book is intended for those who are currently practicing medicine and related disciplines (such as pharmacy, health sciences, nursing sciences, veterinary medicine, and dentistry) as well as those involved in the design and conduct of applied clinical research. Apart from these "users" also "do-ers" of applied clinical research (notably undergraduate students and PhD fellows in medicine and related disciplines) will benefit from the information provided in this book. Clinical epidemiology instructors will find it a valuable resource for their classes.

The purpose of this book is to teach both the "users" and "do-ers" of quantitative clinical research. Principles and methods of clinical epidemiology are used to obtain quantitative evidence on diagnosis, etiology, and prognosis of disease and on the effects of interventions. The contents of this book reflect our teaching experience on the methodology of applied clinical teaching over the last 20 years. It was the ever-advancing development of clinical epidemiological methodology, the increasing discrepancies between our teaching material and existing textbooks of epidemiology, and the many requests from students and practicing physicians for a concise text reflecting our courses that fuelled our decision to prepare this novel textbook.

Throughout this book, we explore the challenges clinicians face in daily practice and the quantitative knowledge required to practice medicine. An important distinction is made between research directed at unraveling causality (notably etiologic research and studies addressing the effects of interventions) and descriptive research aimed at predicting the presence (diagnostic research) or consequences of disease (prognostic research).

To serve both readers who mainly use clinical research findings as well as (inexperienced or more advanced) clinical researchers, the book consists of three parts.

Part 1 (Chapter 1) is an overview of the interplay between relevant clinical knowledge and clinical epidemiology in daily practice. In addition, the principles and methods of clinical epidemiology as well as the four essential types of applied clinical research are introduced: diagnostic, etiologic, prognostic, and intervention research.

Part 2, Chapters 2 through 6, presents the principles of the four major types of clinical research in much more detail. Separate chapters are devoted to research assessing the main effects and adverse effects of interventions, including an introduction to the principles of clinical trials. These five chapters include many practical recommendations for those planning and conducting research in those particular areas.

Part 3, which encompasses Chapters 7 to 12, is directed toward those seeking more detailed information about specific tools applied in clinical epidemiology. These include common study designs (such as meta-analyses, case-control studies, and randomized trials) as well as elementary data-analytical issues.

Every section of the book includes worked-out examples from daily clinical practice and clinically relevant clinical research that can be used as exercises. In addition, an updated selection of exercises for each chapter, including the answers, is provided on the Web site of the Julius Center and the publishers (under Julius' clinical epidemiology/exercises) to facilitate the use of the book in both undergraduate and postgraduate teaching.

We hope that our book will contribute to a better understanding of the strengths of clinical epidemiology as well as help both users and researchers of quantitative clinical research in their endeavors to further improve daily clinical practice.

We realize that this first edition may include inconsistencies and mistakes. We welcome any suggestions from readers to improve its contents.

Foreword

Clinicians often think of epidemiology as something distinct from clinical research. As a consequence of this thinking, epidemiologic methods, disease causation, preventive medicine as well as strategic public health issues have been taught chiefly in epidemiology departments and at schools of public health. Many of these institutions, however, became too isolated from the practice of medicine and the conduct of clinical research. And both camps—epidemiologic research and clinical research—have suffered from this mutual isolation. Epidemiology would be fertilized by close interaction with clinical medicine while offering a powerful toolbox derived from advanced methodologic developments to clinical researchers. Epidemiologic principles and methods are not only integral to public health, but also highly relevant for clinical research. Still today, this fundamental fact is not adequately appreciated by many clinical investigators.

Could epidemiologic methods and clinical epidemiology indeed revolutionize clinical research? Would methodologic rigor, adequate sample size, and skilled statistical analyses allow more rapid progress and quicker implementation of important discoveries? This bold and perhaps naïve idea came to my mind some 25 years ago and my initial hunch that it may be true has grown ever since. Still a practicing surgeon at the time, my own research forced and encouraged some familiarity with the fundamental principles of epidemiology. And this familiarity truly changed the perspectives on my professional performance in the operating room, clinical ward, outpatient departments, emergency units, and in the classroom where I lectured for medical students.

Foremost, my slowly growing familiarity with epidemiologic methodology helped me understand the fundamental prerequisites for causal inference—after all, a successful treatment is little more than a cause of a good outcome. This insight made me increasingly uncertain about the real benefit of our therapeutic, chiefly surgical, interventions and the performance of our diagnostic technologies. This was a time when hip replacement, coronary by-pass surgery, breast conserving surgery, laparoscopic cholecystectomy, kidney transplantation, vascular reconstruction, and radical prostatectomy (just to mention a few examples) transformed our work in the operating room—often without the support or benefit of new technologies from randomized trials. At the same time, computerized tomography, ultrasound, PET scans, and, subsequently, magnetic resonance revolutionized our ability to visualize organs and assess bodily functions. Today, the flow of novel therapeutic and diagnostic techniques is even more intense.

As a practitioner, I navigated through these years with two competing feelings. One was a growing frustration that clinical methods were used and combined so haphazardly; that novel surgical procedures—unlike the strictly regulated approval of new drugs—could be introduced overnight, often with no strategy to quantify risks versus benefits. As a corollary, decisions influencing the life and health of our patients were based on little scientific evidence. But another feeling grew too; a fascination that epidemiologic theory and methodology were directly relevant to advancing the evidence base for clinical practice. After 17 years, I left the operating room peacefully, permanently, and with no subsequent regret to become a full-time epidemiologist.

Persuading clinicians that methods of extraordinary relevance for their research are readily available in the epidemiologic toolbox can be challenging. But trickier still is to provide a readable text that helps them see the light and the opportunities. It is in this context that *Clinical Epidemiology: Principles, Methods, and Applications for Clinical Research* becomes such a tremendously useful addition to the existing literature. I wish that this book had been available to me 25 years ago. I congratulate all those younger colleagues who now receive a firm and stable helping hand in their necessary endeavour to study a wide variety of clinical phenomena in human populations. And I hope that the book will be read also by the growing number of practitioners who need to understand the sophisticated methods used in cutting-edge clinical research.

Hans-Olov Adami
Boston, September 2007

Hans-Olov Adami, MD, PhD, is Professor of Epidemiology and Chairman of the Department of Epidemiology at the Harvard School of Public Health and Professor of Cancer Epidemiology in the Department of Medical Epidemiology and Biostatistics, at the Karolinska Institute, Stockholm, Sweden.

The Julius Center

The Julius Center for Health Sciences and Primary Care (http://www .juliuscenter.nl was established at the University Medical Center Utrecht in December 1996. The Julius Center was built upon previously existing small departments of epidemiology, public health, and clinical epidemiology, and was subsequently expanded with primary care.

The name of the Julius Center was chosen to create a logo for innovative health sciences rather than specifying the disciplines assembled in the center. Hendrik Willem Julius (1901–1971), pictured below, was a professor of health science at Utrecht University during the first half of the 20th century and an early advocate of the clinical trial. Julius never was affiliated with the center. We are honored to use his name for our center with the consent of his children and grandchildren.

Hendrik Willem Julius.

Since its start, the Julius Center has continuously grown in its main domains of research, education, and patient care. A few principles have guided the decisions that shaped the center. One is that epidemiology is a basic medical discipline. This is reflected in the research agenda of the center and the background of its staff, who comprise a fair number of physicians working in productive harmony with epidemiologists from many other biomedical backgrounds. A second principle is the view that clinical epidemiology flourishes best in close approximation and interaction with clinical medicine. Consequently, the center is located in a hospital environment and provides clinical care in primary health care centers within a large, newly-built area of the city of Utecht, while joined appointments of staff further support the continuous interaction with other clinical departments. Finally, a leading principle is that the quality of research by junior fellows as well as by experienced staff is determined by the level of understanding of the principles and methods of epidemiology. To achieve this goal, good education is essential.

When the center had just opened and was still small in size, we began with the development of a common theoretical basis through teaching each other, harmonizing, and updating our views along the way. This has formed the basis for the current epidemiologic curriculum in Utrecht, including the content of the international Master of Science in Epidemiology program offered at Utrecht University and of our teaching of clinical epidemiology to medical students, clinicians, and other health professionals in the Netherlands and abroad.

We believe that a common and consistent set of principles and methods are the strongest assets of epidemiology and the true value clinical epidemiology has to offer to today's applied clinical research.

About the Authors

Diederick E. Grobbee, MD, PhD (1957) was trained in medicine in Utrecht and, after a residency in internal medicine, obtained a PhD in epidemiology at Erasmus University in Rotterdam. His education was continued at McGill University in Montreal and as a visiting Associate Professor at Harvard University School of Public Health. He spent nearly a decade at Erasmus, where he headed the cardiovascular epidemiology group and was appointed Professor of Clinical Epidemiology. He subsequently moved to the University Medical Center Utrecht, to become Professor of Clinical Epidemiology and founder and Chairman of the Julius Center for Health Sciences and Primary Care. He is Program Director of the international MSc Epidemiology Program at Utrecht University and a board member of the Netherlands Institute for Health Sciences. He also is on the board of the Academic Alliance for Clinical Trials and is a board member of the Medical Advisory Council of the Royal Netherlands Academy for Arts and Sciences. He is Editor of the *European Journal of Epidemiology*. His teaching experience includes courses on clinical epidemiology and clinical research methods to various audiences in several countries.

Arno W. Hoes, MD, PhD (1958) studied medicine at the Catholic University Nijmegen. He obtained his PhD degree in clinical epidemiology at the Erasmus Medical Center in Rotterdam. He was further trained in clinical epidemiology at the London School of Hygiene and Tropical Medicine. In 1991, he was appointed Assistant Professor of Clinical Epidemiology and General Practice at both the Department of Epidemiology & Biostatistics and the Department of General Practice at the Erasmus Medical Center. At the latter department, he headed the research line, "Cardiovascular disease in primary care." In 1996, he moved to the Julius Center for Health Sciences and Primary Care of the University Medical Center in Utrecht, where he was appointed Professor of Clinical Epidemiology and Primary Care in 1998. He is currently Director of Research of the Julius Center. His teaching experience includes courses on study design, clinical epidemiology, diagnostic research, drug risk assessment, and cardiovascular disease. Since 1998, he has

Contributors

We thank the following colleagues and friends for their invaluable contributions and critical comments to several of the chapters of this book.

Ale Algra, MD, PhD, Professor of Clinical Epidemiology, the Julius Center for Health Sciences and Department of Neurology, University Medical Center Utrecht; and the Department of Clinical Epidemiology, Leiden University Medical Center, the Netherlands.

Ale Algra has extensive experience with the design, conduct, and analysis of randomized clinical trials in neurovascular disease. His experience and attention to detail shaped Chapter 10.

Huibert Burger, MD, PhD, Associate Professor of Clinical Epidemiology, Department of Clinical Epidemiology and Bioinformatics, University of Groningen Medical Center and the Julius Center for Health Sciences and Primary Care, University Medical Center Utrecht, the Netherlands.

Huibert Burger has a strong interest in the theoretical basis of prediction research. He contributed importantly to Chapter 4 on prognostic research.

Yolanda van der Graaf, MD, PhD, Professor of Clinical Epidemiology, the Julius Center for Health Sciences and Primary Care, and the Department of Radiology, University Medical Center Utrecht, the Netherlands.

Yolanda van de Graaf is one of the most experienced "hands on" clinical epidemiologists in our group and therefore the best equipped to address data analysis from a practical perspective, as is demonstrated by Chapter 12.

Geert JMG. van der Heijden, PhD, Associate Professor of Clinical Epidemiology, the Julius Center for Health Sciences and Primary Care, University Medical Center Utrecht, the Netherlands.

Geert van der Heijden is an evidence-based medicine addict and literature search expert. His knowledge is shared in Chapter 11 on meta-analysis.

Jacobus Lubsen, PhD, Professor of Clinical Epidemiology, Erasmus University Medical School, Rotterdam, the Netherlands.

Koos Lubsen is a longtime teacher and friend. Some of his provocative and lucid ideas can be found in Chapter 11.

Karel G.M. Moons, PhD, Professor of Clinical Epidemiology, the Julius Center for Health Sciences and Primary Care and Department of Anaesthesiology, University Medical Center Utrecht, the Netherlands.

Karel Moons is an expert on diagnostic studies, as he explores the conceptual and theoretical foundations utilizing his extensive practical experience. His views are expressed in Chapter 3 on diagnostic research and he has further contributed to Chapter 4 on prognostic research.

Yvonne T. van der Schouw, PhD, Associate Professor of Epidemiology, the Julius Center for Health Sciences and Primary Care, University Medical Center Utrecht, the Netherlands.

Yvonne van der Schouw has a strong track record in etiologic epidemiologic research. Her work includes cohort studies and randomized trials on the effects of various nutritional factors on health. She provided the examples in Chapter 2.

Acknowledgments

We are indebted to all current and former members of the scientific staff of the Julius Center for their crucial role in advancing the center's conceptual ideas of clinical epidemiology and the conduct of applied clinical research. The development of a joint teaching program shortly after the foundation of the Julius Center marked an important first step in the process that eventually resulted in this textbook. Many staff members contributed to specific sections of this book, and their expertise, devotion, and hard work are greatly appreciated.

We thank our former colleagues at the Department of Epidemiology & Biostatistics of Erasmus Medical Center Rotterdam for their role in the development of our epidemiological thinking and the stimulating discussions (even when we disagreed).

We thank the many students, PhD fellows, clinicians, and participants in our teaching programs in the Netherlands and abroad for their criticism, discussions, and wit that keeps encouraging us to further develop our understanding of clinical epidemiology and improve our teaching methods.

Our thinking about clinical epidemiology was influenced by many scientists. We would like to mention three in particular.

Hans A. Valkenburg laid the foundations for clinical epidemiology in the Netherlands by combining his clinical expertise and knowledge of epidemiology with his entrepreneurship in designing large-scale studies and laboratory facilities in close collaboration with clinical departments. We are proud that we were trained in clinical epidemiology at his Department in Rotterdam. His ideas still serve as a role model for the Julius Center and other clinical epidemiology departments in the Netherlands.

We were profoundly influenced by the wealth of ideas on clinical epidemiology of Olli S. Miettinen. Our many provocative discussions shared with him around the globe not only urged us to remain modest about our own contributions to the discipline, but strongly stimulated us to further explore the foundations of clinical epidemiology and their application in clinical research. We have no doubt that his reading of our texts will induce further stimulating interaction and future adaptations.

We are grateful to Albert Hofman for his friendship and support in a crucial phase of our scientific development. He is at least partly "guilty" in our choice to pursue a career in clinical epidemiology. His contagious enthusiasm about epidemiology and dedication to scientific excellence had a major impact on our work.

Without the relentless efforts of Monique den Hartog and Giene de Vries in the preparation of the manuscript, this book would never have been published. We truly thank them for their important secretarial contributions.

1

Introduction

Epidemiology is occurrence research [Miettinen, 1985]. The object of epidemiologic research is the occurrence of illness and its relation to determinants. Epidemiologic research deals with a wide variety of topics, such as: the causal role of measles virus infection in the development of inflammatory bowel disease in children; the added value of a novel B-type natriuretic peptide bedside test in patients presenting with symptoms suggestive of heart failure; the prognostic implications of the severity of bacterial meningitis on future school performance; and the effect of antibiotics in children with acute otitis media on the duration of complaints. What links all of these is the study and, more precisely, the quantification of the relationship of determinants (in these cases measles infection, the novel bedside test, severity of bacterial meningitis, and antibiotic therapy) with the occurrence of an illness (inflammatory bowel disease, heart failure, school performance, and duration of otitis media complaints). Central to epidemiologic studies in such diverse fields is the emphasis on occurrence relations as objects of research.

The origins of epidemiology lie in unraveling the causes of infectious disease epidemics and the emergence of public health as an empirical discipline. Every student of epidemiology will enjoy reading the pioneer works of John Snow on the mode of transmission of cholera in 19th century London, including the famous words: "In consequence of what I said, the handle of the pump was removed on the following day" [Snow, 1855]. Subsequently, the methods of epidemiology were successfully applied to identifying causes of chronic diseases, such as cardiovascular disease and cancer, and now encompass virtually all fields of medicine.

In recent decades, it has increasingly been acknowledged that the principles and methods of epidemiology may be fruitfully employed in applied clinical research. In parallel with a growing emphasis in medicine to use quantitative evidence to guide patient care and to judge its performance, epidemiology has become one of the fundamental disciplines for patient-oriented research and a cornerstone for evidence-based medicine. Clinical epidemiology deals with questions relevant to clinical practice: questions about diagnosis, causes, prognosis, and treatment of disease. To serve clinical practice best, research should be relevant, valid, and precise (Textbox 1.1). It must be valid (true and precise) because research results eventually will be applied with confidence in daily practice.

TEXTBOX 1.1 Valid and precise.

---

valid

Main Entry: val·id
Pronunciation: 'va-l&d
Function: *adjective*
Etymology: Middle French or Medieval Latin; Middle French *valide*, from Medieval Latin *validus*, from Latin, strong, potent, from *ValEre*

1 : having legal efficacy or force; *especially* : executed with the proper legal authority and formalities <a *valid* contract>

2a : well-grounded or justifiable : being at once relevant and meaningful <a *valid* theory> **b** : logically correct <a *valid* argument> <*valid* inference>

3 : appropriate to the end in view : effective <every craft has its own *valid* methods>

4 *of a taxon* : conforming to accepted principles of sound biological classification

precise

Main Entry: **pre·cise**
Pronunciation: pri-'sIs
Function: *adjective*
Etymology: Middle English, from Middle French *precis*, from Latin *praecisus*, past participate of *praecidere* to cut off, from *prae-* + *caedere* to cut

1 : exactly or sharply defined or stated

2 : minutely exact

3 : strictly conforming to a pattern, standard, or convention

4 : distinguished from every other <at just that *precise* moment>

Source: By permission. From the Merriam-Webster on-line dictionary, © 2007 by Merriam-Webster, Incorporated (*www.merriam-webster.com*)

Clinical Epidemiology

Clinical epidemiology is epidemiology [Grobbee & Miettinen, 1995]. Then why use the term? Clinical epidemiology is not a label to indicate a different discipline or refer to specific aspects of epidemiologic research, such as research on iatrogenic disease, but a statement that marks the application of epidemiologic methods to questions relevant to patient care. Well understood from the perspective of its history, practitioners of epidemiology predominantly have been found in public health or community medicine. Epidemiologic research results have unique value in shaping preventive medicine as well as the search for causes of infectious and chronic disease that affect large numbers in our societies. Yet, with the growing recognition of the importance of probabilistic inference in matters of diagnosis and treatment of individual patients, an obvious interest has grown in the approaches epidemiologic research has to offer in clinical medicine. Use of the term *clinical epidemiology* therefore refers to its relevance in "applied" clinical science; conversely it helps to remind us that the priority in our research agenda must be set with a keen appreciation of what is relevant for patient care. Clinical epidemiology provides a highly useful set of principles and methods for the design and conduct of quantitative clinical research.

Epidemiologic research has largely been devoted to etiologic research. Investigators have built careers and departments' reputations on epidemiologic research into the causes of chronic diseases, while for patient care the ability to establish an individual's diagnosis and prognosis is commonly held to be of greater importance. Still, the work of most MSc and PhD fellows in epidemiology, in particular those working outside of a medical environment, is concentrated on etiology. Perhaps they do not realize that this focus actually restricts the value of epidemiologic research for medical care. Clearly, causal knowledge is relevant, because it may help to prevent disease and find new treatments.

In clinical practice, however, an adequate diagnosis, prediction of the natural course of the illness, and the setting of appropriate indications and contraindications for action are major concerns. These are often established without knowledge of the causes of the illness. If there is a message in clinical epidemiology today that needs reinforcement, it is that more work is needed in diagnostic and prognostic research that, as will be explained later, is *descriptive* rather than *etiologic* (or causal).

Research Relevant to Patient Care

The motive in applied clinical research should be to obtain knowledge relevant to clinical practice. Consequently, understanding the challenges in clinical practice is essential for understanding the objectives of clinical research.

Consider a patient consulting a physician. Most often the reason for consultation is a complaint or symptom suggestive of some illness. For example, a 60-year-old male patient with problems with micturation is referred by his general practitioner to a urologist. For all subsequent action, the point of departure is the patient profile. This patient profile has two components: 1) the clinical profile comprising (among others) the patient's symptoms, signs, and results of diagnostic tests; and 2) the non-clinical profile that includes characteristics such as age, gender, and socioeconomic status. Of these two sets of facts, the clinical profile is temporary and relates to the illness while the non-clinical profile is in the absence of illness and thus relates directly to the bearer of the illness, the patient. Both sets are complementary. Starting from the patient profile, the physician faces a number of challenges. In temporal order these are: 1) interpretation of the clinical profile; 2) explanation of the illness; 3) prediction of course; 4) decision about treatment; and 5) execution of treatment.

The first challenge is to interpret the patient profile and establish a diagnosis. The question to be answered is: "What is the most likely illness, given this patient's profile?" In this process, the doctor identifies the presence of a particular illness in this patient. Commonly, at some point following the diagnosis, an explanation for the illness may be requested (the second challenge). However, while the etiologic question of why this illness has occurred in this patient at this time is obvious, an answer may be impossible to give and quite often is not even necessary for the patient to receive adequate care. For example, appendicitis may be effectively treated by surgery without any understanding of the reasons for its occurrence. Prediction of the course of disease (the third challenge) is usually a much more important task for the physician than a full understanding of its etiology. Certainly, the predicted course is of greatest importance to the patient.

Given the patient's illness, its possible etiology, and the clinical and non-clinical profiles of the patient, what will be the future course of the illness or its manifestations? The prognosis comprises both the simple prediction of the illness's course, given the diagnosis and other patient characteristics (i.e., the predicted course assuming no intervention takes place), as well as the presumed beneficial or adverse effects on that course by appropriate interventions. Note that this ideally includes a comprehensive prediction, given all legitimate clinical actions as well as interventions induced by the patient himself [Hilden & Habbema, 1987]. Clearly, in contemporary medicine the expected course of disease is likely to depend heavily on the availability and choice of treatment. Once this choice has been made (the fourth challenge), execution of treatment naturally follows (the fifth challenge).

A modern physician is a scientific physician. In our era of evidence-based medicine, a physician is taught to base his or her actions on scientific evidence and to develop a scientific attitude even in those (alas) frequent

FIGURE 1.1 Prognosis.

circumstances where data are lacking, incomplete, or may never become available with sufficient precision to guide individual patient care. The mission for clinical epidemiologic research is to add to the knowledge base from which other practitioners of medicine may draw. This mission inherently calls for a multidisciplinary approach with epidemiology providing a well-established complementary set of principles and methods to the general knowledge base and practical expertise. For a physician to meet the challenges of everyday patient care (Table 1.1), knowledge is essential: diagnostic knowledge for the first challenge, etiologic knowledge for the second, and prognostic knowledge (including knowledge about the effects of interventions) for the third. As in applied clinical research in general, the role of clinical epidemiology is to assist in providing scientifically valid and *quantitative* knowledge on diagnosis, etiology, and prognosis of illnesses, including the effects of interventions on their course. This inferential, probabilistic knowledge offers a rational basis for decision-making in patient care. Treatment decisions need quantitative knowledge about the prognosis considering various treatment options combined with an evaluation of the benefits and risks of these options for a particular type of patient. The practicing physician will need to combine this knowledge with experience, discussion with the patient, and skill to arrive at a balanced decision on the best treatment management. These decisions also may be formally addressed in algorithms that are the domain of clinical decision analysis. In clinical decision analyses, results from quantitative applied clinical research serve as the input with estimates of patient outcomes (utilities) and possibly costs of various possible management alternatives as the output. Execution of treatments (challenge 5) requires skill and falls beyond the scope of epidemiologic research.

When designing applied clinical research, the principal objective should be to provide knowledge that is applicable in the practice of medicine. To achieve this end, after the research question is formulated an answer should be given in a way that it is both valid and sufficiently precise. First comes validity, the extent to which a research result is true and free from bias. Valid research results must be sufficiently precise to allow adequate predictions for individual patients or groups of subjects. For example, knowing that the five-year mortality rate after a diagnosis of cancer is validly estimated at 50% is one thing, but when the precision of the estimate ranges between 5% and 80%, the utility of this knowledge is limited for patient care. The design of studies focused on diagnosis, etiology, prognosis, and treatment needs to meet these goals. General and specific design characteristics of clinical epidemiologic research will be discussed in some detail in the next section.

TABLE 1.1   Challenges of Daily Patient Care

Challenge	Question	Needs
Interpret the clinical profile: predict the presence of the illness	What illness best explains the symptoms and signs of the patient?	Diagnostic knowledge
Explanation of the illness	Why did this illness occur in this patient?	Etiologic knowledge
Predict the course of disease	1. What will the future bring for this patient, assuming no intervention takes place? 2. To what extent may the course of disease be affected by treatment?	Prognostic knowledge (including therapeutic knowledge)
Decision about medical action	Which treatment, if any, should be chosen for this particular patient?	Balancing benefits and risks of available options
Execution of medical action	Instigation of treatment.	Skills

Epidemiologic Study Design

Study design in clinical epidemiology has three components: *the theoretical design, the design of data collection, and the design of data analysis* (Textbox 1.2). For some reason, many discussions about study designs seem to concentrate largely on issues of data collection: "Are we going to do a cohort study or a case-control study." How the data will be analyzed is often more emphasized (though, generally to a lesser extent) than theoretical design, despite the latter's overriding importance.

Theoretical Design

The theoretical design of a study starts from a research question. Formulating the research question is of critical importance as it guides the theoretical design and assures that, eventually, the study produces an answer that fits the need of the investigator. Therefore, a research question should be a question and not expressed as a vague ambition. All too often, investigators set out to "examine the association between X and Y." This is anything but a research question and will lead anywhere except to an answer.

For starters, a research question should end with a question mark. An example of a useful research question is: Does five-day treatment with penicillin in children with acute otitis media reduce the duration of complaints? This research question combines three crucial elements: one or more *determinants* (in this case 5-day treatment with penicillin), an *outcome* (the duration of the complaints), and the *domain*. Domain refers to the population (or set of patients), in whom the results can be applied. The domain (in this case, children with acute otitis media) is more broad than the patient population included in the study (children enlisted from 25 primary care practices located in the central region of The Netherlands during the year 2000 who were diagnosed with acute otitis media). Similarly, the domain of the

TEXTBOX 1.2 Epidemiologic study design

- Theoretical design
  Design of the occurrence relation

- Design of data collection
  Design of the conceptual and operational collection of data to document the empirical occurrence relation in a study population

- Design of data analysis
  This includes a description of the data and quantitative estimates of associations

Source: Author.

famous British study in the 1940s addressing the causal role of cigarette smoking in lung cancer was *man*, and not restricted in place or time. The domain for a study is like a pharmaceutical package insert. It specifies the type of patients to whom the results can be applied.

The occurrence relation is central to the theoretical design of a clinical epidemiologic study. The *occurrence relation* is the object of research and relates one or multiple determinants to an outcome. In subsequent phases of the study, the "true" nature and strength of the occurrence relation is documented and quantitatively estimated using empirical data. Occurrence relations in diagnostic, etiologic, prognostic, and intervention research each have particular characteristics, but all have a major impact on the other two components of epidemiologic study design: design of data collection and design of data analysis. To facilitate the theoretical design of a study and determine the (elements of) occurrence relation, a distinction should be made between *descriptive* and *causal* research.

Causal Versus Descriptive Research

By definition, *causal* research aims at explaining a relationship in etiologic terms. It is used in typical etiologic research (such as studies on the causal association between cigarette smoking and lung cancer risk) and also studies that address questions of treatment efficacy and risk. The essence of causal research is that it aims to *explain* the occurrence of an illness. It asks the question, does this factor actually cause the illness? One could imagine the researcher acting as a judge in the courtroom deciding whether the determinants (factors in the case) are guilty of the crime (illness). This implies that the occurrence of the disease could not be explained by some other extraneous reason.

Extraneous determinants are factors that are not part of the object of research; they are outside of the occurrence relation, but may have to be considered in view of their validity. A more common term for an extraneous determinant is *confounder*. When extraneous determinants are not taken into account, the observed relationships between outcome and determinant may not reflect the true relations; there may be underlying associations between both the outcome and the determinant of interest as well as one or multiple extraneous determinants. The relationship can be said to be *confounded*. Consequently, the associations need to be present conditional on the confounding factors—the extraneous determinants—in order to be true. Confounding must be excluded to obtain a valid estimate of the causal relation between the determinant of interest and the outcome.

In *descriptive research*, the aim is to predict rather than explain; this includes diagnostic and prognostic research. In diagnostic research, the determinants typically include elements of the clinical profile, which are signs, symptoms, and test results, with the outcome being the diagnosis of the disease that fits the profile. In *prognostic research*, determinants similarly comprise the clinical profile, including any relevant diagnostic information, with the outcome being the prognosis, for example, expressed by survival, cure, or recurrence of disease.

An essential difference between causal and descriptive research is that in descriptive research no causal relationship between determinant and outcome is assumed. In diagnostic research, determinants that result from the disease are often used to predict its presence. For example, to establish a diagnosis of rheumatoid arthritis, the sedimentation rate may be useful but its elevation clearly results from the disease. Because causal explanation is not necessary, confounding plays no role in descriptive research. It is the rule rather than the exception that multiple determinants are considered at the same time in descriptive research. Yet, none of these determinants is extraneous. All determinant information is used to lead to the best prediction of diagnosis or prognosis.

Elements of the Occurrence Relation

The occurrence relation has a standard set of elements: the outcome, one or multiple determinants (D), and, although they may not always present, one or multiple extraneous factors (confounders or extraneous determinants; ED). The number of determinants and the need to include extraneous factors depends on the research question and whether the research is descriptive or causal. If causal, the relationship between a determinant and an outcome must be present conditional on the existence of extraneous determinants. That is, for the relationship to be truly causal, it needs to be present irrespective of the presence or absence of confounding variables. The relationship between outcome and determinants is quantified by some mathematical function (f). Mathematically, the occurrence relation can be summarized as follows:

Outcome = f *(D | ED)* for causal occurrence relations and
Outcome = f *(D1 − n)* for descriptive occurrence relations.

In the theoretical design, outcome and (extraneous) determinants are first defined conceptually. For example, to answer the question of whether depression is causally related to the occurrence of heart disease, the occurrence relation is defined as,

Heart disease = f (depression | ED)

where ED could include lifestyle factors such as smoking and alcohol but also treatments for depression that might lead to heart disease, such as tricyclic antidepressants.

To allow the collection of empirical data for the study, typically the conceptual definitions of outcome and determinants need to be operationalized to measurable variables. In this example, depression could be measured using the Zung depression scale and heart disease could be operationalized by recording admission to hospital with an acute myocardial infarction.

Often, this step leads to simplification or to measures that are not able to fully capture the conceptual definitions. For example, we may wish to measure quality of life but may need to settle for a crude approximation using a simple 36-item questionnaire. To appreciate the results of a study, it is important to realize that such compromises may have been made.

Design of Data Collection

Now that the overall architecture of the research building is in place, it is time to design how the data will be collected. Clinical epidemiologic research is empirical research, which means that the theoretical occurrence relationships are observed after analyzing empirical data collected from individuals. The true (scientific) nature of the occurrence relation is estimated from the observations. Consequently, an important aspect of the conduct of research is the collection of data that capture the occurrence relation.

There are several ways in which data for a particular study can be collected. The choice will be determined both by the need to obtain a valid estimate of the nature of the occurrence relation and by practical considerations. The former, for example, includes the need to collect full confounder data in causal research. The latter may include restrictions in time or funding that limit the number of options for collecting data. The need to find the truth, and thus the need to never compromise validity, is an essential starting point. Yet, for a given level of validity there may still be several options for data collections.

An inventory of ways to collect data in clinical epidemiologic research and their similarities and distinctions may be found in Chapter 7. In brief, the choices to be made for data collection include the time scale, the nature of the study population, and the option of conducting a study experimentally or non-experimentally. In a cross-sectional study, the follow-up time for a population is zero. But in a longitudinal study, the follow-up time is greater than zero. In a cohort study, a full population sample is studied (*census*). In a case-control study, only specific cases and a sample of controls are studied. In a randomized trial, subjects are experimentally exposed to a particular determinant, say a drug. In an observational cohort study, determinants are studied that are present without any experimental manipulation by the investigator. Aspects of the design of data collection will be discussed in the various chapters on diagnostic, prognostic, and etiologic research and are presented in more detail in the chapters on cohorts, case-control studies, and randomized trials.

Design of Data Analysis

The most difficult parts of designing clinical epidemiologic research are completed when the occurrence relation and the data collection have been designed. In the data analysis, the data of the study are summarized and the relationships between determinants and outcome quantified. Design of data analysis is important because it will determine the utility of the result, so it should maintain the relevance and validity achieved so far. However, in general there are only a few appropriate and feasible ways to analyze data of a given study. Ideally, the design of data analysis follows naturally from the research question, the form of the occurrence relation, and the type of data collected. Some details of the approaches to the design of data analysis can be found in the various chapters on diagnostic, prognostic, and etiologic research, and a summary is presented in Chapter 12.

Diagnostic, Etiologic, Prognostic, and Intervention Research

The major types of clinical epidemiologic research are introduced in Table 1.2 and their distinctions and shared aspects will be emphasized in the sections that follow.

TABLE 1.2 Major Types of Clinical Epidemiologic Research

Type of Research Question	Descriptive/ Causal	Aim (Clinical Challenge)	Relevance
Diagnostic research	Descriptive	To predict the probability of presence of target disease from clinical and non-clinical profile	Relevance for patient and physician to establish diagnosis and guide management
Etiologic research	Causal	To causally explain occurrence of target disease from determinant	Research relevance, may indicate means of prevention and causal intervention
Prognostic research	Descriptive	To predict the course of disease from clinical and non-clinical profile	Relevance for patient and physician to learn about the future and guide management
Intervention research	Causal and descriptive	1. To causally explain the course of disease as influenced by treatment 2. To predict the course of disease given treatment (options) and clinical and non-clinical profile	1. Relevance for research and drug development/ registration 2. Relevance for patient and physician to decide on optimal management

Diagnostic Research

Each day physicians are faced with multiple diagnostic challenges. For any patient presenting with complaints, the aim is to interpret the signs, symptoms, and results of (other) diagnostic tests so that a diagnosis can be established. This diagnostic process is complicated and involves multiple determinants incorporating the clinical profile as well as the non-clinical profile (e.g., age, sex, socioeconomic status). Although the physician often considers more than one diagnosis, the typical question to be answered in clinical practice is whether a certain patient profile is indicative of a particular illness (the outcome). As mentioned earlier, empirical evidence that can guide the clinician in choosing the most efficient diagnostic strategy in relevant patient domains is relatively rare. Clearly, more diagnostic research is needed. Diagnostic research typically aims to quantify the value of combinations of determinants in diagnosing a particular illness and includes studies assessing the value of novel diagnostics tests in addition to readily available tests (such as signs and symptoms).

Consider a 75-year-old man visiting his primary care physician because of increased dyspnea. The patient had a myocardial infarction seven years ago, and his frequent efforts to quit smoking were unsuccessful. Although in view of the impressive smoking history, his physician considers the possibility of chronic obstructive pulmonary disease, the most likely diagnosis appears to be heart failure. Recently, a rapid bedside test to determine the level of B-type natriuretic peptide (BNP), a marker known to be increased in most heart failure patients, has become available and the primary care physician wonders whether such a rapid BNP test would have diagnostic value in this patient's domain.

The research question addressing this issue can be phrased as follows:

What is the value of the novel rapid BNP test *in addition to* signs and symptoms when diagnosing heart failure in patients presenting with dyspnea in primary care?

The multiple determinants include the novel BNP test, the findings from history taking (including known comorbidity), and physical examination, which are available in daily practice anyway; the outcome is a diagnosis of heart failure. Again, the domain should not be too narrow, and could be defined as patients presenting to primary care with dyspnea or, alternatively, all patients presenting to primary care with symptoms suggestive of heart failure. The corresponding occurrence relation can be summarized as the *presence* of heart failure as a function of multiple determinants, including the novel BNP test:

Heart failure = f (BNP, age, sex, prior MI, symptoms, signs, ...)

Chapter 3 examines the specifics of diagnostic research.

Etiologic Research

Clinicians and epidemiologists alike tend to feel most familiar with etiologic research despite its limited direct relevance to patient care and its methodological complexities. As in all epidemiologic studies, starting from the research question, the first step is the design of the occurrence relation. For etiologic research, this includes a consideration of a determinant as well as one or multiple extraneous determinants.

Consider, for example, the causes of childhood inflammatory bowel disease (IBD), particularly to what extent a certain factor (e.g., a measles virus infection) may be responsible for its occurrence. The research question could be formulated as follows:

Does measles virus infection cause IBD in children?

Measles infection and IBD represent the determinant and outcome, respectively, and children are the domain. Suppose that a study is designed to answer this research question. The object of such a study would be an occurrence relation in which the *incidence* of IBD is related to the presence or absence of a preceding viral infection.

To estimate this relation validly, however, the description of the occurrence relation is not complete and should include one or multiple *extraneous determinants* (ED) of the occurrence of childhood inflammatory bowel disease. In this example, these could include nutritional status, socioeconomic factors, and so forth.

The occurrence relation can be depicted as:

IBD = f (measles infection | ED)

A more detailed discussion about etiologic research can be found in Chapter 2.

Prognostic Research

Prognostication forms an essential feature of daily clinical practice. The process of estimating an individual patient's prognosis is illustrated by the following question that is often asked by practicing physicians: "What will happen to this patient with this illness if I do not intervene?" In essence, prognostication implies predicting the future, a difficult task at best. As in the diagnostic process, estimating a patient's prognosis means taking into account multiple potential determinants, some of which pertain to the clinical profile (i.e., markers of the severity of the illness) and some of which refer to the non-clinical profile (i.e., age and sex). Ideally, prognostic evidence should help the clinician to adequately and efficiently predict a clinically relevant prognostic outcome in an *individual* patient. More *general* prognostic information, such as five-year survival of types of cancer and one-year recurrence rates in stroke patients is typically not sufficiently precise. Moreover, several prognostic outcome parameters can be of interest. Apart from survival or specific complications, quality of life indices can be extremely relevant.

Imagine a 10-year-old child with a recent episode of bacterial meningitis. The parents ask the clinical psychologists about the possible longer-term sequelae of their son's illness. They are particularly worried about their child's future school performance. To predict the child's school performance, in this example, five years' time, the psychologist will consider both non-clinical (such as age and previous school performance) and clinical parameters, notably indices of the severity of the meningitis. The clinical psychologist is uncertain which of these latter parameters best predicts future school performance.

An example of a research question of prognostic research addressing this topic is:

> Which combination of indices of disease severity (e.g., duration of symptoms prior to admission because of meningitis, leukocyte count in cerebral spinal fluid, dexamethasone use during admission) best predicts future school performance in children with a recent history of bacterial meningitis?

The determinants include parameters measured during the meningitis episode, the outcome is school performance measured after a certain period (e.g., 5 years) after the illness, and children with recent bacterial meningitis represent the domain.

The occurrence relation is:

> School performance = f (duration of symptoms, leukocyte count, pathogen involved, etc.)

Possibly, other non-clinical potential determinants should be considered in the occurrence relation, such as the child's age, previous school performance, and parents' education. Thus, the research question should be rephrased as: Which combination of parameters best predicts future school performance in children with recent bacterial meningitis?

Chapter 4 includes a thorough presentation of prognostic research.

Intervention Research

An *intervention* is any action taken in medicine to improve the prognosis of a patient. This can include treatment or advice as well as actions aimed at prevention. The most common form of intervention research in medicine is research on treatment effects. There are two reasons why research into the benefits and risks of interventions merits particular attention. One is that the design of intervention research generally requires the design of an occurrence relation that serves both the estimation of the prognostic implication of the intervention and a valid estimation of the causal role of the intervention in that prognosis. In other words, intervention research aims at both predicting prognosis and understanding its etiology (i.e., *etiognosis*).

From the perspective of the patient, the change in prognosis brought about by treatment is of greatest interest. However, from the perspective of, for example, the drug manufacturer or regulator, the question is whether it is the drug and nothing else that improved the prognosis. This questions the causality of the treatment effect. Consequently, the object, data collection, and analysis should comply with the specific requirements of both causal and descriptive research, although typically the requirements of being able to draw causal conclusions by, for example, excluding confounding factors, drive the design. A second reason is that intervention research, particularly its most appreciated form, the randomized trial, can serve as a role model for causal research at large [Miettinen, 1989].

One may question whether causal research that does not take prognostic implications into account has an eventual value in medical knowledge. In intervention studies, principles of both causal and descriptive or, according to Miettinen, "intervention-prognostic" research apply [Miettinen, 2004]. Because the design of data collection and data analysis of etiologic research calls for a strict control of confounding factors, the etiologic outlook of intervention research commonly dominates in intervention studies. However, the challenge for the investigator is not only to provide an answer on etiology but also produce a meaningful estimate of the effect. Thus, intervention research could be designated as etio-prognostic research.

Consider an 18-month-old toddler visiting a primary care physician because of acute otitis media. According to her mother, this is the second episode of otitis; the first episode occurred some nine months ago and lasted ten days. The mother is afraid for continued prolonged periods of complaints and asks for an antibiotic prescription. First, the clinician will estimate the prognosis of the child, taking into account the child's prior medical history, current clinical features (e.g., fever, uni/bilateral ear infection), and other prognostic markers such as age. Then the effects of antibiotic therapy on the prognosis will be estimated. To this end, the causal (i.e., true) effects of antibiotic therapy in young children should be known. The research question of an intervention study providing this evidence is: Does antibiotic therapy reduce the duration of complaints in young children with acute otitis media? Here, antibiotic therapy is the determinant and the number of days until resolution of symptoms is the outcome. The domain is young children (younger than 2 years) with acute otitis media. Although one could argue that the domain may be as large as all children with otitis, the prognosis in young children is considered to be relatively poor and the effects of antibiotics could be different in this subgroup of children. The occurrence relation can be summarized as:

Duration of complaints = f (antibiotic therapy | ED)

As will be explained in detail in Chapter 5, in a typical intervention study, randomization and blinding will minimize any influence of extraneous determinants (ED).

Comparison of Diagnostic and Prognostic Research

Diagnostic and prognostic research shares several characteristics. First and foremost, they are descriptive research [Moons & Grobbee, 2002a]. This has important implications for theoretical design, design of data collection, and design of analysis. As a prelude to a more comprehensive discussion of this research, which will be done in subsequent chapters, a few distinctive features should be mentioned. The occurrence relation in diagnostic and prognostic research is given by the *presence* or *future presence* (*i.e., incidence*) of the outcome in relation to and as a function of one or multiple determinants, respectively. It is exceedingly rare for both diagnostic and prognostic research questions to be restricted to single determinants. In medical practice, a diagnosis or prognosis is hardly ever based on a single indicator. Arguably, certain instances of screening may be exceptions, but more commonly, multiple non-clinical and clinical patient characteristics, including results from diagnostic testing, are used to decide upon the presence of the disease and its prognostic consequences. Unfortunately, one often finds studies addressing the diagnostic capacities of a single test [Moons et al., 1999]. The relevance of research on tests in isolation is markedly limited by the notion that, in the clinical application, it is the added or alternative value of a test that matters rather than its individual merit. For diagnostic or prognostic research to be relevant, all of the putative predictors that are available and considered in a clinical setting need to be included as determinants in the occurrence relation. It is important to realize that theoretically all these determinants have a similar importance. If they predict even in the presence of the other factors they are useful, but if they do not, they are not useful. There are no extraneous determinants (confounders). In other words, confounding is not an issue in descriptive research. Still, it may be relevant to address the value of a test conditional on other determinants. For example, the aim of the investigator may be to determine whether a specific new diagnostic tool has added value or if a less invasive procedure may replace a more invasive one and still maintain the same diagnostic capacity.

Diagnostic and prognostic research both aim for an optimal prediction. In many ways, a prognosis can be viewed as a diagnosis "yet to be made." Where in diagnostic research we attempt to predict the presence of a particular disease, in prognostic research, we attempt to predict the occurrence of a particular disease outcome in the future. The focus of descriptive research could be single or multiple determinants, with the latter being more common. When a prognostic or diagnostic study addresses multiple determinants, there is no inherent determinant hierarchy. The aim is often to reduce a range of available determinants to a subset with the same prognostic or diagnostic value as the full set, or to compare the predictive capacity of a set of determinants inclusive and exclusive of a determinant of particular interest. Inclusion of a larger or smaller number of determinants has no implications for validity as long as the study is large enough to obtain results with sufficient precision. Selection of determinants for inclusion, however, may affect the study's generalizability and thus the relevance of the research. Consider a hospital where magnetic resonance imaging (MRI) scanning is not routinely available in patients admitted to the ICU with head trauma. A study designed to determine which clinical and non-clinical factors may be useful in the diagnostic work-up or prognostication of head trauma patients, which does not include the results of MRI scanning, will provide results that are relevant to similar hospitals despite the potential utility of MRI findings when available.

In addition to shared aspects of the theoretical design of diagnostic and prognostic studies, they have similarities in the design of data collection. Collection of determinant information has a particular feature that discriminates diagnostic and prognostic research from etiologic and intervention research. Etiologic research data on the determinant and confounders must be collected in a strict protocol with a high precision to maximize the opportunity to obtain precise estimates of the true quantitative association with the outcome. Descriptive research data should be collected in agreement with the quality of data collection in practice. Suppose, for example, that particular diagnostic data in a given study are obtained by the most specialized and experienced diagnostician available to the researchers; the importance of the diagnostic indicator is likely to be overestimated relative to the eventual application where, in a routine care setting, average doctors with average capabilities will establish a diagnosis. Note that this makes the use of data collected as part of randomized trials of questionable value in the valid estimation of prognostic factors but those collected in routine care are generally highly suitable for use in descriptive research.

The general approach in prognostic and diagnostic research is to first design the occurrence relation in theoretical and operational terms. Then the data collection is designed, including a choice from different options according to which a study population can be chosen and data collected. The prevalence of the outcome (in diagnostic research) or the incidence of the outcome (in prognostic research) is recorded in a group of patients reflecting the type of patients for which the results of the research are intended to be used. Finally, in the data analysis, the nature and strength of the occurrence relation are calculated by estimating the (regression) coefficients and narrowing the set of determinants to the most informative subset of minimal size.

There are also differences between diagnostic and prognostic research. Diagnostic research is cross-sectional and prognostic research longitudinal.

In a diagnostic study, the outcome is the frequency of the presence of the diagnosis of interest. Prognostic research has no simple single outcome. Rather, the outcome of relevance to the patient is the expected future course of the disease expressed by the expected utility or non-utility. The full prognosis is determined by the utilities of the various possible outcomes together with their respective probabilities. These possible outcomes also include all those resulting from treatment options. Consequently, a prognosis is generally not the probability of a single outcome. However, if only for reasons of feasibility, prognostic research is commonly restricted to a particular outcome.

Comparison of Etiologic and Prognostic Research

In etiologic and prognostic research, the temporal dimension of the occurrence relation is longitudinal. Prognostic and etiologic occurrence relations address the future occurrence of a particular clinical course in relationship to either prognostic or etiologic factors in patients with a certain disease. However, when the incidence of a state or event is studied as a function of an etiologic factor, the assumed relationship of this determinant to the outcome is causative by definition, while in case of prognosis, the prognostic determinants may or may not be causally related to the outcome. For example, Oostenbrink and coworkers [2002a] determined predictors of the occurrence of permanent neurological sequelae after childhood bacterial meningitis. Among the predictors was low body temperature at admission to the hospital. The low temperature is likely to be a marker of severity of the disease rather than causally related to the outcome. Research into the effects of interventions is both etiologic research and prognostic research. In randomized clinical trials—the gold standard for assessment of treatment effects—a prognostic factor (the intervention) is manipulated with the aim of quantifying the causal impact of this factor and estimating its contribution to a change in prognosis.

Because causal explanation has a distinctly different role in etiologic and prognostic research (being absent in the latter), confounding is a critically important concept in etiologic studies and a non-issue in prognostic research as long as causal explanation of effects of intervention is not part of the objective. Etiologic studies typically focus on a single determinant. While in a single study more than one possible causal determinant may be of interest, for each causal determinant there is in principle a unique occurrence relation with a tailored set of confounders to be considered. In the simplest data analytic approach, the disease outcome is assessed in groups of subjects classified in an index category where the determinant is present and a reference category where the determinant is absent. Then the interest is in comparative rates of occurrence of disease across the determinant categories. To infer the true causal difference in the rate of occurrence of a disease, this should be estimated while making distributions of extraneous determinants the same across the determinant categories, that is, estimate the parameters conditional on confounders.

In contrast to etiologic studies, where a single determinant is the determinant of interest, prognostic studies emphasize single or multiple determinants. This does not imply that the investigator may not have a specific interest in a particular determinant. Yet, "science" demands arriving at the best prediction possible and if the investigators' favorite prognostic indicator drops out along the way, so be it. In case the focus is more on a specific new or otherwise interesting putative prognostic determinant, given a set of a priori defined codeterminants, the question will be what the predictive capacity is of the selected prognostic indicator beyond these codeterminants, for example, the added predictive information. A prognostic study by Ingenito et al. [1998] prespecified an added value of measuring preoperative inspiratory lung resistance in predicting the outcome of lung-volume reduction surgery. Here, the occurrence relation was the incidence of increase in forced expiratory volume in one second (FEV_1) after surgery as a function of preoperative inspiratory resistance, conditional on other clinical and non-clinical patient characteristics. Note that it is added value that is at issue, not conditionality on confounding. The range of clinical and non-clinical characteristics included in the study was determined by what was commonly available in that particular clinical setting and therefore relevant in prediction. None of these determinants was extraneous; potentially they all could contribute and no extraneous determinant could be "forgotten" without incurring the risk of producing an invalid result, as may happen in causal research.

In case of the absence of preference for a particular prognostic indicator, the task entailed in the analysis of prognostic studies is to obtain the maximal predictive capacity of a minimal number of predictors without any inherent hierarchy. For example, to assess the risk of death in patients with burn injuries, a group of U.S. investigators had a simple qualitative concern: to reduce a set of potential prognostic codeterminants to a subset with information about prognosis similar to the initial full set. The occurrence relation of this study was the incidence of mortality as a function of clinical and non-clinical characteristics. There were no extraneous determinants [Ryan et al., 1998].

Moving From Research to Practice: Relevance and Generalizability

Similar to other research, the motive for applied clinical studies is to learn about an object. Eventually, knowledge produced by the research needs to be incorporated into a knowledge base that guides daily medical care. During the design and conduct of research, it is important to keep this aim in mind and be aware of the effects that choices in the design of the study may have on the applicability and implementation of the results. In the critical theoretical, initial phase of study design, the occurrence relation is laid out with all of its elements. Following the theoretical design, a plan is made of how to obtain and summarize knowledge on the nature and strength of the occurrence relation from available or induced experience, such as from empirical data collected in groups of subjects. Here, many decisions need to be taken that are separate from the actual way the data are collected. To be able to move from theoretical design to data collection, the occurrence relation needs to be rephrased in both theoretical and operational terms. This will not only point the way to measurement techniques in data collection but also indicate compromises that need to be made to match the ideal format of information on outcome and determinants to what can practically be achieved. For example, suppose we wish to precisely quantify the relationship between presence of heart failure and subsequent loss of patient autonomy and quality of life. In the data collection, we may then have to settle for dyspnea to classify heart failure and the Euroqol questionnaire to assess quality of life [Rasanen et al., 2006]. This need not be a problem, but it is important that these choices are made explicit and recognized in the interpretation of the research. Both the measure of the outcome and the determinant are mere proxies for what we really aim to evaluate. In applied clinical research, it is commonly important to stay close to what matters to patients when deciding upon measures of outcome of diseases. This is not necessarily intuitive to all clinical investigators.

Investigators frequently rely most on what can be quantified in solid measures rather than on what has the biggest impact for a patient. We reviewed studies on new positive inotropic drugs in heart failure [Feenstra et al., 1999]. The profound impacts that congestive heart failure has on life expectancy and quality of life have been a continuous stimulus for the development of new drugs to treat this condition. Despite favorable effects on (aspects of) quality of life in short-term studies, several new agents have been shown to reduce survival rates in mortality trials. However, patients with severe congestive heart failure may experience such incapacitating symptoms that the question should be raised as to whether an improvement in quality of life makes the increased risk of mortality associated with these new agents acceptable. Drugs that improve quality of life at the expense of an increased risk of mortality may be valuable in the treatment of patients with severe congestive heart failure. However, this is only the case if the probability of improvement in quality of life and prolongation of life expectancy for those using the drug exceeds the probability of improvement in quality of life and prolongation of life expectancy for those not using the drug. Unfortunately, most clinical trials in which both mortality and quality of life are evaluated fail to provide information on this composite probability. In clinical research, there is a justified growing emphasis on measures of disease that matter to patients, the importance of which was underlined by the *outcomes movement* and summarized in a seminal article in the *New England Journal of Medicine* [Elwood, 1988].

Questions that trigger applied clinical research result from problems and lack of knowledge perceived in patient care. Certain questions are relevant for particular groups of patients and not to others. Consequently, research findings may be relevant to smaller or larger groups of patients. The essence of scientific research, in contrast to other forms of systematic gathering of data, is that its results can be generalized. The type of knowledge provided by clinical epidemiologic research is inferential, probabilistic knowledge. Scientific knowledge contrasts with factual knowledge because it is not time- and place-specific. It is true for any patient or group of patients as long as the findings, on which the knowledge is based, permit scientific generalization to those patients. The patient is a special case of a category of patients to whom the occurrence relation applies. In the initial theoretical phase of study design, a careful appreciation of the type of patients for which the research needs to be relevant is important. As outlined earlier, the (theoretical) population of patients to which the findings apply is called the *domain* of the study. As stated earlier, the domain description can be viewed as a pharmaceutical package insert of a study ("please use for this type of patient"). When choosing a population for empirical data collection (i.e., the study population), the domain should be kept in mind.

Members of the study population should represent the (virtual) population of the domain. Apart from criteria for selecting a study population that follow from the chosen domain, such as the severity of disease or a certain indication for diagnostic work-up, other restrictions may be necessary for recruiting participants in a study that result from logistic or other circumstances. Many of these additional restrictions, such as the need to live close to the research institution and availability of time for additional diagnostic assessments, will not have an impact on the eventual applicability of the results and therefore will not limit the domain. It is important to appreciate which characteristics of a study population are determined with a view to the intended domain and as such form part of the design, and which characteristics result from reasons beyond the theoretical design. With a view to the study domain, those characteristics of the study population need particular considerations that bear on the generalizability of the empirical relation (Textbox 1.3). The *generalizability* of research results, sometimes referred to as the *external validity*, is the extent to which knowledge obtained in a particular type of patient may be applied to another larger, theoretical, abstract group of patients. Suppose that a study is conducted to determine the value of a certain novel type of surgery in patients with a particular gastrointestinal disease. The results of the study could be that recovery in operated patients of type T is more common than in non-operated ones, conditional on all extraneous determinants (confounders) of

TEXTBOX 1.3 Quotation about generalization

The essence of knowledge is generalization. That fire can be produced by rubbing wood a certain way is a knowledge derived from individual experiences; the statement means that rubbing wood in this way will always produce fire. The art of discovery is therefore the art of generalization. What is irrelevant, such as the particular shape or size of the piece of wood used is to be excluded from the generalization: what is relevant, for example, the dryness of the wood, is to be included in it. The meaning of the term relevant can thus be defined: that is relevant which must be mentioned for the generalization to be valid. The separation of relevant from irrelevant factors is the beginning of knowledge.

Source: Reichenbach H in: The rise of scientific philosophy. New York: Harper and Row. 1965 (Quoted in Rothman, Modern Epidemiology, 1986).

recovery. The conclusion is that operation enhances recovery in patients of type T, without reference to time or place. The results are generalized from the group of patients in which the empirical data were collected to a larger group of theoretical patients representing the domain of the research.

Generalizability is not an objective process that can easily be framed in statistical terms. Moving from time- and place-specific findings to scientific knowledge requires judgement about the potential of other characteristics inherent to the research setting and study population to modify the nature and strength of the relation between determinant(s) and outcomes as estimated in the study. A discussion of the concept of modification is in Chapter 2.

Appreciation of generalizability is essential for scientific inference. Defining the domain of a study as part of the occurrence relation is important because the domain of a relation provides the basis for generalization. As a rule, the utility of research is greater if the domain of the research findings, to which to generalize the estimated relations between outcome and determinants, is broader. Consequently, while the design of the occurrence relation needs to be precise and comprehensive, the domain is generally implicitly or explicitly kept broad. In diagnostic research, the domain is defined by the loosely defined patient profile representing those subjects for whom a particular diagnostic question is relevant. In etiologic research, the domain is formed by people at risk for the illness at issue and with variability of the causal factor at issue. For example, the domain for research on the etiologic role of smoking in lung cancer is all human beings with lungs and the possibility to smoke. In prognostic research, again, the domain is defined by the patient profile of those whom prognostic statements based on the determinants included in the research are considered. In research into treatment effects, the domain is those who may need the treatment. Where most elements of scientific research require maximal specificity, the domain, in general, is loosely defined. Apart from smaller or larger restrictions in the empirical data of a study, either by design or by circumstances, differences will persist among those using the results of research with respect to their willingness to generalize to larger groups. For example, in the absence of results from randomized trials specifically demonstrating the clinical benefits of use of statins in women with elevated cholesterol levels, some people did not accept an indication for use of these drugs in women despite ample evidence of reductions of risk in men with similar risk profiles.

2

Etiologic Research

A 57-year-old female had a heart attack. She never had any symptoms of vascular disease before, is not obese, is a non-smoker, and has normal blood pressure and lipid levels. However, several of her family members had a myocardial infarction at a relatively young age. At the time of the myocardial infarction, she was quickly transported to the hospital and had immediate thrombolysis. The attending cardiologist subsequently put her on a regimen of aspirin and an angiotensin-converting enzyme (ACE) inhibitor.

She visits you to ask what she could do to prevent a future cardiac event. Is there an explanation for her disease? Might it be genetic? Is there anything she should change in her lifestyle? You promise her to have a look at the literature and soon you come across an intriguing report by Sullivan [1981] suggesting that one explanation for women being protected from heart disease before menopause is that they have monthly periods. In some women, the loss of blood would compensate for excessive iron storage. Excessive iron storage could make the heart more vulnerable for ischemia or promote atherosclerosis. Another recent paper by Roest et al. [1999] shows that a relatively common heterozygous form of the gene also coding for hemochromatosis may lead to subclinical cardiac tissue iron accumulation and thereby increase the risk of cardiac events. Apart from a genetic tendency to accumulate iron, it also has been suggested that excess iron storage may result from an inappropriately high intake of iron through the diet. This raises the question whether a high dietary iron intake may be involved in cardiac risk in otherwise low risk individuals.

Etiologic Research in Epidemiology

The origins of today's clinical epidemiology can be found in early research on the causes of common diseases in the population. Initially, the focus was on communicable diseases with classic discoveries like the one by John Snow, who unmasked the Broad Street pump as a source of a cholera epidemic in London even before the notion of germs as a cause of infectious diseases became firmly established (Figure 2.1). Gradually, the domain has broadened with virtually all chronic and acute diseases now being addressed by epidemiologic research. Although there seems to be a common belief that epidemiologic studies alone cannot clarify causal associations, the generally accepted relationships between smoking and lung cancer and the occurrence of vaginal cancer in daughters of diethylstilbestrol (DES) users provide compelling examples to the contrary.

This chapter discusses the principles and methods of etiologic epidemiologic research in a clinical setting and is exemplified by a clinical epidemiologic study on the causal role of excessive iron storage on coronary heart disease risk in women (Textbox 2.1). This cohort study evaluated a large group of women for a baseline of iron metabolism values and other relevant factors who subsequently were followed over time, with the occurrence of myocardial infarction and other manifestations of cardiovascular disease

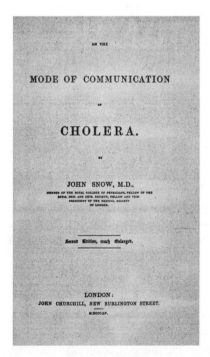

FIGURE 2.1 Cover of John Snow's report, *Mode of Communication: Cholera*, published in 1855 by John Churchill, London. Snow's observations on the method of transfer of this disease virtually ended a London cholera epidemic and laid the foundation for the new science of clinical epidemiology.

TEXTBOX 2.1 Dietary haem iron and coronary heart disease in women

DAPHNE L. VAN DER A   JOANNES J.M. MARX
PETRA H.M. PEETERS   YVONNE T. VAN DER SCHOUW
DIEDERICK E. GROBBEE

AIMS: A role for iron in the risk of ischaemic heart disease has been supported by *in vitro* and *in vivo* studies. We investigated whether dietary haem iron intake is associated with coronary heart disease (CHD) risk in a large population-based cohort of middle-aged women.

METHODS AND RESULTS: We used data of 16, 136 women aged 49–70 years at recruitment between 1993 and 1997. Follow-up was complete until 1 January 2000 and 252 newly diagnosed CHD cases were documented. Cox proportional hazards analysis was used to estimate hazard ratios of CHD for quartiles of haem iron intake, adjusted for cardiovascular and nutritional risk factors. We stratified by the presence of additional cardiovascular risk factors, menstrual periods, and antioxidant intake to investigate the possibility of effect modification. High dietary haem iron intake was associated with a 65% increase in CHD risk [hazard ratio (HR) = 1.65; 95% confidence interval (CI): 1.07–2.53], after adjustment for cardiovascular and nutritional risk factors. This risk was not modified by additional risk factors, menstruation, or antioxidant intake.

CONCLUSION: The results indicate that middle-aged women with a relatively high haem iron intake have an increased risk of CHD.

Source: Van der A, DL, Peeters PHM, Grobbee DE, Marx JJM, Van der Schouw Y. European Heart Journal 2005;26:257–262.

being recorded. As the baseline assessments included measurements of dietary intake, the data allowed a relationship between varying levels of dietary iron intake with the probability of future cardiovascular events to be established.

Theoretical Design

Etiologic epidemiologic research is research into the causes of a health outcome. Its aim is to demonstrate or exclude the relationship between a potential cause and the occurrence of a disease or other health outcome. To achieve this goal, alternative explanations for an apparent link between determinant and outcome need to be excluded in the research. These alternative explanations are offered by relationships due to extraneous determinants (confounders). The form of the etiologic occurrence relation, the object of research, is therefore "outcome as a function of determinant conditional on confounders." The domain, that is, the type of subjects for whom the relation is relevant, is defined by all those capable of having the outcome and are at risk of being exposed to the determinant. So the domain for a study on the role of boxing in causing memory deficits is all those human beings possibly engaged in boxing, which is essentially everyone. The domain for the study in Textbox 2.1 on risks of coronary disease by excessive iron intake is all women and possibly all men, too. The perspective of whether men should be a subset in the domain rests on the degree to which the investigator believes that a risk associated with high iron exposure is something particular to women or is a general feature of Homo sapiens.

Typically, etiologic research focuses on a single determinant at a time. In the example in Textbox 2.1, the emphasis was on haem iron intake operationalized by estimating intake from a food frequency questionnaire. All variables potentially related to both the risk of coronary disease and the levels of iron intake were treated as possible confounders; an elaborate discussion on the definition of confounders is given later in this chapter. In this study on iron intake and heart disease risk, the age at intake, total energy intake, body mass index (BMI), smoking, physical activity, hypertension, diabetes, hypercholesterolemia, energy-adjusted intakes of saturated fat and carbohydrates, fiber, alcohol, β-carotene, vitamin E, and vitamin C intake were considered potential confounders, but when each was taken into account, none changed the risk estimate materially.

In another study addressing the importance of lifestyle in the occurrence of breast cancer, a particular research question might focus on the putative causal role of a high alcohol intake in the occurrence of breast cancer. The occurrence relation would then be *breast cancer as a function of alcohol use conditional on confounders*. The domain would be all women. Among the confounders, smoking would most likely be important. In a second analysis of the same study, the question could be on the causal role of smoking in breast cancer. Now smoking would be the (single) determinant and alcohol presumably among the confounders. The importance of making clear distinctions between determinants and confounders in a given analysis for a given research question is outlined below. Disregarding confounders or having incomplete or suboptimal confounder information may lead to results that are not true and thus invalid. The overriding importance of the need to exclude confounding makes etiologic epidemiologic research particularly difficult.

Courtroom Perspective

If you are doing etiologic research, consider yourself to be a lawyer in a courtroom. You are the prosecutor and your task is to show beyond reasonable doubt that the defendant and not someone else is to blame for the criminal act. Etiologic research is about accusation. As an investigator (author of the study), you must convince the jury (your peers and readers) that the determinant is causally involved in the occurrence of the disease. It is common for an initial report on a causal factor in disease to be superseded by newer research contradicting the initial finding because of evidence on confounders. One report in 1981 [*MacMahon et al.*] suggested a strong relation between coffee use and pancreatic cancer. Since then, however, most studies could not confirm a substantial association, and the overall evidence suggests that coffee consumption is not related to pancreatic cancer risk.

Confounding

Assessment of confounding by detecting the presence of possible extraneous determinants is critical to obtain valid results in etiologic studies. A first step is to clearly decide which determinant is the assumed causal factor of interest. Commonly, diseases are caused by multiple factors that act in concert or separately. In subsequent studies, multiple possible causative agents may be addressed consecutively. At each instant, however, there is typically one determinant of primary etiologic interest while other determinants of the outcome are extraneous to that particular occurrence relation. Extraneous determinants, or confounders, can be very specific to a particular determinant-outcome relation. Potential confounders may or may not distort the relationship between the determinant of interest and the outcome in the data, depending on the presence or absence of associations between these variables.

Frequently, assessment of confounding is proposed by simply determining the links of possible extraneous determinants with both the outcome and the causal determinant of interest. The prevailing view is that, "if a factor X is related to both the determinant and outcome in an occurrence relation, then X is a confounder." Clearly, if a confounder is not related to both outcome and determinant, confounding will not result. However, when a perceived extraneous determinant is simultaneously associated with the outcome and determinant, this does not invariably imply confounding. An example is when the variable is somewhere in the causal pathway and thus *not* extraneous.

For a third variable to act as a confounder in etiologic research, it should be 1) related to the occurrence of the outcome and thus be a determinant of the outcome by itself, 2) associated with the exposure determinant of interest, and 3) extraneous to the occurrence relation. By extraneous, we mean that this variable is *not* an inevitable part of the causal relationship or causal chain between the determinant of interest and the outcome variable (e.g., because it is part of the causal pathway; see below). The terms *confounders* and *extraneous determinants* can be used interchangeably, but extraneous determinant indicates more clearly the type of determinant.

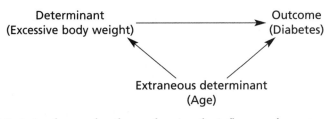

FIGURE 2.2 A simple causal pathway showing the influence of an extraneous determinant on the determinant and outcome.

Assume that you are interested in the (causal) relationship of body weight to the occurrence of diabetes mellitus (Figure 2.2). In a study designed to shed light on the causal role of obesity in diabetes, age is extraneous to the occurrence relation. Because age is known to be related to both body weight and the occurrence of diabetes (note the two arrows), any estimate of a causal effect of excessive body weight in the occurrence of diabetes is likely to be distorted by the effect of age. To validly estimate the true effect of obesity, differences in distributions of age across groups of patients with different body weights should be taken into account either in the design of the data collection or data analysis. To return to the courtroom analogy, you should not blame body weight for the occurrence of diabetes when in fact age is guilty. Extraneous to the occurrence relation also means that the third variable should not be part of the causal chain. If it is part of the causal chain, the variable is an *intermediate factor* rather than an extraneous variable. Such an intermediate factor may induce changes in other factors, which then serve to change the outcome.

An example of the intermediate factor situation is given by the role of high density lipoprotein (HDL) cholesterol levels in the presumed cardioprotective effects of moderate alcohol use. Alcohol use may increase serum HDL cholesterol, which has anti-atherogenic and cardioprotective properties. In a study of the link between alcohol and heart disease, when adjustments are made for differences in serum HDL cholesterol levels between those who do or do not drink alcoholic beverages, an underestimation of the true cardioprotective effect of alcohol will result. Adjustments for *intermediate* factors are inappropriate, because the variable is in the causal chain between the determinant and the outcome and overadjustment will result. "In the causal chain" often implies that the causal determinant influences a certain variable that follows the determinant and forms a true intermediate between determinant and outcome.

Alcohol consumption → HDL cholesterol ↑ → heart disease

Alternatively, a variable could be a *precursor* of the causal determinant of interest and, thus, also part of the causal chain (although not an intermediate in the strict sense) and *not* extraneous to the occurrence relation. For example, when studying the occurrence of heart disease as a function of HDL cholesterol levels conditional of confounders, alcohol intake should *not* be treated as an *extraneous* determinant, in view of the causal pathway depicted in the above equation. Increases in alcohol intake may induce ("precuse") increases in HDL cholesterol.

Note that the relationships between the intermediate factor, the determinant of interest, and the outcome need not necessarily be directly causal. For example, in many circumstances social and economic factors are considered as possible confounders of associations between putative causes of disease and disease outcome. However, social and economic status commonly act as indicators of one or multiple (even unknown) causal factors, such as diet or health care access, rather than being directly causally implicated.

A classical example of a variable that is *not* a confounder although it is (non-causally) associated with both the causal determinant under study and the outcome, is possession of a lighter or matches in the study of smoking as a cause of lung cancer. Clearly, possession of a lighter is related to both the determinant (cigarette smoking) and the outcome (i.e., those carrying a lighter are more likely to develop lung cancer, although, obviously, the matches will not cause the cancer). Consequently, the two arrows do exist. The third prerequisite to be a confounder is not met, however, because carrying a lighter is *not* extraneous to the occurrence relation. Possession of the lighter is a (non-causal) intermediate factor in the causal relationship between cigarette smoking and lung cancer, but not a confounder (see equation below). Consequently, adjustment for carrying a lighter is inappropriate and would artificially dilute the existing association between smoking cigarettes and lung cancer.

Cigarette smoking → carrying a lighter → lung cancer

A study on the risk of congenital malformations as a causal consequence of using certain anti-epileptic drugs may serve as another example of the role of confounding. Specific anti-epileptic drugs are not selected by chance by treating physicians. They tend to be given for certain indications that are related to the type of epilepsy of the mother and her age of onset. These maternal characteristics may themselves constitute risk factors for congenital malformations irrespective of drug use and therefore act as confounders. Consequently, these characteristics are related to both the potentially causal determinant (a specific anti-epileptic drug, say phenobarbital) and the outcome (Figure 2.3), and are possible confounders because they are also extraneous to the occurrence relation under study (and not an intermediate factor).

In this example, the simple ("crude") increased risk for non-spinal malformations in offspring of women using phenobarbital (relative risk 2.0; 95% confidence interval [CI] 1.7–7.1) disappears once maternal characteristics were adjusted for in the analyses (adjusted relative risk 1.2; 95%. CI 0.5–2.1).

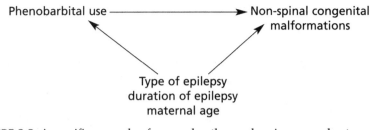

FIGURE 2.3 A specific example of a causal pathway showing several extraneous determinants.

A major problem in the assessment and handling of confounding in etiologic research is the need for knowledge, or lack thereof, about extraneous determinants either conceptually or with regard to their availability in the data. When confounding is suspected and information on putative confounding factors is available in the data, correlation analysis may disclose potential underlying confounding associations. Table 2.1 shows the results from a correlation of several variables in data from a cohort. To determine the (causal) impact of increases of body mass index on blood pressure level, age (as it is significantly correlated with these two variables) acts as a confounder. Heart rate also is related to blood pressure and body mass index but is judged to be an intermediate factor. Number of cigarettes per day is not related to blood pressure or body mass index and is not a confounder.

In this example, systolic blood pressure increased 2 mm Hg per one unit BMI without an adjustment for age ($P < 0.001$), and 1.2 mm Hg per unit with an adjustment for age ($P < 0.001$; results are from linear regression analysis). As expected, the magnitude of the relationship between blood pressure and BMI became smaller when age was taken into account.

More difficult than assessing correlations in the data is to achieve the necessary comprehensive inventory of possible extraneous determinants in the design phase of a study. This requires a good understanding of the nature of the clinical problem and the likely mechanisms that operate.

TABLE 2.1   Correlation of Variables from a Cohort Study

	Systolic BP (mm Hg)	Heart Rate (bmp)	Cigarettes (n)	Age (years)	BMI (K/m²)
Systolic BP	1.0000				
Heart Rate	0.1427*	1.0000			
Cigarettes	−0.0122	0.1349*	1.0000		
Age	0.2879*	−0.0090	−0.1102*	1.0000	
BMI	0.2529*	0.0892*	−0.0411	0.1065*	1.0000

Data are from 1,265 individuals. Pairwise correlations are between blood pressure, heart rate, cigarette smoking, age, and body mass index.

* $P < 0.05$.

Potential confounders need to be identified up front, because when neglected and otherwise missing in the total data collected, it may be impossible to resolve when the data are analyzed. Eventually, it is the investigator's task to completely remove confounding before arriving at any conclusions regarding causality. As an investigator, you can be assured that following the publication in which you, for example, blame sodium intake of causing cardiovascular events, other researchers ("lawyers in the same court room") will challenge such a supposition because of the potential for confounding.

The ongoing debate on the possible increased risk of myocardial infarction in subjects with a high coffee intake may serve as an example. In the mid 1970s, reports were published suggesting that coffee users were at a twofold increased risk of myocardial infarction compared to non-coffee users. The increased risk remained after adjustment for possible confounding factors. Hennekens and coworkers [1976] published a case-control study in which they compared the effects of adjustment for a limited set of extraneous determinants; these included restricted adjustment as in other published reports at the time and adjustment for a more extensive set of possible confounders that included several dietary variables. Cases were male patients who had a fatal myocardial infarction, and controls were sampled from neighbors who remained free from coronary heart disease during the same time period. Information on coffee use and a range of confounders was obtained by interviewing the wives of the myocardial infarction victims and their neighbors (controls). First, an analysis was performed that replicated previous reports with adjustment for a limited set of ten confounders. In this analysis, the relative risk of myocardial infarction for coffee users compared to those who did not drink coffee was 1.8 (95% CI 1.2–2.5). However, when nine additional confounders were taken into account in the analyses, the relative risk was reduced to 1.1 (95% CI 1.6), which showed a non-significant 10% rather than an 80% increased risk. Apparently, in previous work the "adjusted" association was still suffering from "residual" confounding. Subsequent studies with larger numbers of patients and even more extensive adjustment for potential confounders have further reduced the likelihood of a clinically meaningful increased risk of heart disease due to drinking coffee [Grobbee et al., 1990]. A possible exception is the use of so called "boiled" coffee, in the past quite normal in Scandinavia, which has been shown to raise cholesterol and thus may increase the risk of atherosclerosis [Bak & Grobbee, 1989].

One way to invalidate findings in etiologic research is to fail to consider relevant extraneous factors, and an alternative way to produce invalid results is to measure such confounding factors poorly. Adjustment is incomplete when confounders are not taken into account in the data analyses, but the adjustment for confounders in the analysis may be similarly inadequate if the measurement of confounders is not sufficiently comprehensive and precise.

Example: Estrogen and Bone Density

Let us consider a study that assessed whether postmenopausal circulating estrogen levels determine actual bone density [Van Berkum et al., unpublished data]. To this goal, subjects were recruited from a large population study in which plasma estrogen levels were known for all participants. Two groups of participants were selected, one group of women with low circulating estrone levels and one group with high circulating estrone (one of the three estrogen hormones) levels. These two groups were matched for age, age at menopause, and body height. This means that for each woman in the low estrone group, a women in the high estrone group was selected who had a comparable age, age at menopause, and height. When baseline characteristics were compared, the matching variables were expectedly similarly distributed within the two groups. However, body weight and BMI appeared significantly lower in the low estrone group. Consequently, in a simple correlation matrix, obesity would be disclosed as determinant of bone mass as well as being related to estrogen level. Does this make obesity a confounder? The answer to whether obesity must be considered as a confounder has a major impact on the results and inferences from the study.

When adjustments are made in the analyses for differences between the two estrone groups in the BMI, the results look materially different compared to the crude unadjusted analysis (Figure 2.4).

After an adjustment for BMI, none of the initial differences in bone density between low- and high-estrone women remains. However, the question arises as to whether this adjustment is appropriate. Rather, you could argue that differences in circulating estrone levels between women largely reflect differences in body fat, which is the prime site for estrogen production through conversion of androgens in postmenopausal women. While BMI is correlated to both the determinant and the outcome, it does not qualify as an extraneous determinant because it is not extraneous to the occurrence relation of interest. In contrast, the likely mechanism for increased bone density in post-menopause is:

Obesity → higher estrogen production → higher bone density

Obesity precedes higher estrogen production and thus is in the causal chain relating estrogen to bone density. The example illustrates the notion that classification of a factor related to both outcome and determinant as a confounder assumes this factor to be extraneous. Rather than being extraneous, a certain factor may lead to a changed physiology that in turn affects the determinant under study and subsequently the outcome (Figure 2.5).

An important message from this and the alcohol → HDL cholesterol → heart disease example is that judgment of the potential for confounding requires a perspective (knowledge) on possible etiologic mechanisms

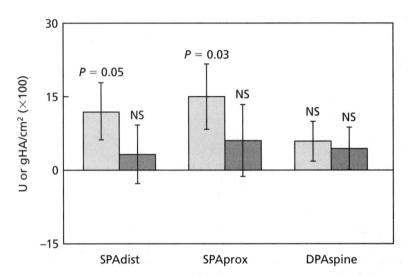

FIGURE 2.4 Do postmenopausal circulating estrogen levels affect bone density? Differences in bone density between high and low estrone groups, with and without adjustment for differences in BMI are shown above. Measurements were made using dual-photon absorptiometry of the spine (DPAspine) and single-photon absorptiometry of the distal and proximal forearm (SPAdist and SPA prox, respectively). Gray bars = crude differences between groups; Black bars ("NS") = differences after adjustment.

involved. This may well create a "Catch 22" situation in which an absence of etiologic insight creates confounding that in turn invalidates subsequent observations. Frequently in etiologic epidemiologic research, initial observations subsequently must be corrected because of expanding knowledge and adjustment for newly recognized confounders [Taubes, 1995]. While assessment of correlations in the data may be useful to detect possibilities for confounding, statistical software is not sufficiently sophisticated to determine the actual confounder. It remains the responsibility of the investigator to exclude confounding in the design and analysis of a study. To decide upon the presence of confounding with confidence, insight into mechanisms involved is required. If a particular determinant that is not the putative causal determinant of interest but is a precursor or intermediary in a causal chain, there is no confounding and making an adjustment in the analysis will lead to over-adjustment. This generally results in an underestimation of the true association between the determinant and the outcome.

Handling of Confounding

Once confounding is suspected, there are several approaches to remove confounding from the observed association. As indicated above, confound-

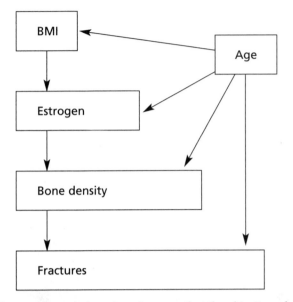

FIGURE 2.5 Determining confounders. Suppose that the objective of your study is to determine the causal role of variation in circulating estrogen levels in the occurrence of bone fractures. You gather a cohort of women and establish a baseline BMI, estrogen levels, and bone density for each. They are followed up for ten years, as you record the occurrence of fractures (outcome) as a function of circulating estrogen levels (determinant), conditional on confounders. Because of the etiologic nature of your research, confounding factors need to be excluded. Age is related with risk of fractures as well as with estrogen levels (and is not in the causal chain) and thus is a confounder. While BMI and bone density both are related to the outcome, they are in the causal chain (fat tissue is a source of estrogen production and bone density is increased by higher circulating estrogen levels). BMI is a precursor and bone density is an intermediate of the association. Consequently, they are not confounding the relationship and their effects should not be removed from the association by adjustments.

ing may occur when a variable is associated with both the determinant of interest and the outcome, and is not part of the causal chain. *Being associated with* implies that the confounder is related to the outcome and that the distribution of the confounder varies across levels of the determinant. To remove confounding requires that the distribution of the confounder is made the same across levels of the determinant. When distributions of the confounder are (made) the same across levels of the determinant, and the determinant outcome relation is still present, we conclude that the relationship is present but conditional on the confounder.

For example, suppose that age is thought to be a confounder of the relationship between gender and stroke risk, implying that age distributions for men and women are different. In order to remove the confounding effect of age, age distributions need to be made similar for men and women. This can be done in a number of ways. First, confounding may be removed by restriction. If only men and women within a small age range are included in the study, the distribution of age across gender is the same and age will not be a confounder. Similarly, men and women may be matched for age. This means that, although the distributions may be wide, they are the same (mean, median, standard deviation) for men and women. Another approach is to analyze the association between gender and stroke risk in separate strata, each of which cover a small age range. Next, the estimates for the strata are pooled using some procedure that weights the information by stratum, such as the Mantel-Haenzel procedure. Finally, essentially the same can be achieved in a multivariate (regression) analysis where age is added to the multivariate model next to the determinant (male/female) and possibly other confounders. In all of these approaches, the presence and strength of the relationship between determinant and outcome are estimated conditional on the confounder(s).

Causality

Etiologic research aims to find causal associations. A determinant is believed to be causally related to an outcome if the association remains when confounding is excluded. Other requirements apply, however, to be confident that the association is indeed causal and to exclude both residual confounding by some unidentified factors and the mere play of chance.

Many criteria have been proposed to make a causal association more probable. These include: a large number of independent studies with consistent results; a temporal relationship where the cause precedes the outcome; a strong association; a dose-response relationship; and biological plausibility. These criteria stem from the work of Hill [1965] and others, but each of the criteria has been challenged and none provides definitive proof. Even a temporal relationship in which the determinant follows the outcome does not rule out the possibility that in other circumstances the determinant could lead to the outcome.

Probably the most limiting factor to disclose causal relationships in epidemiologic studies is the general focus on single determinant outcome relations. Very few diseases are caused by a single factor. For example, many people are exposed to methicillin-resistant *Staphylococcus aureus*. Some bacteria will be colonized and still fewer people will suffer from serious infection. It is likely that genotype modifies the risk of colonization after exposure. The interplay between different factors, possibly through different mechanisms, is the rule rather than the exception in the etiology of disease. Yet other factors, such as the quality of the immune response, will modify the risk of serious infection. The genetic disorder phenylketonuria (PKU) convincingly shows the interaction of genes and environment to cause a disease commonly thought to be purely genetic. Dietary exposure to a particular amino acid gives rise to mental retardation in children with mutations in the *phenylalanine hydroxylase gene* on chromosome 12q23.2 encoding the L-phenylalanine hydroxylase enzyme. The disease is known as phenylketonuria (PKU). Because exposure to both factors is necessary for PKU to occur, infants with the genetic defect are put on a lifelong restricted diet to prevent the development of the disease. Rothman and Greenland [2005] have made important contributions to our understanding of multicausality in epidemiologic research. A full discussion goes beyond the scope of this book. The central principle is that a disease can be caused by more than one causal mechanism, and every causal mechanism involves the joint action of a multitude of component causes (Figure 2.6). As a consequence, particular causal determinants of disease may be neither necessary nor sufficient to produce disease. Nevertheless, a cause need not be necessary or sufficient for its removal to be useful in prevention. For example, alcohol use when driving is neither necessary nor sufficient to lead to car accidents. Yet, prevention of drunk driving will decrease a fair number of casualties. That the cause is not necessary implies that some disease may still occur after the cause is blocked, but a component cause will nevertheless be a necessary cause for some of the cases that occur. When the strength of a causal effect of a certain determinant depends on (or is modified by) the presence or absence of another factor, there is causal, or biologic, interaction or modification. Although modification of a causal association may be very relevant, it may best be viewed as *secondary* to the main determinant-outcome relationship; it adds *detail* to it, albeit sometimes extremely important detail.

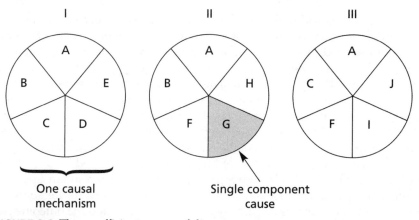

FIGURE 2.6 Three sufficient causes of disease.

Source: Rothman KJ, Greenland S. Causation and causal inference in epidemiology. *Am J Public Health.* 2005;95 Suppl 1:S144–150. Used with permission.

Modification and Interaction

There is a fair degree of confusion about the terms *modification, effect modification,* and *interaction,* their role in epidemiologic research and the importance of interaction between two or more determinants in research of disease mechanisms.

We consider *modification* to be present when the measure of association between a given determinant and outcome is not constant across another subject characteristic [Miettinen, 1985]. Then, that characteristic acts as the *modifier* of the determinant-outcome relationship. In the literature, such a modifier is often referred to as an *effect modifier* because it changes the effect a determinant has on a certain outcome. We prefer the term *modifier,* because the term *effect modifier* implies a causal mechanism underlying the modification. In fact, modification is often studied *without the aim to explain* the mechanism underlying the modification. We propose the term *descriptive* modification in those instances and the term *causal* modification when the objective is indeed to explain the observed modification of the determinant-outcome association (see below).

In statistics, the term *interaction* is merely used to indicate departure from the form of the chosen statistical model. For example, if a multiplicative model explains the data better than a linear model, this is interpreted as the presence of interaction without further causal or other explanation or inference. In epidemiology, the terms interaction and modification are used rather loosely and interchangeably.

Descriptive Modification

We propose to restrict the term *descriptive modification* (or descriptive interaction) to the analysis of the extent to which the strength of a (causal *or* noncausal) determinant-outcome association varies across another factor without the need to explain the nature of that modification. The extent to which the effectiveness of vaccination varies across age groups may serve as an example [Hak et al., 2005]. The only intention here is to determine whether it should be recommended to target the intervention at particular age groups from the perspective of cost effectiveness. There is no need to understand the modification in causal terms. The causal association addressed here concentrates on the effect of the intervention (i.e., influenza vaccination) on the outcome (e.g., survival) only. Modification is examined to learn about differential effects of vaccination across relevant population subgroups such as defined by age. The assessment of modification by age adds detail to the research (on the causal association between vaccination and the outcome parameter) with a view to the practical application of the result.

Descriptive modification may easily occur due to differences in prevalence of the disease across populations or population subgroups. For example, the effectiveness of screening for HIV will be modified by the proportions of hetero- and homosexual individuals in the populations because this will reflect different prevalence rates of the disease. In other words, while the fraction of cases detected will be the same (90%), the absolute number of HIV-infected subjects detected will be modified by the prevalence of homosexual subjects in the population studies. The latter example illustrates that modification may occur both on a relative scale (as in modification by age of the effect of influenza vaccination on survival) and on an absolute scale (the absolute number of newly detected HIV-infected individuals), further exemplifying the complexity of the issue.

Descriptive modification can be equally addressed in etiologic and descriptive studies. An example in descriptive studies is when the question asked whether signs and symptoms of heart failure have another diagnostic value in patients who suffer from chronic lung disease than in patients without this concomitant disease [Rutten et al., 2005a].

Causal Modification

The interest in the *causal modification*, or causal interaction, of a determinant-disease association is of an entirely different nature. Garcia-Closas et al.'s study on the extent to which the presence of a particular genotype increases the risk of bladder cancer resulting from cigarette smoking is an example. Here, two causal mechanisms were addressed. Primarily, the causal association between cigarette smoking and bladder cancer occurrence was assessed but secondly, the authors examined the possible increased sensitivity to cigarette smoke in the presence of the genotype. Garcia-Closas and coworkers [2005] found that persons who were current smokers or had smoked cigarettes in the past had a higher risk of developing bladder cancer. However, the relative risk related to smoking was 2.9-fold increased in those who had the NAT2 slow acetylator genotype and 5.1-fold increased among those with the intermediate or rapid acetylator genotype. In researching the benefits and risks of treatment, etiologic as well as descriptive modifications are often, albeit sometimes implicitly, addressed when subgroups show a higher or lower response to the intervention.

When to Address Modification

Whether modification is examined for a particular occurrence relation depends on the interest and objectives of the investigator. When the appropriate determinant, outcome, and all confounders are considered, the result is valid plus and minus a chance variation, whether or not modifiers are studied. As mentioned above, modifiers add detail that can be either causal or descriptive. For any given determinant-outcome relation, there is an infinite number of potential modifiers. If modification is to be studied, modifiers need to be selected, preferably *a priori*, based on clinical relevance and, in case of causal modification, plausibility. If many potential modifiers are examined without clear *a priori* views on their relevance or plausibility, there are likely to be several false-positive associations. Frequently, investigators are disappointed in their initial negative (overall) findings and start looking next for modifiers. Effectively, they are looking for subgroups of the population characterized by the presence of a modifier in which the determinant-outcome association may still be found. This typically means a search for descriptive modification in the absence of a real view on causal modification. In such cases, causal interpretation is risky. For example, surprisingly, an association is present in women but not in men. What does that mean? If no clear explanation can be given and no previous data have suggested similar gender-specific effects, the result should be considered with great caution when explained in causal terms. Even when the aim is to search for clinically relevant subgroups where the association between the determinant and outcome may be stronger without any causal inference of such modification (i.e., the influenza example), *a priori* determination of a limited number of modifiers is crucial to preclude false-positive identification of modifiers.

A bizarre example of modification detected by unplanned extensive analyses of the data has been reported for the second International Study of Infarct Survival (ISIS) trial (Textbox 2.2). The ISIS trial examined the benefits and risks of intravenous streptokinase, oral aspirin, both, or neither among 17,187 cases of suspected acute myocardial infarction [ISIS-2, 1988]. All ISIS patients had their date of birth entered as an important "identifier." While the overall benefit for aspirin was highly convincing, the subgroup of patients with the astrological star signs Gemini and Libra showed a 9% increased mortality risk for aspirin. Astrological sign actually modified the effect of aspirin! Confounding was unlikely to produce this result because the trial was large and patients were randomized to treatment. Given the number of subgroup analyses in this trial, the finding is most likely the result of chance. Perhaps even more important, the finding is theoretically highly implausible.

The presence or absence of modification—be it descriptive or causal—has a bearing on the domain and the generalizability of research findings. Modifiers point to subdomains, which implies that generalizing results from a study should be different for populations with or without the (particular level of the) modifier. Conversely, when the domain is chosen for a certain occurrence relation and results from a study performed in a subpopulation of that domain are generalized to populations reflecting that domain, the assumption is that the study population does not differ from the domain with regard to determinant-outcome association. Frequently, this is

TEXTBOX 2.2 Astrological daily prediction taking the ISIS trial findings on aspirin into account.

> A loan will be easy to obtain tomorrow but you must have a list of items you own so that you will have something to show as collateral. This loan could be to improve the home or to purchase a car. Things are happening and your career, or path depends upon your own ambition and drive, as well as your ability to be patient and bide your time. You are able to use good common sense to guide you and you can feel the trends and make the right moves. The time is coming soon to take action and get ahead. You may contemplate a career move and next week is a most positive one as you make yourself known. You are advised to use no aspirin.

Source: Author.

assumed rather than studied and therefore views between investigators may vary. For example, in the early days of statin trials for the treatment of elevated serum cholesterol to reduce the risk of cardiovascular disease, the results were largely obtained for men only. As cholesterol is a risk factor for heart disease in men as well as in women, does it follow that women will benefit from statins to the same extent as men? Some investigators argued that there are no reasons to suspect that statins do not work in women. They implicitly assumed that gender is no causal modifier of the relation between statins, cholesterol reduction, and reduction of heart disease risk. Others were hesitant because they did not believe that the effects are similar; they required the formal assessment of the modification, by conducting separate trials in women. Currently, it is well established that statins reduce the risk of heart disease in men as well as women with elevated cholesterol levels. With the results from expanded studies in this trial, it has been well established that the benefits of blood pressure reduction are not causally modified by age. This means that across a wide range of ages, the rate of cardiovascular disease is reduced by 20% to 25% if hypertensive patients are treated with antihypertensive agents. However, there is a descriptive modification, in this case on an absolute scale. Because background rates of cardiovascular disease vary markedly between those below and above age 60 years, the rate difference resulting from treatment is much higher in older patients compared to younger patients (Table 2.2).

TABLE 2.2 A Meta-Analysis of 24 Blood Pressure Trials Involving 68,099 Randomized Patients[1]

Age	Treated Rate/ 1000/Year	Control Rate/ 1000/Year	Rate Ratio	Rate Difference/ 1000/Year
>60	26.0	34.8	0.75	8.8
<60	8.8	11.2	0.79	2.4

"Rate" means rate of cardiovascular disease.
[1]Unpublished results.

Measurement of Modification

Modification is conceptually straightforward. Suppose we study the risk of gastric bleeding for those using aspirin therapy by comparing bleeding rates across users and non-users of aspirin, with adjustments for extraneous determinants related to both aspirin use and the baseline (= before use) risk of bleeding (such as age, comorbidity, and the severity of the disease for which the aspirin was prescribed). If an overall increased risk of bleeding caused by aspirin use is established, a next concern may be to determine which patients treated with high dose aspirin are at a particularly high risk. Certain patients on the same dose of aspirin may be more likely to experience gastric bleeding than others. For example, concurrent use of corticosteroids might enhance the bleeding risk. In other words, steroid use modifies the risk of high dose aspirin as it makes the risk even higher. In this occurrence relation, corticosteroids are (causal) modifiers of the risk of bleeding associated with high dose aspirin use. The modifier changes the measure of association between determinant and outcome. The estimate of the measure of effect depends on the value of the modifier. In this example, suppose that the overall relative risk of bleeding for those taking high dose aspirin compared to low dose aspirin was two; for those taking a corticosteroid that relative risk became four. The modification becomes visible when the association of interest is compared across strata of the modifier.

In etiologic research, analysis of modifiers may help the investigator to understand the complexity of multicausality and causally explain why a particular disease may be more common in certain individuals despite an apparent similar exposure to a determinant. After the unconfounded (raw) measurement of an overall association between a determinant and an outcome, putative modification may be estimated by comparing the measure of association across categories of the modifier. Causal modification also can be studied experimentally. Activated factor VII (FVIIa) is a very potent coagulant and may be a key determinant of the outcome of a cardiovascular event. FVIIa increases in response to dietary fat intake. Mennen and coworkers [1999] studied whether the response of FVIIa to fat intake is modified by the genetic R353Q polymorphism. A fat-rich test breakfast and a control meal was given to 35 women carrying the *Q* allele and 56 women with the *RR* genotype. At 8 AM (after an overnight fast), the first blood sample was taken and within 30 minutes the subjects ate their breakfasts. Additional blood samples were taken at 1 and 3 PM. The mean absolute response of FVIIa was 37.0 U/L in the group with the *RR* genotype and 16.1 U/L (*P* < 0.001) in those carrying the *Q* allele (Figure 2.7).

Good examples of causal modification can be found in genetic epidemiology. Arguably, pharmacogenetics is all about causal modification. The typical research question in pharmacogenetics is whether a certain genotype modifies the response of individuals to a particular drug. A classical example of pharmacogenetic modification is the observation that certain patients show a prolonged respiratory muscular paralysis after succinylcholine (a muscle relaxant) during surgery [Kalow & Staron, 1957]. Subsequently, the genetic bases of the effect was discovered from a mutation that resulted in impaired metabolism by serum cholinesterase in some individuals. Pharmacogenetics also offers ample demonstration of the problem of false positives when large numbers of genetic modifiers are studied.

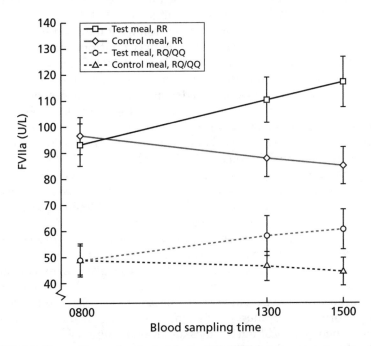

FIGURE 2.7 Comparison of activated factor VII (FVIIa) in women carrying the *Q* allele and those carrying the *RR* genotype before and after a meal.

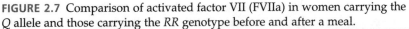

Source: Mennen LI, de Maat MP, Zock P, Grobbee DE, Kok FJ, Kluft C, Schouten EG. Postprandial response of activated factor VII in elderly women depends on the R353Q polymorphism. *Am J Clin Nutr* 1999;70:435–8. Used with permission.

For example, 2,735 individuals on statin therapy, half on atorvastatin and the other half divided among fluvastatin, lovastatin, pravastatin, and simvastatin, were genotyped for 43 single nucleotide polymorphisms (SNPs) in 16 genes that were previously reported to modify the lipid response to statin treatment. The only statistically significant associations with low density lipoprotein-cholesterol (LDL-C) lowering were found for apolipoprotein E2 (apoE2), in which carriers of the rare allele who took atorvastatin lowered their LDL-C by 3.5% more than those homozygous for the common allele, and for rs2032582 (S893A in ABCB1) in which the two groups of homozygotes differed by 3% in LDL-C lowering [Thompson et al., 2005].

The approach to detect modification is to take the modifier into account in the analyses. Typically, modification is addressed by separate analyses among those with and without the modifier. Alternative, so-called *interaction* terms may be included in regression models in the analyses (see Chapter 12).

Modification may act differently depending on the measure of risk, for example, whether relative or absolute measures of the risk association are used. Consider the following example: A disease risk, per 100,000, is 1 for those who are unexposed to two risk factors A and B; it is 2 for those exposed to risk factor A but not to B, and it is 5 per 100,000 for those unexposed to A but exposed to B. You now may ask what the disease risk would be for those who are jointly exposed to both risk factors and whether the risk factors do not interact and, thus, are independent. Because an absence of interaction (or independence) implies that the disease risks are additive the absolute risk for the jointly exposed would, in case of independence, be: $2 + (5 - 1) = 6$ per 100,000. Therefore, if the absolute risk for the jointly exposed was, say, 10, you would conclude that the two risk factors are not independent, or in other words, that modification is present. The modification, or interaction, is visible on an additive scale because: $2 + (5 - 1) = 6 \neq 10$. However, there is no interaction on a multiplicative scale because: $2 \times 5 = 10$ per 100,000; thus, it is the same as the product of the two absolute risks of disease of the individual risk factors [Ahlbom & Alfredsson, 2005].

In etiologic research, investigators often explore effect modification studies on more than one statistical scale, an approach that is likely to increase the rate of false-positive findings. For example, effect modification is examined by using both a multiplicative interaction term in a logistic regression model and a measure of interaction on the additive scale such as the interaction coefficient from an additive relative risk regression model. Starr and McKnight [2004] performed computer simulations to investigate the risk of false-positives when statistical interactions are evaluated by using both type of models. The overall false-positive rate was often greater than 5% when both tests were performed simultaneously. These results provide empiric evidence of the limited validity of a common approach to assess modification.

When the modifiers to be examined as well as the scale on which modification is to be explored have not been specified before analysis, the presence of effect modification should be interpreted particularly cautiously.

The choice of the scale is depending on the aim at which modification is addressed and preferably an *a priori* view on the nature of the modification, additive or multiplicative, and causal or descriptive. In view of the popularity of logistic regression modeling in etiologic epidemiologic research it is quite common to see modification addressed in a multiplicative manner. For example, Hung and coworkers [2006] studied whether polymorphisms in cell cycle control genes are associated with the risk of lung cancer and if they can alter the effect of ionizing radiation (through x-ray) on lung cancer risk. Cell cycle control is important in the repair of DNA damage. It can trigger cell arrest to allow for DNA lesions (e.g., caused by ionizing radiation) to be repaired before the cell continues its normal processes. TP53 plays a key role in cell cycle control. The effect of this polymorphism on lung cancer risk was examined in a multicenter case-control study including 2,238 incident lung cancer cases and 2,289 controls. The data were analyzed using logistic regression models that included a multiplicative interaction term. Persons with the TP53 intron 3 A2A2 genotype (and low number of x-ray exposures) had slightly increased risk of lung cancer compared to those with one or two copies of the A1 genotype (OR = 1.28; 95% CI, 0.67–2.45). Those with a high number of x-ray examinations (> 20; and one or two copies of the A1 genotype) had a 1.3 higher risk than those with a lower number of x-ray examinations (OR = 1.29; 95% CI, 1.07–1.56). The A2A2 genotype in combination with a high number of x-ray examinations raised lung cancer risk significantly (OR = 9.47; 95% CI, 2.59–34.6). This odds ratio is significantly higher than the product of the two risk factors of the individual risk factors. The OR for interaction was 9.47 ÷ (1.28–1.29) = 5.67 (95% CI, 1.33–24.3). The results of this study suggest that sequence variants in TP53 increase the risk of lung cancer and modify the risk conferred by multiple x-ray exposures.

Rothman [2002] has argued that causal modification should be linked to the original scale on which risks are measured. Multiplicative models typically involve logarithmic transformations. Therefore, in his view, causal modification should be examined by studying the presence or absence of additivity of risks. This approach was followed by Patino and coworkers [2005], who examined the extent to which the presence of familial dysfunction modifies the risk of psychosis associated with migration (Table 2.3). To quantify the interaction between family dysfunction and migration, relative risks were calculated for exposure to both migration history and family dysfunction, to family dysfunction only and to migration only, with exposure to neither migration nor family dysfunction as the reference category. The effect when both variables were present was larger than the sum of their independent effects, indicating, in this case, causal interaction.

As long as it is well understood that the choice of the scale on which modification is measured and the selection of the statistical model have an impact on the detection and magnitude of modification, and as long as it is clear why the modification is addressed, there is room for additive as well as multiplicative models.

TABLE 2.3   Migration, Familiar Dysfunction, and Risk of Psychosis

	Odds Ratio for Psychotic Symptoms	
	Crude (95% CI)	Adjusted[1] (95% CI)
Migration history[2]	1.8 (1.1–3.2)	2.4 (1.3–4.3)
Migration history and no family dysfunction[3]	1.2 (0.5–3.2)	1.5 (0.6–3.9)
Family dysfunction and no migration history[3]	1.5 (0.9–2.5)	1.3 (0.7–2.1)
Migration history and family dysfunction[3]	4.0 (2.0–8.2)	4.1 (1.9–8.5)
AP interaction[4]	0.59 (0.02–0.93)	0.58 (0.05–0.91)

CI, confidence interval.

[1]Adjusted for age, gender, psychiatric illness of a parent, and education level of breadwinner.
[2]Reference category is no migration history.
[3]Reference category is no migration history and no family dysfunction.
[4]Attributable proportion (AP) of cases owing to the interaction of migration history and family dysfunction.

Source: Patino LR, Selten JP, Van Engeland H, Duyx JH, Kahn RS, Burger H. Migration, family dysfunction and psychotic symptoms in children and adolescents. *Br J Psychiatry* 2005;186:442–3. Reprinted with permission.

Modifiers and Confounders

Modification is an altogether different issue than confounding in etiologic research. Confounders are inherently and exclusively linked to determinant-outcome relations and need to be adequately and completely handled during the design and analysis of an etiologic study to ensure validity of the findings. In the same study, however, for a given occurrence relation, confounders may also be modifiers. This holds true for both causal and descriptive modifiers. For example, in a non-experimental study on the risk of hemorrhagic stroke in patients receiving warfarin [Fang et al. 2006], age is a confounder when patients using warfarin are generally older and therefore already at a higher risk of stroke (i.e., the outcome). At the same time, however, for two patient groups of different age both using warfarin, the increased risk (the relative risk, the risk difference, or both) of stroke is higher in older patients. Age in this study is both a confounder and a modifier. To fully address confounding and modification of a third variable, the analysis should assess the effect of the determinant both with adjustment for the third variable as well as across the strata of that variable.

An example of physical activity as a modifier but not a confounder in an etiologic study on colon cancer risk is given in Textbox 2.3. This study addressed the role of diet and lifestyle factors in the occurrence of colon cancer. The association between diet and colon cancer appeared not to be confounded by physical activity. The causal impact of a so-called "high risk

TEXTBOX 2.3 Physical activity and colon cancer: Confounding or interaction?

SLATTERY ML, POTTER JD

Health Research Center, Department of Family and Preventive Medicine, University of Utah, Salt Lake City 84108, USA. mslatter@hrc.utah.edu

PURPOSE: Although physical activity has been consistently inversely associated with colon cancer incidence, the association of physical activity with other diet and lifestyle factors that may influence this association is less well understood. Confounding and effect modification are examined to better understand the physical activity and colon cancer association.

METHODS: Based on hypothesized biological mechanisms whereby physical activity may alter risk of colon cancer, we evaluated confounding and effect modification using data collected as part of a case-control study of colon cancer (*N* = 1993 cases and 2410 controls). We examined associations between total energy intake, fiber, calcium, fruit and vegetables, red meat, whole grains as well as dietary patterns along with cigarette smoking, alcohol consumption, BMI, and use of aspirin and/or NSAIDs and physical activity.

RESULTS: No confounding was observed for the physical activity and colon cancer association. However, differences in effects of diet and lifestyle factors were identified depending on level of physical activity. Most striking were statistically significant interactions between physical activity and high-risk dietary pattern and vegetable intake, in that the relative importance of diet was dependent on level of physical activity. The predictive model of colon cancer risk was improved by using an interaction term for physical activity and other variables, including BMI, cigarette smoking, energy intake, dietary fiber, dietary calcium, glycemic index, lutein, folate, vegetable intake, and high-risk diet rather than using models that included these variables as independent predictors with physical activity. In populations where activity levels are high, the estimate of risk associated with high vegetable intake was 0.9 (95% CI 0.6–1.3), whereas in more sedentary populations the estimate of risk associated with high vegetable intake was 0.6 (95% CI 0.5–0.9).

CONCLUSIONS: Physical activity plays an important role in the etiology of colon cancer. Its significance is seen by its consistent association as an independent predictor of colon cancer as well as by its impact on the odds ratios associated with other factors. Given these observations, it is most probable that physical activity operates through multiple biological mechanisms that influence the carcinogenic process.

Source: Slattery ML, Potter JD. Physical Activity and colon cancer: Confounding or interaction?, in Med Sci Sports Exerc. 2002 Jun;34(6):913–9.

dietary pattern," however, was dependent on the level of physical activity. Physical activity level, therefore, acted as a (causal) modifier established on a multiplicative scale.

When causal modification is studied, it should be appreciated that the same principles of etiologic research apply as in typical etiologic studies where a determinant is causally related to an outcome. In other words, alternative explanations that could confound the apparent modification by a particular characteristic should be considered.

Design of Data Collection in Cohort, Case-control, and Experimental Studies

Time

By definition, etiologic studies are longitudinal because the goal is to relate a potentially causal determinant to the future occurrence, for example, the incidence of a disease. This temporal relationship should be incorporated in the design of data collection to ensure that the determinant indeed precedes the development of disease, for example, by means of a cohort study. Consequently, a cross-sectional design, where determinant and outcome are measured at the same point in time, is generally not the preferred approach in etiologic research. Several examples illustrate this point. In studies on dietary habits as a possible cause for cancer, a cross-sectional study design may reveal a positive association between low fat intake and cancer, while in fact the preclinical cancer itself may have caused a change in dietary habits. Such a "which comes first, the chicken or the egg" phenomenon constitutes less of a problem when the etiologic factor cannot change over time (i.e., gender or a genetic trait).

Census or Sampling

The classic approach to collecting data in etiologic epidemiologic research is in a cohort study, where a group of subjects exposed to the causal factor under study interest and a group of unexposed subjects are followed over time to compare the incidence of the outcome of interest. Such a study takes a *census* approach in that in study participants the determinant and outcome and potential confounders (and, if the aim is to study modification, modifiers) are measured. Alternatively, and often more efficiently, information on the determinant and confounders (and possibly modifiers) can be collected in patients with the outcome of interest (the cases) and a *sample* (controls) from the population experience from which these cases arise. The latter approach is called a *case-control study*. A more extensive review of modes of data collection is given in Chapter 7. Cohort studies are described in detail in Chapter 8 and case-control studies in Chapter 9.

Experimental or Non-Experimental

Etiologic research can be conducted non-experimentally or experimentally. *Experimental* means that an investigator manipulates the determinant with the goal of learning about its causal effects. Case-control studies are non-experimental by definition, but cohort studies can either be experimental or non-experimental. The best known type of experimental cohort study is a randomized trial. Randomized trials are particularly suited to study effects of interventions. The principles of intervention research and the conduct of randomized trials are discussed in Chapters 6 and 10.

The study in Textbox 2.1, which addressed the cardiac risks associated with a high haem intake, was a cohort study where determinant, confounder, and outcome data were collected on all members of the cohort. From the above, it is obvious that in an etiologic study data need not only be collected for the determinant and outcome under study, but also for potential confounders and, in case modification is of interest, the effect modifiers.

There are several ways of collecting this information. Participants can be interviewed, face to face or by telephone; they can answer questionnaires at home or under supervision; they can keep diaries; and physical measurements can take place. The chosen method depends on the reliability of the different ways of collecting the data, the feasibility, and affordability. Determinant, confounder, and modifier data are usually collected at the start of the study, that is, at *baseline*. It also is possible for information to be collected from the past. In the cohort study in Textbox 2.1, dietary information was collected for the year prior to enrollment. Another example is when information about reproductive characteristics of women is needed from postmenopausal women. Milestones in their reproductive history such as menarche, menstrual cycles, childbirth, and lactation all happened in the past.

Measurement error is one of the most important problems in the data collection of epidemiologic studies and can lead to spurious associations between determinant and outcome. *Measurement error* occurs when the measurement is not valid, or biased, or when the measurement is not sufficiently precise. Biased or invalid measurements occur when the method used does not measure what the investigator intends to measure. An example is an uncalibrated blood pressure device that systematically measures the blood pressures 10 mm Hg too high. Such an error will impair inference for absolute blood pressure levels. If the measurement is sufficiently precise, however, there is no problem with ranking each study participant correctly in the population distribution. In the example in Textbox 2.1, when the haem iron content is unknown for many foods, this will lead to underestimation of the haem iron intake of essentially all individuals and hence to misclassification of persons with a truly higher intake in categories of low intake. When this occurs to the same extent for persons who develop coronary heart disease as for persons who do not, it will lead to an underestimation of the association. Measurements are not invalid but they are imprecise. Suppose that particular foods are missed exclusively for those who subsequently experience heart disease, which may well be the more likely situation. In this situation, apart from imprecision, the underestimation of intake becomes related to the outcome of interest and the association becomes confounded.

Measurement is as important for the determinant as for the confounders. When there is measurement error for the confounders, the effect of the determinant can not be fully adjusted and this leads to what is called *residual confounding*. Residual confounding leads to biased estimation of the determinant-outcome relationship.

Measures of Association

In cohort studies, participants are followed over time for the outcome to occur. In the example in Textbox 2.1, we collected information on haem iron intake at baseline and then followed our participants for a mean of 4.2 years. During that time, we collected information on the occurrence of coronary heart disease. In the analysis of this type of data, typically the incidence of the outcome is compared between participants with and without the determinant, and usually a relative risk is given as the measure of effect. In our example, we defined four categories of haem iron intake, based on the quartiles of the haem iron distribution in the entire population. Women with a daily haem iron intake of less then 1.28 mg were categorized in the lowest quartile, while women whose daily intake was greater than 2.27 mg were placed in the highest quartile (Table 2.4). Next, we calculated incidences of coronary heart disease for each quartile. When follow-up of the cohort is 100% complete, cumulative incidences can be calculated. Often this is not the case, so incidence densities are calculated, where all individuals contribute observation time (person-years) for as long as they participated in the study. People withdraw from a study for many reasons, and investigators generally do not wait until all participants reach the prespecified endpoint. Under these circumstances, it is more meaningful to calculate

TABLE 2.4   Incidence Densities of Coronary Heart Disease for Haem Iron Intake Quartiles

	Range (mg/day)	*Cases/Person-Years*
Haem iron intake[c]		
Quartile 1	<1.28	54/17,413
Quartile 2	1.28–1.76	53/17,384
Quartile 3	1.76–2.27	57/17,334
Quartile 4	>2.27	88/17,469

incidence densities and conduct a time-to-event analysis (see also Chapter 11). The Cox proportional hazards analysis is the most widely used technique for time-to-event data. This method allows for censoring of survival time for those persons who do not participate in a study until they reach the endpoint. The non-censored "survival" times are usually referred to as *event times*; these result from persons who experience the prespecified endpoint. The Cox proportional hazards analysis estimates the effect of a determinant on the baseline hazard distribution, that is, the survival distribution of completely average persons for whom each predictor variable is equal to the average value of that variable for the entire set of subjects in the study. This baseline survival curve does not need to have a particular form. It can have any shape as long as it starts at 1.0 (or 100%) at time 0 and descends steadily with time. The model estimates hazard ratios, which can be interpreted as risk ratios.

To summarize the risk involved with increasing amounts of haem iron intake, we calculated the hazard ratios, which is the risk of higher intakes compared to a reference level of intake (Table 2.5). Usually persons with no exposure, or with the lowest or highest category of exposure, are considered to be the reference group. The choice of the reference group depends on the study question. In our example, we considered those with the lowest intake of haem iron to be hypothetically the best, and therefore we took the lowest quartile as the reference category. Table 2.5 shows the estimates of relative risk, displayed with various degrees of confounder adjustment.

Our study showed that women with the highest haem iron intake had a 1.65 times higher risk of coronary heart disease than women with the lowest

TABLE 2.5 Hazard Ratios of Coronary Heart Disease for Increasing Haem Iron Intake

Crude Model		Basic Model[a]		Multivariate Model[b]	
HR	95% CI	HR	95% CI	HR	95% CI
1.0	—	1.0	—	1.0	—
0.98	0.67–1.44	1.01	0.68–1.51	1.06	0.71–1.59
1.06	0.73–1.54	1.05	0.71–1.56	1.12	0.74–1.71
1.62	1.16–2.28	1.52	1.06–2.19	1.65	1.07–2.53

[a]Adjusted for age at intake (continuous), BMI (continuous), smoking (current/past/never), physical activity (continuous), hypertension (yes/no), diabetes (yes/no), hypercholesterolemia (yes/no).
[b]Adjusted for age at intake (continuous), total energy intake (continuous), BMI (continuous), smoking (current/past/never), physical activity (continuous), hypertension (yes/no), diabetes (yes/no), hypercholesterolemia (yes/no), energy-adjusted saturated fat intake (continuous), energy-adjusted carbohydrate intake (continuous), energy-adjusted fiber intake (continuous), energy-adjusted alcohol intake (quintiles), energy-adjusted β-carotene intake (continuous), energy-adjusted vitamin E intake (continuous), energy-adjusted vitamin C intake (continuous).

intake. This effect is statistically significant, as the 95% confidence interval for the hazard ratio (1.07–2.53) does not include 1. While the hazard ratio or the relative risk represents the likelihood of disease in individuals with the determinant relative to those without, there is also a measure providing information on the absolute effect of the determinant, or the excess risk of disease in those with compared to those without the determinant. This is the *risk difference* (or the *attributable risk*) and is calculated as the difference of cumulative incidences or incidence densities. In our example, we could calculate the attributable risk as [(88/17,469) – (54/17,413)] = 1.9 per thousand women. From a practical or preventive perspective, it may be useful to estimate the proportion of the incidence of the outcome that is attributable to the determinant: the *attributable risk proportion*. It is calculated as [(1.9/1,000)/ (88/17,469)] * 100 = 37.7%. It also can be interesting to estimate the excess rate of the outcome in the total study population that might be attributed to the determinant. This measure is called the *population attributable risk*, and it indicates the importance of a specific determinant in the causation of a disease outcome. The population attributable risk (PAR) is calculated as the rate of disease in the population minus the rate of disease in the sub-population without the determinant, or alternatively, as the attributable risk multiplied by the proportion of individuals with the outcome in the population. In our example, the PAR is 0.0019 * 0.25 = 4.8 per 10,000 women.

Common Etiologic Questions in Clinical Epidemiology

Despite the overwhelming number of etiologic epidemiologic studies in the literature, the immediate relevance of etiologic information in patient care is often limited. Recall the challenges facing a physician discussed in Chapter 1. From the perspective of the patient as well as the physician, two questions are most important: *"given the patient profile, what is the patient's illness?"* and *"given the patient's illness, its etiology, the clinical and non-clinical profile, etc., what will be the future course of the illness or its manifestations?"* Often it is not necessary to know the cause of the disease to establish its diagnosis or determine its prognosis. For example, in a patient with abdominal complaints, it is important to know that the diagnosis is early colon cancer and subsequently act to improve prognosis by adequate treatment. Yet, etiologic information could help to prevent future occurrences and, in the case of colon cancer, may warrant screening for polyps in family members. Still, many of the most urgent questions that need answering in clinical care are those about optimal diagnostic strategies, better prediction of prognosis, and means to improve the course of the disease. There is, however, a slight subtlety in the nature of question on means to improve prognoses. While the extent to which a certain intervention improves prognosis and is safe is essentially a prognostic question from the viewpoint of patient care, in research on the benefits and risks of treatment it is often also an etiologic question. For example, when a pharmaceutical company launches a research program on a new drug used to treat chronic headache, two questions must be answered. First, does the drug help to relieve headache and, second, is it the drug that causes the benefit or are there alternative explanations? The latter clearly is an etiologic question. For this reason, intervention research is often both prognostic and etiologic. For the same reason, in designing an intervention study all of the principles of etiologic research apply, including the need to fully exclude confounding. Because confounding by indication is a serious problem in intervention research when using data collected from routine care or non-experimental cohort studies, definitive conclusions about the benefits of drug treatment and other interventions can often only be obtained by studying these effects in randomized trials (see Chapters 5 and 10).

A particular category of etiologic questions in clinical medicine are questions about patient safety and iatrogenic (physician-induced) disease. *Primum non nocere* remains the leading principle in patient care. Evidence-based medicine has supported the rational management of patients but also has emphasized the importance of weighing benefits and risks in those instances where treatment options are available. Apart from being effective, medical management needs to be safe. Research into the causes of safety risks of patients cared for in clinical medicine is etiologic research and follows clinical epidemiologic principles of etiologic studies (see Chapter 6). An illustration of the complexities of etiologic research is provided in the next section.

Sample Study

The beneficial effects of moderate alcohol intake on coronary heart disease risk have been clearly established. Whether there is a similar effect of alcohol intake on risk of type 2 diabetes is not yet clear. For the study in Textbox 2.4, data on alcohol intake as well as information on the occurrence of type 2 diabetes were collected as part of a large cohort study initially designed to study the role of diet in cancer occurrence.

Theoretical Design

The research question was, "does moderate alcohol consumption protect against the development of type 2 diabetes?" This translates into the following occurrence relation (incidence of type 2 diabetes) as a function of alcohol intake conditional on confounders. Consideration of confounding is necessary because an etiologic occurrence relation is addressed. The operational definition of the outcome was a first diagnosis of type 2 diabetes as determined using various information sources during follow-up. The measurement of determinant and confounders was operationalized by recording

TEXTBOX 2.4 Alcohol consumption and risk of type 2 diabetes among older women

JOLINE W.J. BEULENS, MSC
RONALD P. STOLK, MD
YVONNE T. VAN DER SCHOUW, PHD

DIEDERICK E. GROBBEE, MD
HENK F.J. HENDRIKS, PHD
MICHIEL L. BOTS, MD

OBJECTIVE: This study aimed to investigate the relation between alcohol consumption and type 2 diabetes among older women.

RESEARCH DESIGN AND METHODS: Between 1993 and 1997, 16,330 women aged 49–70 years and free from diabetes were enrolled in one of the Dutch Prospect-EPIC (European Prospective Study Into Cancer and Nutrition) cohorts and followed for 6.2 years (range 0.1–10.1). At enrollment, women filled in questionnaires and blood samples were collected.

RESULTS: During follow-up, 760 cases of type 2 diabetes were documented. A linear inverse association ($P = 0.007$) between alcohol consumption and type 2 diabetes risk was observed, adjusting for potential confounders. Compared with abstainers, the hazard ratio for type 2 diabetes was 0.86 (95% CI 0.66–1.12) for women consuming 5–30 g alcohol per week, 0.66 (0.48–0.91) for 30–70 g per week, 0.91 (0.67–1.24) for 70–140 g per week, 0.64 (0.44–0.93) for 140–210 g per week, and 0.69 (0.47–1.02) for > 210 g alcohol per week. Beverage type did not influence this association. Lifetime alcohol consumption was associated with type 2 diabetes in a U-shaped fashion.

CONCLUSIONS: Our findings support the evidence of a decreased risk of type 2 diabetes with moderate alcohol consumption and expand this to a population of older women.

all relevant information on past and current alcohol intake, other lifestyle factors, medication use in a questionnaire, and by taking anthropometric measures of the participant during regular visits to the study center.

Design of Data Collection

Data were collected on a cohort of middle-aged and elderly women. Between 1993 and 1997, a total of 50,313 women aged between 49 and 70 years of age who were living in and around Utrecht, the Netherlands, were invited to participate in the study during their routine visit for a screening program for breast cancer. In total, 17,357 women were enrolled in the cohort. At baseline, a general questionnaire containing questions about smoking, behavior (Table 2.6) physical activity, reproductive history, medical history, family history, and medication use, and a food frequency questionnaire about their normal intake during the year prior to enrollment were administered. Height, weight, waist, and hip circumference, and systolic and diastolic blood pressures were measured. For the present analysis, the follow-up period ended on January 1, 2002, after a mean of 6.2 years. During follow-up, questionnaires were sent out at 5-year intervals to inquire about the occurrence of disease, and these contained seven questions about diabetes. A new event of type 2 diabetes during follow-up was defined as a report of this disease in one of two follow-up questionnaires, or a positive urine dipstick sent out with the first follow-up questionnaire, or a diagnosis of type 2 diabetes in the national hospital discharge diagnosis database with which the cohort is linked on an annual basis.

Design of Data Analysis

The principal analysis was performed on the cohort excluding the women who reported diabetes at baseline. This was done because these women might have changed their dietary habits and their alcohol intake as a result of the diagnosis. Although the follow-up was highly complete, it was not possible to keep track of all enrolled women until January 1, 2002, because some of them moved outside of the Netherlands, and a few of them died. Therefore, the follow-up time was calculated individually for every woman. Because the main interest was the causal association between alcohol intake and type 2 diabetes risk, baseline alcohol intake and lifetime alcohol intake were considered to be potential determinants of the outcome. First, the crude incidence density of type 2 diabetes was calculated for four categories of alcohol intake: teetotalers, and those drinking >0 to 4.9 g/day, 5 to 29.9 g/day, and 30 to 69.9 g/day. Univariate risk ratios with 95% confidence intervals were calculated with the Cox proportional hazard analysis, with

TABLE 2.6 Baseline Characteristics* by Alcohol Consumption Categories in 16,330 Dutch Women

	Alcohol Consumption (g/week)						
	Teetotaler	*0–4.9*	*5–29.9*	*30–69.9*	*70–139.9*	*140–209.9*	*≥210*
Participants (n)	1,513	3,115	3,787	2,586	2,384	1,629	1,316
Age (years)[†]	59 ± 6	59 ± 6	58 ± 6	57 ± 6	57 ± 6	57 ± 6	56 ± 6
BMI (kg/m²)[†]	26.9	26.6	26.2	25.8	25.1	25.3	25.3

Data are means ± SD.

*All characteristics are age-adjusted except age.

[†]P value ≤ 0.001 between alcohol intake categories.

teetotalers as the reference group. Next, lifestyle factors and medical information were considered as potential confounders of the observed crude association, because they are other determinants of type 2 diabetes risk and often are associated with alcohol intake. Table 2.6 presents the baseline characteristics of the study population, showing that two important determinants of type 2 diabetes, age and BMI, are also related to baseline alcohol intake. A section of these data are in Table 2.7. The younger and the leaner the participants, the more they drink. Although these associations were tested formally, the presence of confounding is best judged by the changes in the risk estimates rather than by statistical significance. To examine the level of confounding, potential confounders were included in the Cox proportional hazards model, and the extent to which adding these variables to the model materially changed the estimates of the risk ratios was judged. There is no universal definition for a material change in RR, leaving this an arbitrary decision of the investigator. However, commonly 5% to 10% changes in RR are considered large enough to justify adjustment.

Although not displayed in the published article, from Table 2.7 the crude incidence rates and risk ratios for the three categories of alcohol intake compared to teetotalers can easily be calculated to be 1.00 for women drinking 0 to 4.9 g alcohol/day, 0.68 for women drinking 5.0 to 29.9 g alcohol/day, and 0.51 for women drinking 30.0 to 69.9 g alcohol/day. Table 2.7 further shows that adjusting for age and BMI does change the risk estimates quite dramatically, whereas adding additional potential confounders does not result in important changes anymore.

TABLE 2.7   Baseline Alcohol Consumption and Risk of Type 2 Diabetes Among 16,330 Dutch Women

	Alcohol Consumption			
Baseline alcohol consumption (g/day)	0 (teetotaler)	0–4.9	5–29.9	30–69.9
Cases (*n*)	100	211	174	87
Person-years	9,927	19,533	23,755	16,015
Age and BMI adjusted	1.0	1.05 (0.83–1.33)	0.79 (0.61–1.01)	0.65 (0.49–0.87)
Multivariate adjusted*	1.0	1.04 (0.80–1.34)	0.86 (0.66–1.12)	0.66 (0.48–0.91)
Multivariate adjusted†	1.0	1.02 (0.79–1.32)	0.85 (0.65–1.11)	0.64 (0.46–0.89)

Data are means ± SD.
*All characteristics are age-adjusted except age.
†P value ≤ 0.001 between alcohol intake categories.

Implications and Relevance

The results of this study show that moderate alcohol intake protects against development of type 2 diabetes, which was true for baseline alcohol intake as well as lifetime alcohol intake. The type of alcoholic beverage did not make a difference and strongly suggests a protective effect of alcohol itself.

A protective effect of moderate alcohol consumption on cardiovascular disease risk is already well established, just as a close relation of cardiovascular disease to diabetes and other morbidity. You could argue that residual confounding from other comorbidities, notably cardiovascular disease, may be present. However, when excluding cases with cardiovascular disease from the analysis, similar results were obtained.

This study did not specifically address the pathophysiologic mechanism. In a random sample of the population, the relationship between alcohol intake and HDL-C levels was determined, and the expected increasing effect of alcohol was found. Therefore, beneficial effects of alcohol on HDL-C could be part of the mechanism for the protection against type 2 diabetes. However, an increase in insulin sensitivity and anti-inflammatory effects also have been associated with moderate alcohol intake, and might explain the risk reduction of type 2 diabetes [Sierksma et al., 2002].

3

Diagnostic Research

A 55-year-old man visits the general practitioner (GP) because of dyspepsia. He has had these complaints for more than three months, but their frequency and severity have increased over the preceding four weeks. The patient has a history of angina, but did not require sublingual nitroglycerin for more than two years. He is known to the GP as being unsuccessful in his frequent attempts to quit smoking. The GP asks several additional questions related to the nature and severity of the dyspepsia, to estimate the chance that the patient suffers from a peptic ulcer. The GP also asks about possible anginal complaints. A short physical examination reveals nothing except some epigastric discomfort during palpation of the abdomen. The GP considers a peptic ulcer the most likely diagnosis. The probability of a coronary origin of the complaints is deemed very low. The GP decides to test for Helicobacter pylori *serology, to further increase (rule in) or decrease (rule out) the probability of (H. pylori-related) peptic ulcer. The* H. pylori *test turns out to be negative. The GP prescribes an acid-suppressing agent and asks the patient to visit again in a week. When the man visits the GP again, his complaints have virtually disappeared.*

Diagnosis in Clinical Practice

Doctors devote much of their time to diagnosing diseases in patients presenting with particular symptoms or signs. Setting a diagnosis in a patient is important because it directs the physician in making decisions for appropriate patient management and provides insight in the prognosis of the patient (Textbox 3.1).

The diagnostic process in daily practice typically starts with a patient presenting a certain complaint—symptom or sign—which makes the practitioner suspicious of him or her having a particular disorder (target disease) out of a series of possible disorders (differential diagnoses) [Sackett et

TEXTBOX 3.1 Quotation about clinical judgment

Knowing how to live with uncertainty is a central feature of clinical judgment: the skilled physician has learned when to take risks to increase certainty and when to simply tolerate uncertainty.

Riegelman, 1990

Source: Data from Riegelman R. Studying a study and testing a test. Boston: Little, Brown, 1990.

al., 1985]. The target disease can best be viewed as the disorder at which the diagnostic process is initially targeted, either because it is the most serious of the many differential diagnoses ("the one not to miss") or, *a priori*, the most probable one. During the diagnostic process, the physician first estimates the probability, or likelihood, of the presence of the target disease in view of the alternative diagnoses (including the absence of any disease) based on information obtained through history taking, including knowledge about a patient's individual and family's medical history, and physical examination. This is typically an implicit process (Textbox 3.2).

TEXTBOX 3.2 Diagnosis

διά´γνωσις

The term "diagnosis" is a compound of the Greek words διά´ (dia), which means apart or distinction and γνωσις (gnosis) which means knowledge. Diagnosis in medicine can be defined as "the art of distinguishing one disease from the other." (Dorland WAN. *The American Illustrated Medical Dictionary*, 20th Edition. Philadelphia, London: WB Saunders Company, 1944). In clinical practice a diagnosis does not necessarily imply a well-defined, pathophysiologically distinct, disease entity, such as acute myelocyte leukemia, but many diagnoses are set on a much more aggregate level, notably in the beginning of the diagnostic process. For example, a physician on weekend call who speaks to (a family member of) a patient with dyspnea, will first try to set or rule out the diagnosis, "a condition requiring immediate action," before a more precise diagnosis can be made, usually at a later stage. The precision of the diagnosis also depends on the clinical setting. In primary care there often is no need for a very specific diagnosis to decide on the next step [for example, amoxicillin (a small spectrum antibiotic) prescription in a patient with the diagnosis "probable pneumonia" based on signs and symptoms only], whereas in an intensive care setting in a tertiary care hospital, with more virulent bacteria, more antibiotic resistance, and more immunocompromised and seriously ill patients, a more specific diagnosis may be required ("vancomycin-resistant pneumococcal ventilator-associated pneumonia") involving imaging techniques, serology, cultures, and resistance patterns.

Source: Author.

Apart from clinical data about the patient, non-clinical data such as age, gender, and working conditions also may be considered. The estimated probability of the (target) disease will guide the doctor in choosing the most appropriate action. In particular, the physician performs additional diagnostic tests, initiates therapeutic interventions, or, perhaps most importantly, refrains from diagnostic or therapeutic actions for that disease, and probably searches for other underlying diseases. The diagnostic work-up is a continuing process of updating the probability of the (target) disease presence given all available information documented on the patient. The goal of this work-up is to achieve a relatively high or a relatively low probability of a certain diagnosis, that is, the threshold probability beyond or below which a doctor is confident enough about the presence or absence of a certain diagnosis to guide clinical decisions. Threshold probabilities are determined by the consequences of a false-positive or false-negative diagnosis. These critically depend on the anticipated course or prognosis of the diagnosis considered and the potential beneficial and adverse effects of possible additional diagnostic procedures or treatments. Often, history taking and physical examination already provide important and sufficient diagnostic information to rule in or rule out a disease with enough confidence, so that the estimated probability of presence of the disease is below A or above B (Figure 3.1). But when the probability of the disease is estimated to lie in the grey middle area (between A and B), additional diagnostic tests are required to decrease the remaining uncertainty about the presence or absence of the disease. Typically, this additional testing first implies simple, easily available tests, such as blood and urine tests, electrocardiography, or simple im-

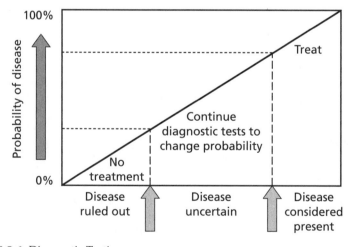

FIGURE 3.1 Diagnostic Testing.

aging techniques like chest x-ray. If after these tests doubt remains, that is, the probability of disease presence has not (yet) crossed the thresholds A or B, more invasive and costly diagnostic procedures are applied such as magnetic resonance imaging (MRI), computed tomography (CT) or positron emission tomography (PET) scanning, arthroscopy, and/or biopsy. This process of diagnostic testing ends, albeit sometimes temporarily, when the estimated probability of the target disease becomes higher or lower than the A or B threshold.

In the example of our patient with complaints of dyspepsia, history taking and physical examination apparently did not provide the doctor with enough information to decide about the initiation of therapeutic interventions, for example, symptomatic treatment with acid-suppressing agents or, alternatively, triple therapy to treat an underlying *H. pylori* infection. In view of the patient burden of invasive *H. pylori* testing (i.e., gastroscopy with biopsy) in combination with the relatively mild complaints and potential benefits of *H. pylori* targeted therapy, the physician decided to perform a noninvasive serology test, although this test is considered less accurate than the gastroscopy. Apparently, the negative test results indeed convinced the physician that the probability of *H. pylori* ulcer disease was lower than the clinically relevant threshold, say 10% to 20%, because triple therapy targeted at *H. pylori* was not initiated. Instead, symptomatic treatment, an acid-suppressing drug, was prescribed. The probability of coronary heart disease—one of the differential diagnoses of a patient with these complaints—as the underlying cause of the complaints also was considered to be very low from the start (far below threshold A for this disease), such that no additional tests for that diagnosis were ordered.

The example may seem subjective, non-quantitative, non-evidence–based, and unscientific, but the diagnostic process in clinical practice often is just that simple. In contrast to many therapeutic interventions, quantitative evidence of the value of diagnostic tests and certainly of the *added* value of a test beyond previous, more simple test results, is often lacking. Given the paramount importance of diagnosing in every day practice, there is an urgent need for research providing such quantitative knowledge [Knottnerus, 2002b; Grobbee, 2004].

The diagnostic process thus is a multivariable concern. It typically involves the documentation and interpretation of multiple test results (or diagnostic determinants), including non-clinical patient information [Moons et al., 1999]. In practice, hardly any diagnosis is based on a single diagnostic test. The number of diagnostic tests applied in everyday practice may differ considerably and depends, for example, on the targeted disease, patient characteristics, and the diagnostic certainty required to decide on patient management (Textbox 3.3). Importantly, a natural hierarchy of testing exists. Almost without exception, any diagnostic work-up starts with non-burdening tests such as history taking and physical examination, followed by simple laboratory or imaging tests, and eventually more burdening and expensive tests, such as imaging techniques requiring contrast fluids or biopsies. Subsequent test results are always interpreted in the context of previous diagnostic information [Moons et al., 1999; Moons & Grobbee, 2002a]. For example, the test result "presence of chest pain," is obviously interpreted differently in a 5-year-old girl than in a 60-year-old man with a history of myocardial infarction. The challenge of the physician lies in predicting the probability of the absence or presence of a disease based on all documented test results. This requires knowledge about the contribution of each test result to the probability estimation. The diagnostic value of the *H. pylori* test in the example above is negligible if it adds nothing to the findings offered by the few minutes of history taking and physical examination; information that is always acquired by every physician anyway. More technically, the *H. pylori* test is worthless if the test result does not change (increase or decrease) the probability of presence of peptic ulcer disease as based on the results from history taking and physical examination. Importantly, in case the next step in clinical management is already decided upon (when the disease probability is below A or above B in Figure 3.1), one may (if not *should*) refrain from additional testing.

The works of the 18th century Scottish pastor and mathematician, Thomas Bayes, have been instrumental in the development of a more scien-

TEXTBOX 3.3 Primum non nocere

Primum on nocere (first do not harm) refers to the principle that doctors should always take into account the possible harm of their actions in patients, and that an intervention with an obvious potential of harm should not be initiated, notably when the benefits of the intervention are small or uncertain. Although this Hippocratic principle is most often used in discussions on the effects of therapeutic interventions, it equally applies to diagnostic tests, especially for the more invasive and burdening tests. When the management of a patient has been determined, additional diagnostic tests obviously have no benefit to guide this decision and could therefore only be harmful, albeit sometimes to the health care budget only. In daily practice many diagnostic tests are being performed that have no potential consequences for patient management. Especially when additional test ordering is relatively easy, for example, serum parameters and imaging such as x-rays, the potential consequences for patient management, as well as possible harm, are not always taken into account. In a patient with a rib contusion as a result of a fall, an x-ray to rule out a rib fracture is useless, because the test result will not influence treatment (i.e., rest with painkillers). The challenge of the physician in any diagnostic process thus not only lies in choosing the optimal diagnostic tests and in what order, but also in knowing when to stop testing.

Source: Author.

tific approach towards the diagnostic process in clinical practice. He established a mathematical basis for diagnostic inference. Bayes recognized the sequential and probabilistic nature in the diagnostic process. He emphasized the importance of prior probabilities, that is, the probability of the presence of a target diagnosis *before any* (subsequent) tests are performed, perhaps even before patient history and physical examination. He also recognized that, based on subsequent test results, doctors will update this prior probability to a *posterior* probability. The well-known *Bayes' rule* formally quantifies the association between the prior probability of a disease and the properties (sensitivity and specificity or likelihood ratio) of the additional test on the one hand, and the posterior probability of disease presence on the other (Textbox 3.4). Although it has repeatedly been shown that this mathematical rule does often not hold—since the underlying assumption of constant sensitivity and specificity or likelihood ratio across patient subgroups is not realistic in most situations [Hlatky et al., 1984; Detrano et al., 1988; Moons et al., 1997; Diamond, 1992], the rule has been crucial in understanding the probabilistic and stepwise nature of diagnostic reasoning in clinical practice.

We should emphasize that setting a diagnosis in itself is not a therapeutic intervention. It is a vehicle to guide therapies. An established diagnosis is a label that, despite being highly valued by medical professionals, is of no consequence to a patient other than to set the optimal therapy and to obtain a first estimate of the expected course of the complaints. Accordingly, a diagnostic test commonly has no direct therapeutic effects and therefore does not directly influence a patient's prognosis. Once a diagnosis, or rather the probability of the most likely diagnosis, is established and an assessment of the probable course of disease in the light of different treatment alternatives (including no treatment) has been made, a treatment decision will be taken to eventually improve patient outcome.

To summarize, the diagnostic process in clinical practice has the following characteristics:

1. A diagnosis starts with a patient presenting a complaint (symptom and/or sign) suggestive of a certain disease to be diagnosed.
2. The subsequent work-up is a multivariable process. It involves multiple diagnostic determinants (tests) that are applied in a logical order: from age, gender, medical history, and signs and symptoms, to more complicated, invasive, and costly tests.
3. Setting or ruling out a diagnosis is a probabilistic action in which the probability of the presence or absence of the disease is central. This probability is continuously updated based on subsequent diagnostic test results.
4. The true diagnostic value of a test is determined by the extent to which it provides diagnostic information beyond earlier tests, that is,

TEXTBOX 3.4 Example of a Two-By-Two Table with Test Results and Bayes' Rule

Test characteristics of test (T) N-terminal pro B-type natriuretic peptide (NT-proBNP; cut-off 36 pmol/L)) in the detection of heart failure in primary care patients with conditions known to be associated with a high prevalence of heart failure.

	NT-proBNP positive (T+)	NT-proBNP negative (T−)	Total
Heart failure present (D+)	9	0	9
Heart failure absent (D−)	69	55	124
	78	55	133

where sensitivity = P(T+|D+) = 9/9=100%; specificity = P(T−|D−) = 55/124 = 44%; positive predictive value = P(D+|T+) = 9/78 = 12%; negative predictive value = P(D−|T−) = 55/55 = 100%; likelihood ratio positive test (LR+) = P(T+|D+)/[1 − P(T+|D−)] = (9/9)/(69/124) = 1.8; likelihood ratio negative test (LR−) = [(1 − P(T+|D+)]/[P(T−|D−)] = (0/9)/(55/124) = 0.

Bayes' rule:

$$P(D+|T+) = \frac{P(D+)*P(T+|D+)}{P(D+)*[P(T+|D+)] + P(D−)*P(T+|D−)} = $$ (Eq. 1)

$$P(D+|T+) = \frac{P(D+)*\text{sensitivity}}{P(D+)*\text{sensitivity} + [1 − (P(D+)]*(1 − \text{specificity})} = \frac{9/133 * 1}{9/133 * 1 + 124/133 * 0.56} = 0.12 = 12\%$$

and

$$P(D−|T+) = \frac{P(D−)*P(T+|D−)}{P(D+)*[P(T+|D+) + P(D−)*P(T+|D−)]} = $$ (Eq. 2)

$$P(D−|T+) = \frac{P(D−)*(1 − \text{specificity})}{P(D+)*\text{sensitivity} + [1 − (P(D+)]*(1 − \text{specificity})} = \frac{124/133 * 0.56}{9/133 * 1 + 124/133 * 0.56} = 0.88 = 88\%$$

Alternative (so-called odds) notation of Bayes' rule $\rightarrow$ (1) divided by (2):

$$\frac{P(D+|T+)}{P(D-|T+)} = \frac{P(D+)}{P(D-)} * \frac{P(T+|D+)}{P(T+|D-)} = \frac{P(D+)}{P(D-)} * LR+ \rightarrow$$

Posterior odds $(D+|T+)$ = prior odds $* LR+$

Note: $Odds(D+)/[1 - P(D+)] \rightarrow P(D+) = Odds(D+)/[1 + Odds(D+)]$

For sequential diagnostic tests, Bayes' rule theoretically can be simply extended:

$$\frac{P(D+|T_1+, T_2+, T_3+)}{P(D-|T_1+, T_2+, T_3+)} = \frac{P(D+)}{P(D-)} * LR(T_1+|D+) * LR(T_2+|D+) * LR(T_3+|D+)$$

Note that this form of Bayes' rule assumes that the results of test 1 to test 3 are independent of each other. However, it has been shown that this assumption in practice typically does not hold, as test results are often mutually related simply because they are reflections of the same underlying disease (see text).

Source: Author.

materially changes the probability estimation of disease presence based on previous test results.

5. The goal of the diagnostic process is to eventually rule in or out the disease with enough confidence to take clinical decisions. This requires precise estimates of the probability of the presence of the target disease(s).

Finally, the difference between *diagnosing* and *screening for* a disease should be recognized. The former starts with a patient presenting with a particular symptom and sign suspected of a particular disease and is inherently multivariable. Screening for a disease may start with non-symptomatic individuals and is in principle univariable. Examples include phenylketonuria screening in newborns and breast cancer screening in middle-aged women, where a single diagnostic test is performed in all subjects irrespective of symptoms or signs. In this chapter, we will deal with *diagnosing* exclusively.

From Diagnosis in Clinical Practice to Diagnostic Research

Diagnostic research should be aimed at improving the diagnostic process in clinical practice. Typically it focuses on identifying combination(s) of tests that have the largest diagnostic yield. In clinical epidemiologic terms; the occurrence relation of diagnostic research predicts the probability of the presence of the disease of interest as a function of multiple (though preferably not too many) diagnostic determinants, in the relevant domain. The domain is defined by patients suspected of that particular disease. Diagnostic determinants typically include findings from history taking (including age, gender, symptoms, and known comorbidity) and physical examination (signs), and if applicable and necessary, the findings from more advanced diagnostic testing.

The diagnostic process and thus diagnostic research is predictive or descriptive by nature, as its object is prediction of the yet unknown presence of the underlying disease. The goal is not to explain the cause of the disease under study. Consequently, confounding variables, that is, factors that may distort a causal relationship between a particular causal determinant and an outcome, do not play a role in diagnostic research and are not part of the occurrence relation. This is in sharp contrast to etiologic research where confounders are of critical importance. In diagnostic research, all other determinants merely serve as additional diagnostic test results that may be helpful in further distinguishing between those with and without the disease. Importantly, diagnostic research should be performed in close adherence to daily clinical practice to ensure applicability of the findings. Thus, the typical features of the diagnostic process outlined above should be taken into account in the design of the study. This has important consequences for the choice of the study population, the diagnostic determinants to be evaluated, their hierarchy and temporal sequence of measurement, and the data analysis.

Diagnostic Research Versus Test Research

Alas, many published "diagnostic studies" are better characterized as "test research." The main objective of test research is to assess whether a *single* diagnostic test (index test) adequately discriminates between the presence or absence of a particular disease [Moons et al., 2004a]. Often these studies include a group of patients with the disease of interest (as determined by a so-called reference or *gold standard*) and a group of patients without this disease in whom the results of the index test are measured. Typically, the results of the index test are categorized as positive or negative and the study results are summarized in a 2×2 contingency table (Textbox 3.4). The table in this box allows for calculation of the four classical measures to estimate diagnostic accuracy in test research. These are:

1. Sensitivity [P(T+ I D+)]; probability (P) of a positive test (T+) given presence of the disease (D+) (the true positive rate);
2. Specificity [P(T– I D–)]; probability of a negative test (T–) in those without disease (D–) (the true negative rate);
3. Positive predictive value [P(D+ I T+)]; probability of the presence of disease in those with a positive test result;
4. Negative predictive value [P(D– I T–)]; probability of absence of disease in those with a negative test result.

Other—though less often applied—parameters include the likelihood ratio of a positive test (the probability of a positive test in the diseased divided by the probability of a positive test in the non-diseased), the likelihood ratio of a negative test (i.e., the probability of a negative test in the diseased divided by the probability of a negative test in the non-diseased), or the odds ratio (which can be calculated as the ratio of the former two). The latter is seldom applied but it is a frequently used measure in diagnostic meta-analyses. If the index test results are not dichotomous but measured on a continuous scale, receiver operating characteristic (ROC) curves can be produced, based on sensitivity and specificity of the different cut-off values of the diagnostic test to be evaluated [Hanley and McNeil, 1982; Harrell et al., 1982].

Test research, which refers to studies focusing on the quantification of the diagnostic accuracy of a particular test, varies from the main principle of clinically relevant diagnostic research in that they should mimic clinical practice. First and foremost, they do not recognize the fact that the diagnostic process by definition involves multiple tests or incorporates the natural hierarchy of diagnostic testing in practice. Second, these studies typically do not include representatives of the relevant patient domain, that is, patients presenting with symptoms and signs suggestive of the disease. Rather, one selects a group of patients with evident disease and a group of non-diseased patients; sometimes these are healthy individuals who are not even aware of the disease under study. Both types of patient selection, however, lead to biased estimates of the test's performance (see section on Bias in Diagnostic Research, p. 83). Finally, there is a clear difference in the occurrence relation between clinically relevant diagnostic research and test research that is aimed at quantifying a single test's characteristics (usually sensitivity and specificity).

The occurrence relation of test research on a test's sensitivity or specificity in fact can be described as:

$$P(T) = f(D)$$

where T is the probability (0%–100%) of a positive or negative result, respectively, of the single test under study, and D the presence or absence of disease, respectively.

Test research that is mainly focused on predictive values of a single test is relatively rare. The occurrence relations of studies estimating the probability of (presence of/absence of) disease (0%–100%) as a function of the single test result can be summarized as:

$$P(D) = f(T)$$

The occurrence relation of clinically relevant diagnostic research (see also below) can be summarized as:

$$P(D) = f(T1, T2, T3, \ldots Tn)$$

where P(D) signifies the probability of the disease of interest (range 0%–100%) and T1 to Tn are the multiple diagnostic tests or determinants being studied.

A study to determine the value of plasma N-terminal pro B-type natriuretic peptide (NT-proBNP) levels in diagnosing heart failure may serve as an example of a diagnostic study primarily presented as test research. NT-proBNP, a neuropeptide produced in the human cardiac ventricle as a result of increasing pressure, was assessed in a sample of 133 primary care patients [Hobbs et al., 2002]. Selection of these patients was based on the presence of a condition known to be associated with a higher prevalence of heart failure (i.e., a history of myocardial infarction, angina, hypertension, or diabetes), and the study was not restricted to the clinically more relevant group of patients presenting with complaints (i.e., fatigue or dyspnea) suggestive of heart failure.

Textbox 3.4 summarizes the main results. In addition, Bayes' rule, calculating the post-test probability (or odds) of disease as the product of the pre-test probability (or odds) and the test's likelihood ratio are illustrated using the data derived from this study.

It was concluded from the study that NT-proBNP has value in the diagnosis of heart failure. Its main use would be to rule out heart failure in patients with suspected heart failure in which normal concentrations of NT-proBNP are found. Several remarks can be made about this study, most of which were recognized by the authors. First, the focus of this study on the NT-proBNP test as a single test to diagnose or rule out heart failure does not reflect the diagnostic approach in clinical practice. NT-proBNP will never be applied as the sole diagnostic test in diagnosing heart failure. Simpler diagnostic tools inevitably are used first, notably information on age, sex, comorbidity, and symptoms and signs, before additional tests, such as NT-proBNP and perhaps electrocardiography, or even echocardiography [Rutten et al., 2005b]. The clinically more relevant research aim would thus be to assess whether NT-proBNP appreciably adds to the diagnostic information that is readily available in real clinical care.

This can only be achieved by comparing the diagnostic performance of two diagnostic strategies: one including all diagnostic information available to the physician before BNP measurement is executed, and one including the same information plus the NT-proBNP levels. In doing so, the multivariable nature of the diagnostic process in clinical practice is taken into account as well as the inherent hierarchy of diagnostic testing. It should be emphasized that the authors indeed did perform a multivariable logistic regression analysis to determine whether a model including sex, history of myocardial infarction or diabetes, Q waves or bundle branch block pattern on electrocardiogram, and NT-proBNP performed better in diagnosing heart failure than a similar model excluding NT-proBNP. Nonetheless, the *added* diagnostic value of NT-proBNP was not emphasized in the presentation of the results or in the conclusion, nor were symptoms and signs included as possible "diagnostic tests."

In addition, the study population included in the study can be criticized. The ability of a diagnostic test or combination of tests to distinguish between diseased and non-diseased should be studied in those patients in whom the diagnostic problem truly exists. In other words, the patients should be representatives of the domain of patients suspected of that disease and in whom the physician generally considers diagnostic testing to ensure applicability of the findings. This is crucial because the value of diagnostic tests critically depends on the patient mix (Textbox 3.5). Most patients included in the NT-proBNP study (i.e., mainly patients with conditions known to be associated with a high prevalence of heart failure) were not representative of the clinically relevant domain of patients visiting their primary care physician with symptoms and signs suggestive of heart failure. Thus, the applicability of the findings to patients encountered in daily practice is limited.

The focus on the quantification of the value of a single test to diagnose or rule out a disease and the common preoccupation of such research with a test's sensitivity and specificity are typical of prevailing diagnostic research [Moons et al., 2004a].

TEXTBOX 3.5 Sensitivity and specificity are not constant

Are sensitivity and specificity given properties of a diagnostic test, and do predictive values critically depend on the prevalence of the disease?

The common emphasis on sensitivity and specificity in the presentation of diagnostic studies is at least partly attributable to the notion that predictive values critically depend on the population studied, whereas sensitivity and specificity are considered to be (more or less) constant [Moons & Harrell, 2003]. There is no doubt that predictive values of diagnostic tests are influenced by the patient domain. This may be best illustrated by comparing the performance of a test in primary and secondary care. Because of the inherent higher prevalence of the relevant disease in suspected patients in secondary care compared to primary care (because of the referral process), positive predictive values are commonly higher in secondary care (i.e., fewer false-positives) than in primary care (more false-positives), while negative predictive values are usually higher in primary care (fewer false-negatives). Sensitivity, specificity, and likelihood ratios indeed are not directly influenced by the prevalence of the disease because these parameters are conditional upon the presence of absence of disease. It has been shown extensively, however, that they vary according to differences in the severity of disease and thus—one might say—indirectly across the prevalence of the disease [Hlatky et al., 1984; Detrano et al., 1988; Moons et al., 1997; Diamond, 1992]. For example, in secondary care, relatively more advanced disease stages will be presented, with usually higher levels of the diagnostic markers or more index test positives. This in turn could result in a higher sensitivity in secondary care than in primary care and a higher specificity in primary care.

Source: Knottnerus JA. Between iatrotropic stimulus and interiatric referral: the domain of primary care research. J Clin Epidemiol 2002a;55:1201–6.

The common focus on sensitivity and specificity is also illustrated by the following, intuitively attractive, but in our view incorrect statements found in classical textbooks in clinical epidemiology or biostatistics:

Identify the sensitivity and specificity of the sign, symptom, or diagnostic test you plan to use. Many are already published and sub specialists worth their salt ought either to know them from their field or be able to track them down [Sackett et al., 1985].

and

For every laboratory test or diagnostic procedure there is a set of fundamental questions that should be asked. Firstly, if the disease is present, what is the probability that the test result will be positive? This leads to the notion of the sensitivity of the test. Secondly, if the disease is absent, what is the probability that the test result will be negative? This question refers to the specificity of the test [Campbell & Machin, 1990].

As the goal of setting a diagnosis in patients is to estimate the probability of disease from the diagnostic test results, the parameters of interest undoubtedly are the posterior probabilities or predictive values, which directly reflect the diagnostic probabilities needed for decision-making in clinical practice. Indeed, patients do not enter a physician's office saying, "I have been diagnosed with this particular disease and would like to know whether the available tests are positive; please give me the sensitivity." For the doctor, the sensitivity is similarly uninformative. The still common focus on probabilities of test results given the presence or absence of disease—sensitivity and specificity—is clearly unjustified from a clinical point of view. It should be emphasized that in the NT-proBNP study example, the authors stated that their main conclusion (that heart failure can be excluded in those with normal NT-proBNP values) was indeed based on the excellent negative predictive value. In our experience, researchers as well as journal editors are reluctant to dismiss the sensitivity and specificity as the most important parameters in diagnostic research, as is also reflected in the recent Standards for Reporting of Diagnostic Accuracy (STARD) guideline for the critical appraisal of diagnostic studies [Bossuyt et al., 2003a, 2003b].

A first step to prevent the continued focus on these measures when judging the value of diagnostic tests is to change the order in which the traditional parameters are presented, and to present predictive values first [Moons & Harrell, 2003; Rutten et al., 2006]. Diagnostic knowledge is not provided by answering the question, "How good is this test?" Diagnostic knowledge is the information needed to answer the question, "What is the probability of the presence of a specific disease given these test results?"

Notwithstanding its limitations, test research—focusing on estimating the accuracy of a single test to diagnose a disease—may offer relevant information. Most notably, it is helpful in the developmental phase of a new diagnostic test, when the accuracy of the test is yet unknown. One will often first assess whether the test provides different results in those *with* overt disease and those *without* this disease, sometimes even using healthy control subjects [Fryback & Thornbury, 1991; Moons & Grobbee, 2002a]. Furthermore, test research can be valuable in the realm of screening for a particular disorder in asymptomatic individuals. In this context, no test results other than the single screening test are considered. Depending on the type of screening not even age and gender may need to be accounted for [Moons et al., 2004a].

Rational Diagnostic Research

Because the object of diagnosis in practice is to predict the probability of the presence of disease from multiple diagnostic test results, the rational design of diagnostic research is very much determined by the understanding, if not mimicking, of everyday practice [Moons & Grobbee, 2005]. In the following, the three components of clinical epidemiologic diagnostic study design will be discussed: theoretical design, design of data collection, and design of data analysis.

Theoretical Design

The occurrence relation of a diagnostic study is:

$$P(D) = f(T1, T2, T3, \ldots Tn)$$

where P(D) is the probability of the disease and T1 to Tn the multiple diagnostic test results. The domain of any diagnostic occurrence relation typically includes patients suspected of a particular disease, usually defined by the presence (or combination) of particular symptom(s) and/or sign(s) that have led to consultation of a physician. In this context, the research objective can be to assess the optimal diagnostic strategy; that is, to determine which combination of diagnostic determinants in what order most adequately estimate the probability of disease presence, theoretically ranging from 0% to 100%. The goal can be to assess whether a certain, often newly developed, diagnostic test provides additional diagnostic value in clinical practice. Added value means that which is relative to the currently available or previously applied diagnostic tests. This implies a comparison of two occurrence relations: one excluding and one including the new test. Also, one could aim to compare two tests or different combinations of tests. For example, when a (new) less burdening or inexpensive test serves as an alternative for another established diagnostic test. This implies a comparison of an occurrence relation with the routinely available test(s) and a second occurrence relation including the alternative or new test in addition to the same routine tests.

The relevance of quantifying to what extent a particular diagnostic test or test strategy leads to optimal estimation (prediction) of the presence of a disease depends on the clinical consequences (i.e., targeted therapy) once the diagnosis has been established. Sometimes this may not be clear, such as when a new test provides truly novel disease information that potentially offers other treatment choices compared to the currently available test. An example is functional imaging with PET in diagnosing pancreatic cancer for which CT is the widely accepted gold standard. Compared to CT, PET may especially be helpful in detecting smaller lesions and distant metastases. Application of PET may lead to other diagnostic classifications that would require initiating other treatment options that have the potential different patient outcomes than the use of CT [Biesheuvel et al., 2006; Bossuyt et al., 2000; Lord et al., 2006]. In such a situation, studies may be conducted to estimate the (additional) benefit of a new diagnostic test (or strategy) on the patients' prognosis (e.g., in terms of morbidity, mortality, or quality of life), rather than doing a (cross-sectional) study comparing the diagnostic accuracy of PET with CT as the reference standard. Although inspired by a diagnostic question, such studies are not simply predictive. They become analogous to studies assessing the effects of therapeutic interventions on patient outcome and, consequently, carry the characteristics of intervention research. In intervention research the aim is to explain (Does addition of this test cause an improvement in patients' prognosis?) rather than predict (Does this test improve the estimation of the probability of the presence of a certain disease?). Thus, confounding becomes an issue, because one wishes to ensure that the observed effects are indeed causally related, that is, fully attributable, to the diagnostic test or strategy. Remember that you are in court and guilt must be proven beyond a reasonable doubt. All of this has important consequences for the theoretical design (notably for the outcome definition), the design of data collection (where randomized trials with a relevant time horizon may be an attractive option), and the data analysis (see Textbox 3.6). For the purpose of understanding the principles of clinical epidemiologic study design, this category of *diagnostic intervention* studies is not addressed in detail in this chapter; Chapters 5 and 10 discuss the

TEXTBOX 3.6 Typical diagnostic research versus diagnostic intervention research

Illustration of the difference between typical diagnostic research, assessing the contribution of multiple diagnostic determinants to the estimation (prediction) of the presence of a certain disease and "diagnostic intervention research" aimed at estimating (in this case explaining) the effect of diagnostic tests (plus subsequent interventions) on the patients' prognosis. The latter type of research becomes intervention research, requiring taking extraneous determinants (i.e., confounders) into account.

Diagnostic study

Diagnosis = $f\, T_{1-n}$
Where T is diagnostic determinant

Covers bold part

Diagnostic question → **diagnostic strategy** → **diagnosis** → intervention → outcome

Diagnostic Intervention study

Prognosis (disease outcome) = $(fT_{1-n}) + (fI \mid EF)$
Where T is diagnostic determinant, I is intervention following diagnosis and EF are extraneous factors.

Covers bold part

Diagnostic question → **diagnostic strategy** → **diagnosis** → **intervention** → **outcome**

Source: Author.

principles of intervention studies as do other papers [Biesheuvel et al., 2006; Bossuyt et al., 2000; Lord et al., 2006].

Design of Data Collection

Time

The object of the diagnostic process is cross-sectional by definition. It estimates (predicts) the probability of the *presence* of a disease (i.e., prevalence) rather than its future occurrence. Accordingly, the data for diagnostic studies are collected cross-sectionally. The determinant(s)—that is, the diagnostic test results—and the outcome—the presence or absence of the target disease as determined by the so-called reference standard—are theoretically determined at the same time. This is the moment that the patient presents with the symptoms or signs suggestive of the disease (t = 0). Even when the definitive diagnosis may take some time to become known, for example, when several days or even weeks are needed before all relevant tests have been performed and interpreted or when a "wait and see" period of time is used to set the final diagnosis (Textbox 3.6), these findings are used to establish that the diagnosis present at time is zero in diagnostic research.

Census or Sampling

Generally, a cross-sectional diagnostic study takes a census approach in which all consecutive patients suspected of a certain disease and fulfilling the predefined inclusion criteria are included. The potentially relevant diagnostic determinants under study as well as the "true" presence or absence of the target disease are measured in *all* patients.

Although more commonly found in etiologic research, a case-control study can offer a valid and more efficient alternative. In a diagnostic case-control study (which is a cross-sectional case-control study), all patients suspected of the target disease who are (eventually) diagnosed with the disease ("cases") are studied in detail, together with *a sample* of those suspected of the disease who turn out to be free from the target disease ("controls"). This usually implies that some determinants (notably the most expensive or patient-burdening ones) will be measured in cases and controls only, while the outcome (reference standard; and often the more readily available diagnostic determinants) will be assessed in all patients suspected of the target disease. This method will provide accurate estimates of the diagnostic accuracy of the test (or diagnostic strategy of interest) and for the relevant patient domain. The approach is similar to case-control studies in other research areas, notably in etiologic research (see Chapters 2 and 9). As in diagnostic research, the goal is to obtain absolute probabilities of disease presence given the determinants, in the data analysis portion of a diagnostic case-control study, the sampling fraction of the (cases and) controls should always be accounted for. A diagnostic case-control study offers a particularly attractive option when the measurement or documentation of one or more of the diagnostic tests under study are time-consuming or expensive. Examples are in measuring certain blood parameters, micro array testing, or the reading of imaging tests [Rutjes et al., 2005]. Diagnostic case-control studies are still relatively rare, despite their efficiency. In the example in Textbox 3.7, a

---

TEXTBOX 3.7 Example of a diagnostic case-control study

BACKGROUND: Information about the diagnostic value of cardiovascular magnetic resonance imaging (CMR) in detecting heart failure is scarce, and virtually lacking in patients with a diagnosis of chronic obstructive pulmonary disease (COPD).

AIM: To determine which results from CMR provide (additional) diagnostic information for identifying heart failure in patients with stable COPD.

METHODS: Participants were recruited from a cohort of 405 patients aged 65 years or over, with a general practitioner's diagnosis of COPD. After an extensive diagnostic assessment, the diagnosis of heart failure was established by an expert panel, using all available diagnostic information, including echocardiography, but without natriuretic peptide measurements (amino-terminal proB-type natriuretic peptide). In a nested case-control study design, 37 COPD patients with heart failure (cases) and a random sample of 41 COPD patients without heart failure (controls) received additional CMR measurements within three weeks from the panel meeting, before therapy was eventually changed. The diagnostic value of CMR measurements for heart failure was quantified using univariate and multivariate logistic modelling and area under the receiver operating characteristic curves (ROC-area) analysis.

RESULTS: Of the CMR measurements, left ventricular ejection fraction (LVEF) < 45% had the best test characteristics with a positive predictive value of 1.0 (95% CI 0.92–1.0), and a negative predictive value of 0.87 (95% CI 0.83–0.90). A 'CMR' model based on CMR parameters only (LVEF, indexed left and right atrial volume, and left ventricular end-systolic diameter) had an ROC-area of 0.88. These CMR measurements had significantly more additional diagnostic value beyond clinical signs and symptoms (ROC-area 0.91) than NT-proBNP (ROC-area 0.80), or electrocardiography (ROC-area 0.77). Further addition of NT-proBNP or electrocardiography had no independent value beyond the diagnostic model based on signs, symptoms, and CMR parameters.

CONCLUSIONS: CMR is the test with the highest diagnostic value in identifying heart failure in stable COPD patients, and could be an attractive alternative for echocardiography in these notoriously difficult to investigate group of patients.

Source: Author.

case-control approach was chosen to assess the added value of cardiac magnetic resonance (CMR) imaging in diagnosing heart failure in patients known to have chronic obstructive pulmonary disease. Because of the costs, time, and patient burden involved, CMT measurements were performed in all patients with heart failure (cases) and a sample of the remainder of the participants (controls) only [Rutten, 2005c].

Confusingly, diagnostic studies comparing test results in a group of patients with the disease under study—often those in an advanced stage of disease severity—with test results in a group of patients with absence of this disease without reference to a well-defined group of patients suspected of this disease, tend to be referred to as case-control studies as well, as nicely summarized by Rutjes et al. [2005]. This also holds true for studies comparing a sample of patients with the disease and a group of healthy individuals sampled from the general population. As discussed above, such studies will bias the estimates of diagnostic accuracy of the tests being studied and compromise the generalizability of the study results. This is because the cases and certainly the healthy controls do not reflect the relevant patient domain, which is all those suspected of having the disease for whom the tests are intended. However, we recall that these studies may provide information on the *potential* value of a new test early in its development. If a test is incapable of distinguishing those with severe disease from healthy individuals, it is unlikely to be useful in diagnosing the disease in patients suspected of the disease when addressed with a proper study design [Fryback & Thornbury, 1991; Moons & Grobbee, 2002a].

Experimental or Observational Research

Setting a diagnosis is not an aim in itself, but a vehicle to guide patient management and treatment in particular. The ultimate goal of diagnostic testing is to improve patient outcome. Hence, it has widely been advocated that when establishing a test's diagnostic accuracy, the impact of the test on patient outcome also must be quantified. Consequently, the characteristics of intervention research, notably a randomized design, have been proposed for diagnostic research questions as well [Bossuyt et al., 2000; Biesheuvel et al., 2006; Lord et al., 2006].

Commonly, however, patient outcome is not considered in diagnostic research. The aim usually is to quantify whether new diagnostic tests or strategies can replace currently applied tests or strategies. Replacement is typically indicated if the test or strategy under study is at least as accurate, in that it produces similar or better diagnostic classifications of the disease, while decreasing patient burden and/or costs. If a cross-sectional diagnostic study has indicated that the tests under study can similarly or better classify the presence or absence of the disease, the effect of those tests on patient outcome can usually be validly established without the need for a subsequent follow-up study on patient outcome. After all, earlier studies often adequately quantified the effects on patient outcome of the available treatment(s) for that disease. Using simple statistical or decision modeling techniques, one can combine the results of the cross-sectional diagnostic accuracy study and of those randomized therapeutic intervention studies. Hence, a test's effect on patient outcome can be quantified if 1) a cross-sectional accuracy study has shown that the index test or diagnostic strategy adequately detects the presence or absence of the target disease and 2) the effects of available therapeutic interventions in that disease on patient outcome are known, preferably from randomized trials. In such instances, diagnostic research does not require an additional intervention randomized comparison between two test-treatment strategies, one without and one with the test under study, to establish the test's effect on patient outcome.

An example in which a randomized study was not necessary to quantify the effect of the new test on patient outcome is the immunoassay test for the detection of *H. pylori* infection that was cross-sectionally compared with the established reference (a combination of rapid urease test, urea breath test, and histology) [Weijnen et al., 2001]. The new test indeed could substitute for the more costly and invasive reference, as it provided similar diagnostic accuracy or classifications. As consensus exists about the therapeutic management of patients infected with *H. pylori* (based on randomized clinical trials establishing the efficacy of treatment [McColl, 2002]), a subsequent randomized follow-up study to quantify the effects of using the new immunoassay test on patient outcome was not needed.

Another example comes from diagnosing deep vein thrombosis (DVT). The accuracy of repeated real-time B-mode compression ultrasonography of the lower legs was compared with venography, which was the existing reference at the time [Lensing et al., 1989]. It was found that the ultrasonography method was as accurate as the venography to include or exclude DVT. Hence, venography has been widely replaced by repeated ultrasonography as the reference method for detecting DVT, without the need of randomized trials comparing the effects of venography plus treatment versus ultrasonography plus treatment on patient outcome.

There are situations in which randomized follow-up studies on patient outcome are needed to properly quantify the consequences of a novel diagnostic test or strategy on patient outcome [Bossuyt et al., 2000; Biesheuvel et al., 2006; Lord et al., 2006]. Notably, when a new diagnostic technology under study might be "better," to the extent that it provides new information potentially leading to other treatment choices, than the existing tests or strategy, a randomized trial may be useful. As described above, functional imaging with PET in diagnosing pancreatic cancer, for which CT is the current reference, offers an example. Also, when there is no direct link between the result of the new diagnostic test under study and an established treatment indication, such as the finding of non-calcified small nodules (less than 5.0 mm) when screening for lung cancer with low-dose spiral CT scanning, an experimental approach quantifying the effect on patient outcome may be required. Finally, the diagnostic technology under study itself may have direct therapeutic properties and change patient outcome. Such procedures are rare, but salpingography to determine patency of the uteral tubes is an example.

When performing a randomized trial to determine the impact of a diagnostic test or strategy on patient outcome, an initially *diagnostic* research question is transformed into *therapeutic* research question (with the goal of establishing causality) with corresponding consequences for the design of the study. A disadvantage of a randomized approach to directly quantify the contribution of a diagnostic test and treatment on patient outcome is that it often addresses diagnosis and treatment as a single combined strategy, a "package deal." This makes it impossible to determine afterwards whether a positive effect on patient outcome was attributed solely to the improved diagnosis by using the test under study or to the chosen (new) treatment strategies.

Study Population

A diagnostic test or strategy should be able to distinguish between those with the target disease and those without, among subjects representing the relevant clinical domain. The domain is thus defined by patients suspected of a particular disease based on the signs and symptoms presented. Consequently, patients in whom the presence of disease has already been established or in whom the probability of the disease is considered high enough to initiate adequate therapeutic actions, fall outside the domain, just as patients where the probability of disease is deemed too low to warrant additional diagnostic tests. Furthermore, we recommend that investigators restrict domain definitions, and thus the study population, to the setting or level of care (e.g., primary or secondary care), as the diagnostic accuracy and combinations of these tests usually vary across care settings [Oudega et al., 2005a; Knottnerus, 2002a]. This is a consequence of differences in the distribution of severity of the disease across the different settings.

The study population should reflect the domain. There is no need for the study population to form a "representative," let alone a random selection of representatives from the domain. The population of a study could be defined as: all consecutive patients suspected of the disease of interest that present themselves to one of the participating centers during a defined period and in whom the additional diagnostic tests under investigation are considered. Exclusion criteria should be few to ensure wide applicability of the findings. They would typically include alarm symptoms requiring immediate action or referral (e.g., melena in the dyspepsia example in the beginning of this chapter) and contraindications for one of the major diagnostic determinants (tests) involved (e.g., as claustrophobia for MRI assessments). One could argue that "patients suspected of the disease" as an inclusion criterion is too subjective, so in many studies the definition includes symptoms and signs often accompanying the disease. For example, a study to address the added value of a novel test to diagnose or exclude myocardial infarction could include "patients with symptoms suggestive of myocardial infarction." Alternatively, the study population can be defined as "patients with chest pain or discomfort" or a combination of the two, "patients with chest pain of discomfort or other symptoms and signs compatible with a myocardial infarction."

Diagnostic Determinants

As the diagnosis in practice is typically made on the basis of multiple diagnostic determinants, all test results that are or could potentially be used in practice should be considered and measured in each patient. Starting with patient history and physical examination, subsequent tests need to be measured to determine their *added* value. In the earlier example of the *H. pylori* test to diagnose peptic ulcer, the main signs and symptoms as well as the *H. pylori* test would have to be included as potential determinants. There is, however, a limit to the number of tests that can be included in a study, because of logistic reasons and the larger sample size that is required with each additional test that is considered (see below). Hence, the choice of the determinants to be included should be based on both the available literature and a thorough understanding of clinical practice.

Because the quality of the determinant information in a study should resemble the quality of this information in daily clinical practice, one could argue that all determinants should be measured by the participating physicians according to usual care; without efforts to standardize or improve the diagnostic assessment. In a study involving multiple sites and physicians, this may significantly increase interobserver variability in the diagnostic testing, which could underestimate the potential diagnostic value of (combinations of) test results, although the study would indicate the current average value of the tests in clinical practice. Moreover, this effect is likely to be larger for more subjective tests, such as auscultation of the lungs. An alternative would be to train the physicians to apply a standardized diagnostic assessment. One example is to make sure that history taking and physical examination are done in a similar manner in all patients. One may also ask experts in the field to do the diagnostic tests under study. This, however, has the disadvantage that it will likely overestimate the diagnostic accuracy of the tests in daily practice and reduce the applicability of the study results. For a multicenter, multi-doctor study, we recommend a pragmatic approach where all diagnostic determinants are assessed as much as possible according to daily practice and by the practicing physicians involved, with efforts to standardize measurements.

Outcome

The outcome in diagnostic research is typically dichotomous: the presence or absence of the disease of interest. Although sometimes outcomes on higher aggregate levels are used (e.g., the presence of any life-threatening condition), the usual outcome is the presence versus absence of a well-defined diagnosis (e.g., myocardial infarction or pneumonia). As discussed above, in clinical practice commonly more than one disease is considered in a patient presenting with particular symptoms and signs, that is, the so-called *differential diagnosis* [Sackett et al., 1985]. Accordingly, the outcome should often be polytomous rather than dichotomous. Attempts have been made to study and analyze polytomous outcomes in a single (multivariable) diagnostic study, but the design of these studies, particularly in the design of the data analysis, is complicated. Further methodological developments to adequately deal with polytomous or perhaps ordinal diagnostic outcomes are awaited [Harrell, 2001]. Hence, the general approach in diagnostic research is to study dichotomous outcomes, which most often will be the presence versus absence of the target disease.

In diagnostic research, as in each epidemiologic study, adequate assessment of the outcome is crucial. The outcome should be measured as accurately as possible and with the best available methods. The term most often applied to indicate the ideal diagnostic outcome is *gold standard*, referring to the virtually non-existent situation where measuring the disease is devoid of false-negatives and false-positives. More recently, the more appropriate term *reference standard* was introduced to indicate the non-golden properties of almost all diagnostic procedures in today's practice, including procedures like biopsy combined with histologic confirmation for cancer diagnoses. Very few diagnostic procedures do not require human interpretation. Moreover, the term *reference standard* directly illustrates the essence of diagnostic studies, which is the value of (or combinations of) diagnostic determinants assessed *with reference to* the diagnostic outcome.

Deciding on the reference standard is a crucial but difficult task in diagnostic research. The reference standard is the best procedure(s) that exists at the time of study initiation to determine the presence (or absence) of the target disease. The word *best* in this context means the measurement of disease that best guides subsequent medical action. Hence, the reference method to be used in a diagnostic study may very well include one or a combination of (expensive and complicated) tests that are not routinely available or applied in everyday clinical practice. Note that this contrasts with the assessment of the diagnostic determinants of interest, which should more or less mimic daily practice to enhance generalizability of study results to daily practice.

Preferably, the final diagnosis should be established independently from the results of the diagnostic tests under study. Commonly, the observer who assesses the final diagnosis using the reference method is blinded for *all* of the test results under study. If this blinding is not guaranteed, the information provided by the preceding tests may implicitly or explicitly be used in the assessment of the final diagnosis by the reference method. Consequently, the two information sources cannot be distinguished and the estimates of accuracy of the tests being studied may be biased. Although theoretically this bias can lead to both an under- and overestimation of the accuracy of the evaluated tests, it commonly results in an overestimation; the final diagnosis may be guided to some extent by the results of the test under evaluation, artificially decreasing the number of false-positive and false-negative results. This kind of bias is often referred to as diagnostic review or incorporation bias [Sackett et al., 1985; Swets, 1988; Begg & Metz, 1990; Ransohoff & Feinstein, 1978].

The possibility to blind the outcome assessors for the results of the tests under study depends on the type of reference standard applied. It is surely feasible if the reference standard consists of a completely separate test, for example, imaging techniques or serum levels of a marker. Because this kind of reference test is not available for many diseases (e.g., psychiatric disorders), it is infeasible or even unethical to apply (notably when the test is invasive and patient burdening) so next-best solutions should be sought. In particular, an approach involving a so-called *consensus diagnosis* determined by an outcome panel often is applied; these often are combined with a clinical follow-up period to further promote an adequate assessment of the outcome [Swets, 1988; Moons & Grobbee, 2002b; Begg, 1990]. Outcome panels consist of a (usually unequal) number of experts on the clinical problem. During consensus meetings, the panel establishes the final diagnosis in each study patient based on as much patient information as possible. This includes information from patient history, physical examination, and all additional tests. Often, any clinically relevant information from each patient (e.g., future diagnostic tests and diagnoses, response to treatment targeted at the outcome disease) during a defined follow-up period is forwarded to the outcome panel in order to allow for a better judgment on whether the target disease was present at the time of (initial) presentation [Moons & Grobbee, 2002b]. When using a consensus diagnosis based on all available information as the reference standard, the test results studied as potential diagnostic determinants are also included ("incorporated") in the outcome assessment. As mentioned earlier, this may lead to bias ("incorporation bias"). To fully prevent incorporation bias, the outcome panel should decide on the final diagnosis without knowledge of the results of the tests under study. This may seem an attractive solution, but limiting the information forwarded to the panel may increase misclassification in the outcome assessment with varying and unpredictable consequences, that is, an over- or underestimation of the diagnostic value of the tests under study. Incorporation bias commonly leads to an overestimation of the value of the tests under study that can be considered when interpreting the study data.

There are no general solutions to this dilemma that is inherent to using a consensus diagnosis as the reference standard. The pros and cons of excluding or including the results from all or some of the tests under study in the assessment of the final diagnosis by the outcome panel should be weighed in each particular study. Consider a study that aims to assess which combination of tests from patient history and physical examination best predicts the presence of heart failure in patients suspected of the syndrome, and whether plasma BNP levels or echocardiography have added diagnostic value. As in several earlier studies on suspected heart failure, an outcome panel can determine the "true" presence or absence of heart failure [Moons & Grobbee, 2002b]. When studying the accuracy of an index test known to receive much weight in the consensus judgment (in this example echocardiography and to a lesser extent BNP levels), it is preferable *not to use* these tests in the assessment of the final diagnosis. Inclusion of this test in the consensus diagnosis undoubtedly will overestimate its diagnostic value. Doing so requires that the remaining diagnostic information, including clinical follow-up data, enables the panel to accurately categorize patients by those with and without heart failure. Non-availability of the BNP levels will probably not pose a major problem, but withholding the echocardiographic findings from the outcome panel may seriously endanger the validity of the outcome assessment. Consequently, we may be able to quantify the added value of BNP levels, but not of the echocardiogram. Alternatively, the outcome panel could judge the presence or absence of heart failure first without considering the echocardiographic findings and then subsequently with the echocardiography results. Comparing the outcome classification according to both approaches may provide some insight in the effect of incorporation bias on the (boundaries of the) accuracy of the test under study, in this case echocardiography.

As mentioned earlier, in certain situations it is not feasible or even unethical to apply the best available reference method in all study patients at the time of presentation, in particular when the reference test is invasive and may lead to complications. For example, this applies to studies on the diagnosis of pulmonary embolism, where it may be unethical to perform pulmonary angiography in all suspected patients, including those with a negative ventilation-perfusion lung scan result. In studies on the diagnosis of malignancies, it is often difficult to establish or rule out a malignancy at t = 0 even when multiple tests, including sophisticated imaging techniques, are performed. Under these circumstances, a clinical follow-up period may offer useful information. It should be emphasized here that a clinical follow-up period is applied to assess at the time of presentation of the complaints (t = 0) whether the disease of interest was indeed present or not. It is then assumed that the natural history of the (untreated) target disease implies that the target disease was present but unrecognized at t = 0. A clinical follow-up period to establish a diagnosis has been successfully applied in studies on the accuracy of diagnostic tests for a variety of diseases, including pulmonary embolism, bacterial meningitis, and certain types of cancer. For example, Fijten et al. [1995] studied which signs and symptoms were helpful in ruling out colorectal cancer in patients presenting with fecal blood loss in primary care. It was impossible to perform colonoscopies and additional imaging or surgery in all participants to rule in or out a malignancy. Therefore, all patients were followed for an additional period of at least 12 months after inclusion in the study, assuming that colorectal cancer detected during the follow-up period would indicate presence of the cancer at baseline (t = 0). Obviously, the follow-up period should be limited in length, especially in diseases with a relatively high incidence, to prevent new cases from are being counted as prevalent ones. The acceptable clinical follow-up period varies and depends on the natural history and incidence of the disease studied. A 6- to 12-month period is often encountered in the literature for cancer studies. For venous thromboembolism this is usually three months, and in the study of bacterial meningitis it was one week.

Besides documenting the natural history of a disease one may also document the response to treatment targeted at the outcome diagnosis and use this information to determine whether the target disease was present at t = 0. Response to therapy may be helpful in excluding (in the case of no response) or confirming (in the case of a beneficial effect on symptoms) the target disease. In these situations, one should be aware that response following therapy provides no definite proof of the disease, because the response could result from other factors. Similarly, non-response does not preclude the presence of the disease at t = 0. Examples of using the response to empirical treatment to confirm a diagnosis are studies in suspected heart failure. In fact, clinical response to targeted therapy is included in the current criteria for heart failure as an adjunct to signs and symptoms and echocardiography (Table 3.1).

TABLE 3.1 Definition of Heart Failure According to the European Society of Cardiology

I. Symptoms of heart failure (at rest or during exercise)

and

II. Objective evidence (preferably by echocardiography) or cardiac dysfunction (systolic and/or diastolic at rest, and in cases where the diagnosis is in doubt)

and

III. Response to treatment directed towards heart failure

Criteria I and II should be fulfilled in all cases.

Bias in Diagnostic Research

As outlined earlier in this book, bias affects the validity of a study. Bias is systematic error. To decide about the validity of a particular study, the critical reader should answer the following question: are the quantitative results, whether relative risk, odds ratio, predictive values, and ROC area or multivariable regression coefficients, correct in the patient population in whom the study was performed? Consideration of the applicability of the (valid) results to the more abstract domain of the study is a matter of generalizability of the results and not of validity. In this respect, the still common use of the term *internal* validity to indicate validity and *external* validity to indicate generalizability or applicability is unfortunate. Bias in diagnostic research occurs in those circumstances where the results are distorted because of flaws in the study design. Usually in the design of data collection but possibly also in the data analysis (see below). From available articles and textbook chapters on the methodology of diagnostic research, one can easily produce an extensive list of types of potential biases in diagnostic research, including rather illustrious sounding biases such as centripetal bias, patient filtering bias, diagnostic safety bias, co-intervention bias, inter-observer variability bias, intra-observer variability bias, and temporal effects bias. The use of so many terms, which often refer to the same phenomenon, carries the danger of complicating the understanding of the methodology of diagnostic studies. The recent STARD guideline also aimed to reduce this confusion [Bossuyt et al., 2003a, 2003b]. As in all types of research examined in this book, a distinction will be made between two main types of bias, that is, confounding bias and "other forms" of bias. Within the latter category, however, some biases typical to diagnostic research will be exemplified, and the terms often used in the literature will be mentioned, albeit that the use of these specific terms is discouraged.

Confounding

Confounding is bias that leads to erroneous conclusions of causality in etiologic research. As diagnostic research is predictive or descriptive, confounding or its exclusion plays no role. Although there may be similarities in the multivariable data analysis of diagnostic and prognostic research on the one hand and research unraveling causality on the other, the purpose is profoundly different. In causal research, a multivariable approach is used to *explain* whether the occurrence of an outcome can truly be attributed to a particular determinant by adjusting for other risk factors. In diagnostic and prognostic research, the mission is "simply" to *predict*—as accurately as possible—the probability of presence (in the case of diagnosis) or incidence (in the case of prognosis) of outcomes using multiple predictors. The motive is not to explain the disease occurrence; causality is of no concern. All variables potentially associated with the outcome, causally or non-causally, can be considered in a diagnostic (or prognostic) study. Most diagnostic determinants—such as blood markers, imaging parameters, or histopathology results—will be consequences of this disease and can thus never be a cause of the disease.

Other Biases

Certain other biases may particularly affect diagnostic research. The two most important ones are discussed below.

1. Knowledge of results from diagnostic tests (determinants) influences patient selection to undergo subsequent tests including the reference test(s).

In routine care, not every patient suspected of a particular disease undergoes the entire diagnostic work-up. Referral to subsequent testing is always based on previous test results. Hence, only a selected sample undergoes further testing or disease verification, including the reference test. In diagnostic research, ideally *all* patients undergo the entire diagnostic work-up, including the reference test, to determine the final diagnosis. It has been shown extensively that selective referral or work-up or disease verification leads to biased estimates of the accuracy of the tests under study, and still occurs in many (up to about 25%) of the published diagnostic studies [Lijmer et al., 1999; Rutjes et al., 2005; Whiting et al., 2004]. However, we prefer to discourage all of this different terminology for the same bias or problem, because it adds to the confusion surrounding diagnostic research. To prevent this bias, outcome assessment ("verification") should be ensured in all patients in the design of data collection. This means that each study patient undergoes the reference test(s). If this is not feasible or deemed unethical, a clinical follow-up period and/or outcome panel to ultimately determine the presence or absence of the target disease in all patients could offer a solution (see above).

2. Knowledge of the results of the diagnostic determinants influences the result of the outcome assessment.

As stated earlier, this bias is often categorized in the diagnostic literature as "incorporation bias" and "diagnostic review bias." This bias particularly occurs when there is no objective reference and a consensus (panel) diagnosis uses a "reference standard" that is partly based on results from the diagnostic tests studied on their performance. These results are therefore "incorporated" into the reference standard. Information bias also can occur without the use of a consensus approach. The term *diagnostic review bias* is often used to indicate bias that occurs when the assessor of the reference test(s) is aware of the results of one or more of the diagnostic determinants studies. Obviously, this is more likely when the reference test is not 24 carat gold. Such bias should always be considered when the interpretation of the reference method is subject to (intra and inter) observer variation, a common situation, and is less likely when reference tests include more "objective" testing, such as biochemical parameters [Moons & Grobbee, 2002b]. This bias only can be prevented fully by rigorous blinding of those involved in establishing the definitive diagnosis to the results of all diagnostic tests to be evaluated.

Design of Data Analysis

Objective of the Analysis

Analysis of data from multivariable diagnostic studies serves a number of purposes: 1) to show which potential diagnostic determinants independently contribute to the estimation of the probability of disease presence (i.e., which determinants change the probability of disease presence?); 2) to quantify to what extent these contributing determinants change the probability of disease presence (i.e., to estimate the relative weights of these determinants); 3) to develop and validate a diagnostic model or rule to facilitate the estimation of the probability of disease given the combination of test results in individual patients in clinical practice [Moons et al., 2004a].

Whether all three goals can or should be pursued depends on the motive of the study. If the aim is only to determine whether a particular test has added value or may replace another existing test, then goal three may not be relevant. Furthermore, prior knowledge and the amount and type of study data determine whether goals 2 and 3 should be addressed, as we will discuss below. We do not intend to provide full details on the statistical analysis of diagnostic data. For this we refer to the (statistical) literature.

Required Number of Subjects

The multivariable character of diagnostic research creates problems for the estimation of the required number of study subjects. Power calculations do exist for test research, that is, studies aiming to estimate the diagnostic value (e.g., sensitivity, specificity, likelihood ratio, or ROC area) of a single test or to compare the properties of two single tests [Simel et al., 1991; Hanley & McNeil, 1983]. For multivariable studies that aim to quantify the independent contribution of each test with sufficient precision, no straightforward methods to estimate the required patient number are available. Several authors have stipulated, however, that in multivariable prediction research, including diagnostic studies, for each determinant (or diagnostic test) studied at least ten subjects are needed in the smallest category of the outcome variable to allow proper statistical modeling. In case of the typical dichotomous outcome, that is, those with or without the disease, this usually implies ten individuals with the disease [Harrell et al., 1996; Peduzzi et al., 1996]. If the number of potential determinants is much larger than 10% of the number of diseased, the analysis tends to result in too optimistic of a diagnostic accuracy of an eventually developed diagnostic strategy or model. The expected number of patients with the target disease thus limits the number of determinants to be analyzed and what might be inferred from a study.

Univariable Analysis

Before proceeding to multivariable analyses, we recommend to first perform a univariable analysis in which each individual potential determinant is related to the outcome. Biostatisticians often refer to this type of analysis as a *bivariate analysis* because the association between two variables (determinant and outcome) is studied. In diagnostic research, categorical determinants with more than two categories and continuous determinants are often dichotomized by introducing a threshold. This commonly leads to loss of information [Royston et al., 2006]. For example, dichotomizing the body temperature > 37° Celsius (C) as test positive and ≤ 37° Celsius as test negative implies that the diagnostic implications for a person with a temperature of 37.5°C is the same as for a person with 41°C. Second, the resulting association heavily depends on the threshold applied. This may explain why different studies of the same diagnostic test yield different associations. The aim of the univariable analysis is to obtain insight in the association of each potential determinant (test) and the presence or absence of the disease. Although it is common to (only) include in the multivariable analysis the determinants that show statistical significance (P-value < 0.05) in univariable analysis, it may lead to optimistic estimates of the accuracy of a diagnostic model (see below) [Harrell, 2001; Steyerberg et al., 2000; Sun et al., 1996]. This chance of "optimism" increases when the number of potential determinants clearly exceeds the "1 to 10 rule" described earlier. It is therefore recommended to use a more liberal selection criterion, for example, $P < 0.20, 0.25$, or an even higher threshold. The downside to this is that more determinants will qualify for multivariable analysis, requiring the need for so-called internal validation and penalization or shrinkage methods that we will discuss later in this chapter. Alternatively, univariable analyses may guide combination and clustering of determinants, ideally influenced by prior knowledge of the most important determinants. Methods have been developed to incorporate prior knowledge into the selection of predictors [Harrell, 2001; Steyerberg et al., 2004]. Finally, univariable analysis is useful to determine the number of missing values for each determinant and for the outcome, and whether these missing values are missing completely at random, or rather missing at random (MAR) or missing not at random (MNAR). The nature and implications of these different forms of missing data are discussed in Chapter 2 as well as methods available to deal with missing values in diagnostic and other multivariable prediction research.

Multivariable Analysis

Diagnostic practice is probabilistic, multivariable, and sequential. Consequently, the multivariable analysis is the main component of diagnostic data analysis. In the multivariable analysis, the probability of disease is related to *combinations* of multiple diagnostic determinants, in various orders. Multivariable analysis can accommodate the order in which tests are used in practice and will show which (combination of) tests truly contributes to the diagnostic probability estimation. To address the chronology and sequence of testing in clinical practice, the accuracy of combinations of easily obtainable determinants should be estimated first and subsequently the added value of the more burdening and costly tests [Moons et al., 1999].

Logistic regression modeling is the generally accepted statistical method for multivariable diagnostic studies with a dichotomous outcome [Hosmer & Lemeshow, 1989; Harrell, 2001]. Other statistical methods, such as neural networks and classification and regression trees (CART), have been advocated, but these received much criticism as both often result in overly optimistic results [Harrell, 2001; Tu, 1996]. Therefore, we will focus on the use of logistic regression models for multivariable diagnostic research.

The determinants included in the first multivariable logistic regression model are usually selected on the basis of both prior knowledge and (with care) the results of univariable analysis. Also, the first model tends to concentrate on determinants that are easy to obtain in practice. Hence, this model typically includes test results from history taking and physical examination [Moons et al., 2004a; Moons et al., 1999]. A logistic regression model estimates the log odds (*logit*) of the disease probability as a function of one or more predictors:

$$\log [\textit{probability (outcome event)/probability (non-event)}] =$$
$$\beta_0 + \beta_1 * T_1 + \ldots \beta_n * T_n = \textit{linear predictor} \tag{Eq. 1}$$

in which β_0 is the intercept and β_1 to β_6 are regression coefficients of T_1 to T_n. T_1 to T_n are the results of the diagnostic determinants (tests) obtained from patient history and physical examination. The sum of the intercept and regression coefficients multiplied by the predictor values is called the linear predictor (*lp*) [Harrell et al., 1996]. A regression coefficient can be interpreted as the log odds of the outcome event relative to a non-event per unit increase in a specific test; in case of a dichotomous test the log odds of the outcome event for a positive relative to a negative test. The odds ratio can be computed as the antilog of the regression coefficient [exp(β)]. Equation 1 can be rewritten to estimate the probability of the outcome event for an individual patient:

probability (disease presence) =
$$exp(\beta_0 + \beta_1 * T_1 + \ldots \beta_n * T_n)/[1 + exp(\beta_0 + \beta_1 * T_1 + \ldots \beta_n * T_n)] =$$
$$1/\{1 + exp[-(lp)]\} \tag{Eq. 2}$$

Accordingly, the probability of absence of disease can be estimated as:

probability (disease absence) = 1 − probability (disease presence) (Eq. 3)

The next step is remove the non-contributing or non-significant determinants to obtain a reduced model with a similar diagnostic performance as
the full model. Non-contributing tests are manually (one by one) excluded
using the log likelihood ratio test, again at a liberal level. For example, diagnostic tests could be excluded if the significance level exceeds, say 0.10 or
0.15. This leads to a so-called reduced model that includes only those history and physical determinants that independently contribute to the probability estimation. The regression coefficient of each determinant reflects its
independent contribution (weight) to the outcome probability (see equation 1).

The next step is to estimate the diagnostic accuracy of this reduced multivariable model. The accuracy of a model is commonly estimated by two
parameters: the calibration (reliability or goodness of fit) and the discrimination [Hosmer & Lemeshow, 1989; Harrell, 2001]. Calibration is measured
by the level of agreement between the disease probabilities estimated by the
model versus the observed disease frequencies. Good calibration means
that the estimated probability of disease presence is similar to the observed
proportion in patient subgroups, for example, 20 equal groups of the distribution of estimated disease probabilities after ordering from 0 to 1. The best
way to examine this is by a graphical comparison. Figure 3.2 shows a calibration plot of a "reduced diagnostic history and physical model" for the diagnosis of deep vein thrombosis (DVT) estimated from 400 primary care
patients suspected of DVT. Ideally, the slope of the calibration plot is 1 and
the intercept 0. The presented model includes six patient history and physical examination determinants, taking the form of equation 1. The calibration of this model was very good, as the predicted probabilities are very
similar to the observed disease prevalence across the entire distribution.
Figure 3.2 shows a slight overestimation by the model in those patients in
the lower estimated disease probability range.

A frequently used statistic to assess whether a multivariable model shows
good calibration is the so-called *goodness-of-fit* test. A statistically significant (P
< 0.05) test indicates marked differences between predicted and observed
probabilities and thus poor calibration [Hosmer, 1989]. This test, however,
often lacks statistical power to determine important deviations from poor calibration because the P-value is seldom less than 0.05 [Harrell, 2001; Hosmer
& Lemeshow, 1989]. We therefore recommend that the investigator closely examine the calibration plot to determine a model's calibration.

The discrimination of a multivariable model refers to the model's ability to discriminate between subjects with and without the disease. This is estimated with the area under the Receiver Operating Characteristic (ROC)
curve or the c-index (index of concordance) of the model [Harrell et al.,

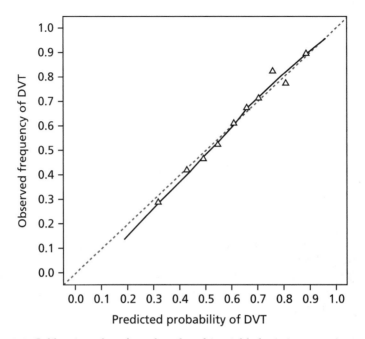

FIGURE 3.2 Calibration plot of a reduced multivariable logistic regression model, including six determinants from patient history and physical examination to estimate the probability of the presence of DVT in 400 patients suspected of DVT at 12 months of follow-up. The dotted line represents the line of identity, that is, perfect model calibration. All triangles represent 10% of the patients. The triangle on the left end represents the 10% with the lowest predicted probability of disease, with the mean predicted probability (32%) on the x-axis and a somewhat lower observed prevalence of DVT (28%) in the same patients on the y-axis.

1982; Hanley & McNeil, 1982]. Figure 3.3 shows the ROC curve of the "reduced multivariable history and physical examination model" (red curve). A multivariable model in fact can be considered a "single" test, existing of several component tests, with the model's estimated probability of disease presence (using equation 2) as the "single" test result. The ROC curve exhibits the sensitivity ("true positive rate") and 1 – specificity ("false positive rate") of the model for each possible threshold in the range of "estimated probabilities." The area under the ROC curve reflects the overall discriminative value of the model, irrespective of the chosen threshold. It exhibits the extent to which the model can discriminate between subjects with and without the target disease. The diagonal line reflects the worst model or test. For each threshold, the number of correctly diagnosed patients equals the number of false diagnoses, that is, no discriminating value and an ROC area of 0.5 ("half of the square"). In other words, the probability of a false and

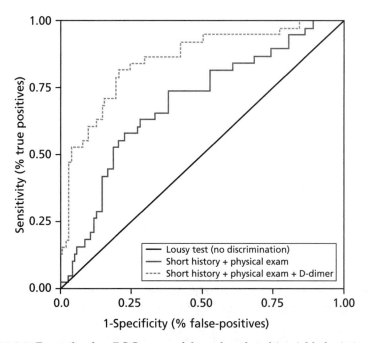

FIGURE 3.3 Example of an ROC curve of the reduced multivariable logistic regression model, including the same six determinants as in Figure 3.2. The ROC area of the "reduced history + physical model" (red) was 0.70 (95% confidence interval [CI], 0.66–0.74) and of the same model added with the D-dimer assay (green) 0.84 (95% CI, 0.80–0.88).

true diagnosis is both 50%, a model that is no better than flipping a coin. The best model is reflected by the "curve" that runs from the lower left to the upper left and upper right corners, yielding an ROC area of 1.0 ("the entire square"). Note that for this model a threshold can be chosen that leads to a sensitivity and specificity of both 1.0. Hence, the more the ROC curve is in the left upper corner—the higher the area under the curve (the closer to 1.0)—the higher the discriminative value of the model. More exactly defined, the ROC area is the probability that for each (randomly) chosen pair of a diseased and non-diseased subject, the model estimates a higher probability for the diseased than for the non-diseased individual [Harrell et al., 1982; Hanley & McNeil, 1982].

The next step is to extend the "reduced history + physical model" by the subsequent test from the work-up in our example study on DVT (see also below); this was the D-dimer assay. This shows the assay's added value in the probability estimation, using the same statistical procedures as described above. Whether the D-dimer test is a truly independent predictor is estimated again by the log likelihood ratio test [Harrell et al., 2001; Hosmer

& Lemeshow, 1989]. Next, the calibration and discrimination of the extended model are examined. The calibration of this extended model was good (data not shown), and the discriminatory value was high (ROC area 0.84; Figure 3.3). Methods have been proposed to formally estimate the precision of differences in ROC area, in this case 0.84 − 0.70 = 0.14, by calculating the 95% confidence interval or P-value of this difference. In this calculation, one needs to account for the correlation between both models ("tests") as they are based on the same subjects [Hanley & McNeil, 1983]. In our example study, the confidence intervals did not overlap, indicating a significant added value at the 0.05 level.

This process of model extension can be repeated for each subsequent test. Moreover, all of the above analytical techniques can be used to compare the difference in the (added) diagnostic value of two tests separately when the aim is to choose between the two or to compare the diagnostic accuracy of various test orders. We should emphasize that the ROC area of a multivariable diagnostic model or even a single diagnostic test has no direct clinical meaning. It addresses the overall value of diagnostic models or tests, irrespective of the chosen threshold. Moreover, it can be used to compare the overall discriminative value of different diagnostic models, strategies, or tests.

This example exemplifies the need for multivariable diagnostic research. A comparison between models including fewer or additional tests enables the investigator to learn not only about the added value of tests but also about the relevance of moving from simple to more advanced testing in practice. It should be noted that the data analysis as outlined above only quantifies which (subsequent) tests have independent or incremental value in the diagnostic probability estimation and thus should be included in the final diagnostic model from an *accuracy* point of view. It might still be relevant to judge whether the increase in accuracy of the test outweighs its costs and patient burden. This weighing can be done formally, including a full cost-effectiveness or cost-minimization analysis accounting for the consequences and utilities of false-positive and false-negative diagnoses. This enters the realm of medical decision-making and medical technology assessment and is not covered here.

The multivariable analysis can be used to create a clinical prediction rule that can be used in clinical practice to estimate the probability that an individual patient has the target disease given his or her documented test results. There are various examples of such multivariable diagnostic rules: a rule for diagnosing the presence or absence of DVT [Wells et al., 1997; Oudega et al., 2005b], the Apgar score [Apgar, 1953], pulmonary embolism [Wells et al., 1997], conjunctivitis [Rietveld et al., 2004], and bacterial meningitis [Oostenbrink et al., 2001]. There are various ways to present a diagnostic rule in a publication and to enhance its use in clinical practice as we will describe below.

Internal Validation and Shrinkage of the Diagnostic Model

An initial prediction model commonly shows a too optimistic discrimination (ROC area relatively high, closer to 1.0) and calibration (slope close to 1.0 and intercept close to 0) when it is applied to the data from which it is derived, the derivation or development data set. The model is so-called *overfitted*. This means that the model's predicted probabilities will be too extreme ("too high for the diseased and too low for the non-diseased") when the model is applied to new patients. There it will usually yield less extreme predicted probabilities and thus poorer calibration (slope commonly lower than 1.0 and an intercept different from 0) and discrimination (lower ROC area) [Harrell, 2001; Steyerberg et al., 2003; Van Houwelingen, 2001]. The amount of optimism (overfitting) in both calibration and discrimination can be estimated using so-called *internal validation* methods. Here *internal* means that no new data are used, just data from the derivation set.

The most widely used internal validation methods are the split-sample, cross-validation, and bootstrapping methods [Harrell, 2001]. In the first two, part of the derivation data set (e.g., a random sample of 75% or a sample based on the time of inclusion in the study) is used for model development. The remainder (e.g., 25%) is applied for estimating the model's accuracy. With bootstrapping, first a model is developed (fitted) on the full sample as described above. In brief, multiple random samples (e.g., 100) are then drawn with replacement from the full sample. On each bootstrap sample, the model is redeveloped. The calibration (i.e., slope and intercept of the calibration plot) and discrimination (ROC area) of each bootstrap model are then compared to the corresponding estimates of the bootstrap models when applied (tested) in the original full sample. These differences can be averaged, and they provide an indication of the average optimism of the bootstrap models. This average optimism in discrimination and calibration can be used to adjust the original model estimated in the full sample, that is, adjusting or shrinking the regression coefficients and ROC area. Application of the shrunken model (regression coefficients) in new patients will generally yield better (less optimistic) calibration, and the adjusted discrimination (ROC area) better approximates the discrimination that can be expected in new patients [Harrell, 2001; Steyerberg et al., 2001b; van Houwelingen, 2001]. Bootstrapping is preferred over split-sample or cross-validation as an internal validation tool as it is more efficient. Bootstrapping uses all patient data for model development and for the model validation. Most importantly, however, all steps in the model's development, including decisions on the transformation, clustering, and re-coding of variables as well as on the selection of variables (both in the univariable and multivariable analysis) can and should be redone in every bootstrap sample [Harrell, 2001; Steyerberg et al., 2003] Bootstrapping techniques have become widely available in standard statistical software packages, such as STATA, SAS, and S-plus. Other methods for shrinkage or penalizing a model for potential overfitting are the use of a heuristic shrinkage factor [Copas, 1983; van Houwelingen & LeCessie, 1990] and the use of penalized estimation methods [van Houwelingen, 2001; Harrell, 2001; Moons et al., 2004b].

Inferences From Multivariable Analysis

The lower the number of study patients, the higher the number of candidate determinants, and the more *predictor-selection-techniques-based-on-P-values* are used, the larger the chance of optimism of the final diagnostic model and the need for bootstrapping and shrinkage. Under certain extreme circumstances, even bootstrapping and shrinkage techniques cannot account for all optimism [Steyerberg et al., 2003; Bleeker et al., 2003]. The analysis and inferences then should be more cautious. Preferably one should not try to goal 3 described above, but restrict the analysis to investigate those that may be independent predictors of the presence or absence of the disease (goal 1) and estimate their shrunken relative weights (goal 2). If nonetheless after bootstrapping and shrinkage a full model is reported, we advise investigators to stress the need for future studies focused on confirming the observed predictor-outcome associations, and to estimate the calibration and discrimination of these predictors in new patient samples.

Prediction Rules and Scores

A diagnostic model developed to assist in setting a diagnosis in individual patients can be presented (or reported) in three ways. The most precise method is to report the original (untransformed) logistic model with the shrunken regression coefficients and corresponding discrimination and calibration of the model. This presentation has the form of equation 1. Readers may apply this model directly to estimate an individual patient's probability of the disease by multiplying the patients' test results by corresponding coefficients, summing these up, and taking the antilog of the sum using equation 2. This, however, requires a calculator or computerized patient record, which are not always available in clinical practice. To improve the applicability of a multivariable model in practice, one can use the (shrunken) regression coefficients to create a nomogram, as shown in Figure 3.4. This is rarely done, although the creation of a nomogram has become easy with the statistical package S-plus [Harrell, 2001].

A final method to present a prediction model and to facilitate its implementation is a so-called *simplified risk score* or *scoring rule*. The original (shrunken) regression coefficients (method 1, equation 1) are then transformed to rounded numbers that are easily added together. This is commonly done by dividing them by the smallest regression coefficient,

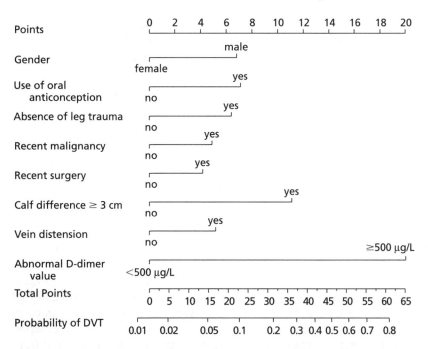

FIGURE 3.4 Nomogram of a diagnostic model used to estimate the probability of DVT in suspected patients. To use this nomogram, a man (who corresponds to seven points from the "Points" scale at the top of the figure), who (obviously) does not use oral contraception (0 points), has no leg trauma (6 points), and no recent malignancy (0 points), underwent surgery in the past 3 months (11 points), has a difference in calf circumference of more than 3 cm (11 points), no vein distension (0 points), and a D-dimer concentration of < or ≥ 500 μg/L (20 points), receives a "Total Points" score of 48. The lower two scales of the graphic show that this score corresponds to a probability of DVT of about 0.55 (or 55%).

multiplying by 10, and rounding to the nearest integer. The reporting of a simplified rule must be accompanied by the observed disease frequencies across score categories, as we will show in the example below. This simplification of a risk score will lead to some loss of information and thus some loss in diagnostic accuracy, because the original regression coefficients are simplified and rounded. However, this loss in precision usually does not affect clinical relevance. Ideally, the loss in precision should be minimal, with the simplified risk score as accurate as the original model but more easy to use. To allow readers to choose, we recommend the report to include both the original untransformed model plus the corresponding accuracy measures, and the simplified risk score with its ROC area.

We add one final note about the presentation of multivariable models. As explained earlier, an ROC area only reflects the overall discriminative value of a model and has no direct relevance and meaning to clinical practice in terms of absolute disease probabilities. A clinically relevant question remains, "above which probability one may consider the target disease as being present or absent?" This, in fact, defines thresholds A and B depicted in Figure 3.1. Methods to formally quantify the optimal probability thresholds are beyond the scope of this book. However, when a model is presented as a simplified rule (method 3 above), we recommend that the report presents the observed distribution of diseased and non-diseased patients across various score categories of the rule to aid readers in choosing the most relevant score threshold.

External Validation

The possible optimism of a diagnostic model may be addressed by internal validation, but generally *external* validation, that is, using *new* data, is necessary before a model can be used in practice with confidence [Justice et al., 1999; Altman & Royston, 2000a; Reilly & Evans, 2006]. *External validation* is the application and testing of the model in new patients. The term external refers to the use of data from subjects who were not included in the study in which the prediction model was developed. So defined, external validation can be performed, for example, in patients from the same centers but from a later period than during which the derivation study was conducted, or in patients from other centers or even another country [Justice et al., 1999; Reilly & Evans, 2006]. External validation studies are clearly warranted when one aims to apply a model in another setting (e.g., transporting a model from secondary to primary care) or in patient subgroups that were not included in the development study (e.g., transporting a model from adults to children) [Knottnerus, 2002a; Oudega et al., 2005a].

Too often, researchers use their data only to develop their own diagnostic model, without even mentioning—let alone validating—previous models. This is unfortunate as prior knowledge is not optimally used. Moreover, recent insights show that in the case where a prediction (diagnostic or prognostic) model performs less accurately in a validation population, the model can easily be adjusted based on the new data to improve its accuracy in that population [Steyerberg et al., 2004]. For example, the original Framingham coronary risk prediction model and the Gail breast cancer model were adjusted based on later findings and validation studies [Grundy et al., 1998; Costantino et al., 1999]. An adjusted model will then be based on both the development and the validation data set, which will further improve its stability and applicability to other populations. The adjustments may vary from parsimonious techniques such as updating the intercept of the model for differences in outcome frequency, via adjusting the originally estimated regression coefficients of the determinants in the model, to even adding new determinants to the model. It has been shown that simple updating methods are often sufficient and thus preferable to the more extensive model adjustments, however [Steyerberg et al., 2004; Janssen et al., 2007].

With these advances, the future may be one in which prediction models—provided that they are correctly developed—are continuously validated and updated if needed. This resembles cumulative meta-analyses in therapeutic research (see Chapter 11). Obviously, the more diverse the settings in which a model is validated and updated, the more likely it will generalize to new settings. The question arises as to how many validations and adjustments are needed before it is justified to implement a prediction model in daily practice. Currently there is no simple answer. "Stopping rules" for validating and updating prediction models should be developed for this purpose.

Application of Study Results in Practice

Why are prediction models constantly used in, for example, weather forecasting and economics (albeit with varying success), while they still have limited application in medicine? There may be several reasons. First, prediction models are often too complex for daily use in clinical settings that are not supported by computer technology. This may improve with the introduction of computerized patient records but also may require a change in attitude by practicing physicians. Second, because diagnostic (and prognostic) models often are not routinely validated in other populations, clinicians may—but perhaps should not—trust the probabilities provided by these models. External validation studies as described above are still scarce. Even less often are models validated or tested for their ability to change clinicians' decisions, not to mention their ability to improve a patient's prognosis [Stiell et al., 1995]. Reilly and Evans [2006] nicely summarized the consecutive levels of validating or testing prediction models before using them in practice. There are no formal criteria to judge the generalizability of diagnostic study results, but a few rules of thumb can be given. Generalizability of a diagnostic model is first and foremost determined by its use in the appropriate domain of patients suspected of having the target disease. Second, it is commonly determined by the setting (primary, secondary, tertiary care) in which the model was developed and perhaps validated. For example, particular symptoms or signs presented by patients in an academic hospital may be less relevant in patient populations from a general hospital or from primary care and vice versa [Knottnerus, 2002a]. This recently has been shown for extrapolation of a diagnostic rule for DVT developed in secondary care patients to primary care patients [Oudega et al., 2005a]. Third, generalizability is determined by the tests included in the final model. For example, the inclusion of particular advanced tests, such as spiral CT scanning, may lead to a limited applicability of the model to other patient populations or settings.

A final reason why diagnostic models are often not applied in daily practice is that clinicians may find it difficult to include explicit predicted probabilities in their decision-making, more because many doctors are reluctant to accept that a simplified mathematical formula replaces their clinical experience, skills, and complicated diagnostic reasoning in everyday patient care. The latter opinion clearly is a misunderstanding. Diagnostic rules are tools that should be used to aid physicians in their daily tasks, indeed, to help them cope with their complicated diagnostic challenges. Such tools are not meant to be a substitute for clinical experience and skills, but to strengthen them.

Sample Study

Recognition and ruling out of deep vein thrombosis (DVT) may be difficult when the analysis is based on history taking and physical examination alone, because a variety of non-thrombotic disorders can mimic the presentation of DVT. An adequate diagnosis in patients presenting with symptoms suggestive of DVT (usually a painful, swollen leg) is crucial because of the risk of potentially fatal pulmonary embolism when DVT is not adequately treated with anticoagulants. False-positive diagnoses also should be avoided because of the bleeding risk associated with anticoagulant therapy. The availability of the D-dimer tests in serum clearly improved the accuracy of diagnosing and ruling out DVT in suspected patients (Textbox 3.8). Algorithms, including clinical assessment (i.e., signs and symptoms) and D-dimer testing, are available that are widely applied in clinical practice and recommended in current guidelines. The most famous of these, the Wells rule, was developed and validated in secondary care settings [Wells et al., 1997]. Recent research has demonstrated that the Wells cannot adequately rule out DVT in patients suspected of DVT in primary care as too many (16%) patients in the low risk category (Wells score below 1) still had DVT [Oudega et al., 2005a]. The goal of the study presented here was to develop the optimal diagnostic strategy, preferably by way of a diagnostic rule, to be applied in primary care [Oudega et al., 2005b].

Theoretical Design

The research question was: Which combination of diagnostic determinants best estimates the probability of DVT in patients suspected of DVT in primary care?

Determinants considered included demographics, medical history, signs, and symptoms as well as the D-dimer test result. The occurrence relation can be summarized as:

TEXTBOX 3.8   Ruling out deep venous thrombosis in primary care: A simple diagnostic algorithm including D-dimer testing

In primary care, the physician has to decide which patients have to be referred for further diagnostic work-up. At present, only in 20% to 30% of the referred patients the diagnosis DVT is confirmed. This puts a burden on both patients and health care budgets. The question arises whether the diagnostic work-up and referral of patients suspected of DVT in primary care could be more efficient. A simple diagnostic decision rule developed in primary care is required to safely exclude the presence of DVT in patients suspected of DVT, without the need for referral. In a cross-sectional study, we investigated the data of 1295 consecutive patients consulting their primary care physician with symptoms suggestive of DVT, to develop and validate a simple diagnostic decision rule to safely exclude the presence of DVT. Independent diagnostic indicators of the presence of DVT were male gender, oral contraceptive use, presence of malignancy, recent surgery, absence of leg trauma, vein distension, calf difference and D-dimer test result. Application of this rule could reduce the number of referrals by at least 23% while only 0.7% of the patients with a DVT would not be referred. We conclude that by using eight simple diagnostic indicators from patient history, physical examination and the result of D-dimer testing, it is possible to safely rule out DVT in a large number of patients in primary care, reducing unnecessary patient burden and health care costs.

Source: Oudega R, Moons KGM, Hoes AW. A simple diagnostic rule to exclude deep vein thrombosis in primary care. Thromb Haemost 2005b;94:200-5.

P (DVT) = f (d1, d2, d3, . . . dn)

where d1 . . . dn refer to the D-dimer test result in addition to a total of 16 history or physical examination determinants.

The domain of the study consisted of patients presenting to primary care with symptoms suggestive of DVT.

Design of the Data Collection

Data were collected cross-sectionally. Participating primary care physicians were asked to include all patients in whom the presence of DVT was suspected during an inclusion period of 17 months. All 17 diagnostic determinants and the reference standard (see below) were assessed in all included patients. Thus, the time dimension of data collection was zero, a census (and no sampling) approach was taken and the study was observational (and not experimental).

The inclusion criterion was phrased as "all patients aged 18 years or older in whom the primary care physician suspected deep vein thrombosis," while in the information forwarded to the primary care physician, suspicion of DVT was explicitly defined as at least one of the following symptoms or signs of the lower extremities: swelling, redness, and/or pain. Exclusion criteria included a duration of the symptoms exceeding 30 days and suspicion of pulmonary embolism. In total, 110 primary care physicians in three regions of the central part of the Netherlands, each served by one hospital, were involved.

All items from history and physical examination were recorded in the case record form by the patient's primary care physician. The D-dimer test and the reference standard (real time B-mode compression ultrasonography) were performed in the adherent hospital. In patients with a normal compression ultrasonography, the procedure was repeated after seven days to definitely rule out DVT. The diagnostic determinants under study and the result from the reference standard were recorded in all 1,295 included patients.

Design of the Data Analysis

The (multivariable) analysis started with an overall logistic regression model including all 16 history and physical findings to determine which of these independently contributed to the presence or absence of proximal DVT; logistic regression analysis was used. Model reduction was performed by excluding variables from the model with a P-value > 0.10 based on the log likelihood ratio test. Subsequently, the D-dimer test was added to the reduced "history + physical" model to quantify its incremental value, which resulted in the final model. The calibration and ROC area of both models (with and without D-dimer) were estimated. Bootstrapping techniques, repeating the entire modeling process, were used to internally validate the final model and to adjust the estimated performance of the model for optimism. The model's performance obtained after bootstrapping was considered to approximate the expected performance in similar future patients. To construct an easily applicable diagnostic rule, the regression coefficients of the variables in the final model were transformed to integers according to their relative contributions (regression coefficients) to the probability estimation. Finally, after estimating the score for each patient, the absolute percentages of correctly diagnosed patients across score categories were estimated. One hundred and twenty-seven subjects had missing values for one or more tests under study. Per predictor, on average, 2% to 3% of the values were missing. As data were not missing completely at random (MCAR), deleting subjects with a missing value would lead not only to a loss of statistical power but also to biased results. To decrease bias and increase statistical efficiency, the missing values were imputed.

Results and Implications

Of the 1,295 patients included, 289 had DVT (prevalence 22%). An abnormal D-dimer level was by far the strongest determinant of the presence of DVT (univariable odds ratio of about 35.7; 95% CI, 13.3–100.0). In multivariable analysis, seven of the history and physical examination items were independent predictors of DVT: male gender, use of oral contraceptives, presence of malignancy, recent surgery, absence of leg trauma, vein distension, and a difference in calf circumference of 3 cm or more. The ROC of this model was 0.68 (95% CI, 0.65–0.71). The multivariable model including these seven determinants plus the D-dimer test had an ROC area of 0.80 before and 0.78 (95% CI, 0.75–0.81) after bootstrapping and shrinkage, with an odds ratio of the D-dimer assay (after shrinkage) of 20.3 (8.3–49.9). This indicates a substantial added value. The calibration plot—after bootstrapping—of the final model showed good calibration; the *P*-value of the goodness of fit test was 0.56 (far from statistically significant).

The final, untransformed model after shrinkage was:

Probability of DVT = 1/[1 + exp– (–5.47 + 0·59*male gender + 0·75*OC use + 0·42*presence of malignancy + 0·38*recent surgery + 0·60*absence of leg trauma + 0 · 48*vein distension + 1·13*calf difference ≥ 3cm + 3·01*abnormal D-dimer)]

To facilitate application of this model in daily practice, the following simplified scoring rule was derived:

Score = 1*male gender + 1*oral contraceptive use + 1*presence of malignancy + 1*recent surgery + 1*absence of leg trauma + 1*vein distension + 2*difference in calf circumference ≥ 3 cm + 6*abnormal D-dimer test

The score ranged from 0 to 13 points, and the ROC area of the simplified rule was (also) 0.78. Table 3.2 shows the number of participants and probability of DVT in different categories of the risk score.

As an example, a woman using oral contraceptives who was without a leg trauma but had vein distension and a negative D-dimer test would

TABLE 3.2   DVT Probability by Risk Score

Risk	Score Range	Number of Patients		DVT Present	
Very low	0–3	293	(23%)	2	(0.7%)
Low	4–6	66	(5%)	3	(4.5%)
Moderate	7–9	663	(51%)	144	(21.7%)
High	10–13	273	(21%)	140	(51.3%)
Total	0–13	1,295		289	(22.0%)

receive a score of 3 $(0 + 1 + 0 + 0 + 1 + 1 + 0 + 0)$, corresponding with a very low estimated probability of DVT of 0.7%.

It was concluded from the study that a simple diagnostic algorithm based on history taking, physical examination, and D-dimer testing can be helpful in safely ruling out DVT in primary care and thus would reduce the number of unnecessary referrals for suspected deep venous thrombosis.

Currently, the accuracy of this simplified rule was externally validated in three regions in the Netherlands to gain confidence that the number of suspected patients that is not referred for ultrasonography because of a risk score of ≤ 3 but still have DVT is indeed very low. The rule has been included in the current primary care clinical guideline on suspected DVT in the Netherlands.

4

Prognostic Research

A 40-year-old woman diagnosed with rheumatoid arthritis contacts her rheumatologist for a routine follow-up visit. This woman keeps well-informed about her disorder and recently learned that patients suffering from rheumatoid arthritis are at an elevated risk of infections [Doran et al., 2002]. She asks her rheumatologist if there is any reason to worry. Her doctor responds by stating that her patient raises a relevant issue, because she has been using corticosteroids since the last visit a couple of months ago. These medications are notorious for increasing infection risk.

To become better informed about her patient's risk to contract an infection, the rheumatologist searches for extra-articular manifestations of rheumatoid arthritis, such as skin abnormalities (cutaneous vasculitis), which are also associated with a higher infection risk. She observes none. Still, the rheumatologist feels uncertain about the probability that future infections will occur in her patient. She decides to draw blood and send it to the lab for a leukocyte count. No leukopenia is found. Now the rheumatologist feels confident enough to reassure her patient and does not schedule more frequent follow-up visits than those initially planned.

Prognosis in Clinical Practice

In clinical epidemiology, research questions arise from clinical practice and the answers must serve that practice. Therefore, a discussion of the motive, aim, and process of setting a prognosis in practice is essential before discussing the particulars of prognostic research.

Motive and Aim of Prognosis

Prognoses are made to inform patients and physicians. Like all humans, patients have a natural interest in their future health. This not only reflects a basic need for certainty, but it also enables people to rationally anticipate on the future and thereby make plans. Consequently, patients will be eager to elicit a statement from their doctor about his or her prognosis. In the context of medical practice, a prognosis may refer to all elements of future health. These include not only direct manifestations of disease such as mortality, pain, or other direct physical or psychological sequelae, but also adverse effects of treatment, treatment response, or failure; limitations in psychosocial or societal functioning; disease recurrence; the future need for invasive diagnostic procedures; and other concerns. For physicians, a patient's prognosis is of key clinical importance; prognostication is a core activity. The prognosis of a patient with a given diagnosis forms the point of departure for all subsequent aspects of patient management. Prognosis guides subsequent medical actions such as monitoring the course of disease, the planning of future interventions as well as the decision to refrain from interventions (Textbox 4.1).

One of the motives for a physician to be interested in the patient's prognosis is that many treatments tend to become more (cost) effective as the prognosis worsens, which means that patients with a poor prognosis have

---

TEXTBOX 4.1 Definition

Prognosis in clinical practice can be defined as a prediction of the course or outcome of a certain illness, in a certain patient. It combines the ancient Greek word προ, meaning beforehand, and γνωσις, meaning knowledge. Although prognoses are all around us, such as weather forecasts and corporate finance projections, the word has a medical connotation. After setting a diagnosis, and perhaps making a statement on the surmised etiology of the patient's illness, making a prognosis ("prognostication") is the next challenge a physician faces. Accurate prognostic knowledge is of critical importance to both patients and physicians. Although perhaps obvious, it must be stressed that a person does not require an established illness or disease to have a prognosis. For instance, life expectancy typically is a prognosis relevant to all human beings, diseased and non-diseased. Preventive medicine is concerned with intervening upon those who are still free of disease, yet have a higher risk of developing a particular disease, that is those with a poor prognosis. In the medical context and of clinical epidemiology, however, prognosis is commonly defined as the course and outcome of a given illness in an individual patient.

Source: Author.

more to gain. For instance, in patients diagnosed with myocardial infarction having a low mortality risk (defined as a one-year risk below 10%), the benefit of reperfusion therapy expressed as the reduction in the absolute risk of mortality has been shown to be less than 3%. For those with a poorer prognosis, say a mortality risk of 25%, the mortality risk reduction is much higher, about 15% (range 25%–10%) [Boersma & Simons, 1997]. In other instances, a poor prognosis may call for withholding a certain treatment, a relatively common situation in surgery and intensive care medicine. Also, the acceptability of a therapy with serious adverse effects often depends on a patient's prognosis. In women diagnosed with breast cancer, the risk of recurrence of a cancerous tumor determines whether or not systemic adjuvant therapy is initiated [Joensuu et al., 2004]. If the prognosis is favorable, where the recurrence risk is low, the burden of systemic therapy may not outweigh its benefits.

Thus, prognostication often implies answering the question, "What is the predicted course of the disease in this patient in case I do not intervene?" It is crucial in the decision to initiate or refrain from therapeutic interventions. Predicting an individual patient's response to a certain therapy also involves prognostication, because the typical aim of the intervention is to improve prognosis. Denys et al. [2003] developed a risk score to estimate the response to pharmacotherapy in patients treated for obsessive-compulsive disorders. A combination of patient characteristics available at treatment initiation adequately predicted a patient's drug response. This type of score enables the physician to selectively treat those most likely to benefit from treatment, which yields an increased treatment efficiency and limits unnecessary drug use.

In practice, patient management is hardly ever based on the expected probability that a patient develops a single prognostic outcome. Instead, physicians base their decision to start a certain treatment in a given patient commonly on several prognoses. In fact, for adequate actions, a physician is faced with the considerable challenge to make reliable predictions for virtually all relevant patient outcomes, to assess their utilities (i.e., hazards and benefits), and to weigh and combine these outcomes in discussions with the patient. For instance, in a patient suffering from multiple sclerosis, adequate medical action will be based not only on the predicted mortality risk but also on the risk of future urinary incontinence, dysarthria, visual acuity, and impairments in activities of daily life, among other contraindications. It also should be emphasized that prognostication is not a "once in the course of illness activity." It is commonly repeated in order to monitor a patient's condition in consideration of eventual treatment alterations, and, of course, to regularly inform ("update") the patient. After all, the word *doctor* stems from the Latin word *doctrina*, meaning *teacher*.

Comprehensive, precise, and repeated evidence-based prognostication is the ultimate aim. However, this often may be unattainable in daily practice, primarily due to a lack of adequate evidence from scientific prognostic research. In addition, there are practical obstacles; multiple or complex risk calculations at the bedside are often incompatible with the time constraints in medical practice.

Format of Prognoses

As the future cannot be predicted with 100% certainty, a prognosis is inherently probabilistic. Therefore, prognoses are formulated in terms reflecting uncertainty, that is, risks or probabilities. For example, short-term mortality in a patient with a recent diagnosis of severe heart failure may be expressed as *likely*, *uncertain*, or *unlikely*. Preferably, a prognosis is expressed in exact quantitative terms, such as a period specific absolute risk. For instance, the ten-year survival rate for a woman between 50 and 70 years of age with node-negative breast cancer with a tumor diameter less than 10 millimeters, is 93% [Joensuu et al., 2004].

Clinically relevant prognoses are to be expressed as absolute risks, or absolute risk categories. Relative risks have no relevance to patients or physicians without reference to absolute probabilities. For instance, the knowledge that a certain patient characteristic is associated with a twofold risk (i.e., relative risk of 2) of a certain outcome has no meaning, unless the probability of the outcome in patients without the characteristic is known; clearly, doubling of this probability will have a different impact on patient management when it is very low, say 0.1%, than when it is much higher, say 10%. Therefore, the preferred format of a prognosis is an absolute risk. Sometimes it is not the probability of the occurrence of a certain event that is to be predicted but rather the level of a future continuous outcome, for instance, perceived pain or quality of life as measured on a scale ranging from 0 to 100.

Approaches to Prognostication

There are at least three different approaches to making a prognosis. The first is to base prognosis on mechanistic and pathophysiological insight, an approach that fits the educational experience of most doctors. Although mechanistic and pathophysiological knowledge may be useful in prognostication, it rarely enables a doctor to effectively discriminate patients who have a high risk from those with a low risk of developing a certain outcome. This is because disease outcomes are generally determined by multiple, interrelated, complex, and largely unknown biological factors and processes with large between-subjects-variability [Moons et al., 2005]. In addition, knowledge about underlying mechanisms is not always available and if available is often difficult to measure. Remarkably, however, in many instances accurate prognostic predictions may be obtained by combining several easy-to-assess clinical and non-clinical characteristics of the patient, characteristics that are often not causally linked to the course of disease. For example, hip fracture can be accurately predicted from age, gender, height, use of a walking aid, cigarette smoking, and body weight [Burger et al., 1999]. Probably these predictors correlate with parameters involved in the causal mechanism underlying fracture risk, that is, low bone density, impaired bone quality, impact on the hip bone from a fall, and postural instability.

Second, clinical experience is a frequently used source of prognostic knowledge. Suppose that a cardiologist observes that women diagnosed with heart failure return to the hospital less frequently than men. Obviously, this observation—even when confirmed by colleagues—may be the result of a truly worse prognosis in men than in women. Several other phenomena, however, may have led to a similar observation. Examples are (1) that survival in women with heart failure actually may be worse than in men, leading to fewer readmissions; (2) women with similar symptoms of worsening heart failure are less likely to be referred to hospital; or (3) the observation may be wrong. Although clinical experience is of paramount importance in the prognostication in daily practice, prognostic research may be useful to confirm or refute and, preferably, quantify prognostic associations.

The third approach is an example of prognostication fuelled by empirical prognostic research: the use an explicit risk score or prediction model or rule containing multiple prognostic determinants, representing the values of the predictors, and their quantitative relation to a certain prognostically relevant outcome. A good example of an explicit prognostic model is the Apgar score for estimating the probability of neonatal mortality [Apgar, 1953; Casey et al., 2001]. It formally describes how several characteristics of the newborn relate to the probability of dying during the first 28 days after birth. Each characteristic is assigned a score 0 for absent, a score 1 for doubtful, and a score 2 for definitely present. As there are five characteristics, the total score ranges from 0 to 10. Interestingly, the Apgar score (Table 4.1) was already used worldwide decades before its high predictive power for neonatal mortality was confirmed in a formal prognostic study.

In practice, the three approaches discussed above are often used simultaneously. It is unlikely that a physician estimates a prognosis based on a prediction model only. The aim of any prediction model in any medical field is not meant to take over the job of the physician. The intension is to guide physicians in their decision-making based on more objectively estimated probabilities as a supplement to any other relevant information, including clinical experience and pathophysiological knowledge [Christensen, 2004; Concato et al., 1993; Feinstein, 1994].

Prognostication Is a Multivariable Process

It is common practice in the medical literature as well as during clinical rounds to refer to the prognosis of a disease rather than to the prognosis of

TABLE 4.1 Apgar Score

Signs	0	1	2
Heartbeat per minute	Absent	Slow (<100)	Over 100
Respiratory effort	Absent	Slow, irregular	Good, crying
Muscle tone	Limp	Some flexion of extremities	Active motion
Reflex irritability	No response	Grimace	Cry or cough
Color	Blue or pale	Body pink, extremities blue	Completely pink

Casey BM, McIntire DD, Leveno KJ. The continuing value of the Apgar score for the assessment of newborn infants. N Engl J Med 2001;344:467–71.

a patient: "The prognosis of pancreatic cancer is poor"; "Concussion most often leaves no lasting neurological problems"; or, more quantitatively, "Five year survival in osteosarcoma approximates 40%." These so-called *textbook prognoses* are not individualized prognoses but merely average prognoses. They are imprecise because many patients will deviate substantially from the average patient, and they are clinically of limited value because the aim of prognostication—individual risk prediction—cannot be attained. Typically, the prognosis of an individual patient, say five-year survival, is determined by a variety of patient characteristics, and not just by a single item such as a diagnosis of osteosarcoma. A combination of prognostic determinants is often referred to as a *risk profile*. This profile usually comprises both non-clinical characteristics such as age and gender, and clinical characteristics such as the diagnosis, symptoms, signs, possible etiology, blood or urine tests, and other tests such as imaging or pathology. Thus, prognosis is rarely adequately estimated by a single prognostic predictor. Physicians—implicitly or explicitly—use multiple predictors to estimate a patient's prognosis [Braitman & Davidoff, 1996; Concato, 2001]. Adequate prognostication thus requires knowledge about the occurrence of future outcomes given combinations, of prognostic predictors. This knowledge in turn requires prognostic studies that follow a multivariable approach in design and analysis to determine which predictors are associated, and to what extent, with clinically relevant outcomes, to provide outcome probabilities for different predictor combinations, and to develop tools to estimate these outcome probabilities in daily practice. These tools, often referred to as *clinical prediction models, predictions rules, prognostic indices,* or *risk scores* enable physicians to explicitly transform combinations of values of the identified prognostic determinants documented in an individual patient, to an absolute probability of developing the disease-related event in the future. Similar tools based on multiple determinants are also applied in diagnosis (Chapter 3) [Laupacis et al., 1997; Randolph et al., 1998].

Added Prognostic Value

As in diagnosis, a logical hierarchy in all available prognostic determinants exists based on everyday practice. Preferably, a doctor will first try to estimate a patient's prognosis based on a combination of a limited number of non-patient–burdening, easily measurable variables, typically obtained by history taking (including known comorbidity) and physical examination. Before using more cumbersome or costly prognostic markers (e.g., blood tests and imaging), a doctor should be convinced that the additional test indeed has added predictive value beyond the more easily obtained prognostic predictors. Unfortunately, recent overviews have shown that in most prognostic studies, single rather than multiple predictors are investigated, and that the *added* value of a novel, potentially valuable prognostic marker is not assessed [Burton & Altman, 2004; Riley et al., 2003]. Yet medical practice slowly shifts from implicit to explicit prognostication, including appreciation of multivariable prediction models, and allows for quantification of an individual patient's probability to develop a certain outcome within a defined time period. A recent example is the indication for cholesterol-lowering drug therapy in men or women without prior cardiovascular disease. Formerly based on cholesterol level only, recent international guidelines included cardiovascular score (e.g., those based on the Framingham Heart study) to predict a person's probability to develop cardiovascular disease during the next ten years, based on parameters of age, gender, blood pressure level, smoking habits, glucose tolerance, and, as only one of the prognostic markers, cholesterol level [Kannel et al., 1976]. Other examples of prognostic models in medicine are the above-mentioned breast cancer model [Galea et al., 1992] and Apgar score [Apgar, 1953; Casey et al., 2001], the Acute Physiology and Chronic Health Evaluation (APACHE) score [Knaus et al., 1991], the Simplified Acute Physiology Score (SAPS) [Le Gall et al., 1993], and rules for predicting the occurrence of postoperative nausea and vomiting [Van de Bosch et al., 2005] or postoperative pain [Kalkman et al., 2003].

An example of a more recently developed prognostic score is an algorithm predicting the probability of severe early postoperative pain [Kalkman et al., 2003]. Items included in that score are age, preoperative pain, anxiety level, and the type of surgery. As shown in Table 4.2, the lowest total score (0) yields an estimated probability of postoperative pain of 3%, while a high score of 73 corresponds to an 80% probability of postoperative pain.

TABLE 4.2 Prognostic score for preoperatively predicting the probability of severe early postoperative pain

Sex	Points	Pain score	Points	Anxiety level of patients (APAIS)	Points		Total Points	Probability of postoperative pain
Male	0	0	0	4–5	0		0	
Female	3	1	2	6–7	2		11	0.03
		2	4	8–9	3		22	0.05
Age (years)		3	6	10–11	5		34	0.10
15–19	17	4	8	12–13	6		41	0.20
20–24	16	5	10	14–15	8		48	0.30
25–29	15	6	12	16–17	9		53	0.40
30–34	13	7	14	18–19	11		59	0.50
35–39	12	8	16	12			65	0.60
40–44	11	9	18				73	0.70
45–49	10	10	20	**Information seeking behavior of patients** (APAIS)				0.80
50–54	9			2	9			
55–59	8	**Surgery type**		3	8			
60–64	7	Ophthamology	0	4	7			
65–69	6	Laporoscopy	5	5	6			
70–74	4	Ear/nose/throat	8	6	5			
75–79	3	Orthopedic	14	7	3			
80–84	2	Abdominal	18	8	2			
85–89	1	Other	7	9	1			
≥90	0			10	0			
		Incision size						
		Small	0					
		Medium-large	3					

This article was published in *Pain*, 105, Kalkman CJ, Visser K, Moen J, Bonsel GJ, Grobbee DE, Moons KG. Preoperative prediction of severe postoperative pain. pp. 415–23. Copyright Elsevier 2003.

From Prognosis in Clinical Practice to Prognostic Research

In prognostication, the estimation of the likelihood of a certain medical condition does not address the present (as in diagnosis) but the future. A prognosis therefore may be viewed as a diagnosis in the future. Consequently, it is not surprising that prognostic research shares many characteristics with diagnostic research. However, prognostic research is inherently longitudinal, more often deals with continuous outcomes, such as measures of pain or quality of life, and multiple outcomes, for example, survival and quality of life. Also, as prognostic outcomes inherently involve time, prognostic predictions are generally less accurate than diagnostic predictions, particularly if they predict outcomes occurring a few years later (Textbox 4.2).

Predictive Nature of Prognostic Research

The purpose of prognostic research is the prediction of the future occurrence of a certain health outcome in a subject or patient encountered in clinical practice. This aim matches the application of prognostic knowledge, which is to guide patient management. This goal is predictive or descriptive (i.e., non-causal), which most fundamentally distinguishes prognostic research from causal research, that is, etiologic and intervention research.

The purely predictive aim of prognostic research is shared with diagnostic research and—as described in Chapter 3—has major implications for the design, conduct, and reporting of research.

In etiologic research, the mission is to assess whether an outcome occurrence can be causally attributed to a particular risk factor, which typically requires an adjustment for confounders. The physician aims to *explain* the occurrence of a certain outcome. For instance, in a study assessing whether unfavorable coping style and low social support in patients with HIV-1 infection are causally related to progression to AIDS, adjustments were made for race and antiviral medications because they were considered potential confounders [Leserman et al., 2000]. Adjustment for confounders is essential to prove causality. Often, etiologic research is motivated by the prospect of new (preventive) interventions. This was explicitly expressed in the conclusion section of Lesserman et al.'s study: "Further research is needed to determine if treatments based on these findings might alter the clinical course of HIV-1 infection." Prognostic research aims to *predict* as accurately as possible the probability or risk of future occurrence of a certain outcome as a function of multiple predictors. The aim is not to *explain* the outcome.

As there is no central factor or determinant whose causal effect must be isolated from the effects of other variables, confounding is not an issue in prediction research. In addition to the predictive aim, the requirement of

TEXTBOX 4.2 Application of Prognostic Scores: Hospital Audits

Prognostic information is not only used to guide individual decisions but also to make proper adjustments for "case mix" when comparing the performances of different hospitals. The aim of these comparisons is to make *causal* inferences about the care given, that is to assess whether differences in performance are due to differences in quality of care. This can only be accomplished if the analyses are adequately adjusted for the confounding effect of initial prognosis. Prognostic models, that are in itself the results of descriptive research, can be helpful in achieving this.

A good example comes from a study by the International Neonatal Network. In this study, a scoring system to predict mortality in preterm neonates with low birth weight admitted to neonatal intensive care units was developed [The International Neonatal Network, 1993]. The scoring system, denoted as the CRIB score, included birth weight, duration of gestation, congenital malformations, and several physiologic parameters measured during the first 12 hours of life. It showed excellent predictive accuracy with an area under the receiver operating characteristic (ROC) curve of 0.9. Apart from developing this score for the purpose of helping doctors to make mortality predictions in individual neonates, the authors aimed to compare the performance of the intensive care units of tertiary hospitals with those of non-tertiary hospitals, as reflected by their relative neonatal mortality rates. Because the initial prognosis of neonates admitted to tertiary hospitals may be different from that of neonates referred to non-tertiary hospitals, these causal analyses were performed adjusting for the confounding effect of initial mortality risk as indicated by the CRIB score. It appeared that only after adjustment for CRIB score, tertiary hospitals showed convincingly less mortality than the non-tertiary hospitals. This example illustrates that adjustment for initial prognosis or "case mix" is essential when performance audits are carried out. Yet, the validity of this approach is highly dependent on the degree to which the prognostic scores used to adjust for confounding adequately capture prognosis.

Source: Author.

practical applicability of prognostic study results is shared with diagnostic research. To this end, the domain is usually given by patients presenting with a certain disorder in a certain setting. Prognostic determinants are characteristics typically assessed during history taking, physical examination, blood tests, imaging, and other test results. But they also may include treatments currently used (or used in the past) by the patient. Furthermore, to increase the likelihood that prognostic study results can be translated to everyday practice, the study should be performed in and mimic practice. Finally, results should be expressed as absolute risks in order to be informative for patient and doctor in deciding about patient management. In the

HIV example above, instead of an etiological research question, one could also imagine a prognostic research question. For example, does coping style in addition to other prognostic items, such as age, gender, and leukocyte counts, predict the development of AIDS? In this example, all variables would be considered as prognostic determinants.

Appraisal of Prevailing Prognostic Research

Many studies labeled as *prognostic studies* actually are not prognostic studies as defined above, but etiologic studies of diseased patients. The researcher is interested in the causal association between a particular determinant and an outcome in patients with a certain disease, rather than in the combined predictive accuracy of multiple determinants in predicting the future development of that disease. This is also reflected in a recent appraisal of the quality of individual studies in systematic reviews of prognostic studies in which "adequate adjustment for confounders" was considered an important item [Hayden et al., 2006]. However, as mentioned earlier, confounding—defined as the undesired influence of other risk factors on the (causal) association between the determinant and outcome—is a hallmark of causal research, while not relevant in prognostic research. Thus, in appraising a study designated as a *prognostic study*, it is essential that the aim of the study is completely clear: to predict or to explain (i.e., address causality of) an outcome. In the following, the term *prognostic study* is reserved for a study with a purely predictive aim.

Commonly, prognostic studies, although valuable in themselves, do not produce results that directly allow the establishment of accurate individualized prognoses in future patients in daily practice. This relates to several issues. First it is not always recognized that for the results to be relevant to individual patient management, period-specific absolute risks based on a combination of prognostic markers should be obtainable from the published report of the prognostic study. As an example, El-Metwally and colleagues [2005] studied the short- and long-term prognoses of preadolescent lower limb pain and assessed factors that contributed to pain persistence. While they did report period-specific absolute risks ("of the baseline students with lower limb pain, 32% reported pain persistence at 1-year follow-up and 31% reported pain recurrence at 4-year follow-up"), these risks are average risks that do not allow for individual prognostication. Although they did study the association of specific prognostic factors with pain recurrence during the four-year follow-up period, unfortunately the authors only reported relative risks (e.g., a twofold risk in the presence compared to the absence of the factor), while absolute risks are clearly more relevant.

Another study concluded that symptomatic deep-vein thrombosis carries a high risk of recurrent thromboembolism, especially for patients without transient risk factors, and that this observation challenges the widely adopted short course of anticoagulant therapy (patient management). This typically suggests a predictive aim [Prandoni et al., 1997]. Yet, similar to the study on limb pain, only average absolute risks and (adjusted) relative risks were presented, rather than absolute outcome probabilities within a defined time period for different predictor combinations. A somewhat adapted data analytic strategy (see below, Design of Data Analysis) would have provided absolute risks more relevant for patient and doctor.

In Textbox 4.3, the abstract of a paper presenting a prognostic study on the value of gene-expression profiles in predicting distant metastasis in patients with lymph-node-negative primary breast cancer is shown [Whang Y, et al., 2005]. However, the study was primarily designed and analyzed as an etiologic study. For example, the authors adjusted for potential confounders, and *hazard ratios* were presented as the main finding. In a true prognostic study, confounding is not relevant and the added value of these gene-expression profiles in estimating the *absolute* probability of developing distant metastasis should be determined. Instead of considering, for example, age as a potential confounder, this characteristic should be considered as a potentially useful prognostic determinant. Whether the 76-gene signature has any prognostic value *in addition* to age and other easily measurable prognostic factors is of primary interest, but such an analysis was not presented.

A second problem of many prognostic studies is that often prognostic variables are included based on measurements that are not feasible in everyday practice. As a consequence, the practical application of the resulting prognostic model may be hampered. An example is the use of an extensive questionnaire to assess the personality trait neuroticism in the prognostication of depression [O'Leary & Costello, 2001].

Third, in the case where the interest of prognostic research lies in the prognostic value of a particular new marker, researchers often fail to assess the marker's *added* predictive value. For example, Leslie and colleagues [2007] aimed to assess osteoporotic fracture prediction with dual-energy x-ray absorptiometry (DXA) in a large clinical cohort. While a valuable study, unfortunately it does not address the key clinical question in this context; whether DXA measurement has prognostic value *in addition to* more conventional and easy-to-assess predictors such as age, gender, smoking habits, and body weight. Furthermore, this study also only presented age-adjusted hazard ratios (relative risks) for fracture rather than absolute risks. Finally, prognostic studies that do develop a multivariable prediction model or rule seldom validate the model internally (that is, within their own data) or externally by testing the accuracy of the model in another population reflecting the same domain.

Fortunately, an increasing number of well-designed and reported prognostic studies is being published that do enable physicians to reliably esti-

TEXTBOX 4.3 Study on the prognostic value of gene-expression profiles in predicting distant metastasis in patients with lymph-node-negative primary breast cancer

Summary

Background: Genome-wide measures of gene expression can identify patterns of gene activity that subclassify tumors and might provide a better means than is currently available for individual risk assessment in patients with lymph-node-negative breast cancer.

Methods: We analyzed, with Affymetrix Human U133a GeneChips, the expression of 22,000 transcripts from total RNA of frozen tumor samples from 286 lymph-node-negative patients who had not received adjuvant systemic treatments.

Findings: In a training set of 115 tumors, we identified a 76-gene signature consisting of 60 genes for patients positive for estrogen receptors (ER) and 16 genes for ER-negative patients. This signature showed 93% sensitivity and 48% specificity in a subsequent independent testing set of 171 lymph-node-negative patients. The gene profile was highly informative in identifying patients who developed distant metastases within 5 years (hazard ratio 5·67 [95% CI 2·46–12·4]), even when corrected for traditional prognostic factors in multivariate analysis (5·55 [2·46–12·15]). The 76-gene profile also represented a strong prognostic factor for the development of metastasis in the subgroups of 84 premenopausal patients (9·60 [2·28–40·5]), 87 postmenopausal patients (4·04 [1·57–10·4]), and 79 patients with tumors of 10–12 mm (14·1 [3·34–59·2]), a group of patients for whom prediction of prognosis is especially difficult.

Interpretation: The identified signature provides a power tool for identification of patients at high risk of distant recurrence. The ability to identify patients who have a favorable prognosis could, after independent confirmation, allow clinicians to avoid adjuvant systemic therapy or to choose less aggressive therapeutic options.

Source: Whang Y, Klein JG, Zhang Y, Sieuwerts AM, Look MP, Yang F, Talantov D, Timmermans M, Meijer-van Gelder ME, Yu J, Jatkoe T, Berns EM, Atkins D, Foekens JA. Gene-expression profiles to predict distant metastasis of lymph-node-negative primary breast cancer. Lancet 2005; 365:671–9.

mate an individual patient's absolute risk of developing a particular outcome within a defined time period in a practical manner. A recent example is a study by Steyerberg et al. [2006]. The rationale of this study was that surgery for esophageal cancer has curative potential but the procedure also is associated with considerable perioperative risks. Patients with very high mortality risks as estimated before surgery therefore may not be eligible for this operation. Analyses in this study focused on optimizing predictive accuracy and the presentation of the results were in line with the objective of determining individual absolute risk predictions facilitating patient selection and thus more targeted management. In this study, a chart with the estimated risks according to the presence of several prognostic predictors was combined into a single score. Another recent study from Hong Kong, in which a prognostic model for patients with severe acute respiratory syndrome (SARS) was developed and validated, also yielded results that can be directly applied in medical practice [Cowling et al., 2006].

Rational Prognostic Research

Once it is recognized that the aim of prognostication is to stratify patients according to their absolute risk of a certain future relevant health event, based on their clinical and non-clinical profile, the three components of epidemiologic study design (theoretical design, design of data collection, and design of data analysis) follow logically.

Theoretical Design

The object of medical prognostication is to predict the future occurrence of a health-related outcome based on the patient's clinical and non-clinical profile. Outcomes may include a particular event such as death, disease recurrence, or complication, but also continuous or quantitative outcomes such as pain or quality of life. As noted already, the architecture of prognostic research strongly resembles that of diagnostic research. The major difference is that time or follow-up is elementary to prognostic research, whereas diagnostic research is inherently cross sectional. The occurrence relation of prognostic research is given by:

Incidence $O = f (d1, d2, d3, \ldots dn)$

where O signifies the outcome (occurrence of an event or realization of a quantitative parameter) at a future time point t, and d1 . . . dn represent the potential prognostic determinants measured at one (or more) time point(s) before t.

The domain of a prognostic occurrence relationship includes individuals who are at risk of developing the outcome of interest and is usually defined by the presence of a particular condition. This condition can be an illness but also can be those undergoing surgery, being pregnant, or "being a newborn." Consequently, patients with a zero or 100% probability of developing the outcome are not part of the domain. An example of individuals that were at a 100% risk of developing the outcome and thus did not belong to the study domain is the group newborns with inevitably lethal conditions in a study evaluating a risk score for the prediction of "in-hospital mortality" in newborns [The International Neonatal Network, 1993]. Generalization of the risk score to these children is invalid and clearly irrelevant because application of the risk score in these newborns cannot have any bearing on patient management.

The typical *research objective* of prognostic research is to assess which of the potential prognostic determinants under study indeed contribute to the prediction of the (future) outcome. As described above, the aim also can be to assess whether a new prognostic marker provides additional predictive value beyond the available predictors. Furthermore, it may include comparison of the predictive accuracy of two (new) markers. Both require a comparison of the predictive accuracy of two occurrence relations: one with the new predictor and one without, and one with marker one and one with marker two, respectively.

Design of Data Collection

The main objective of a prognostic study is to provide quantitative knowledge about the occurrence of a health outcome in a predefined time period as a function of multiple predictors. The following sections discuss the most important aspects of designing the data collection.

Time

The object of the prognostic process is inherently longitudinal. Accordingly, prognostic research follows a longitudinal design in which the determinants or prognostic predictors are measured before the outcome is observed. The time period needed to observe the outcome occurrence or outcome development may vary between several hours (e.g., in case of early postoperative complications), to days, weeks, months, or years.

Census or Sampling

As the outcomes of prognostic studies are generally to be expressed in *absolute* terms, the design most suitable to address prognostic questions is a cohort study in which all patients with a certain condition are followed for some time to monitor the development of the outcome; this uses a census approach. Preferably, the data are collected prospectively rather than retrospectively because this allows for optimal measurement of predictors and outcome, and adequate (i.e., complete) follow-up. Typically, all consecutive patients with a particular condition who are at risk to develop the outcome of interest (i.e., are part of the domain) are included. The potential prognostic determinants as well as the outcome are measured in *all* patients.

As in diagnostic research, sometimes a case control design (and thus a sampling rather than a census approach) is used in prognostic research.

This is done for efficiency reasons, when measurement of one of more of the prognostic determinants is patient burdening or expensive or when the prognostic outcome is rare. However, this design does not allow for an estimation of absolute risks of an outcome when cases and controls are obtained from a source population of unknown size. But when the sampling fraction of the controls (i.e., the proportion of the population experience of the entire cohort that is sampled in the controls) is known, the true denominators, and thus absolute risks, can be estimated by reconstructing the 2 × 2 table. These case-control studies *nested* within a cohort are explained in more detail in Chapter 9 [Iglesias de Sol et al., 2001; Moons & Grobbee, 2002].

Experimental or Observational Studies

Almost all prognostic studies are observational, where a well-defined group of patients with a certain condition are followed for a period of time to monitor the occurrence of the outcome. The researcher observes and measures the non-clinical and clinical parameters anticipated to be of prognostic significance. These potential prognostic determinants are not influenced (let alone randomly allocated) by the researcher. However, as in diagnostic research, one could imagine that prognostic studies involve experimentation, for example, when comparing the impact on a certain outcome (say mortality) of the use two prognostic risk scores by randomly allocating the two rules to individual physicians or patients [Reilly & Evans, 2006].

Alternatively, however, randomized trials can serve as a vehicle for prognostic research. Then the study population of the trial is taken as a plain cohort where the prognostic determinants of interest are just observed and not influenced by the researcher. Consequently, a prognostic study within a trial bears a greater resemblance to an observational rather than a typical experimental study. The issue continuing to be debated is whether one should limit the prognostic analysis to the trial participants in the reference group, that is, those who did not undergo the randomly allocated prognosis-modifying intervention. In the case of an ineffective intervention, most researchers will include both the intervention and reference cohort in the prognostic study, while where the intervention is beneficial or harmful, only the reference group is included. Is should be emphasized, however, that even in cases of no observed effect of the randomly allocated intervention, they can modify the association of the prognostic determinants with the outcome. To study such effect modification, one could perform separate prognostic analyses in the two comparison groups of the trial, guided by tests for interaction (see Chapter 2) between the intervention and the (other) prognostic predictors. Certainly, both analyses may provide clinically useful information: the prognostic study within the placebo group of a trial will help physicians to accurately estimate the prognosis in a patient with a certain condition if no intervention was to be initiated (i.e., the natural history of a disease or condition) and can be instrumental in deciding about treatment initiation. A prognostic analysis within the treated patient group will facilitate quantification of the expected course (in terms of absolute risks) in an individual patient following treatment. A recent example of a prognostic study performed within a trial is shown in Textbox 4.4, which attempted to help physicians to identify those children with acute otitis media prone to experience prolonged complaints (and thus may require closer monitoring or antibiotic treatment). Rovers et al. [2007] performed a prognostic analysis in a data set including the placebo groups of all available randomized trials assessing the effect of antibiotic treatment in children with acute otitis

TEXTBOX 4.4 Predictors of a prolonged course in children with acute otitis media: an individual patient meta-analysis

Rovers MM, Glasziou P, Appelman CL, Burke P, McCormick DP, Damoiseaux RA, Little P, Le Saux N, Hoes AW. Pediatrics 2007; 119:579–85.

Background: Currently there are no tools to discriminate between children with mild, self-limiting episodes of acute otitis media (AOM) and those at risk of a prolonged course.

Methods: In an individual patient data meta-analysis with the control groups of 6 randomised controlled trials (n = 824 children with acute otitis media, aged 6 months to 12 years), we determined the predictors of poor short term outcome in children with AOM. The primary outcome was a prolonged course of AOM, which was defined as fever and/or pain at 3–7 days.

Main findings: Of the 824 included children, 303 (37%) had pain and/or fever at 3–7 days. Independent predictors for a prolonged course were age < 2 years and bilateral AOM. The absolute risks of pain and/or fever at 3–7 days in children aged less than 2 years with bilateral AOM (20% of all children) was 55%, and in children aged 2 years or older with unilateral AOM 25% (47% of all children).

Interpretation: The risk of a prolonged course was two times higher in children aged less than 2 years with bilateral AOM than in children aged 2 years or older with unilateral AOM. Clinicians can use these features to advise parents and to follow these children more actively.

media. An obvious advantage of such an analysis is the availability of high-quality data. On the other hand, however, the findings following from this approach may have restricted generalizability due to commonly strict in/exclusion criteria applied in the trials [Marsoni & Valsecchi, 1991; Kiemeney et al., 1994]. Moreover, the high-quality data on prognostic determinants may be a blessing in disguise, because in the real-life application the available clinical information may be of lower quality and the predictors thus will show reduced prognostic performance.

Study Population

As in all types of epidemiological research, the study population should be a representative for the domain. Prognostic predictors, models, or strategies are investigated on their ability to predict as accurately as possible a future health outcome. Accordingly, and as noted before, the domain of a prognostic study is formed by individuals who are at risk for developing that outcome. Patients who already developed the outcome or in whom the probability is considered so low ("zero") that the physician does not even consider estimating this probability fall outside the domain, because subsequent patient management (e.g., to initiate or refrain from therapeutic actions) is evident. Furthermore, as in diagnostic research, we recommend restricting domain definitions and thus study populations in prognostic research to the setting of care (notably primary or secondary care) of interest, due to known differences in predictive accuracy of determinants across care settings [Oudega et al., 2005a; Knottnerus, 2002a]. Finally, we recall that a study population does not necessarily have to be a random sample from the full population representing the domain, as long as characteristics of the study population that may affect the generalizability of the findings to the relevant domain are carefully considered. Indeed, the selection or recruitment of any study population is often restricted by logistic circumstances, such as necessity of patients to live near the research center or the availability of time to participate in the study. These characteristics are often unlikely to influence the applicability and generalization of study findings. It is challenging to appreciate which characteristics truly affect the generalizability of results obtained from a particular study population. This appreciation usually requires knowledge of those characteristics (*effect modifiers*) that may modify the nature and strength of the estimated associations between the prognostic determinants and outcome. Therefore, generalizability from study population to domain is not an objective process that can be framed in statistical terms. Generalizability is a matter of reasoning, requiring external knowledge and subjective judgment. The question to be answered is whether in other types of subjects from the domain who were not represented in the study population the same prognostic predictors would be found with the same predictive values.

Prognostic Determinants (Predictors)

As in diagnostic studies, prognostic studies should mirror real-life situations and consider multiple predictors. Predictors under study can be obtained from patient history (each question is a potential predictor), physical examination, additional testing such as imaging results and biological markers, characteristics of (severity of) the disease, and also may include the interventions the patient received. Determinants included in a prognostic study should be clearly defined, and their measurement should be sufficiently reproducible to enhance application of study results to daily practice. This notably applies when treatments are studied as potential predictors [Simon & Altman, 1994] but also to predictors that require subjective interpretation, such as imaging test results, to avoid studying the predictive ability of the observer rather than of the predictors. Predictors should preferably be measured using methods applicable—or potentially applicable—to daily practice, again to enhance generalizability and to prevent too optimistic predictive accuracy of predictors than can be expected in real-life situations. Applying specialized measurement techniques that are not easily replicated in medical practice may yield optimistic predictive accuracy. In itself, specialized measurement of predictors is not necessarily a limitation of prediction research. This argument may even be turned around: if substantially better predictions are obtained with specialized or more elaborate measurements, this may call for such measurements, if feasible, in everyday clinical practice. Feasibility plays an important role in choosing determinants to be included in prognostic research. One could decide to study proxy or surrogate predictors if the underlying predictor is too cumbersome to measure; for example, the color of the newborn rather than oxygen saturation is included in the Apgar score.

All predictors that are considered to be predictive are usually measured and analyzed in each subject of the study population. This can be done with a view to chronological hierarchy in clinical practice, starting with history and physical examination tests. Subsequent predictors will be measured in each subject if the aim is to determine the (added) predictive value of such predictors. However, we do warn against the inclusion of large numbers of determinants in prognostic research for the same reasons as are discussed in Chapter 3. Hence, the choice of the predictors under study should be based on both available literature and a thorough understanding of clinical practice [Steyerberg et al., 2000; Harrell et al., 1996].

Outcome

The outcome in prognostic research is typically dichotomous: the occurrence, in this case the incidence (yes/no) of the event of interest. In addition, prognostic outcomes may comprise continuous variables such as tumor growth, pain, or quality of life, rather than incidence or non-occurrence of a particular event. In both instances, we recommend that the researcher study outcomes that really matter to patients, such as remission of disease, survival, complications, pain, or quality of life. One preferably should not study so-called proxy or intermediate outcomes such as joint space in patients with osteoarthritis of the knee (instead of pain, the ability to walk, or quality of life), unless a clear causal relationship between such an intermediate outcome and outcomes more relevant for patients has been established. The latter may apply for the use of CD4 count as a prognostic outcome (rather than the occurrence of AIDS or even death) in HIV studies.

As in all research, criteria defining the absence or presence of the outcome as well as the measurement tools used should be described in detail. Importantly, the outcome occurrence is assessed as accurately as possible, with the best available methods to prevent misclassification, even if this requires measurements that are never done in clinical practice. Note again that, as in diagnostic research, this contrasts with the assessment of the determinants that should mimic methods used in daily practice.

The time period during which the outcome occurrence is measured requires special attention. Predicting an outcome occurrence over a three-month period typically yields different predictors or different predictor-outcome associations than prediction of the same outcome after five years. Like in weather and stock value forecasting, prediction over a shorter period is commonly less cumbersome than prediction over a longer period.

Finally, as in most research, outcomes should be measured without knowledge of the predictors under study to prevent self-fulfilling prophecies, particularly if the outcome measurement requires observer interpretation. For example, the presence of those determinants believed to be associated with the prognostic outcome may influence the decision to consider the outcome to have occurred. This bias can cause under- or overestimation of the predictive accuracy of predictors, but commonly leads to overestimation, and can be prevented by blinding the assessors of the outcome to the values of the prognostic determinants [Moons et al., 2002c; Loy & Irwig, 2004]. Blinding is not necessary for mortality or other outcomes that can be measured without misclassification.

Bias in Prognostic Research

Confounding Bias

In prognostic research, the interest is in the joint predictive accuracy of multiple predictors. As stated earlier, there is no central determinant for which the relationship to the outcome should be causally isolated from other outcome predictors as in causal research. Confounding thus is not an issue in prognostic research, as in all types of prediction research.

Other Biases

While confounding does not play a role in prediction research, other biases certainly do. Bias that may occur when the outcome assessor is aware of the determinants was discussed in the last paragraph as well as in Chapter 3. In addition, selective loss to follow-up (and thus non-assessment of the outcome parameter) of those patients with certain values of prognostic determinants may lead to considerable bias; typically, the prognostic value of that determinant will be underestimated if loss to follow-up is related to a poorer prognosis (e.g., in case of hospital admission or death) and overestimated when loss to follow-up is higher in those with a more favorable course of the condition. This may be the case when patients relocate to another area. This type of bias resembles the disturbance that may occur in trials if no intention to treat analysis is performed (see Chapter 10).

Design of Data Analysis

Analysis Objective

The aims of the data analysis in multivariable prognostic research are similar to multivariable diagnostic research, except for the dimension of time: to provide knowledge about which potential predictors, causal or non-causal, independently contribute to the outcome prediction, and to what extent. Also, one may aim to develop and validate a multivariable prediction model or rule to predict the outcome given predictor combinations. Which goal to pursue again depends on the amount of data and prior knowledge; these are addressed in Chapter 3 as well as on the eventual intended use of research results. Also, the parameters of the required number of subjects and data analytical steps of prognostic studies are similar to diagnostic studies. For example, to guide decision-making in individual patients, the analysis and reporting of prognostic studies concentrates on *absolute* risk estimates (in prognostic studies on incidence and in diagnostic studies on prevalence) of an outcome given combinations of predictors and their values. In view of the large similarities of the analysis of prognostic and diagnostic studies, we will concentrate on the few differences that exist between the two types of studies and further refer to Chapter 3.

Different Outcomes

In contrast to diagnostic research where the outcome is typically dichotomous, prognostic research can distinguish between various types of outcomes. The first and most frequently encountered type of outcome is the occurrence (yes/no) of an event within a specific period of time, for example, occurrence of a certain complication within three months, where (ideally) each included patient has been followed for at least this period. The cumulative incidence, expressed as a probability between 0% and 100%, of the dichotomous outcome at a certain time point (t) is to be predicted using predictors measured before t. For these outcomes, the analysis is identical to the analysis in diagnostic research. The second most frequently encountered outcome in prognostic research is the occurrence of a particular outcome event over a (usually) longer period of time, where the follow-up time may differ substantially between study participants. Here, the time to occurrence of the event can be predicted using the Kaplan-Meier method or Cox proportional hazard modeling. It is also possible to predict the absolute risk of a certain outcome within multiple time frames (e.g., 3 months, 6 months, 1 and 3 years), albeit that the maximum time period is determined by the maximum follow-up period of the included patients (see also the worked-out example at the end of this chapter). Other, less frequently encountered outcomes in prognostic prediction studies are continuous variables [Harrell, 2001], such as the level of pain or tumor size at t, and—as in diagnostic research—polytomous (nominal) outcomes [Biesheuvel et al., 2007] or ordinal outcomes [Harrell et al., 1998], such as the Glasgow Outcome Scale collapsed into three (ordinal) levels: death, survival with major disability, and functional recovery [Cremer et al., 2006].

Required Number of Subjects

As for diagnostic research, the multivariable character of prognostic research creates problems to estimate the required number of study subjects; there are no straightforward commonly accepted methods. Ideally, prognostic studies have several hundred outcome events [Simon & Altman, 1994; Harrell, 2001]. Like for all dichotomous outcomes analyzed with multivariable logistic regression analysis (see Chapter 3), various studies showed that for the analysis of time-to-event outcomes using Cox proportional hazard modeling, at least ten subjects in the smallest of the outcome categories (i.e., either with or without the event during the study period) are needed for proper statistical modeling [Concato et al., 1995; Peduzzi et al., 1995]. The same applies to ordinal and polytomous outcomes [Biesheuvel et al., 2007].

For continuous outcomes, the required number of subjects may be estimated crudely by performing a sample size calculation for the t-test situation where the two groups are characterized by the most important dichotomous predictor. Another approach, more directed at the use of multiple linear regression modeling, is to define the allowable limit in the number of covariates (or rather, degrees of freedom) for the model by dividing the number of subjects by 15 [Harrell, 2001]. For more sophisticated approaches, we refer our readers to the article by Dupont and Plummer [1998].

Statistical Analysis

The two most frequently applied outcomes in prognostic research are (1) dichotomous outcomes within a certain time period (cumulative incidence) and (2) time to event outcomes.

Modeling of the cumulative incidence of a dichotomous outcome at t1 using logistic regression is discussed in Chapters 3 and 12.

For time-to-event outcomes, also denoted as survival type outcomes, the univariable analysis can be performed using the Kaplan-Meier method (see Chapter 12). Similar to the analysis of dichotomous outcomes, the observed probabilities depend on the threshold values of the predictor. Unfortunately, the construction of an ROC-curve is not straightforward because the outcomes of the censored patients are unknown. The so-called *concordance-statistic* (c-statistic), however, easily can be calculated and its value has the same interpretation as the area under the ROC-curve. For the multivariable analysis of time-to-event data using Cox proportional hazard modeling, we refer to the worked-out example below.

When the outcome is continuous, for example, tumor size, univariable and multivariable analyses are usually carried out using linear regression modeling. The discriminatory power of a linear regression model can be assessed from the squared multiple correlation coefficient (R^2), also known as the *explained variance* [Harrell et al., 1996; Harrell, 2001]. Detailed information on the analysis of continuous as well ordinal and polytomous outcomes is available in the literature [Harrell, 2001; Roukema et al., 2007; Biesheuvel et al., 2007].

Internal Validation and Shrinkage of the Developed Prognostic Model

If the number of potential predictors in multivariable logistic regression modeling is much larger than the number of outcomes or subjects, any fitted model will result in a too optimistic predictive accuracy (see Chapter 3). The internal validation and shrinkage of a multivariable logistic, Cox proportional hazard, and linear, ordinal, and polytomous models are similar, as has been described in Chapter 3 for diagnostic research [Harrell, 2001; Steyerberg et al., 2000; Steyerberg et al., 2001a].

Other Relevant Data Analysis Issues

Because the relevant issues pertaining to reporting of study results, external validation of the developed model, and application of a final model in clinical practice are similar for prognostic and diagnostic research, we refer you to Chapter 3 for further details on these issues.

Worked-Out Example

This example is based on a study conducted by Spijker and colleagues [2006]. This example illustrates the design of data analysis in the case of time-to-event data which include: how to obtain absolute risks from a Cox proportional hazard model; how to shrink coefficients; how to assess discriminatory power; and how to calculate (theoretical) sensitivity and specificity using the predictive values. Useful methodological considerations underlying this example can be found in the literature [Vergouwe et al., 2002; Harrell, 2001; Altman & Andersen, 1989; Van Houwelingen & Le Cessie, 1990; Steyerberg et al., 2000; Steyerberg et al., 2001b].

Rationale for the Study

Persistence of a major depressive episode (MDE) is a common and serious problem. If the persistence risk can be estimated accurately, treatment may be tailored to an individual patient's needs. If the risk of persistence is small, a policy of watchful waiting might be adopted while a high risk of persistence may call for immediate and possibly more aggressive treatment (e.g., antidepressant drug therapy in combination with psychotherapy). Setting a prognosis in individual cases with MDE, however, is notoriously difficult and lacks a sound empirical basis. Although many studies among depressed patients identified predictors of depression persistence, the analyses and presentation of the results do not allow prediction of the absolute risk in individual patients in daily practice [Sargeant et al., 1990].

Theoretical Design

The study objective was to construct a score that allows prediction of major depressive episode (MDE) persistence over 12 months in individuals with MDE, using determinants of persistence identified in previous research. The prognostic determinants considered were measures of social support, somatic disorders, depression severity and recurrence, and duration of previous episodes.

The occurrence relation can be represented as follows:

Persistence after 12 months = $f(d_{1-6})$

The domain in this study was confined to those individuals from the general population suffering from depression.

Design of Data Collection

This cohort study was performed using data collected between 1996 and 1999 in a general population survey [Netherlands Mental Health Survey and Incidence Study (NEMESIS)] [Ten Have et al., 2005]. Two hundred and fifty patients diagnosed with MDE according to the *Diagnostic and Statistical Manual of Mental Disorders*, version 3 revised (DSM-III-R) criteria, as assessed with the Composite International Diagnostic Interview, were identified. For these patients, all information on the predictors under study was recorded. In an interview 0.5 to 24 months after the diagnosis (this variability was due to logistic reasons), the duration of depression was assessed using the Life Chart Interview.

Design of Data Analysis

First, a univariable analysis for each predictor was carried out to "keep in touch with the data." Then a multivariable Cox proportional hazards regression model with time to recovery (i.e., no more persistence) as the outcome variable and the six predefined predictors as the independent variables was run. The Cox model, instead of the usual logistic regression model, was applied to account for the varying follow-up times across patients.

The aim of the analysis was to calculate the absolute 12-month risk of not having recovered, that is, the probability of depression persistence 12 months after the diagnosis for individual patients. This appears to be not straightforward, as the Cox regression procedure yields actual survival estimates [S(t)] only. These estimates represent the predicted risks of depression persistence for each patient given the patient's follow-up time and values of the prognostic determinants.

Actual survival estimates are defined as:

$$S(t) = S_0(t)^{\exp(LP)}$$

where the linear predictor (LP) is $\beta_1{}^*X_1 + \beta_2{}^*X_2 + \ldots \beta_n{}^*X_n$, with the Xs denoting the predictor values of a patient and the βs denoting the regression coefficients.

The baseline survival function $S_0(t)$ is the time-dependent cumulative risk of persistence of depression for a person with none of the predictors present, that is, the LP being zero and thus $S_0(t) = S(t)$.

The baseline survival function $[S_0(t)]$ can be calculated by remolding the above formula as follows: $S_0(t) = S(t)^{1/\exp(LP)}$. This calculation allowed us to calculate the cumulative 12-month baseline risk from the database for those patients who actually had 12 months of follow-up $[S_0(12\text{ months})]$. In our study, this value appeared to be 0.2029 (20.3%). The final step is to calculate the 12-month risk for all patients using this $S_0(12\text{ months})$ and an individual's LP, the latter thus representing the individual patient's part of the risk.

In the formula, $S(12\text{ months}) = S_0(12\text{ months})^{\exp(LP)} = S_0(0.2029)^{\exp(LP)}$.

The 12-month time span was primarily chosen on clinical grounds but also because at that follow-up time, the number of patients at risk (of recovery) was still sufficiently large. To evaluate the calibration of the model, that is, to assess the extent to which the model predictions are in agreement with the observed probabilities, we calculated the Kaplan-Meier estimate of the 12-month risk of depression persistence for each decile of predicted risk and compared these using a scatter diagram.

As a next step, the discriminatory power of the model was quantified. Because the outcomes of the censored patients are unknown, the construction of a ROC-curve for the evaluation of discriminatory power, such as those calculated for logistic regression models, is impossible. However, the c-statistic can be calculated. It is numerical and, with regard to interpretation, equal to the area under the ROC-curve; it reflects the probability that for a random pair of patients, the one who has the outcome event first has the highest predicted probability. The concordance statistic (as the area under the ROC-curve) is an overall measure of discriminatory power. A value of 0.5 indicates no discrimination and a value of 1.0 indicates perfect discrimination between those developing and not developing the study outcome, in this case depression persistence during the defined time period [Altman & Royston, 2000a]. Both the regression coefficients and therefore also the hazard ratios [i.e., exp (regression coefficient), which is interpreted as a relative risk] with their 95% confidence intervals as well as the concordance-statistic, were adjusted for over-fitting or over-optimism using bootstrapping techniques [Efron & Tibshirani, 1993]. To this end, 100 random bootstrap samples with replacement were drawn from the data set with complete data on all predictors ($N = 250$). The model's predictive performance after bootstrapping is the performance that can be expected when the model is applied to future similar populations.

To construct an easily applicable "persistence of depression score," each coefficient from the model was transformed to a rounded number. As the coefficients reflect the relative weight of each variable in the prediction, they were transformed to a number of points in a uniform way, that is, each coefficient was divided by the coefficient closest to zero, in this case –.107. The number of points was subsequently rounded to the nearest integer. The total score for each individual patient was determined by assigning the points for each variable present and adding them up.

The predicted probability of persistence of depression at 12 months follow-up was presented according to four broad categories of the risk score for reasons of statistical stability and practical applicability. The categories were arbitrarily chosen with a view to reasonable size of each category as well as clinical sensibility. Next, the score was transformed to a dichotomous "prognostic test," allowing each patient to be classified as *high* or *low* risk of depression persistence. Sensitivity, specificity, and the positive and negative predictive value of categorized values of the score were calculated for the same cut-offs of the score as those used to delineate the scoring categories. Data were analyzed using SPSS 12.0 and S-plus 2000 software programs.

Results

Follow-up time ranged from 0.5 to 24 months and 187 subjects out of the total population ($N = 250$) recovered. The final proportional hazards regression model appeared to be reasonably calibrated as the predicted and observed probabilities were similar over the entire range (Figure 4.1).

The shrinkage factor for the coefficients that was obtained from the bootstrap process was 0.91. The results presented are based on the findings after shrinkage. Coefficients from the model as well as the hazard ratios as measures of relative risk are displayed in Table 4.3, together with the risk points per predictor.

Table 4.4 shows the relationship between categories of the score, the observed risk, and the predicted risk of MDE persistence after one year. The mean risk was 23% and the predicted risks increased from 7% to 40% with increasing score categories and were generally well in agreement with the observed risk. From Table 4.4, it can also be seen that the patient introduced above has a 29% risk of persistence of depression. The overall discriminatory power of the score was fair with a c-statistic of 0.68. For specific cutoffs, the sensitivity, specificity, and predictive values are shown in Table 4.4.

If, for instance, a cut-off ≥ 5 is chosen as the threshold for a high risk of persistence and thus requires more intense treatment, 69% (sensitivity) of those who would still suffer depression after one year will have received this treatment. Yet, 12% (1-NPV) of those who did not undergo the more intense treatment because their test was negative will still have depression.

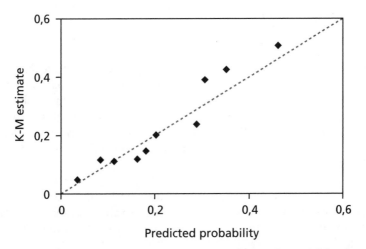

FIGURE 4.1 Calibration plot of the Cox proportional hazards model for the prediction of depression persistence at 12 months of follow-up. The dotted line represents the line of identity, that is, perfect model calibration.

TABLE 4.3   Multivariable predictors of recovery from depression at 12 months

Predictor	Coefficient	Hazard ratio (95% confidence interval)	Contribution to risk score
Somatic disorder	–0,319	0.73 (0.54 – 0.97)	3
Medium social support	–0,107	0.90 (0.64 – 1.27)	1
Low social support	–0,420	0.66 (0.46 – 0.95)	4
Severe depression	–0,314	0.73 (0.53 – 1.01)	3
Recurrent depression	0,392	1.48 (1.10 – 1.99)	–4
Long duration previous episodes	–0,426	0.65 (0.48 – 0.89)	4

Total risk score = physical illness*3 + medium social support + low social support*4 + severe depression*3 – recurrent depression*4 + long duration previous episodes*4.

The total risk score was calculated using the formula at the bottom of the table. For instance, a subject with a severe and recurrent MDE, with a comorbid somatic disorder and low social support, has a score of +3 – 4 + 3 + 4 = 6 points.

Spijker J, de Graaf R, Ormel J, Nolen WA, Grobbee DE, Burger H. The persistence of depression score. Acta Psychiatr Scand 2006;114:411–6.

TABLE 4.4   Prognostic test characteristics for 12-month depression persistence

Cut-off score	N (%)	Sensitivity	Specificity	PPV	1-NPV
≥ 2	184 (74%)	93%	32%	27%	7%
≥ 5	109 (44%)	69%	63%	34%	12%
≥ 8	49 (20%)	36%	85%	40%	17%

Spijker J, de Graaf R, Ormel J, Nolen WA, Grobbee DE, Burger H. The persistence of depression score. Acta Psychiatr Scand 2006;114:411–6.

It should be noted that the discriminatory power of the resulting score is modest with a c-statistic of 0.68, in particular when compared with c-statistics or, equivalently, areas under the curve of the ROC-curve obtained in many diagnostic studies. However, it must be kept in mind that by nature of the close temporal relationship between predictors and outcome, measures of discrimination generally achieve higher values in the diagnostic than the prognostic setting.

It was concluded that the study yielded a risk score for the prediction of persistence of MDE in the general population with depression with reasonable performance. The score may be of value to clinical practice in providing a rational basis for treatment decisions, but validation in that setting is required.

Concluding Remarks

Prognostic research shows a large similarity to diagnostic research; in fact, prognoses can be seen as diagnoses in the future. Most importantly, they are both variants of prediction research. The applicability of prediction in diagnostic and prognostic research critically depends on several precautions:

1. Assemble a patient population that reflects a carefully determined domain in clinical practice.
2. Measure potential predictors using similar methods as in clinical practice.
3. Measure a clinically relevant outcome as accurately as possible.
4. In the analysis, use absolute rather than relative risk values.
5. Do not worry about confounding, as it is a non-issue in prediction research.
6. Do not start with too many predictors relative to the number of outcome events or subjects.
7. Include predictors in the model that add to the predictive power of the model, but beware of data-driven selection of predictors. This generally argues against stepwise regression models.
8. Take care that in the presentation the absolute risks can be calculated for (all) predictor combinations in a practical way, for instance, using a risk score or nomogram.
9. Assess the discriminatory power and the calibration of the prediction model.
10. Take care that the model is internally validated and corrected (shrunk) for over-optimism, for example, by bootstrapping, heuristic shrinkage methods, or penalized regression modeling.
11. Apply the model to a different population representing the same domain for (external) validation.

Implementation of well conducted prediction research may greatly contribute to the efficiency of medical practice, thereby reducing the suffering from disease. Undoubtedly, the introduction of computerized patient records will further increase the interest in multivariable prediction models as described here, because their development, validation, and application in research settings as well as in routine care becomes much more feasible.

5

Intervention Research: Intended Effects

Effective treatment is the stronghold of modern medicine. Despite all other types of care clinical medicine has to offer, patients and physicians alike expect first and foremost that diseases can be cured and symptoms relieved by appropriate intervention. Evidence-based treatment—or prevention for that matter—demands the unequivocal demonstration by empirical research of the efficacy and safety of the intervention. In general, any intervention is characterized by intended and unintended effects, where the intended effects are those for which the treatment is given. The intended effect is the main effect. However, any intervention also has unintended effects. These may range from relatively trivial discipline required by the patient to potentially life-threatening adverse drug reactions. Ideally, intended effects should be highly common, predictable, and large, and unintended effects rare and mild. Drugs and other interventions vary markedly with regard to the relative frequency and severity of unintended effects just as drugs vary in effectiveness with regard to their intended effects. Intervention research aims to quantify the full spectrum of relevant effects of intervention. However, the approaches to demonstrating the intended or primary effects generally differ from those to demonstrate safety. This chapter concentrates on intended effects while the study of unintended effects is discussed in Chapter 6.

Research on the benefits and risks of interventions is central to current clinical epidemiological research. For centuries, the field of medicine has grown with very limited possibilities to offer adequate treatment. This has dramatically changed in recent decades. Rapidly expanding pharmacopeias and advances in surgical techniques are equally progressing with an increasing emphasis on less invasive techniques. *Intervention* is a general term for an action intended to change the prognosis in a patient and includes drug treatment, surgery, physiotherapy, lifestyle interventions such as physical exercise, and preventive actions such as vaccination. To treat a patient with confidence, the physician needs to know about the potential benefit of the treatment (i.e., the intended or main effects of the intervention), which must be weighed against possible risks (i.e., unintended or side effects of the intervention). Increasingly, cost considerations also play a role when choices are made between different treatment options. The deliberate decision not to treat or to postpone treatment can be viewed as an intervention. Money is not only an issue from the perspective of the fair and efficient use of available resources, it is an important driving force for the development and marketing of new treatments. Pharmaceutical and other manufacturers producing medical devices increasingly emphasize their compassion with patients as a motive for their search for new compounds, but they typically—and understandably—have their shareholders and profits as their main focus. This elevates research on treatment effects to an arena in which huge interests play a role. As a consequence, much more than in any other area of medical research, the quality and reliability of intervention research has been the topic of major interest and development. The result is a highly sophisticated set of principles and methods that guide intervention research.

In intervention research, the principles of etiologic and prognostic research combine. Intervention research is commonly causal research, because it is the true effect of the intervention that needs to be estimated free from confounding variables. Intervention research commonly is also prognostic. In order to use an intervention in medical practice, it is important to know as precisely as possible the absolute benefits and risks that a patient may experience.

For example, a one-year mortality is expected to decrease from 30% to 10% (intended or main effect), while the risk of developing orthostatic hypotension (unintended or side effect) is 10%. To serve clinical decisions of treatment best, intervention research in general and clinical trials in particular should be viewed as the means to measure the effects of interventions. It is generally not sufficient to know whether a treatment works. What is needed is a valid estimate of the size of the effects. In clinical epidemiologic intervention research, randomized controlled trials (RCTs) play an essential role, not only because they are often considered the only approach to definitively demonstrate the magnitude of benefits of treatment, but also because RCTs offer a role model for causal research. The principles of the design of randomized trials are quite straightforward. When appropriately understood, they also will greatly help to improve causal research under those circumstances where a randomized trial cannot be conducted. To understand the nature of trials is to understand unconfounded observation.

Effects of Intervention

The challenges of scientific inference on the effects of intervention can be illustrated by a simple example in which a physician is considering using a new drug to treat high blood pressure in a group of his patients. The drug has been handed to him by a sales representative, who promised a rapid decline in blood pressure for most patients, with excellent tolerability. Let us assume that the physician decides to try out the drug on the next 20 or so patients who visit his office with a first diagnosis of hypertension. He carefully records each patient's baseline blood pressure level and asks them to return a number of times for remeasurement in the next weeks. His experience with these patients is summarized in Figure 5.1.

The physician is satisfied. A gradual decline in systolic blood pressure is shown in his patients. Moreover, most were very pleased with the drug because the treatment had few side effects; one patient mentioned the development of mild sleeping disturbances. Would it be wise to conclude that the drug works, is well tolerated, and can now become part of routine treatment with confidence? Clearly not. There are a number of reasons why the observed response may not adequately reflect the effect caused by the drug. In order to use the drug as a preferred treatment in similar future patients, it is necessary to be assured that the response resulted from the pharmacological agent and does not reflect other mechanisms. Although a patient may not care why the reduction occurred as long as the hypertension was treated, from a sensible medical viewpoint it is necessary to know whether the effect can be attributed to the drug. If it is not, then additional costs are

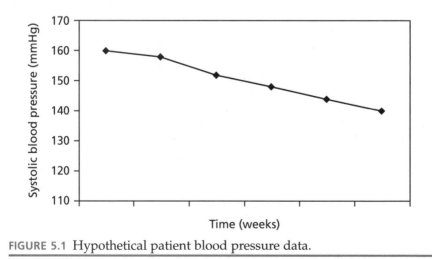

FIGURE 5.1 Hypothetical patient blood pressure data.

generated, the patients is medicalized, and side effects may be induced without a sound scientific justification. Let us examine alternative explanations for the observation made by the physician.

Natural History

The first question to be answered is whether the same blood pressure response would have been observed when no treatment was given. In other words, is it possible that the natural history of the disease would explain the change over time? *Natural history* is the variability in symptoms and signs of a disease not explained by treatment, which is the prognosis of the disease in the absence of treatment. Many factors can cause changes in the presence or manifestations of disease and even more mechanisms that lead to changes in an individual's course of disease are not understood. Still, the force of natural history can be very powerful. In a study of over a 1000 women in Sweden with symptoms suggestive of urinary tract infection, confirmed with urine cultures, the spontaneous cure rate of symptoms was 28% after the first week, and 37% had neither symptoms nor bacteriuria after five to seven weeks [Ferry et al., 2004]. Spontaneous remission or cure of symptoms or conditions may occur in many diseases and in research aimed at quantifying treatment effects, there is no exception to the rule that the effect of treatment needs to be separated from the natural course of the disease, such as the course of the disease in the absence of treatment. As the natural history of disease is difficult—if not impossible—to predict, there is no way its effect can be estimated in a single patient.

An important component of natural history is created by regression to the mean. *Regression to the mean* occurs for any measure of disease (severity) or other patient variable and can be explained from a combination of intraindividual variability and selection. The way regression to the mean works is simple. If patients are selected according to their relatively high or low values of a characteristic that shows intraindividual variability, the value of that variable on remeasurement will be lower or higher, respectively. The cause of the intraindividual variability is irrelevant. It can be a reflection of variation in the measurement, circadian patterns, or some other unknown, biological mechanism. The magnitude of the effect depends on the magnitude of variability and the level of selection.

This can be illustrated by the classification of individuals as hypertensive and the subsequent remeasurement of blood pressure in the selected group (Figure 5.2). Suppose that all individuals are selected with an initial systolic blood pressure at or above 140 mm Hg. Because blood pressure shows a certain degree of variability in all subjects, some of these individuals will have blood pressure levels above their average level at the time of the measurement. These individuals are more likely to have lower than higher blood pressure levels at a subsequent measurement. Individuals who

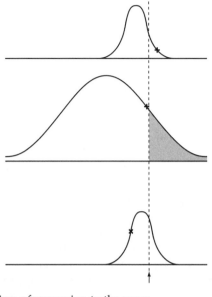

FIGURE 5.2 Mechanism of regression to the mean.

had a blood pressure below their usual average level and below the cut-off point at the time of the first measurement were not selected and will not be invited for remeasurement. As a consequence, those subjects classified too low, relative to their usual blood pressure, will not be remeasured, while those individuals in whom the observed value was too high relative to their usual blood pressure level will be remeasured along with all those whose measured blood pressure adequately reflected their usual pressure. Because the selected population subgroup includes more subjects whose blood pressure will be lower on remeasurement than subjects whose blood pressure will be higher at the time of remeasurement, the average blood pressure of the selected population will fall. Regression to the mean is the inevitable consequence of selection based on a variable that shows variation. Virtually all variables that are measured in clinical research show some degree of intraindividual variability. Also, variables that appear stone solid, such as height or bone density, show some variability when measured in groups, if only because measurement errors can never be completely excluded and these will lead to some degree of variability. Clearly, the issue is more prominent for measures that are inherently variable such as blood pressure, temperature, or measures of pain. The first report of regression to the mean dates back to the work of Francis Galton [1886], who authored the paper entitled, "Regression Towards Mediocrity in Hereditary Stature." Galton related the heights of children to the average height of their parents, which he called the mid-parent height (Figure 5.3).

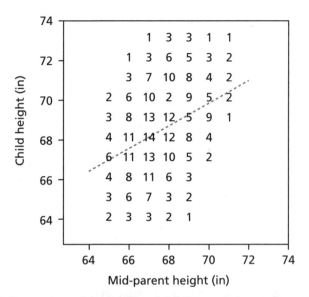

FIGURE 5.3 Comparison of the heights of children to their parents made by Francis Galton (1822–1911). Diagonal line shows the average height.

Source: Bland JM, Altman DG. Statistic notes: regression towards the mean. BMJ 1994:308:1499.

Children and parents had the same mean height of 68.2 inches. The ranges differed, however, because the mid-parent height was an average of two observations and thus had its range reduced. Now, consider those parents with a relatively high mid-height between 70 and 71 inches. The mean height of their children was 69.5 inches, which was closer to the mean height of all children than the mean height of their parents was to the mean height of all parents. Galton called this phenomenon *regression towards mediocrity*. The term was coined with this report, but the observation is different from what is currently considered regression to the mean because this concerned the full population without selection. The principle, however, is the same.

Regression to the mean is not an exclusive phenomenon in epidemiological research. Consider, for example, students who take a clinical epidemiology exam. Students who receive an unexpected, extremely low score will probably get a better score when they repeat the exam, even when they put no further effort into understanding the topic. It is likely that some bad luck was involved in getting the exceptional score, and this bad luck is unlikely to occur for a second time in a row, given the usual (higher) score in this student. It is a common mistake in everyday life to assign a causal role to something apparently related to the observed effect but in reality is likely due to regression. Take, for example, the case of the poor badminton champion from Kuala Lumpur (Textbox 5.1). Some of this champion's predecessors

TEXTBOX 5.1 Depression toward the mean in badminton

KUALA LUMPUR: Prime Minister Datuk Seri Dr Mahathir Mohamad congratulated Malaysian shuttler Mohd Hafiz Hashim for his achievement but warned that he should not be "spoilt" with gifts like previous champions.

Dr Mahathir said people should remember what had happened to previous champions when they were spoilt with gifts of land, money and other items.

"I hope the states will not start giving acres of land and money in the millions, because they all seem not to be able to play badminton after that," he said after taking part in the last dry run and dress rehearsal for the 13th NAM Summit at the PWTC yesterday.

Source: Modified from "Mahathir asks states not to 'spoil' Hafiz," The Star Online, 2/18/2003.

very likely achieved greater than their usual level of performances because of a lucky play of chance, and their subsequent downfall was attributed to the "spoiling" by gifts of appreciation.

In medicine, regression to the mean is also known as "the doctors' friend." General practitioners (GPs) use time as one of their main tools is differentiating between serious and less serious problems. Worried mothers call their GP when they measure a high temperature in their sick child. When the doctor arrives or the parents and child arrive at the emergency room, the temperature often has fallen. People tend to self-select themselves at peak levels of symptoms, such as temperature, cough, depressive symptoms, and pain. Many will show "spontaneous" decline because of regression to the mean. The solution in practice is to wait and remeasure. Similarly, in research the approach to removing regression to the mean is to remeasure and select only those who show stable levels of, for example, elevated blood pressure before entering into a study.

Regression to the mean is but one component of natural history and it is an entirely statistical phenomenon. There are many other factors that may influence the natural history that are linked to the outcome by some pathophysiological mechanism. When this is known, we may try to adjust our observation for this knowledge. Typically, however, determinants of natural history are unknown and cannot simply be subtracted from the observed effect.

Extraneous Effects

A second reason why the physician observed a seeming response to the drug may be that other determinants of blood pressure changed concomitantly. The patients were told that they had high blood pressure and that this is a risk factor for stroke and a myocardial infarction that should be treated. This information could motivate patients to try to adjust their lifestyle. They may have improved their diet, started exercising, or reduced alcohol intake. All of these actions also may have reduced the blood pressure. These effects are called *extraneous* because they are outside of the effect of interest, namely the drug effect. In a study, we may attempt to measure extraneous effects and take these into account in the observation, but this requires that the effects are known and measurable.

There is one particularly well known extraneous effect that is so closely linked to the intervention that it generally cannot be directly measured or separated from the drug effect: the *placebo effect*. Placebo effects can result simply from contact with physicians when a diagnosis or simple attention from a respected professional alleviates anxiety. As Hróbjartsson [1996] puts it, "Any therapeutic meeting between a conscious patient and a doctor has the potential of initiating a placebo effect." In research, obtaining informed consent has been shown to induce a placebo effect. There is a wealth of literature on placebo effects and considerable dispute on the mechanism of action. Clearly, psychological mechanisms are likely to play a role, and certain personality characteristics have been particularly related to strong placebo responses [Swartzman & Burkell, 1998]. However, well-documented seemingly pharmacologic actions are related to placebo responses. For example, the placebo response to placebo-induced analgesia can be reversed by naloxone, an opioid antagonist [Fields & Price, 1997]. Obviously, the type of outcome that is being studied is related to the presence and magnitude of a placebo response. Outcomes that are more subjective, such as anxiety or mood, will be more prone to placebo effects. Expectation also powerfully influences how subjects respond to either an inert or active substance. In a study where subjects were given sugar water but were told that it was an emetic, 80% of patients responded by vomiting [Hahn, 1997].

Placebo effects are, to a greater or lesser extent, an inherent component of interventions and they will obscure the measurement of the intervention effect of interest, such as the pharmacological action of a drug. This may or may not be a problem in intervention research. Again, from the perspective of the patient, it does not really matter whether the relief results in part from a placebo effect of the drug. Cure is cure. Similarly, from the viewpoint of the physician, the placebo effect may be a welcome additional benefit of an intervention. Even for an investigator studying the benefits of treatment, the placebo effect can be accepted as something that is inseparable from the drug effect and therefore should be included in the overall estimate of the benefit of one treatment compared to another (e.g., non-drug) treatment strategy. Different treatments may have different placebo effects and this will also explain differences in benefits when employed in real life. In other words, the need to exclude placebo effects in research on benefits and risks of interventions is not a given and depends on the objectives of the investigator. Although many believe that the best evidence for treatment effects comes from trials in which a placebo effect has been ruled out by comparing treatment to placebo treatment, there are good examples of research where potential placebo effects were included in the measured treatment effect that provide a more meaningful result than when placebo effects were removed. The motives and consequences of research that does or does not separate the pharmacological from the placebo effects were well outlined in a classic paper by Schwarz and Lellouch [1967] on pragmatic and explanatory trials. Their article gives an example from a real case in which a decision needed to be made between different options to determine the benefits of a drug aimed at sensitizing cancer patients for required radiotherapy. The assumption was that when patients were pretreated with the drug, the effect of the radiotherapy was enhanced. The investigators decided to do a randomized comparison between usual therapy and the new treatment scheme. For the usual therapy arm of the study, there were two options (Figure 5.4, taken from the original report by Schwarz and Lellouch). One option was to just treat the patients as usual, which implied the immediate treatment with radiotherapy. The alternative option was to first give a placebo drug and then start radiotherapy. In the second option, placebo effects from the drug would be removed from the comparison. However, radiotherapy would be put at a disadvantage because compared to the usual approach the installment of radiotherapy would be delayed. In contrast, in the first option the new approach would be compared to the optimal way to deliver radiotherapy without the sensitizing drug, but placebo effects could not be ruled out. Given that the new drug was not without side effects, a distinction between real and placebo benefits seemed important. There is no single best solution to this problem. Probably, when little is known from a drug, first a comparison with placebo is necessary to determine the true pharmacological action devoid from placebo effects. Next is to establish its value in real life to a comparison with the best standard treatment, in this case immediate radiotherapy. The result of either comparison also determines the relevance of the answer.

Suppose that in the blinded comparison radiotherapy still is shown to be superior. Now, a comparison with immediate radiotherapy is not needed because, if anything, the effect would be even more beneficial than when combined with the drug period. In their article, the authors propose the term *explanatory* for a trial in which placebo effects are removed and the term *pragmatic* for a study in which placebo and other extraneous effects are taken as part of the overall treatment response and are accepted in a comparison to an alternative treatment option. There are many circumstances in which the true effects, without placebo effects, of a drug are well established and where a pragmatic trial will deliver a result that better reflects the anticipated effect in real life than an explanatory trial. In some cases, the apparent "main" intervention is not even the most important part of the strat-

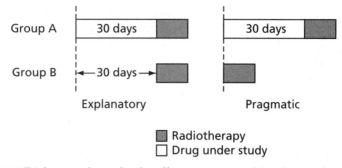

FIGURE 5.4 Trial arms where placebo effects are removed (explanatory) and where the placebo effect was considered to be part of the overall treatment (pragmatic).

Schwartz D, Lellouch J. Explanatory and pragmatic attitudes in therapeutic trials. J Chron Dis 1967:20:637–48.

egy. For example, in a pragmatic randomized trial comparing the effect of minimally invasive coronary bypass surgery to conventional bypass grafting on post-surgery cognitive decline, the assumption was that the necessary use of a cardiopulmonary pump during conventional surgery was the most important component of the intervention with regard to adverse effects on cognitive function [Van Dijk et al., 2002].

Unfortunately, the term *pragmatic* sounds somewhat less scientific and rigorous and some investigators are hesitant to refrain from rigorous placebo control in their research. In doing so, they may eventually produce results that do not adequately address the question that medical practitioners need to have answered. It is important to understand that removal of placebo and other extraneous effects is a deliberate decision that an investigator needs to make in the design of a study and that pragmatic studies often may be the preferred option. There is ample confusion about the nature of pragmatic intervention research. For example, some authors propose that explanatory studies "recruit as homogeneous a population as possible and aim primarily to further scientific knowledge" or that "in a pragmatic trial it is neither necessary nor always desirable for all subjects to complete the trial in the group to which they were allocated" [Roland & Torgerson, 1998]. These views are erroneous. The homogeneity of the study population may affect the generalizability and speaks on the domain of a study irrespective of whether a trial is pragmatic or explanatory. In both explanatory and pragmatic trials, patients sometimes complete the study in the group to which they were not randomized; for example, they may need the treatment originally allocated to the other groups and thus "cross over" from one treatment arm to the other. This is common and not a problem as long as the patients are analyzed according to allocated treatment, that is, by "intention to treat." Pragmatic or explanatory does not speak on methodologic rigor or the scientific value of the knowledge that is generated. The distinction between pragmatic and explanatory trials reflects the nature of the comparison that is being made. In pragmatic studies, the treatment response is the total difference between two treatments (i.e., treatment strategies), including treatment and associated placebo or other extraneous effects, and this will often better reflect the likely response in practice.

Observer Effects

The third, and last, reason for a difference in the observed response to treatment and the true treatment effect lies in the influence of the observer/researcher or the patient being observed (Figure 5.5).

Without deliberate intention, the observer may favorably interpret the report of a patient or adjust (round up or down) measurement results to better values. The observer effect is that which an observer or the observed participant has on the particular observations made. Observer bias is a systematic effect that moves the observed effect from the true effect. Observer effects may well reflect an interaction between observer and patient. For example, a physician has just received a sample of a new drug that is reputed to work exceptionally well in cases of chronic sleeping problems. When Mrs. Jones visits his surgery again with a long-lasting complaint of sleeping problems

FIGURE 5.5 Observer–observee difference in perceived response to treatment.

so far resistant to any medication, the doctor proposes this new miracle drug, which may offer a last resort. At the next visit, Mrs. Jones may be inclined not to disappoint her doctor again and gives a somewhat positively colored account of her sleeping history in the last couple of weeks. At the same time, the physician is reluctant to accept yet another failure of treatment in this patient. Together they create a biased observation of an otherwise unchanged problem. Just like for placebo effects, the magnitude of the potential for observer effects will depend on the type of observation that is being made. The "softer" the outcome, the more room for observer effects. In a study on the benefits of a drug in patients with ischemic cardiac disease, measures of quality of life and angina will be more susceptible for observer bias than vital status or myocardial infarction, although the latter is also sufficiently subjective to be affected. For example, disagreement in the determination of electrocardiographic ST segment elevation by emergency physicians occurs frequently and is related to the amount of ST segment elevation present on the electrocardiogram.

Treatment Effect

Despite all of the reasons why an observed treatment effect need not necessarily show the benefit of the treatment per se, obviously there is the possibility that what effect is being observed is entirely or in part the result of the treatment. In intervention research, the mission is to extract from the observation the component in which we are interested. This can only be achieved by comparing a group of patients who are being treated to a group of patients who are not treated or are treated differently. There is no way in which a valid estimate of the effect of a drug or other treatment can be obtained from observing treated patients only. Consequently, in the example of the physician trying out a new antihypertensive drug, there is no way that the true effect of the new drug can be made from the overall observation. A comparative study is needed. The treatment effect and the three alternative explanations for the observed treatment response (natural history, extraneous effects, and observer effects) as well as the handling of the latter three in research can be illustrated by a simple equation.* In a comparative study where a treatment, say a drug named "R_x," is compared to no treatment at all, the responses in the index (i.e., treated) group can be summarized as follows:

$$OEi = R_x + NHi + EFi + Obi$$

where OEi is the observed effect, R_x is the treatment effect, NHi is the effect of natural history, EFi is the effect of extraneous factors including placebo effects, and OBi is the observer effect in the treated group.

---

*Lubsen J, de Lang R. Klinisch genes middelen onderzoek. Utecht: Binge, 1987.

The corresponding equation in the reference (r) group not receiving the intervention is:

OEr = NHr + EFr + OBr

When the interest is in the treatment effect per se, in this example the single pharmacological effect of the drug, R_x, OEi − OEr needs to equal R_x. To achieve this end, the other terms need to cancel out. Consequently, NHi needs to equal NHe, EFi needs to equal EFr, and OBi needs to equal OBr.

The equation for a comparison between two treatments is the same except that after cancelling out the other terms, OEi − OEe now equals R_xi − R_xr, that is, the net benefit of the index treatment over the other.

The principles of intervention research can be summarized as ways to make all terms in the equation in the two groups the same, except for the treatment term. This means that natural history, extraneous effects, and observer effects are made the same in the groups that are compared. Note that one way to achieve comparability of natural history, extraneous effects, and observation is by removing them completely from the study. However, this is generally impossible to achieve. Rather, by accepting these effects but by assuring that they cancel out in the observation, a valid estimate of the treatment effect is obtained.

Comparability of Natural History

Comparability of natural history is a *conditio sine qua non* (Latin legal term meaning "without which it could not be") in intervention research. Because natural history may be highly variable between individuals, an intervention effect estimated from research that includes effects from natural history cannot be generalized to what can be expected in practice. Consequently, it is of critical importance that in a comparison between two or more groups to estimate the effect of an intervention, the effects of natural history are the same in all groups.

There are several ways in which this can be achieved. First, a *quasi-experimental study* can be conducted where the participants in the groups are carefully selected in such a way that each group represents the same distribution of natural histories. For example, in a comparison of two anti-cancer drugs for treatment of leukemia, patients in the two groups can be deliberately selected in such a way so that they have a similar age, proportion of males, severity of the disease, and so on. One could even go as far as to closely match each individual in the index group to an individual from the reference group according to characteristics expected to be related to prognostic characteristics expected to determine natural history. This will improve the probability that, in the absence of treatment, the two groups would show the same natural history and, therefore, the observed difference in response would not reflect a difference in natural history. A related approach would be to restrict the entire study population to a highly homogeneous group of patients who, because of their similarity, are expected to all have a highly similar prognosis (natural history). Alternatively, no preselection is made and patients receive treatment as deemed by the physician but prognostic indicators are recorded in detail. Clearly, initiation of a specific intervention in daily practice is everything but random because physicians tend to treat those patients with a relatively poor prognosis earlier. Therefore, in the analysis of the data from the study, multivariate adjustments should be made to remove the effect of differences in natural history from the comparison.

A necessary requirement for either of these approaches is that all relevant prognostic factors that could be different between the groups are known and can be measured validly. In addition, the source population of patients should be large enough to make preselection and matching possible. Similarly, for multivariate analysis, the size of the study population should be large enough to allow statistical adjustments. The overriding problem, however, is that knowledge on all relevant prognostic factors is typically limited. A variable that is not known or measured cannot be taken into account in preselecting study groups nor can it be controlled in the analysis. This holds true for any causal research where the effect of an exposure needs to be separated from other related but confounding determinants of the outcome. However, the problem in intervention research is accentuated because of the complexity of the decision to treat patients. In setting an indication for prescribing a drug to a patient, the treating physician will take many factors into consideration such as the severity of the disease, the likelihood of good tolerance and compliance, the experience in this patient with previous treatments, and so forth. When groups of patients with the same disease but with and without a prescription for treatment by a physician are compared, they are probably different in many ways, some of which can be measured while others are very implicit and neither reflected in the patient file nor measurable by taking additional efforts. The indication for treatment (i.e., the composite of reasons to initiate it) is a very strong prognostic indicator. If a patient is judged to have an indication to use a drug, this patient would probably have a more severe untreated prognosis than a patient with the same diagnosis in which the physician has decided to wait before deciding on drug treatment. The effect on natural history of the presence or absence of a pertinent indication in patients with the same disease who are or are not treated is termed *confounding by indication* [Grobbee & Hoes, 1997].

Figure 5.6 shows that the reasons underlying the decision to initiate treatment are important potential confounders. These reasons, often related to patient characteristics such as severity of disease, by definition are associated with the probability of receiving the intervention (illustrated by the exclamation mark). If these reasons are also related the probability of

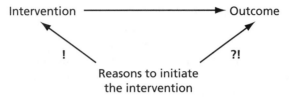

FIGURE 5.6 Reasons underlying the decision to initiate treatment are important potential confounders.

developing the outcome, which is the case where patients with more severe disease are more prone to receive the intervention, then the right arrow also exists. Consequently, confounding will occur.

Although many drugs can affect the course of a disease positively, the outcome in people with that disease compared with those who do not have it or have a less severe form may be worse or, at best, similar. Confounding by indication can completely obscure an intervention effect when treated and untreated patients are compared who do or do not receive the intervention in routine care. To illustrate this effect, Table 5.1 shows the risks for cardiovascular mortality in women with hypertension who participated in a population-based cohort study and were either treated or not treated by their physicians.

The crude rate ratio for mortality was 1, suggesting that the treatment had no effect because the treated and untreated hypertensive groups had the same cardiovascular mortality risk. However, when adjustments were made for a number of factors that were expected to be related to both the indication for treatment and cardiovascular mortality, and thus possibly confounding the comparison, the rate ratio dropped in a way that was compatible with the rate for a benefit of treatment.

Whether the adjusted rate ratio reflects the true treatment effect depends on whether an adjustment was made for all of the differences in confounding variables between the treated and untreated groups. This conclusion is very difficult to make. Confounding by indication commonly creates insurmountable problems for non-randomized research on treatment effects.

TABLE 5.1   Crude and adjusted rate ratios for death from cardiovascular causes in untreated and drug treated women that were all hypertensive according to common criteria

	Rate ratio (95% CI)
Crude value	1.0 (0.6 to 1.5)
Adjusted for:	
Age	0.7 (0.4 to 1.1)
+ Body mass index, pulse rate	0.6 (0.4 to 1.0)
+ Smoking, lipid concentrations	0.6 (0.4 to 0.9)
+ Diabetes	0.5 (0.3 to 0.9)

Valid inferences can much more likely be drawn under those rare circumstances in which (1) groups of patients with the same indications but different treatments can be compared and (2) residual dissimilarities in characteristics in patients receiving different treatments for the same indications are known, adequately measured, and can be adjusted for. For example, Psaty et al. [1995] compared the effects of several antihypertensive drugs on the risk of angina and myocardial infarction. In a case control study, they selected patients who all shared the indication for drug treatment for hypertension. Consequently, both cases and controls had this indication. In addition, they took ample measures to exclude residual confounding by indication, notably in the design of data analysis.

Apart from the reasons to start an intervention ("indication"), reasons to refrain from initiating the intervention may act as confounding variables. This is sometimes referred to as *confounding by contraindication*. Just as for confounding by indication (see Figure 5.6), these reasons (e.g., patient characteristics known to increase the risk of developing unintended or side effects of the intervention) will be associated with the probability of receiving the intervention, albeit that here the association represented by the left arrow will be inverse. If these reasons *not* to start the intervention are also associated with the probability of developing the outcome of interest, (i.e., the right arrow exists), then confounding is very likely to occur. Such confounding by contraindication is illustrated in a study on risk factors for death in patients taking ibopamine, after its use was restricted in early 1995. [Feenstra H, Grobbee D.E., in 't Veld B.A., Stricker, B.H. Confounding by contraindication in a nationwide study of risk for death in patients taking ibopamine. Ann Int Med 2001;134:56g72]. In a comparison between patients with an index date before and those with an index date after September 8, 1995, the relative risk for death associated with current use of ibopamine was 3.02 (95% CI, 2.12–4.30) compared with 0.71 (CI, 0.53–0.96), respectively. The marked inversion of the relative risk estimate is very likely the result of a changed practice in the use of (relative) contraindications in these patients. Apparently, ibopamide was preferentially prescribed to patients with a much lower mortality risk after 1995 than in the preceding period. Consequently, the observed mortality risk in users of ibopamide was reduced. We will only use the term *confounding by indication* (where indication is then defined as reasons to initiate *or refrain* from a certain intervention) to indicate circumstances when the reasons to start or *not* to initiate the intervention are also related to the (beneficial or unfavorable) outcome of interest, and, thus, confounding may occur.

Randomization

The most effective way to resolve the problem of confounding by indication and other confounding effects of differences in natural history in a comparative study is by randomization (Figure 5.7). Randomization means that the

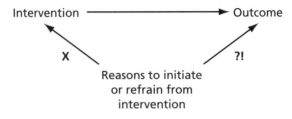

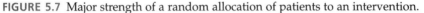

FIGURE 5.7 Major strength of a random allocation of patients to an intervention.

treatment is allocated at random to individual participants in a study. Any resulting difference in prognosis in the absence of treatment between randomized groups is the sole result of random imbalances. The risk of remaining prognostic differences is thus inversely related to the size of the population that is randomized.

Figure 5.7 shows the major strength of random allocation of patients to an intervention. Because of randomization, the distribution of all (known and unknown) reasons to start or not to start an intervention that would operate in daily practice (and that may be related to the occurrence of the outcome) are made similarly in the two comparison groups. Consequently, there will no association between (contra)indications and the probability of receiving the intervention: the left arrow does not exist and there will be no confounding. Obviously, patients with an unequivocal indication or clear contraindication cannot be randomized and would in any event not reflect the domain of a study to determine the effects of an intervention.

Typically, randomizing groups of 50 or more subjects to two treatment arms effectively makes the groups comparable in prognosis. The most attractive feature of randomization is that it makes groups comparable for known as well as unknown variables affecting natural history. The first account on randomization as a preferred allocation scheme in the design of experiments came from Sir Ronald A. Fisher [1935]. One of his books describes how to test the claim, using the example of a certain lady who said that she could distinguish by the flavor of her tea alone whether the milk or the tea was first placed in the cup. By randomizing the order in which the tea was made, Fisher was able to test if she could actually distinguish between the teas. To test the lady, eight cups of different teas were prepared, four with the tea poured into the cup first, and four with milk added first, and they were presented in random order. She correctly identified the full order, which led to a P-value of 0.01 (had she made one error, the P-value would have been 0.24). Note that this example also illustrates the first use of the so-called $n = 1$ *trial*, which is a randomized trial in a single subject.

The problems of confounding by natural history in treated and untreated patients and the prospects of randomization led Bradford-Hill and co-workers [1948] to be among the first to use randomized allocation to treatment in medical research in the Medical Research Council (MRC) investigation into streptomycin treatment of pulmonary tuberculosis published in the *British Medical Journal*. Randomization rapidly became popular and soon became the standard for treatment allocation in experimental comparisons of treatment effects. A *randomized study*, better known as a *randomized trial*, is a prospective and experimental study by definition. Allocation to treatment is not based on a clinical indication motivated by the care for the patient but by a random process in patients that all share the indication and are free from contraindications, with the aim to learn about the effects of the intervention.

There are added benefits from randomization in a comparative study. One is that it provides the statistical basis for statistical testing [Fisher, 1925]. A second consequence of randomization is that it enables blinding of participants and investigators for treatment status because the result from the allocation is unpredictable. But by far the most important reason to randomize is that it assures comparability of natural history. It should be noted that randomization provides no guarantee that important differences in prognostic factors between randomized groups cannot occur. You may just have bad luck as randomization is by nature a random process. Or groups may just be too small. The likelihood of randomly creating groups with the same distribution of men and women when only two males and six females are randomized is clearly small. Several techniques (apart from including more subjects) can prevent randomly occurring differences in important prognostic factors across randomized groups. For example, by first separating the study population in subgroups that share similar characteristics, such as a group of male and female participants, next randomize within each of the groups and then combine the individual patients again in the eventual treatment arms. Using this so-called *stratified randomization* scheme reduces the chance that marked differences in, for example, the proportion of males and females occurs by chance during randomization. More details on randomization are found in Chapter 10.

A consequence of randomization is that statistical tests can theoretically not be used to judge eventual imbalances between groups after randomization. In a baseline table of a trial, when summarizing the relevant patient characteristics at the start of the study (t0), judgment is needed to decide whether differences between groups are large enough to create problems in the comparison. There, *P*-values to "test" whether observed differences are attributable to chance (given the "null-hypothesis" of no difference between the groups) have no meaning and should not be reported, because any difference by definition results from chance, as long as the randomization has been carried out without manipulation. If major differences in prognostically relevant baseline characteristics are present despite adequate randomization, the potential impact on the results is often estimated by comparing the results with and without adjustment for these baseline differences. The choice of whether to adjust for baseline differences at t0 is difficult. Adjustments only can be made for observed differences in measured baseline variables and while no differences may exist in relevant variables that were not measured at baseline. Then, an adjustment could even induce dissimilarities in some prognostic variables. Any adjustment for baseline differences has an arbitrary component and may thus reduce the credibility of the results.

Comparability of Extraneous Effects

While comparability of natural history is mandatory in a comparative study on treatment effects, the extent to which extraneous effects should be the same in the comparison groups is a matter of choice. As discussed above, in an explanatory trial, every effort should be made to exclude extraneous effects, including placebo effects. In a non-experimental study, this is difficult to achieve. There, placebo effects only can be conquered when two or more treatments are compared that have similar placebo effects. In a randomized trial, placebo treatment and blinding are the two tools that ensure comparability of extraneous effects. Treatment can be compared with placebo treatment without disclosure of the allocation to the patient or the investigator. This makes the study *blinded*, either single (patient) or double (patient and observer) blinded, depending on how many parties remain ignorant about the allocation. In an explanatory trial, blinding is crucial to yield explanatory results while in pragmatic studies, extraneous effects are accepted as being inherently part of the intervention strategy and the use of placebo and blinding is not indicated (Figure 5.8).

Sometimes a choice can be made between an explanatory or a pragmatic trial for the same intervention. This choice will depend on the research question and the relevance for either type of answer in view of the aim of the investigator. For certain types of interventions, however, the obvious choice is a pragmatic study. This applies, for example, for research in which very different interventions are compared. When the question is addressed of whether the preferred mode of treatment of patients with coronary artery disease is by drugs or surgery, two different strategies are compared. The investigator will accept that surgery comes along with anesthesia and hospitalization while drug treatment does not. While it cannot be excluded that aspects of the surgical procedure beyond the mere creation of an arterial bypass may have an effect on prognosis, this is accepted as an inseparable component of the strategy. While perhaps conceptually extraneous, these components should not be considered as such in the comparison of the two strategies. This is very common in clinical research where different strategies are compared such as physiotherapy versus watchful waiting

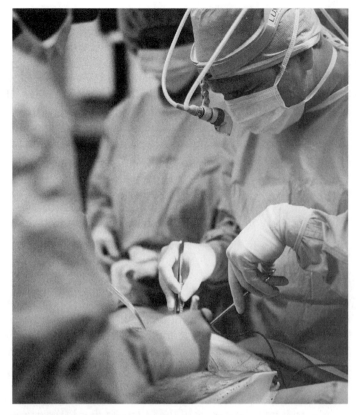

FIGURE 5.8 Tim O'Dogerty, M.D., supervises a placebo transplantation.

in low back pain, psychotherapy or drug treatment in anxiety disorders, and surgery or bed rest in hernia or lifestyle intervention in diabetes.

Comparability of Observations

There are a number of ways to prevent or limit observer effects. First, hard outcomes can be applied. When hard outcomes are used that can be measured objectively, such as mortality, incomparability of observations will be limited. Often, however, softer and more subjective outcomes may be more relevant for the research. Alternatively, the measurement can be highly protocolized and standardized, which will limit the room for subjective interpretation. This will help but is not foolproof.

A more rigorous way to prevent observer effects is to separate the observation from knowledge of the intervention. By blinding the observer for the assigned treatment, the observation will not be systematically different according to treatment status even if the measurement is sensitive to subjective interpretation. To further reduce the impact of the observer, the patient also can be blinded for the intervention. Another way to separate observation from intervention knowledge is to have an observer who plays no role in the treatment. For example, in a study on the effects of different drugs on glucose control in diabetic patients, the laboratory technician measuring HbA1C need not be informed about which intervention the patients receive. Similarly, a radiologist can judge the presence of vertebral fractures in osteoporotic women participating in a trial on a new anti-osteoporotic treatment without being informed about the mode of treatment the women receive. Note that even in a trial that should preferably be pragmatic, one may very well decide to conduct a blinded trial because of the type of outcome involved and achieve comparability of observations.

Limits to Trials

The principles of randomized trials can be fully understood by appreciation of the comparability requirements. Randomization assures comparability of natural history (NHi = NHr). Blinding and use of placebo ensures comparability for extraneous effects (EFi = EFr). Blinding also prevents observer bias due to differential observations or measurements in either group (Obi = OBr). While comparability for natural history is always needed for a valid estimation of the treatment effect, the need for blinding varies according to the objective of the trial and the nature of the outcome that is measured. In the case of a pragmatic study, extraneous effects are included in the treatment comparison and placebo treatment is not needed. Still, blinding may be desirable to ensure unbiased outcome assessment. With very solid outcome measures, observer effects may be negligible so blinding also is unnecessary.

For a trial that needs to be blinded because of the outcome measure but its goal is to provide pragmatic knowledge, an option is to make the trial only partly blinded. For example, it could be open for the patients but blind for the observers. Because confounding by differences in natural history, in particular confounding by indication, is a major problem in non-randomized comparisons (where allocation of treatments is done by the doctor in daily practice), the use of non-experimental studies to assess the benefits of treatment has major disadvantages. The randomized trial is generally the preferred option to quantify intended treatment effects.

However, there are many reasons why randomized trials, although preferred, cannot be conducted, and an alternative non-experimental approach needs to be sought. First, the necessary number of participants needed in a particular trial may be too large to be feasible. This applies to studies where the outcome, although important, occurs at a low rate; an example is when preventive treatments are studied in low-risk populations.

Low outcome rates are a particular problem in research on side effects of treatment and are discussed in Chapter 6. Take, for example, the relationship between diethylstilbestrol (DES) and vaginal cancer in daughters of users (see also Table 6.1, page 172). Vaginal cancer, even in the exposed group, is extremely rare. Alternatively, the expected difference in the rate of events between two interventions that are being compared may be very small, for example, when two active treatments are compared but one is only slightly better than the other. The latter situation is increasingly common for research on new treatments for an indication where an effective intervention already exists. For example, when two effective antihypertensive drugs are compared in a hypertensive population, it may take a very big study to demonstrate a small, albeit meaningful, difference in efficacy. Apart from practical restrictions, a randomized trial simply might be too expensive or time-consuming. Randomized trials need considerable budgets, particularly when they are large and of long duration, which is quite common for so-called phase three drug research necessary during the Food and Drug Association (FDA) or European Medicines Agency (EMEA) approval process before marketing. Time may be a problem in itself, for example, when an answer to a question on the effect of a treatment needs to be obtained quickly and results cannot wait for a long-term trial to be completed. This is more often the case in research on side effects than on main effects. If, for example, a life-threatening side effect is suspected, adequate and timely action may be warranted and non-experimental studies may be necessary to provide the relevant scientific evidence (see Chapter 6). Another problem with the duration of trials is that they are less suited for outcomes that take many years or even generations to occur. Randomized trials usually can run a couple of years at maximum. Longer trials become too expensive, but also with time the number of people who drop out of the study may become unacceptably high. Recall the diethylstilbestrol example; even if vaginal cancer in the daughters of users of this drug is a common outcome, it would be difficult to perform a trial because the follow-up period spans an entire generation.

In circumstances where the sample size, money, or the duration of follow-up poses no insurmountable problems, random allocation of patients may be problematic. For example, random allocation of a lifestyle intervention, such as heavy alcohol use or smoking, is generally impossible. Moreover, "true" blinding in a trial may be difficult to achieve. A trial can be nicely blinded on the surface, but in reality participants or investigators may well be able to recognize the allocated treatment. In the large, three-armed Women's Health Initiative trial, examining the effect of long-term postmenopausal hormone therapy on cardiovascular and other outcomes, over 40% of participants correctly identified the allocated treatment. Knowledge of randomized treatment may affect the likelihood of noticing or diagnosing an outcome event and may thus severely invalidate the comparison (Table 5.2), as has been worked out by Garbe and Suissa [2004].

TABLE 5.2 Illustration of detection bias for the ratio of AMI stratified by blinding status of exposure, assuming the unblinded subjects were 1.2, 1.5, and 1.8 times more likely to be diagnosed than the blinded study subjects

	Estrogen + progestin			Placebo			Rate ratio
	Cases	n	Rate[a]	Cases	n	Rate[a]	
All subjects	164	8506	19.3	122	8102	15.1	1.28
First stratification by exposure blinding (assuming 20% unrecognized MI[b])							
Blinded	89	5062	17.6	112	7554	14.8	1.19
Unblinded	75	3444	21.8	10	548	18.2	1.19
Ratio of diagnostic likelihood			1.2			1.2	
Second stratification by exposure blinding (assuming 33% unrecognized MI[b])							
Blinded	81	5062	16.0	110	7554	14.6	1.10
Unblinded	83	3444	24.1	12	548	21.9	1.10
Ratio of diagnostic likelihood			1.5			1.5	
Third stratification by exposure blinding (assuming 44% unrecognized MI[a])							
Blinded	74	5062	14.6	108	7554	14.3	1.02
Unblinded	90	3444	26.1	14	548	25.5	1.02
Ratio of diagnostic likelihood			1.8			1.8	

[a]Rate as cumulative incidence of acute MI per 1000.

[b]The detection rates of 22%–44% relate to the proportion of incident MIs that remain clinically unrecognized at the time they occur but can be detected by ECG (Sheifer et al., 2001).

Garbe E, Suissa S. Issues to debate on the Women's Health Initiative (*WHI) study: Hormone replacement therapy and acute coronary outcomes: methodological issues between randomized and observational studies. Hum Reprod 2004;19:8–13.

Another possible limitation of trials is that they tend to include highly selected patients and not those patients who are most likely to receive the intervention in daily practice. Typically, randomized trials include younger, healthier patients who have less co-morbidity and co-medications, and who are more compliant than real-life patients. Evidently, this has no bearing on the validity of the results (it can actually be helpful to include a homogeneous population) but may limit the generalizability of the findings to the relevant clinical domain. This only occurs, however, when the differences in characteristics of trial populations and patients in daily practice modify the effect of the intervention. For example, the earlier trials on drug therapy in heart failure included mostly relatively young patients with little co-morbidity, whereas the typical heart failure patients are older and have multiple co-morbidities. Generalizability of the findings of the earlier studies to the elderly has long been debated. Currently, trials are being conducted among the very old to provide evidence of the efficacy of heart failure therapy in this large group of patients

Finally, a trial involving randomized allocation and possibly blinding may be deemed to be unethical. An example is when there are highly suggestive data to support the marked superiority of a new treatment, particularly in a situation where no alternative treatments are available for a very serious disease. Unfortunately, the presence of weak data from flawed research sometimes prohibits a decent trial, leaving medical practitioners without a sound basis for treatment decisions. Sir Austin Bradford Hill [1951] succinctly summarized the problem of publication of questionable but suggestive data on treatment benefits:

> "If a treatment cannot ethically be withheld then clearly no controlled trial can be instituted. All the more important is it, therefore, that a trial should be begun at the earliest opportunity, before there is inconclusive though suggestive evidence of the value of treatment. Not infrequently, however, clinical workers publish favourable results on three or four cases and conclude their article by suggesting that this is the mode of choice, or that what now is required is a trial on an adequate scale. They do not seem to realize that by their very publication they have vastly increased difficulties of the trial or, indeed, made it impossible."

Random allocation can only be justified if there is a sufficient uncertainty about the superiority and safety of one treatment over another.

When no randomized trial can be conducted, the effects of intervention need to be studied using non-experimental studies, usually cohort or case-control studies. (A detailed discussion on cohort and case-control studies is in Chapters 8 and 9.) The results of non-experimental intervention studies are not inherently less valid than the results of trials. However, it is much more difficult to adhere to the comparability requirements in non-experimental research. This already has been discussed for the problem of confounding by indication that will prohibit non-experimental studies for many interventions. However, the impossibility of using a placebo and blind participants in a non-experimental study may make the outcome assessment problematic and leave room for observer bias. Absence of blinding also leads to research that is invariably pragmatic but this need not be a major problem in view of the aim of the study.

To overcome the problem of incomparability of natural history for a concurrent comparison of treated and untreated subjects, sometimes the use of a *historic control group* may offer a solution. This is acceptable if there is assurance that the historic group of patients who were all untreated (e.g., because the treatment has only recently become available) is comparable with regard to all characteristics that determine the severity and thus the natural history of the disease. In other words, the historic cohort and the current cohort of patients should have shown the same prognosis if treatment would not have been given.

Jones and co-workers [1982] decided to study the benefits of Inosiplex (isoprinosine) therapy in patients with subacute sclerosing panencephalitis (sspe) a very rare dementing and fatal illness possibly related to a slow virus infection. Power calculations suggested that close to 100 patients would be needed in each arm of a randomized trial, a number that was unlikely to be recruited in a reasonable time period. Consequently, a multicenter non-randomized study was conducted which included all 98 patients admitted to 28 medical centers in the United States and Canada between 1971 and 1980. As a reference, three groups of *historical* untreated control patients were selected who were drawn from medical registries in the preceding time period during which no effective treatment was available. The results were highly suggestive of a marked effect of the treatment (see Figure 5.9).

To judge the validity of the conclusion, however, assurance is needed that the groups were comparable with regard to natural history, extraneous effects, and observer effects. The natural history may well have changed over several decades. Also, extraneous factors may be different for the historic and current cohorts. The quality of care and supporting treatments may have changed survival patterns over the year even when the true natural history remained unchanged. Even observer effects cannot be ruled out. It is possible that in the registries only patients with a severe prognosis were listed while milder cases remained undetected.

In the current cohort, every effort was made to include all patients with a diagnosis. Selective mortality follow-up could well explain a marked difference in survival rates. For a more detailed discussion of the limitations and implications of this study, see Hoehler et al. [1984].

When the prognosis of patients is very stable or highly predictable, a *before-after study* can be conducted as an alternative to randomized parallel comparisons. This is a cohort study where the patients form their own his-

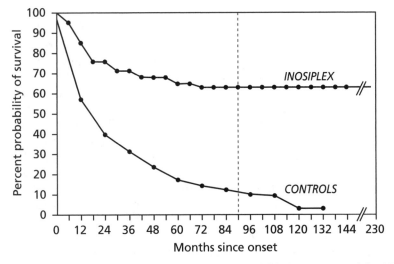

FIGURE 5.9 Life table profiles for 98 inosiplex-treated SSPE patients and for 333 composite SSPE controls (Israeli, Lebanese, and U.S. registry patients).

Reproduced with permission from: Jones CE, Dyken PR, Hutten Locher PR, Jabour JT, Maxwell KW. Inosiplex therapy in subactute sclerosing panencephalitis. Lancet 1982;319:1035.

toric comparison group. For example, to determine the effect of hip replacement surgery in patients with a highly compromised functional status due to severe hip arthritis, it is reasonable to assume that, in the absence of treatment, the functional status would not improve. If a clear improvement after surgery is observed, this may safely be attributed to the intervention. Similarly, antagonism of opioid intoxication in a comatose patient with naloxone does not require a concurrent randomized comparison to allow estimation of the effect of the treatment.

The Randomized Trial as a Paradigm for Etiologic Research

The principles of randomized trials are governed by the need to determine the causal role of the intervention in changing the prognosis of patients. Causal explanation requires the exclusion of confounding and other types of bias. Bias in comparing treatment effects across treated and untreated or differently treated patients, may arise from different distributions of prognostic factors, differences in extraneous effects, and differences in observations of outcomes across the comparative groups. In a randomized trial, problems of confounding are effectively handled by randomization and blinding. The same confounders obviously are relevant in any etiologic study. It may help the investigator, as a mental experiment, to imagine the way a trial would be conducted, also in cases where a randomized trial is infeasible. Using the randomized trial as a paradigm for non-experimental research may be particularly helpful to detect problems of confounding and to indicate ways for their control [Miettinen, 1989].

There is more that can be learned about the design of non-experimental studies from randomized trials. There is a common misappreciation of the relation between the way a study population is selected and the extent to which findings in the research can be generalized to other populations. In theory, findings in one population can be generalized to other populations as long as differences between populations do not modify the nature of the determinant-outcome relation. The finding of the causal relation between certain genetic sequences and retina pigmentation observed in a population of children can be generalized to elderly subjects without problem because despite the vast difference in characteristics of the two populations, these are judged not to modify the relationship between genes and eye color [Rudakis et al., 2003].

The randomized trial typically uses a highly selective population that is eventually randomized. The Multiple Risk Factor Intervention Trial (MRFIT) was a randomized primary prevention trial designed to test the effect of multifactor intervention on mortality from coronary heart disease [Neaton et al., 1987]. Before randomization, men were seen at three screening visits to establish eligibility. A total of 361,662 men were screened and 12,866 men were randomized. While less than 10% of all those screened were included, the results were judged to be relevant for all men (and even for women) who need risk factor intervention. Indeed, selection may or may not affect generalizability depending on the effect of the selection on the distribution of variables that have an impact on the relationship between intervention and outcome, and thus are modifiers of the intervention outcome relation. In other words, selection bias is determined by the extent to which the trial population and the population to whom the findings are generalized differ in modifiers of the intervention effect. In a non-experimental etiologic study, just like in a trial, the study population should be expressly defined and selected to enable generalization to the domain.

Study populations in etiologic research can be highly selective. Moreover, selectivity can make etiologic research much more effective. There is a persistent view that the ideal study population is a random sample from a population. This view is deeply rooted in statistics where estimates of the mean value of a population, such as height in Japanese males, are best obtained from a random sample of that population. The objective of such estimation, however, is altogether different from an epidemiologic study that aims at finding the genetic basis for differences in height among Japanese males. Here, rather than a random sample, it would probably be much more effective to select males at the extremes of the height distribution for genetic analyses. Again, the randomized trial serves as a role model. In a trial, the determinant distribution is deliberately chosen by (random) allocation. There is clearly no complete representation of the source population in the determinant distribution. Similarly, in a trial the determinant contrast is created by design and does not depend upon a given distribution in a sample. In a trial on the benefits of cholesterol reduction, cholesterol is reduced in one arm of the trial by allocation to statins while in the other arm the natural history of the cholesterol levels is followed. Then why study a random population sample, with the full cholesterol distribution, in a cohort study to determine the relationship between elevated cholesterol and heart disease risk? The middle part of the distribution adds little information to the research. In a trial, the reference category is explicitly defined and large contrasts are generally created to make the study efficient. The only requirement is that exposure is contrasted to non-exposure, while taking into account the potential for bias, notably confounding. There is no reason not to apply the same principles in non-experimental research.

6

Intervention Research: Side Effects

A 75-year-old woman, known to have rheumatoid arthritis since approximately ten years of age, visits her doctor because of increasing joint pain. She has been taking non-steroidal anti-inflammatory drugs (NSAIDs) for many years. In the past, several NSAIDs were stopped and replaced by others because she suffered from dyspepsia attributed to the drugs. Three years ago she developed a peptic ulcer. Currently, she receives ibuprofen, which she uses on a daily basis in conjunction with a proton pump inhibitor to prevent NSAID-induced gastrointestinal side effects. Because of the current severity of the complaints, the doctor decides to switch to Metoo-coxib®, a novel cyclooxygenase (COX)-2 inhibitor, with powerful analgesic properties and believed to cause less gastrointestinal side effects than classic NSAIDs. COX-2 selective inhibitors were developed as an alternative for classic (non-selective) NSAIDs because COX-1 inhibition exerted by the latter drugs decreases the natural protective mucus lining of the stomach. Indeed, within a month the pain decreases considerably and no gastrointestinal side effects are encountered. Consequently, the proton pump inhibitor is withdrawn. After three months, however, the woman suffers from a myocardial infarction. This certainly comes as a surprise, because apart from advanced age, no cardiovascular risk factors are present. Doctor and patient wonder whether the myocardial infarction was caused by Metoo-coxib®.

Interventions (treatments) in clinical practice are meant to improve a patient's prognosis. After careful consideration of the expected natural course of a patient's complaint or disease (prognostication), a physician has to decide whether, and to what extent, a particular intervention is likely to improve this prognosis. In this decision, knowing the anticipated *intended* (or *main*) *effects* of the intervention is essential.

In the example in this chapter's opening paragraph, the doctor presumably believes that the joint pain of the patient would increase or last an unacceptably long time, pressuring the prescription of a different, novel, and apparently stronger painkiller. The alleged stronger analgesic properties of the novel drug should be based on evidence from valid research on the *intended* effect (see Chapter 5). Apart from the primary (or intended effect) of an intervention, however, *unintended* (or *side effects*) could, and in fact should play an important role in the decision to initiate or refrain from an intervention (Textbox 6.1).

Only when the expected benefits are likely to outweigh the anticipated harmful effects will initiation of the intervention be justifiable. In the case of the elderly woman with arthritis, the impressive history of gastrointestinal effects that occurred during the use of previous NSAIDs presumably also contributed to the initiation of Metoo-coxib®, as it was believed to confer fewer gastrointestinal side effects. The latter decision also should be based on solid evidence that the incidence of unintended gastrointestinal effects is lower when patients take Metoo-coxib® than classical NSAIDs. Quantification of the side effects of interventions, however, is notoriously difficult most notably because randomized trials, the paradigm method to measure intended effects of interventions, are often less suited to assess unintended effects. This chapter discusses the strengths and limitations of methods to quantify the risks of interventions.

TEXTBOX 6.1 Side effects of interventions: terminology

Multiple terms for side effects of interventions are used in the literature. A short list is provided below. These include unintended effects, side effects, harm, adverse effects, risks, and, in the case of pharmaceutical interventions, adverse drug reactions (ADRs) or adverse drug events.

In our view, the term *unintended effects* as opposed to intended effects, best reflects the essence of these intervention effects [Miettinen, 1983]. Pharmacovigilance is the term increasingly being applied to indicate the methodology or discipline or, if one wishes, art, to assess side effects of pharmacological interventions. Alternatively, drug risk assessment, post-marketing surveillance, and pharmacoepidemiology are terms often applied, although the latter often also encompasses nonexperimental research on the use of drugs in daily practice (drug utilization) and on intended effects. [Strom, 2005]

Source: Author created.

Research on Side Effects of Interventions

With the emergence of multiple interventions in clinical medicine, particularly pharmaceutical interventions, the need to prove the effects of these treatment options greatly increased. Simultaneously, federal regulation passed in the 19th and first half of the 20th century to ensure the health interests of the consumers of drugs and foods has facilitated quality assurance for pharmaceuticals and, albeit at a later stage, the methodological development of studies assessing the intended and unintended effects of interventions (Textbox 6.2). It took several disasters before drug risk assessment became a mandatory step to obtain marketing authorization of a drug; research became an important tool in monitoring the safety of the application of the drug in daily practice, both before and after marketing authorization.

The thalidomide tragedy dramatically changed the way a drug's primary and side effects are assessed. In 1954, the small German firm Chemie Grünenthal patented the sedative thalidomide. Although no apparent beneficial effects were observed in test animals, the absence of side effects, even

TEXTBOX 6.2 Side effect of cannabis

Napoleon Bonaparte presumably was among the first to ban a drug (in this case: herbal) intervention because of serious side effects. While in Egypt around 1800 the French occupying forces indulged in the use of cannabis, either through smoking or consumption of hashish-containing beverages. He prohibited the use of cannabis in 1800:

"It is forbidden in all of Egypt to use certain Moslem beverages made with hashish or likewise to inhale the smoke from seeds of hashish. Habitual drinkers and smokers of this plant lose their reason and are victims of violent delirium which is the lot of those who give themselves full to excesses of all sorts."

(Quoted in P. Allain, Hallucinogens et societe (Paris: Payot, 1973), p. 184.

www.druglibrary.org/Schaffer/hemp/history/first12000/8.htm (accessed February 2007).

Although Napoleon undoubtedly interpreted the observed effects of cannabis as side effects, the question remains whether the effects were indeed considered "unintended" by the consumers. The fact that consumption of hashish was reported by some to increase after the official prohibition illustrates that the effects may, to some extent at least, have been "intended."

Source: Quoted in P. Allain, Hallucinogens et societe (Paris: Payot, 1973), p. 184. Available at: *www.druglibrary.org/Schaffer/hemp /history/first12000/8.htm* Accessed in February, 2007.

with very high dosages, fueled the impression that the drug was harmless [Silverman, 2002]. The potential hypnotic effect of the drug was revealed after free samples of the (at that time unlicensed) drug were distributed. The drug was licensed in Germany in 1957 and sold as a non-prescription drug because of its presumed safety. Within a few years, the drug was by far the most often used sedative. Sold in more than 40 countries around the world, thalidomide was quick to be marketed as the anti-emetic drug of choice for pregnant women with morning sickness. About a year after its release, however, a neurologist noticed peripheral neuritis in patients who received the drug. Even when reports of this side effect were accumulating rapidly, the company denied any association between thalidomide and this possible side effect. In 1960, marketing authorization was sought in the United States. Interestingly, at that time only proof of safety (rather than clinical trials to demonstrate efficacy) of a drug was required for approval by the Federal Drug Administration (FDA). By the end of 1961, the first reports of in increasing number of children with birth defects were published. These defects included phocomelia, a very rare malformation characterized by severe stunting of the limbs; children had flippers instead of limbs. In December, the pediatrician Lenz presented a series of 161 phocomelia cases linked with thalidomide in an article in a German newspaper (excerpt in Textbox 6.3) and the story drew a lot of attention. As a consequence, the firm withdrew thalidomide from the German market before it was approved by the FDA. Exact statistics are unknown, but it has been estimated that 8,000 to 12,000 infants developed phocomelia because of their mother's use of thalidomide during pregnancy.

Despite its dramatic past, thalidomide received a marketing authorization in the late 1990s, with the caveat that it only could be applied under strict conditions and its use in pregnant women was absolutely contraindicated. The drug is currently applied for several disorders, including erythema nodosum leprosum, a severe complication of leprosy and multiple myeloma. The beneficial effects of thalidomide have been attributed to its tumor necrosis factor-alpha (TNF-α) lowering properties.

The thalidomide and other tragedies from pharmaceutical use clearly show the importance of weighing the risks and benefits of interventions before marketing (i.e., widespread application) as well as in the physician's decision, after licensing, to initiate the intervention in individual patients in daily practice. This requires empirical evidence of the expected intended and unintended effects of the intervention and, thus, valid studies. Naturally, researchers and definitely those employed by the manufacturers of the interventions, are more likely to direct their research efforts at the intended effects of interventions than at possible side effects. In addition, quantifying the risks of interventions is often more complicated than estimating their benefits, because the research paradigm to determine effects of intervention—the

TEXTBOX 6.3 Malformations caused by drugs in pregnancy

Prof. Dr. W. Lenz, Munster/Westf, Germany

Up to 1961, only a few cases of malformations in man have been attributed to drugs, notably aminopterin (Thiersch, 1952;[1] and 1960;[2] Meltzer, 1956;[3] Warkany et al., 1959[4]), busulfan (Diamond et al. 1960[5]), androgens and progestogens (Wilkins, 1960[6]), cortisone (Bongiovanni & McPadden, 1960[7]), quinine (Brebe, 1952;[8] Uhlig, 1957;[9] & Eindorfer, 1953[10]), insulin (Wickes, 1954[11]), and tolbutamide (Larsson & Sterky, 1960[12]).

A causal relationship has been well established only for aminopterin and for the androgenic and gestagenic hormones. A few cases of cleft palate following high doses of cortisone administered in early pregnancy . . . insulin and kept under close supervision throughout pregnancy. Any striking teratogenic effect could not, under these circumstances, escape attention. Cardiac, skeletal, and multiple major malformations do occur with increased incidence in children of diabetic women. This association is, however, independent from insulin treatment (Pedersen et al, 1964[24]). Even insulin shock treatment in pregnant psychotic patients does not usually produce malformations, although there is a suggestion that it might occasionally do so (Sobel, 1960[25]). The case for the teratogenic action of tolbutamide in man is equally weak (Sterne and Lavieuville, 1964[26]).

Source: Lenz W. Am J Dis Child, 1966;112:99–106.

randomized trial—is less suited to evaluate unintended effects. In this chapter, the methods available to assess side effects of interventions are presented. Most examples in this chapter are drawn from studies on the side effects of drug interventions, but the same principles also hold for surgical, lifestyle, and other health care interventions.

Studies on Side Effects of Interventions: Causal Research

When the goal is to quantify the association of a specific intervention with the occurrence of an unintended outcome (side effect), the main challenge of the researcher lies in establishing causality. As in research on intended (main) effects of intervention (Chapter 5), the *causal* influence of the intervention on a patient's prognosis is the object of study. Although such studies also bear characteristics of prediction (in this case prognostic) research

(Chapter 4), because knowledge about the influence of the intervention according to the probability (range 0%–100%) of developing a specific (untoward) event is instrumental in guiding patient management, their primary aim is to prove or repudiate causality. In designing studies to quantify the causal association of an intervention with a side effect, the analogy of a court room is even more self-evident than on the study of intended effects. Here the researcher (prosecutor) will have to prove beyond reasonable doubt that the intervention caused the side effect and that the observed "crime" (side effect) was not committed by other factors. Be assured that, in the case of a major blockbuster drug from a large pharmaceutical company, there will be a well-selected group of real-life lawyers carefully scrutinizing your study. Consequently, as explained in detail in Chapter 5, achieving comparability of natural history, extraneous factors, and observation is essential. In particular, the influence of potential confounders should be prevented or accounted for in a later stage of the investigation. In this process, consideration of the confounding triangle may be helpful (Figure 6.1).

Critical evaluation of the two arrows in Figure 6.1, that is, the association of potential confounders with both the exposure to the intervention and the side effect, is essential. In daily practice, as in the study of main effects of interventions, the reasons an intervention is initiated in or withheld from patients (i.e., relative or absolute indications or contraindications) are by definition associated with exposure to the intervention [Grobbee & Hoes, 1997]. Consequently, the left arrow in Figure 6.1 exists unless allocation of the intervention is a random process. As explained earlier, the latter typically only occurs when the researcher ensures comparability of natural history in those who do or do not receive the intervention *randomization*, that is, by performing a randomized controlled trial. The presence or absence of a relationship between the reasons to initiate the intervention (the indication) and the side effect (the arrow on the right) determines the potential for *confounding by indication*. Similarly, when drugs are particularly used by patients at a higher (or lower) risk of developing the side effect of interest than patients not receiving the intervention, failure to take this confounding into

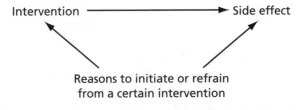

FIGURE 6.1 Reasons to initiate or refrain from a particular intervention.

TEXTBOX 6.4 Merck found Liable in Vioxx Case

Texas Jury Awards Widow $253 Million

by Mark Kaufman
Washington Post Staff Writer
Saturday, August 20, 2005; Page A01

After less than 11 hours of deliberation, a Texas jury yesterday found Merck & Co. responsible for the death of a 59-year-old triathlete who was taking the company's once-popular painkiller, Vioxx.

The jury hearing the first Vioxx case to go to trial awarded the man's widow $253.4 million in punitive and compensatory damages—a sharp rebuke to an industry leader that enjoyed an unusually favorable public image before the Vioxx debacle began to unfold one year ago.

Source: Kaufman, M. Washington Post, Aug 10, 2005, p. A01.

account will bias the study findings. When, for example, COX-2 inhibitors are (for some reason) preferentially prescribed to patients with an unfavorable cardiovascular risk profile, comparison of the incidence of myocardial infarction of patients receiving the drug (such as the 75-year-old woman in the earlier example) with those not using the drug in daily practice may reveal an increased risk of this side effect. At least part of this increased risk will be attributable to confounding by indication.

Textbox 6.4 is an excerpt from a *Washington Post* article from August 20, 2005. Apparently, the judge considered the causal relationship between the use of rofecoxib, a generic COX-2 inhibitor, and the untimely death of the athlete proven. Rofecoxib was withdrawn from the market by the manufacturer in September 2004, after a randomized trial showed an increased risk of cardiovascular disease among rofecoxib users [Bresalier et al., 2005].

The importance of taking confounding into account in research on side effects of intervention and possible bias attributable to initiation of (drug) intervention in high-risk patients is clearly exemplified by the following quote from John Urquhart: *Did the drug bring the problem to the patient or did the patient bring the problem to the drug?* (sic).

As in all types of research aimed at quantifying causal associations, confounding in the assessment of side effects of interventions can be accounted for either in the design of data collection or in the design of data analysis. The potential for confounding, however, critically depends on the type of side effect involved: type A or type B [Rawlins & Thompson, 1977].

Type A and Type B Side Effects

Type A Side Effects

Type A side effects result from the primary action of the intervention and can be considered an exaggerated intended effect. Type A side effects are usually common, dose-dependent, occur gradually (insidious from a very mild to—often with increasing dosages—more serious presentation), and are in principle predictable. Lowering of the intervention's dosage will usually take the side effect away. Type A side effects also may occur at recommended dosages of the intervention, for example, when the drug metabolizes at a lower rate.

A classic example of a type A side effect is bleeding resulting from anticoagulant therapy. The side effect results from the intended effect of the drug (i.e., its anticoagulant property), is fairly common, usually occurs in a mild form such as bruises (but sometimes fatal hemorrhage may develop), and is to a certain extent predictable because risk factors for bleeding during anticoagulant use are known. These include age, dosage, alcohol use, tendency to fall, and other relevant comorbidity. The predictability of side effects is important, because knowledge about these risk factors will cause physicians to refrain from prescribing the intervention in high-risk patients. This "good clinical practice" on the one hand will prevent side effects to occur in some patients. However, on the other hand, such preferential (non-)prescribing should be taken into account when estimating the association between the intervention and such a side effect. Uncritical comparison of the incidence of the side effect among those receiving the drug and a group of patients not receiving the drug will dilute the association. Obviously such confounding (often referred to as *confounding by contraindication*, see Chapter 5) should be accounted for in the design of the study.

Because type A side effects are closely related to the intended effects of an intervention, patient characteristics associated with the initiation of an intervention may be predictive of the probability of developing both intended and unintended effects. Consequently, confounding by indication threatens the validity of any study assessing type A side effects. This is illustrated in Figure 6.2.

Because in Figure 6.2 the left arrow exists by definition (see exclamation mark), any association between one of the determinants of prescribing anticoagulants with the side effect of interest may induce confounding. Multiple patient characteristics will influence the decision to start an intervention in clinical practice (e.g., elderly, men, those at increased cardiovascular risk, and those with clear indications such as atrial fibrillation are more likely to receive anticoagulants), so it seems justified to consider confounding by indication as a given. At least one of these determinants (here, for example, age) is apt to be associated with the probability of developing the side effect.

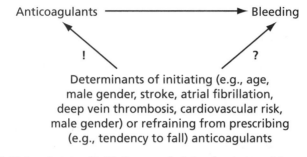

FIGURE 6.2 Determinants of initiating or refraining from prescribing anticoaguants.

Thus, one should always take measures to prevent or adjust for confounding in the assessment of type A side effects.

Type B Side Effects

In contrast to type A side effects, type B side effects do not result from the primary action of an intervention and, in fact, often the mechanism underlying a typical type B side effect remains unknown. Type B side effects are rare, not dose-dependent, are an all-or-none phenomenon, and cannot be predicted. Classical examples of type B side effects are anaphylactic shock, aplasia, or other idiosyncratic reactions following the administration of certain drugs. The all-or-none phenomenon refers to the fact that type B side effects either do not occur or present themselves insidiously as a full-blown event, irrespective of the dosage. The unpredictability of such side effects is crucial in the understanding of the potential of confounding in research directed at these side effects. Consider a study quantifying the association between the use of an antihypertensive drug enalapril [one of the first angiotensin-converting-enzyme (ACE) inhibitors] and the occurrence of angioedema (Figure 6.3). This is a rare event characterized by swelling around the eyes and lips, which in severe cases also may involve the throat, a side effect that is potentially fatal.

Again, determinants of enalapril prescription (blood pressure level, levels of other cardiovascular risk factors, and relevant comorbidity such as heart failure or diabetes) will influence the use of the drug in clinical practice (left arrow in Figure 6.3). In contrast to type A side effects, these patient characteristics are very unlikely to be associated with the outcome. For example, blood pressure, cholesterol levels, and diabetes are not related to the risk of developing angioedema. Consequently, the arrow on the right in Figure 6.3 is non-existent and confounding is not a problem in such type B side effects [Miettinen, 1982; Vandenbroucke, 2006].

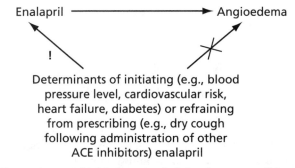

FIGURE 6.3 Determinants of initiating or refraining from prescribing enalapril.

Measures to prevent confounding are therefore not necessary in type B side effects, albeit that one has to be absolutely sure that characteristics of recipients of the intervention are indeed not related to the adverse event.

Other Side Effects

Unfortunately, many side effects are neither typical type A nor typical type B side effects. For example, gynacomastia as a side effect of the use of cimetidine, an anti-ulcer drug type A mechanism related to the action of the drug (albeit not to the primary action of the drug) has been identified and the effect seems to be dose-related [Garcia Rodriguez, 1994]. The dose-related effect, typically a type A phenomenon, is counterbalanced by the unpredictability of the side effect, type B characteristic. In addition, some side effects that were first considered clear type B side effects may develop into type A side effects at a later stage, for example, when the underlying mechanism and predictors of the side effects become known.

An example is the abstract in Textbox 6.5. With the first reports of angina pectoris or myocardial infarction in recipients of sumatriptan, a then novel anti-migraine drug, these rare events were primarily considered type B side effects (see also the wording *unknown* in the abstract) [Ottervanger et al., 1993]. With accumulating evidence, however, the effect was shown to be related to the primary action of the drug, that is, its vasoconstrictive properties, and also the predictability of the side effect increased. Currently this adverse drug reaction is primarily considered a type A effect, although the side effect remains, fortunately, rare.

Also, myocardial infarction as a possible consequence of Metoo-coxib®, the drug introduced in the beginning of this chapter, carries more characteristics of a type A than a type B side effect. COX-2 inhibition promotes platelet aggregation because of inhibition of endothelial prostacyclin, while COX-1 inhibition inhibits aggregation because of inhibition of platelet thromboxane

TEXTBOX 6.5 Example of a type A adverse drug reaction that was first considered a type B side effect

---

Transmural myocardial infarction with sumatriptan

J.P. Ottervanger   H.J.A. Paalman
G.L. Boxma   B.H.Ch. Stricker

For sumatriptan, tightness in the chest caused by an unknown mechanism has been reported in 3%–5% of users. We describe a 47-year-old woman with an acute myocardial infarction after administration of sumatriptan 6 mg subcutaneously for cluster headache. The patient had no history of underlying ischaemic heart disease or Prinzmetal's angina. She recovered without complications.

Source: Reprinted from The Lancet, Vol. 341. Ottervanger JP, Paalman HJA, Boxma GL, Stricker BHCh. Transmural myocardial infarction with sumatriptan. 861-2. 1993 with permission from Elsevier.

synthesis. Thus, selective COX-2 inhibition was expected to increase platelet aggregation and this indeed may promote thrombus formation and eventually myocardial infarction. The observed dose response relationship further illustrates that myocardial infarction may be a type B side effect [Andersohn et al., 2006]. Consequently, confounding by indication may pose an important threat to the validity of research on this potential side effect of Metoo-coxib® or other COX-2 inhibitors.

Theoretical Design

The occurrence relation of research on side effects of an intervention closely resembles that of research on main effects of interventions:

Side effect = f (intervention | EF)

Because the primary goal is to assess causality, the occurrence relation should be estimated conditional on confounders (external factors; EF).

The domain usually includes patients with an indication for the intervention (e.g., a specific disease), or defined more broadly, patients in whom a physician considers to initiate the intervention.

In the Metoo-coxib® example, the occurrence relation would be,

Myocardial infarction = f (Metoo-coxib® | EF)

and the domain is defined as a patient with osteoarthritis (or perhaps other diseases) requiring analgesics.

Design of Data Collection

Time

As for studies assessing the primary effect of interventions, the time dimension for research on side effects is larger than zero. The aim is to establish whether a specific intervention is related to the *future* occurrence of a certain effect. In principle, therefore, research on side effects is longitudinal.

Census or Sampling

In contrast to diagnostic studies and research on the primary effects of interventions, studies addressing side effects of interventions relatively often take a sampling instead of a census approach. There are several reasons why case-control studies are attractive here. First, sampling is efficient when the side effect is rare, as is typically the case in type B side effects. A census approach would imply following-up very large numbers of patients receiving or not receiving the treatment. Alternatively, one may hypothetically define a "swimming pool" consisting of patients with diseases requiring analgesics, and only study in detail those developing the side effect (i.e., cases) during the study period and a sample representative of that swimming pool (i.e., controls). Obviously, the definition of the swimming pool (study base) critically depends on the domain of the study. Methods to validly sample from the study base, which can be either a cohort or a dynamic population, are explained in detail in Chapter 9. Case-control studies are efficient also when the measurement of the determinant and other relevant characteristics, such as potential confounders and effect modifiers, is expensive, time consuming, or patient-burdening. For example when detailed information, including dosage, duration of use, compliance to medications (including Metoo-coxib®), and relevant comorbidity is difficult to obtain, a case-control study should be considered. In addition, when side effects take a long time to develop or when the time from exposure to the intervention and the occurrence of the side effect are unknown, a case-control approach is attractive.

The classic example of a case-control study establishing the causal association between the use of the estrogen diethylstilboestrol (DES) in mothers and the occurrence of clear-cell adenocarcinoma of the vagina in their daughters illustrates the strengths of case-control studies; a census approach would require an unrealistic follow-up time lasting one generation and a huge study population because vaginal carcinoma is extremely rare. Table 6.1 is the original table with the results of that case-control study from 1971 [Herbst et al., 1971].

In that study, eight cases were compared with 32 matched controls. The mothers of seven of the eight daughters had received DES (a drug primarily

TABLE 6.1 Summary of data comparing patients with matched controls

Case no.	Maternal age (yr) Case	Mean of 4 controls	Maternal smoking Case	Control	Bleeding in this pregnancy Case	Control	Any prior pregnancy loss Case	Control	Estrogen given in this pregnancy Case	Control	Breast feeding Case	Control	Intra-uterine x-ray exposure Case	Control
1	25	32	Yes	2/4	No	0/4	Yes	1/4	Yes	0/4	No	0/4	No	1/4
2	30	30	Yes	3/4	No	0/4	Yes	1/4	Yes	0/4	No	1/4	No	0/4
3	22	31	Yes	1/4	Yes	0/4	No	1/4	Yes	0/4	Yes	0/4	No	0/4
4	33	30	Yes	3/4	No	0/4	No	0/4	Yes	0/4	Yes	2/4	No	0/4
5	22	27	Yes	3/4	Yes	1/4	Yes	1/4	No	0/4	No	0/4	No	0/4
6	21	29	Yes	3/4	Yes	0/4	Yes	0/4	Yes	0/4	No	0/4	No	1/4
7	30	27	No	3/4	No	0/4	Yes	1/4	Yes	0/4	Yes	0/4	No	1/4
8	26	28	Yes	3/4	No	0/4	Yes	0/4	Yes	0/4	No	0/4	Yes	1/4
Total			7/8	21/32	3/8	1/32	6/8	5/32	7/8	0/32	3/8	3/32	1/8	4/32
Mean	26.1	29.3												
Chi Square (1 df)[a]			4.52		4.52		7.16		23.22		2.35		0	
P-value	0.53		0.53		<0.05		<0.01		<0.00001		0.20			
	(N.S.)†		(N.S.)								(N.S.)		(N.S.)	

[a]Matched control chi-square test used is described by Pike & Morrow. †Standard error of difference 1.7 yr (paired t-test); N.S. = not statistically significant.

Herbst AL, Ulfelder H, Poskanzer DC. Adenocarcinoma of the vagina. Association of maternal stilbestrol therapy with tumor appearance in young women. N Engl J Med 1971;284:878–81. Copyright © 1971. Massachusetts Medical Society. All rights reserved.

prescribed for women with habitual abortion to prevent future fetal loss) during pregnancy, whereas none of the mothers of the 32 control daughters had used DES. Although no quantitative measure of association was reported, and in fact the odds ratio could not be calculated because its numerator included 0 and the odds ratio reached infinity, it was not difficult to conclude that DES increases the risk of vaginal carcinoma in daughters. When assuming that the mother of one control received DES during pregnancy, the odds ratio would be $(7 \times 31)/(1 \times 1) = 217$, still indicating a more than 200-fold risk.

Experimental or Observational Study

The main challenge of research on side effects of interventions lies in proving beyond reasonable doubt that the intervention is causally involved in the occurrence of the outcome. As was explained in detail in Chapter 5 on the primary effects of interventions, an experimental approach (i.e., a randomized controlled trial) best ensures that the outcome is indeed attributable to the intervention, mainly because randomization will achieve comparability of natural history of those who do and do not receive the intervention and, thus, confounding by indication is prevented. Moreover, randomized controlled trials, when properly conducted, will also achieve the other two "comparabilities," that is, comparability of extraneous effects and comparability of observations, which are necessary to prove that the intervention is "guilty" (see Chapter 5). However, there are several reasons why this paradigm to assess causality in intervention research is less suitable when the aim is to establish side effects.

Circumstances under which randomized trials are not suited for the study of side effects are situations where case-control studies are particularly efficient: when the side effect is rare and when the time between exposure to the intervention and the development of the side effect is very long. There is no doubt that a randomized trial to estimate the risk of vaginal carcinoma in daughters of mothers exposed to DES during pregnancy is not feasible because it would be an unrealistically large trial with an unachievable follow-up period. Also, when the time from exposure to the side effect is unknown, randomized trials are of limited value. In fact, one of the major strengths of *observational* studies on side effects is that they can determine the influence of the duration of the exposure on the occurrence of the side effect [Miettinen, 1989].

Table 6.2 shows that the number of patients required in each of the two arms of a randomized trial to detect a relative risk of 2 (with a type 1 error of 0.05, and type 2 error of 0.20) increases dramatically when the incidence of the side effect becomes rare.

Type B side effects are especially difficult to detect in a randomized trial because the frequency of the outcome, such as anaphylactic shock in those

TABLE 6.2 Risk of outcome in control group and number required in each group

Risk of Outcome in Control Group	Number Required in Each Group
50%	8
25%	55
10%	198
5%	435
1%	2331
0.1%	23,661
0.01%	236,961

not receiving the drug under study or an alternative intervention, is usually lower than 0.1% or even 0.01%.

There are also ethical constraints in conducting randomized trials to quantify the occurrence of side effects, most notably when risk assessment is the primary aim of the trial and suspicion has been raised. For some interventions, random allocation is downright impossible. One cannot envision a trial involving random allocation of patients smoking 40 cigarettes for 40 years to quantify the increased lung cancer risk or a trial randomly allocating participants to a sedentary life to estimate its deleterious effects on cardiovascular health. Moreover, imagine a trialist asking potential participants whether they would be willing to participate in a study designed to determine if Metoo-coxib® increases the risk of myocardial infarction and that their probability of being randomly allocated to receive the drug for a couple of years is 50%. Few patients would sign an informed consent for that study. Whether the Ethics Committee would permit such a trial to be launched clearly depends on the magnitude of the beneficial effects of Metoo-coxib® relative to its comparator substance, a placebo, or another NSAID. When an intervention has proven efficacy, placebo-controlled trials will often be considered unethical and active comparators will have to be included. Obviously, side effects should be recorded in all randomized trials primarily aimed at assessing the beneficial effects of interventions, notably of drug interventions. Certainly premarketing (Phases 2 and 3) trials, however, will often lack statistical power to detect less common side effects. A postmarketing (Phase 4) trial is an important tool in drug risk assessment because these trials are larger than premarketing trials. With the combination of multiple similar trials in meta-analyses (Chapter 11), the power can be further increased, sometimes even allowing the detection of rare type B side effects.

An example of a randomized trial that was designed to also quantify the occurrence of side effects of an intervention is shown in Table 6.3. A large placebo-controlled randomized trial was performed to assess both the main effects and side effects of an influenza vaccination in the elderly. The rationale for that study was provided by the alleged low efficacy and the existing fear for systemic side effects that were both believed to underlie the low vaccination rate in older adults at that time. A separate article [Govaert et al., 1993] was devoted to the side effects of influenza vaccination and the main results are summarized in Table 6.3.

Although local side effects, such as swelling and itching, were much more common in the influenza than in the placebo group, the frequencies of systemic reactions did not differ appreciably, in particular among those older adults with established cardiovascular, pulmonary, or kidney disease (i.e., patients who were at *potential* risk). The power in this latter group was too low, however, to detect small differences between the groups. The comforting results of this Dutch study have probably significantly contributed to the currently high (> 80%) vaccination coverage among the elderly in The Netherlands.

A final disadvantage of randomized trials is their tendency to include highly selected patient populations. Although this bears on the generalizability of the findings rather than on the validity of the study, it may seriously hamper the wider applicability of the results, in particular with regard to side effects of interventions. As explained in Chapters 1 and 5, restriction of study populations (e.g., men within a certain age range) may increase the feasibility and validity of a study and, as long as the research findings can be expected to be similar in other groups of patients not included (e.g., men of other ages and women), this will not restrict the applicability of the findings. There is ample evidence that for many interventions, the primary effects are not modified by age and gender, particularly when these effects are measured as a relative risk reduction (i.e., relative risks). For example, treatment with cholesterol-lowering statins reduces the incidence of cardiovascular disease by approximately 30% across a wide age range, irrespective of gender and prior cardiovascular disease [LaRosa & Vupputuri, 1999].

Side effects, however, tend to occur more often in certain patient categories, typically children or older patients with comorbidities who are taking multiple drugs. Pregnant women are a particularly vulnerable group. Thus, excluding these "real-life" patients from the study population may dilute the association between an intervention and the side effect, and will limit the generalizability and clinical relevance of the findings. To learn whether an intervention causes a side effect in clinical practice requires the inclusion of patients using the drug in daily practice. Randomized trials including highly restricted patient populations often are of limited value to address the risk of side effects. Trials on the effect of anticoagulant treatments in patients with atrial fibrillation may serve as an example. Most of these trials were primarily conducted to assess the beneficial (e.g., cerebrovascular event-reducing) effects of these drugs, and patients were selected such that their risk of bleeding (a type A side effect) was minimized

TABLE 6.3 Numbers (percentages) of all patients* at potential risk who reported local or systemic adverse reactions

Reactions	Vaccine group		Placebo group		P-value	
	All patients (n = 904)	Patients at potential risk (n = 246)	All patients (n = 902)	Patients at potential risk (n = 234)	All patients	Patients at potential risk
Local Reactions:	158 (17.5)	52 (21.1)	66 (7.3)	20 (8.5)	< 0.001	< 0.001
Swelling	66 (7.3)	25 (10.2)	8 (0.9)	2 (0.9)	< 0.001	< 0.001
Itching	41 (4.5)	18 (7.3)	13 (1.4)	6 (2.6)	< 0.001	0.02
Warm feeling	43 (4.8)	17 (6.9)	14 (1.6)	4 (1.7)	< 0.001	0.01
Pain when touched	94 (10.4)	30 (12.2)	29 (3.2)	10 (4.3)	< 0.001	0.00
Constant pain	17 (1.9)	6 (2.4)	8 (0.9)	3 (1.3)	0.07	0.50
Discomfort	23 (2.5)	4 (1.6)	19 (2.1)	4 (1.7)	0.53	1.00
Systemic Reactions:	99 (11.0)	27 (11.0)	85 (9.4)	28 (12.0)	0.34	0.73
Fever	12 (1.3)	2 (0.8)	6 (0.7)	2 (0.9)	0.15	1.00
Headache	44 (4.9)	13 (5.3)	35 (3.9)	15 (6.4)	0.30	0.60
Malaise	58 (6.4)	14 (5.7)	50 (5.5)	17 (7.3)	0.45	0.50
Other complaints	33 (3.7)	8 (3.3)	31 (3.4)	11 (4.7)	0.82	0.56
All reactions	210 (23.2)	61 (24.8)	127 (14.1)	38 (16.2)	< 0.001	0.02

Thirty-two subjects were excluded because of incomplete data, ten of whom were at potential risk.

Govaert TM, Dinant GJ, Aretz K, Masurel N, Sprenger MJ, Knottnerus JA. Adverse reactions to influenza vaccine in elderly people: Randomised double blind placebo controlled trial. BMJ 1993;307:988–90

TEXTBOX 6.6 Exclusion criteria for the AFASAK-2 study

Systolic blood pressure > 180 mm Hg
Diastolic blood pressure > 100 mm Hg
Mitral stenosis
Alcoholism
Dementia
Psychiatric disease
Lone atrial fibrillation in patients < 60 years of age
Contraindications for warfarin therapy
Contraindications for aspirin therapy
Warfarin therapy based on other medical conditions
Thromboembolic event in the preceding 6 months
Foreign language
Pregnancy and breastfeeding
Chronic nonsteroidal anti-inflammatory drug therapy

Source: Author.

[Koefoed et al., 1995]. For example, patients with conditions requiring permanent NSAID therapy and regular alcohol users were excluded. Consequently, the observed risk in many of those trials was lower than the risk observed in daily practice. Textbox 6.6 describes an example of the exclusion criteria from one of these studies, the AFASAK-2 study.

Although multiple exclusion criteria can be very helpful and justified to optimize safety of participants in an efficacy trial, they also may lead to inadequate estimates of the side effects occurring in daily practice where patients will be treated outside the domain of the study.

In a randomized study specifically designed to compare gastrointestinal side effects in those receiving rofecoxib (the first marketed COX-2 inhibitor) and the NSAID naproxen, recipients of the COX-2 inhibitor experienced a 50% lower risk of gastrointestinal side effects (Table 6.4) [Bombardier et al., 2000].

This trial among patients with rheumatoid arthritis shows the strength of randomized trials in estimating the risk of relatively frequent side effects (e.g., 4 per 100 patient years in the naproxen group). It also exemplifies that when trials are large enough, they may be instrumental in detecting even relatively rare side effects. In this study including 8076 randomized patients, the risk of myocardial infarction was lower in the naproxen group (0.1%) than in the rofecoxib users (0.4%; relative risk 0.2; 95% CI 0.1–0.7). It took several more years, however, before another trial, this one in patients with colorectal adenoma, confirmed the increased risk of cardiovascular events among rofecoxib users, urging the firm to withdraw the drug from the market [Bresalier et al., 2005].

TABLE 6.4 Incidence of gastrointestinal events in the treatment groups

Type of event	Rofecoxib group (N = 4047)	Naproxen group (N = 4029)	Rofecoxib group (N = 4047)	Naproxen group (N = 4029)	Relative risk (95% CI)*	P-value
	no. with event		rate/100 patient-yr			
Confirmed upper gastrointestinal events	56	121	2.1	4.5	0.5 (0.3–0.6)	< 0.001
Complicated confirmed upper gastrointestinal events	16	37	0.6	1.4	0.4 (0.2–0.8)	0.005
Confirmed and unconfirmed upper gastrointestinal events†	58	132	2.2	4.9	0.4 (0.3–0.6)	< 0.001
Complicated confirmed and unconfirmed upper gastrointestinal events‡	17	42	0.6	1.6	0.4 (0.2–0.7)	0.002
All episodes of gastrointestinal bleeding	31	82	1.1	3.0	0.4 (0.3–0.6)	< 0.001

*CI denotes confidence interval.

†The analysis includes 13 events that were reported by investigators but were considered to be unconfirmed by the end-point committee.

‡The analysis includes six events that were reported by investigators but were considered to be unconfirmed by the end-point committee.

Bombardier C, Laine L, Reicin A, Shapiro D, Burgos-Vargas R, Davis B, Day R, Ferraz MB, Hawkey CJ, Hochberg MC, Kvien TK, Schnitzer TJ; VIGOR Study Group. Comparison of upper gastrointestinal toxicity of rofecoxib and naproxen in patients with rheumatoid arthritis. VIGOR Study Group, N Engl J Med 2000;343:1520–8.

Given the limitations of randomized trials to detect side effects of interventions, notably when these are rare, observational (i.e., non-experimental) studies provide an important alternative. To allow for valid conclusions regarding the causal relationship between the intervention and the side effect, however, these should be designed such that comparability of natural history, observations, and extraneous factors is ensured (see Chapter 5). Notably, achieving comparability of natural history, that is, preventing confounding, is often very difficult. In this process a thought experiment, taking the randomized trial as a paradigm for observational research, can be very useful [Miettinen, 1989]. In the following, different approaches to prevent or limit incomparability of observations, extraneous effects, and natural history will be discussed in some detail.

Comparability in Observational Research

Researching Observations of Side Effects

Blinding is the generally accepted method to achieve comparability of observations between those receiving the interventions and the comparison group. In a randomized trial, tools (notably the use of a placebo) are available to keep all those involved in measuring the outcome (i.e., the observer, but possibly also the patients and doctors or other health care workers when they can influence the measurements) blinded to treatment allocation. In observational research, usually only part of the observations can be blinded. In a cohort study examining the effect of Metoo-coxib® on the risk of myocardial infarction, for example, one could blind the researchers involved in adjudication of the outcome by deleting all information pertaining to the medication used by the patients from the data forwarded to them. If, however, the use of COX-2 inhibitors urges health care workers (and patients) to be more perceptive of signs of possible myocardial infarction, leading more often to ordering tests to establish or rule out the disease, incomparability of observations may artificially inflate the drug's risk. Alternatively, one could choose the technique to measure the outcome such that observer bias is minimized. For example, automated biochemical measurements do not require blinding, albeit that in daily practice, routine ordering of such tests may very well be influenced by the intervention the patient receives. Finally, a *hard outcome*, such as death, will increase comparability of observations. But even when comparability is achieved, incomparability of extraneous effects may still endanger the validity of the study.

Researching Extraneous Effects

As in research on intended effects of interventions, one should first establish which part of the intervention is considered extraneous to the occurrence relation before the design of data collection is determined. When the goal is to quantify the causal relationship between the pharmacological substrate of a drug and an unintended outcome, as will often be the case in drug risk assessment, all other effects of receiving a drug (such as the extra time spent by the prescribing physician, possible comedication, and accompanying lifestyle changes) are extraneous and should be accounted for in the design of the study, typically in the design of data collection. As discussed earlier, the main tool to achieve comparability of extraneous effects in randomized trials—a placebo or sham intervention—is unattainable in observational research. In principle, the observational counterpart of placebo treatment is *selectivity* in the formation of the intervention and reference categories of the determinant. Ideally, the extraneous effects of these categories should be comparable or absent. This is more likely to be achieved by comparing two drug interventions with similar indications, for example, two individual COX-2 inhibitors, then by contrasting the use of Metoo-coxib® to non-use of a COX-2 inhibitor. Comparison of those receiving the intervention under study with those *not* receiving any intervention may lead to considerable incomparability. Obviously, comparison of Metoo-coxib® treated patients with patients not receiving any analgesics may affect validity because of incomparability of extraneous effects, when those receiving Metoo-coxib® are more likely to comply to healthy lifestyle habits influencing the risk of myocardial infarction or because they visit their treating physician more regularly. The choice of an appropriate reference category for the determinant is also important to deal with the major threat to the validity of observational studies on the effects of interventions: incomparability of natural history. How to prevent such confounding in research on side effects will be discussed in the next section.

Natural History and Side Effects

Incomparability of natural history (i.e., confounding) is the most critical threat to the validity of most observational studies on the effects of interventions. Fortunately, several methods, both in the design of data collection and the design of data analysis, are available to limit or even prevent confounding. However, before embarking on a crusade of measures to reduce confounding in an observational study, one should first decide whether confounding is indeed likely. As explained earlier, the probability of confounding critically depends on the association between the reasons (including patient characteristics) to prescribe (or refrain from prescribing) a certain intervention with the outcome involved, that is, on the existence of the right arrow in the "confounder triangle" (see Figure 6.1). When such an association is non-existent, as will be the case in typical type B side effects such as anaphylactic shock or angioedema, confounding is a non-issue.

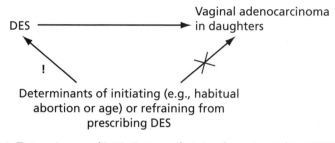

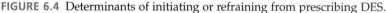

FIGURE 6.4 Determinants of initiating or refraining from prescribing DES.

Consider once again the example of the use of DES in mothers and the occurrence of vaginal carcinoma in their daughters. The "confounder triangle" of the occurrence relation is shown in Figure 6.4.

The patient characteristics influencing the physician to initiate or refrain from prescribing the drug, including habitual abortion (the indication for the drug) or age, by definition, will be related to the probability of receiving the intervention (left arrow exists). These or other patient characteristics related to the initiation of the drug are very unlikely to also determine the occurrence of vaginal carcinoma in their daughters (i.e., the right arrow is absent). Consequently, there is no confounding. In non-type A side effects [and also intended (main) effects on an intervention], the right arrow is much more likely to exist so confounding should be dealt with appropriately. Even then, however, a detailed discussion of the probability of confounding can be very helpful.

Deep vein thrombosis (DVT) as a side effect of different types of second versus third generation oral contraceptives serves as another example. DVT could be considered a type A side effect because the underlying mechanism is understood [Kemmeren et al., 2004] and the side effect may be predicted to a certain extent. As third generation oral contraceptives were initially expected to be safer, they could preferentially have been prescribed to women who had an increased risk for vascular effects of oral contraceptives, for example, those with a history of thrombosis. Nevertheless, confounding need not be an issue as long as the reasons to prescribe a second or third generation oral contraceptive are *not* related to the risk for venous thrombosis. To confidently exclude such a relationship is a difficult task, however, and requires detailed knowledge about the determinants of DVT and the distribution of these characteristics among women receiving second or third generation oral contraceptives in daily practice. Often, showing that measures to limit confounding do not materially influence the observed risk of the side effect is the only way to convince the readership that confounding indeed did not occur [Lidegaard et al., 2002].

Methods to Limit Confounding

Observational Studies on Side Effects of Interventions

As in many type A side effects, when confounding cannot be excluded beforehand, multiple methods can be applied to establish or approach comparability of natural history. Most studies apply multiple methods simultaneously to achieve comparability of natural history in observational research on side effects. Some of these methods are summarized in Textbox 6.7. The same methods also can be used to limit confounding in observational studies on the *main effects* of interventions, although major confounding may remain present because the reasons to initiate an intervention are, by definition, almost always related to the outcome (i.e., its intended) effect and many may be implicit or unmeasured (Chapter 5) [Hak et al., 2002]. Such massive confounding often poses insurmountable validity problems [Vandenbroucke, 2004].

Limiting Confounding in the Design of Data Collection

Restriction of the Study Population

An important tool to prevent confounding is to choose the study population so that the baseline risk of the outcome (side effect) is more or less similar in all participants. This could be achieved, at least in part, by restricting the study population to those patients *with a similar indication* but *without contraindications* for the intervention under study. The former restriction is obvious; it primarily reflects the typical domain of a study on the effects of

TEXTBOX 6.7 Means to limit confounding by indication in observational studies on side effects of interventions

In the design of data collection

1. Restriction of the study population
2. Selectivity in reference categories of determinant
3. Matching of those with and without the determinants
4. Pseudorandomization using instrumental variables

In the design of data analysis

1. Multivariate analyses
2. Propensity scores

Source: Author.

interventions. It will be difficult to exclude that some of the reasons to start an intervention, for example, the severity of the disease, are related to the risk of experiencing the side effect. Restriction to those without contraindications (or more specifically, those without predictors of the side effect under study) seems straightforward, but the operationalization of this may be rather difficult. The essence of the latter restriction is that in the remainder of the study population, the reasons for the intervention to not be prescribed will not be based on the risk for side effect [Jick & Vessey, 1978]. It should be emphasized that not all reasons to initiate or refrain from an intervention in daily practice are known and measurable, let alone that their possible association with the occurrence of the side effect has been established. Consequently, residual confounding can never be excluded. Those receiving or not receiving the intervention in the restricted study population may still differ in characteristics that may be related to both the prescription of the intervention and the outcome, and thus act as confounders.

In a nested case-control study with the objective to quantify the risk of myocardial infarction or sudden cardiac death of COX-2 inhibitors, the study population was a cohort comprised of patients who filled at least one prescription of a COX-2 inhibitor or other NSAID(s) [Graham et al., 2005]. Thus, all participants had (or had in the past) an indication for a painkiller and did not have a clear contraindication for NSAIDs. Nevertheless, there may be reasons to choose a specific NSAID within the indicated population, and if these reasons are related to the risk of myocardial infarction or sudden cardiac death, then confounding will result. Although restriction can be a powerful means to limit confounding, additional methods are usually required to preclude residual confounding.

Selectivity in the Reference Categories of the Determinant

Obviously, the determinant of the occurrence relation is the intervention studied, in our example, the use of Metoo-coxib®. In other words, exposure is defined as the use of this drug. The definition of the reference category is less straightforward, however. Simply including patients not receiving the intervention (non-use of Metoo-coxib®) carries the danger of including many patients outside the relevant domain, that is, those not even having an indication for analgesics (see the previous section on restriction). Even when the indications are not related to the side effect (and therefore are not confounders), the generalizability of the findings to the relevant patient domain may become problematic. When designing the data collection, this domain [e.g., those requiring (with an indication for) analgesics] should be carefully considered. Although theoretically, non-use of analgesics *within* this domain could be taken as the reference category when calculating the risk of myocardial infarction during Metoo-coxib® use, non-users of analgesics remain an atypical, small subgroup among the domain of those indicated for these drugs. When the reasons to refrain from prescribing analgesics in this group (i.e., a history of peptic ulcer) are associated with the risk of the side effect, confounding will occur. Choosing another drug with similar indications and contraindications (and preferable even within the same drug class) as the reference category of the determinants is an attractive approach to prevent confounding; patients receiving Metoo-coxib® are likely to be quite comparable to patients receiving an alternative COX-2 inhibitor, and one may even assume that the decision to prescribe one of the two will not be related to patient characteristics but is influenced by other factors (e.g., a visit by the company representative or pricing of the drug) unrelated to the risk of the side effect. Even when comparing individual drugs with similar indications and contraindications, confounding could occur and residual confounding should be considered.

In the earlier nested case-control study, the risk of myocardial infarction or sudden cardiac death in recipients of rofecoxib was compared to those receiving celecoxib, another COX-2 inhibitor. Patient characteristics of rofecoxib and celecoxib users were expected to be similar, and a relationship between preferential prescription of one of these drugs and cardiovascular risk (and thus the side effect) was considered unlikely. Close comparison of the control patients (within this case-control study), however, revealed that celecoxib was prescribed more often to patients with relatively high cardiovascular risks (Table 6.5).

Interestingly, tables comparing characteristics among determinant categories are not often presented in case-control studies despite the fact that the data can be very helpful in identifying potential confounding by indication. Table 6.5 shows that, for unknown reasons, celecoxib was prescribed to older patients and those with more unfavorable cardiovascular risk profiles. The unadjusted comparison of rofecoxib and celecoxib users therefore yielded a lower odds ratio (OR; as an approximation of the relative risk) of myocardial infarction or sudden cardiac death (OR 1.32) than after an adjustment for confounders (OR 1.59).

In many studies on side effects, *ex-users* of the intervention are taken as the reference exposure category. The rationale behind this approach is the ease with which a cohort of patients receiving the intervention (often a drug) can be identified (e.g., by using routinely available clinical, insurance, or pharmacy data) and the notion that these patients have (or had) an indication (and not an important contraindication) for the intervention. It should be emphasized, however, that ex-users of an intervention represent a rather specific group of patients. For example, cessation of an intervention could have been related to the occurrence of side effects or ineffectiveness of the therapy. In addition, the severity of the disease is likely to be less in ex-recipients of the intervention. Therefore, we hesitate to recommend including ex-users as the reference category in research on side effects because of the potential for confounding.

TABLE 6.5 Selected characteristics of controls from the case-control study receiving different COX-2 inhibitors or NSAIDs and ex-users ("remote use") of these drugs [Graham, 2005]

	Celecoxib (n = 491)	Ibuprofen (n = 2573)	Naproxen (n = 1409)	Rofecoxib (n = 196)	Remote use (n = 18720)
Age (years)	73.4 (8.5)	66.9 (11.3)	68.4 (10.9)	72.1 (9.9)	66.4 (11.7)
Men	245 (50%)	1591 (62%)	801 (57%)	91 (46%)	11,807 (63%)
Cardiovascular risk score	4.21 (3.24)	3.11 (3.14)	3.22 (3.15)	3.14 (3.16)	2.91 (3.16)
Cardiovascular admissions in past year	31 (6%)	59 (2%)	51 (4%)	5 (3%)	581 (3%)
Cardiovascular drug use in past year	373 (76%)	1535 (60%)	876 (62%)	129 (656%)	10,388 (55%)
Angiotensin-converting-enzyme inhibitor	140 (29%)	512 (20%)	301 (21%)	43 (22%)	3555 (19%)
Angiotensin-receptor blocker	29 (6%)	33 (1%)	28 (2%)	2 (1%)	348 (2%)

Graham DJ, Campen D, Hui R, Spence M, Cheetham C, Levy G, Shoor S, Ray WA. Risk of acute myocardial infarction and sudden cardiac death in patients treated with cyclo-oxygenase 2 selective and non-selective non-steroidal anti-inflammatory drugs: Nested-case-control study. Lancet 2005;365:475–81.

In the nested case-control study, ex-users were treated as a separate reference group. Table 6.5 clearly shows, however, that these ex-users ("remote use") differ considerably from the current users of analgesics. Cardiovascular risk and the prevalence of comorbidity were the lowest factors among ex-users, indicating the larger potential for confounding in the comparison with this reference group.

Matching Those with and without the Determinants

Matching patients receiving the intervention with those in the reference group of the determinant/exposure is another option that can limit confounding. Usually, for each patient exposed to the determinant, a patient in the reference category is sought who has similar values of one or more characteristics (i.e., matching factors) considered to act as important confounders. This will result in equal distribution of these confounders among the two comparison groups. Intuitively, this is an attractive approach because it *seems* to mimic the randomization procedure in a trial. The matching procedure, however, will only be able to achieve comparability for known and adequately measurable confounders, while randomization will prevent any (known and unknown) confounding. Moreover, matching may pose logistical problems, particularly when multiple matching factors are involved. Matching on more than two patient characteristics is therefore generally not feasible. Alternatively, one could match those receiving the intervention and those in the reference category according to a composite score (i.e., the propensity score), encompassing multiple potential confounders. (The propensity score method is discussed later in this chapter.) It should be emphasized that matching of patients exposed to the intervention with patients in the reference category of the determinant (which is usually done in a cohort study) is completely different than matching of cases and controls in a case-control study. As explained in detail in Chapter 9, matching of cases and controls is counterintuitive because those developing the outcome (i.e., the cases) should naturally differ from those not (yet) experiencing the outcome (controls) in all risk factors for the outcome. In fact, such matching often is artificial and may induce rather than prevent confounding (see Chapter 9).

Pseudorandomization Using Instrumental Variables

Another method is believed to limit (or even prevent) both known and unknown confounding in observational causal research: pseudorandomization using an instrumental variable. A so-called *instrumental variable* is strongly related to exposure to the determinant but *not* to the study outcome. Categorizing study participants according to this instrumental variable implies that, if indeed the instrumental variable is not associated with the probability of developing the outcome, all potential confounders are equally distributed among the categories of the instrumental variable [Martens et al., 2006]. A study on the effects of more intensified treatment (including cardiac catheterization) on mortality in patients with myocardial infarction was one of the first to apply this method [McClellan, 1994]. Distance to the hospital was used as an instrumental variable as it was considered to be closely related to the chance of undergoing this procedure (i.e., more likely when the distance is shorter), while the distance to the hospital itself was judged not to be related to mortality (or health status). Theoretically, comparison of patients living close to a hospital with those living farther away would provide for an unconfounded estimate of the effect of more intensified treatment of myocardial infarction on mortality.

The instrumental variable method has been applied in research on side effects of interventions. Brookhart et al. [2006] used the physician's preference to COX-2 inhibitors or other NSAIDs as an instrumental variable to compare the risk of gastrointestinal side effects of these drugs. Textbox 6.8

TEXTBOX 6.8 The instrumental variable method

Background: Postmarketing observational studies of the safety and effectiveness of prescription medications are critically important but fraught with methodological problems. The data sources available for such research often lack information on indications and other important confounders for the drug exposure under study. Instrumental variable methods have been proposed as a potential approach to control confounding by indication in non-experimental studies of treatment effects; however, good instruments are hard to find.

Methods: We propose an instrument for use in pharmacoepidemiology that is based on a time-varying estimate of the prescribing physician's preference for one drug relative to a competing therapy. The use of this instrument is illustrated in a study comparing the effect of exposure to COX-2 inhibitors with nonselective, nonsteroidal anti-inflammatory medications on gastrointestinal complications.

Results: Using conventional multivariable regression adjusting for 17 potential confounders, we found no protective effect due to COX-2 use within 120 days from the initial exposure (risk difference = −0.06 per 100 patients; 95% confidence interval = −0.26 to 0.14). However, the proposed instrumental variable method attributed a protective effect to COX-2 exposure (−1.31 per 100 patients; −2.42 to −0.20) compatible with randomized trial results (−0.65 per 100 patients; −1.08 to −0.22).

Conclusions: The instrumental variable method that we have proposed appears to have substantially reduced the bias due to unobserved confounding. However, more work needs to be done to understand the sensitivity of this approach to possible violations of the instrumental variable assumptions.

Source: Brookhart MA, Wang PS, Solomon DH, Schneeweiss S. Evaluating short-term drug effects using a physician-specific prescribing preference as an instrumental variable. Epidemiology 2000, 17;268–75. Reproduced with permission.

is the abstract of their study; it illustrates both the potential strength and the uncertainties of the method.

Although instrumental variables appear to offer a rather ideal solution to the danger of (known and even unknown) confounding in observational causal research, instrumental variables may be hard to find in a particular study. Most notably, it is difficult to prove that the main assumption underlying this method holds true, namely, that the instrumental variable is not related to the occurrence of the outcome. Nevertheless, the method deserves further study.

Limiting Confounding in the Design of Data Analyses

Multivariate Analyses

Ways to adjust for confounders in the data analyses (i.e., stratified analyses or multiple regression techniques) are briefly discussed in Chapters 2 (etiology) and 12 (data analysis). The essence is that potential confounders should be identified in advance and measured appropriately, and then the observed crude association of the intervention and the outcome (side effect) is adjusted using available statistical techniques. There is no consensus about the way to select confounders and how to build a multivariable model. Usually, the decision to adjust for a potential confounder is based on a close examination of its relationship with both the determinants and the outcome in the database of the study. Often, all confounders are included in a multiple regression model all at once or researchers develop computer models to build the multivariable model using statistical reasons to include or exclude a potential confounder. However, we recommend that confounders be included one at a time, starting with the strongest confounder based on clinical expertise and the univariate analysis. Then the effect of each included confounder on the risk estimate can be evaluated. Moreover, the methodical single inclusion of confounders may indicate the potential for residual confounding. If, for example, the risk estimate remains stable after inclusion of the first major confounders even after inclusion of additional confounders, one may argue that any unmeasured or unknown confounder is unlikely to result in a major change in the risk estimate. The advantage of subsequent inclusion of individual confounders in a multiple regression model is illustrated in our case-control study on the risk of sudden death in hypertensive patients using non-potassium sparing diuretics compared to other antihypertensives (Table 6.6).

It should be noted that in cases where an adjustment for many potential confounders is anticipated, both stratification and multiple regression techniques may become problematic, the latter because the assumptions underlying the regression model often become untenable. Use of a single score summarizing patient characteristics that may act as confounders has been advocated as a better alternative [Miettinen, 1976a; Jick et al., 1973]. In particular, the use of so-called *propensity scores* has increased in recent years.

TABLE 6.6 Risk of sudden cardiac death among patients with hypertension receiving non-potassium sparing diuretics (NPSD) compared to other antihypertensive drugs. Results of multivariable logistic regression analysis. Subsequent inclusion of the first (strongest) confounders yielded the expected changes in the risk estimate. Inclusion of additional confounders hardly changed the odds ratio, indicating that residual confounding may be limited

Potential confounders included in the model	Odds ratio (95%) of sudden cardiac death for NPSD versus other antihypertensives
Crude	1.7 (0.9–3.1)
+ Prior myocardial infarction	2.0 (1.1–3.8)
+ Heart failure	2.0 (1.0–3.9)
+ Angina	2.1 (1.1–4.1)
+ Stroke	2.1 (1.0–4.1)
+ Arrhythmias	2.1 (1.1–4.1)
+ Claudication	2.1 (1.1–4.2)
+ Diabetes	2.1 (1.0–4.1)
+ Obstructive pulmonary disease	2.2 (1.1–4.6)
+ Cigarette smoking	2.2 (1.1–4.4)
+ Hypercholesterolemia	2.2 (1.1–4.5)
+ Mean blood pressure prior 5 years	2.2 (1.1–4.6)

Hoes AW, Grobbee DE, Lubsen J, Man in 't Veld AJ, van der Does E, Hofman A. Diuretics, beta-blockers, and the risk for sudden cardiac death in hypertensive patients. Ann Intern Med 1995a;123:481–7.

Propensity Scores

The *propensity score* represents the probability of receiving the intervention. It often results from a multiple logistic regression analysis including patient characteristics believed to be related to initiation of the intervention as independent variables and exposure to the intervention as the dependent variable. Rubin and Rosenbaum [1984] were the first to summarize all characteristics related to the initiation (or non-initiation) of the intervention in a propensity score. In the Metoo-coxib® example, this would imply that a score predicting the use of Metoo-cox® instead of the reference exposure (e.g., other NSAIDS) would first be derived. After a propensity score is calculated for each participant, one can adjust for this score through simple stratification or regression analysis including one covariate (the score). Matching each patient using Metoo-coxib® with a patient receiving another NSAID according to the individual propensity score is an alternative [Rubin, 1997]. The popularity of the propensity score in drug risk assessment has increased rapidly in recent years. The method, however, has its inherent limitations. These include the complexity of developing appropriate propensity scores (in fact, many studies fail to report in detail how the score was derived) and the fact that only known and measurable patient characteristics can be accounted for.

Table 6.7 compares several available methods to limit confounding in observational studies assessing effect of interventions. The example is taken from a study on the (beneficial) effect of influenza vaccination on influenza complications, including death [Hak et al., 2002]. The methods compared include restriction (in age categories), individual matching ("quasi-

TABLE 6.7 Methods to limit confounding

Study population and analysis	Adjusted for	Odds ratio (95% CI)
Adult patients (18–102 y, n = 1696) Conventional control: MLR*	Crude value	1.14 (0.84 to 1.55)
	+ Age (in years)	0.87 (0.64 to 1.20)
	+ Disease (asthma/COPD)	0.82 (0.59 to 1.13)
	+ GP visits (in number)	0.76 (0.54 to 1.05)
	+ Remaining factors	0.76 (0.54 to 1.06)
Elderly patients (65–102 y, n = 630) Conventional control: MLR*	Crude value	0.57 (0.35 to 0.93)
	+ Age (in years)	0.56 (0.35 to 0.92)
	+ Disease (asthma/COPD)	0.53 (0.32 to 0.87)
	+ GP visits (in number)	0.50 (0.30 to 0.83)
	+ Remaining factors	0.50 (0.29 to 0.83)
Younger patients (18–64 y, n = 1066) Conventional control: MLR*	Crude value	1.27 (0.84 to 1.94)
	+ Age (in years)	1.11 (0.73 to 1.70)
	+ Disease (asthma/COPD)	1.08 (0.70 to 1.66)
	+ GP visits (in number)	0.94 (0.61 to 1.47)
	+ Remaining factors	0.94 (0.60 to 1.45)
Quasi-experiment (18–64 y, n = 676) Conventional control: MCLR†	Matched crude value	0.90 (0.63 to 1.52)
	+ Age/disease/GP visits + Remaining factors	0.89 (0.52 to 1.54)
Younger patients (18–64 y, n = 1066) Propensity score: MCLR†	Matched crude value	0.87 (0.56 to 1.35)
	+ Age/disease/GP visits + Remaining factors	0.86 (0.55 to 1.35)

*MLR, multivariate logistic regression analysis; †MCLR, multivariable conditional logistic regression.

Hak E, Verheij TJ, Grobbee DE, Nichol KL, Hoes AW. Confounding by indication in non-experimental evaluation of vaccine effectiveness: the example of prevention of influenza complications. J Epidemiol Community Health 2002;56:951–5.

experiment"), inclusion of individual confounders in a multiple regression analysis, and the propensity score method. Because influenza vaccination is expected to reduce complications, the crude odds ratio of 1.14 indicates confounding by indication.

Restriction of the study population to certain age categories and inclusion of a few confounders in a multiple regression model reduced confounding dramatically (OR < 1.0). Also, individual matching according to different confounders (quasi-experiment) or on the propensity score clearly reduced confounding, while inclusion of additional potential confounders did not change the risk estimate.

Health Care Databases as a Framework for Research on Side Effects of Interventions

As discussed in this chapter, most studies on side effects of interventions are observational, require very large sample sizes, long follow-up periods, and include identification and valid measurements of confounders to ensure their validity. The fact that the availability of many large-scale, longitudinal, computerized health care databases (including routinely collected data on interventions received, patient characteristics, and patient outcomes) have greatly facilitated the conduct research of side effects is, therefore, hardly surprising. Several health care databases have proven to be invaluable in quantifying risks of intervention, particularly of drugs. These include (1) health maintenance organizations (HMO), such as the Kaiser Permanente Medical Care Program and Group Health Cooperative (GHC) of Puget Sound, Seattle, in the United States; (2) general practice research databases, for example in the United Kingdom (GPRD) and The Netherlands (IPCI); and (3) pharmacy databases combined with hospital discharge diagnoses, such as the Institute for Drug Outcome Research (PHARMO), also located in The Netherlands. Examples from these databases include studies on the unintended effects of COX-2 inhibitors [Graham et al., 2005], estrogen replacement therapy [Heckbert et al., 1997], statins [van de Garde et al., 2006], antipsychotics [Straus et al., 2004], and quinolones [Erkens et al., 2002]. A more general discussion of the advantages and disadvantages of routine health care databases is presented in Chapter 8.

In Textbox 6.9, some characteristics of the Kaiser Permanente Medical Care Program, which started in 1961, are shown [Selby et al., 2005].

Obviously, the suitability of these databases critically depends on the quality of the (usually routinely collected) relevant data. In particular, the use of the intervention (including dosage and duration), the outcome and potential confounders, including comedication, comorbidity, and other relevant patient characteristics, should be assessed validly. The availability of

TEXTBOX 6.9 Kaiser Permanente Medical Care Program

Total number of enrollees	8.2 million
Enrollees in Northern California	3.2 million
Initiation of the program	1961
Selected databases available	Information includes:
Membership database	Enrollment status, source of insurance
Demographic database	Name, birthdate, sex, address, physical disabilities
Hospitalizations	ICD coded hospital discharge diagnoses
Outpatient visits	Date, ICD-coded diagnoses, provider
Laboratory results	Chemistry, hematology, microbiology, pathology, etc.
Prescriptions	Name, drug code, dosage, dispensing, costs
Disease registries	Cancer, diabetes, AIDS, ICD cause of death registries

Source: Author.

prescription-filling data from pharmacies is crucial as are high-quality coding systems for relevant diagnoses. The latter is much more problematic; one simply cannot expect that all diagnoses are coded correctly by treating physicians in daily practice and selectivity in the diagnoses used (i.e., restriction to those requiring additional diagnostic testing or the more severe outcomes) is important. The main advantages of HMO databases are that enrollees will typically visit those physicians, hospitals, and pharmacists affiliated with the organization and that complete coverage of all available health information of its members can be ensured. The health care system in some European countries, such as Great Britain and The Netherlands, greatly increases the value of general practice databases. In these countries, all inhabitants are enlisted with one computerized general practice, fill their prescription at one computerized pharmacy, and the general practitioner has a gate-keeping function where referral to hospital specialists is initiated by the general practitioner and all relevant information (including hospital discharge letters) are available in the general practice database [van der Lei et al., 1993]. Despite the value of these databases, some information, such as more subjective diagnoses (e.g., dyspepsia, depression), lifestyle parameters (e.g., smoking, alcohol use), ethnicity, and socioeconomic status is notoriously difficult to obtain validly, if they are available at all. If such information is required to limit confounding, the validity of the study is at stake. Consequently, these databases are particularly suited to assess type B side effects, where confounding generally does not play a role.

7

Design of
Data Collection

The design of data collection is an element of critical importance in the successful design of clinical epidemiological studies. The prime consideration in choosing from different options to collect data is the expected quality of the results of the data analyses in terms of relevance, validity, and precision. The relevance is first and foremost determined by the research question with the type of subjects from whom data are collected adequately reflecting the domain. Next, a number of issues are important. Time constraints and budgetary aspects of a study may impact the choice of study population and type of data collection. For example, when a widely used drug is becoming suspected of a serious side effect, it is usually impossible to postpone action for a number of years before a study yields results. Also, lack of money may force an investigator to limit the number of measurements or the size of the group of patients who can be studied. Sometimes ethical limitations apply, for example, when an investigator wants to examine whether particularly high doses of radiotherapy induce secondary tumors in patients treated for a primary cancer. The investigator should preferably use data at hand rather than wait until a next group of patients is exposed. There is no unique optimal way to collect data for each research question in any study.

In contrast to the sometimes fiercely voiced belief that the most reliable results are obtained in a randomized trial, there are many examples of bad trials and much better "non-trials," and there are obvious instances where a trial is not feasible or otherwise not justified. This chapter discusses some general aspects of the design of data collection, with the goal of offering a consistent and comprehensive taxonomy without confusing terminology. In clinical epidemiology, all studies can be classified according to three characteristics: time, census or sampling, and experimental or observational.

Time

Time is an essential aspect of data collection. The time between collection of determinant and outcome information can be zero or larger than zero. When data on determinant and outcome are measured simultaneously, the time axis of the study is zero and the study is called *cross-sectional*. In all other study type the time axis is larger than zero. Furthermore, both determinant and outcome data already may or may not be available at the start of the study. If the data have been recorded in the past they are collected retrospectively and the study is *retrospective*. When the data are yet to be collected and recorded for both outcome and determinants when the study is started, the data are collected prospectively and the study is termed *prospective*. Combinations of retrospective and prospective data collection can occur.

There are no inherent implications for the validity of a study when data are not prospectively collected. Still, frequently authors as well as readers use and interpret the term *retrospective* as a negative qualification. Retrospective should only be taken with caution if a similar study with a prospective data collection would provide data that are qualitatively or quantitatively better. For example, in an etiological study, the available data may lack information on certain confounders or have confounder information that is less precise than necessary for full adjustment. Results from such a study may be biased or contain residual confounding that would not apply if data had been collected prospectively.

Alternatively, data on certain outcomes may be lacking. The results would then necessarily be restricted to inference on the outcomes that are in the data. While restricted, the research may still be valid and relevant. In descriptive research, the lack of particular data may create even fewer problems because the need for full confounder information is not a concern. Consider a study on the value of exercise testing in the diagnostic workup of patients suspected of ischemic coronary disease. An available database may not include results from troponin measurements, which are being used in some clinics to assist the diagnosis in these patients. Consequently, the added value of exercise testing in the presence of troponin measurements cannot be studied. Still, the results may be very useful to position exercise testing for those clinics that have no access to troponin measurements in these patients.

Retrospective data collection may suffer more from missing data in a proportion of the study population than data that are purposely collected prospectively. Missing data, for example, are a typical problem for routine clinical data that were stored before they were used for research. Here, the size of the problem depends on the magnitude of the data that are missing. Depending on the size of the overall study and the completeness of other data, the problem of missing data may be reduced or overcome by estimating the value of the missing data points, for example, by *multiple imputation*.

The principle of imputation is based on the view that if sufficient information on a certain subject is available the value of unobserved variables may be estimated with confidence. For example, suppose that in an existing database the data on body weight is missing for some individuals. With the use of available data on height, age, gender, and ethnicity, a reliable estimate of an individual's body weight may be obtained through regression modeling. Provided that the number of missing data is not too high, say less than 10% for a few variables, valid analyses may be done on all subjects. For a more elaborate discussion on missing data in routine care databases and how to deal with it, see Chapter 8.

It is important to realize that the time dimension of a study is not necessarily the same as the time dimension of the object of research. With the exception of diagnostic research, where diagnostic determinants and the outcome occur at the same time, all determinant outcome relations are prospective by nature. Take for example a study on the relationship between the *BCR-ABL* gene and leukemia that is conducted with a time axis of zero (e.g., cross-sectionally). Genes are measured in patients with and without the disease. While in this study determinant and outcome information was collected simultaneously, the inference of an increased risk of leukemia in those with the *p210 BCR-ABL* gene points at a prospective relationship: those with the gene have an increased risk of acquiring the disease in the future. Retrospective and prospective thus refer to the timing of data collection. Literally, historical cohort would be a better name than retrospective cohort because it more directly speaks to the operational aspect of the study. However, the term retrospective is much more commonly used.

Census or Sampling

The paradigm of epidemiologic research is the *cohort study*. A cohort is a group of subjects from whom data are collected. The word *cohort* is derived from Roman antiquity where a cohort was a body of about 300 to 600 soldiers; the tenth part of a legion. Once part of the cohort, there was no escape, you always remained a member. Now that you are reading this book, you are part of the cohort of readers who read the book. You will never get rid of that qualifying event.

In epidemiologic research, the qualifying event for becoming member of a cohort is typically that a subject is selected together with a smaller or larger group of other individuals to become part of a study population that is then studied over time. Sometimes, subjects can enter and leave a study population, as for example the population of a town that is followed over time. As the months and years go by, people will move into the town and become part of the study population while others will leave. Such a study population is called a *dynamic population*. The membership of a cohort is fixed while dynamic populations may change. The sometimes used term *dynamic cohort* is an oxymoron. It has also become common to use the term *cohort studies* for dynamic population studies and we do so throughout this book.

In studies of cohorts and dynamic populations, epidemiologic analyses will compare the development of disease outcomes across categories of a determinant. For example, if the risk of heart disease is elevated among those with high blood homocysteine levels, the rates of disease will be higher in those with a high baseline homocysteine level compared to those with a low baseline homocysteine level. This is epidemiologic research in its most simple form. Clearly, when the causal role of high homocysteine in the occurrence of heart disease needs to be clarified, a number of confounders must be taken into account simultaneously.

Sometimes investigators may face the need to follow a large population to be able to address particular rare outcomes, for example, in the study of the gene–environment interaction and the occurrence of Hodgkin lymphoma. To determine genetic abnormalities in the whole population would create insurmountable expenses. An alternative is to wait until cases of lymphoma occur and perform genetic analyses only in those with the disease and in a random sample of the remainder of the population. The purpose of the population sample is straightforward. If a valid sample is taken and the sample is sufficiently large, the distribution of determinants (and confounders) in the sample will reliably reflect the distributions in the population from whom the sample was drawn. In other words, the sample provides the same information as the much larger full population would have given. Across categories of the determinant in the combined samples of diseased subjects and controls, relative rates and risks can now be calculated with adjustments for confounders where appropriate. In this approach, rather than examining the entire population (census), an equally informative subgroup of the population is studied (sampling). Such a study is called a *case-control study*.

There is no innate reason why the results of a case-control study should be different than when the whole population is analyzed as long as the researcher adheres to some fundamental principles. The main principle in sampling is that determinants are sampled without any relationship to outcomes, and that outcomes are sampled without relationship to the determinant. If not, then the relationships may be biased. Suppose, for example, that only cases of Hodgkin disease are sampled that are known to have the oncogene *BCL11A*. It will come as no surprise that this gene will show an increased risk even though it may not play a role in reality. Because in a case-control study generally determinant information is collected after the cases and controls have been sampled, it is particularly the problem of biased sampling of cases or controls rather than biased measurement of determinants that may occur. For example, in some situations, cases may only become known to the investigator when they have certain determinants; a physician may be less suspicious of gastrointestinal (GI) bleeding problems in patients using a new non-steroidal anti-inflammatory drug (NSAID) that is marketed as much safer than another older brand. In contrast, when examining patients using the older drugs the same physician may be more suspicious and thus discover more cases of minor bleeding. If a case-control study were to be conducted using the cases noted in this physician's practice over a period of time, a relationship will have been introduced in favor of the newer drug which is not necessarily true.

Another issue in case-control studies compared to full cohort analyses is that the number of controls that is sampled needs to be sufficiently large to obtain adequate precision. There is no general rule about how large a control sample needs to be. Given that all cases that arise in a population are included in the research, this will depend on the strength of the relation that is being studied and the frequency that particular determinants of interest occur in the population. Generally, when a control sample four times the size of the case series is drawn, the population distributions can be estimated with sufficient precision.

Frequently, in a case-control study the actual size of the population from which cases and controls are drawn is not exactly known. For example, in a well known case-control study on the risk of vaginal cancer in female daughters of mothers exposed to DES use, a case series was collected and a number of controls without any reference to the size of the population from which the cases and controls originated (Figure 7.1). If the population size is not known, a limitation of the study is that no estimates of absolute risk can be obtained, such as for example, rate differences. Then, only relative measures of notable odds ratios may be obtained. However, in those instances where cases and controls are sampled from a cohort of known size, the same absolute and relative measures of disease risk can be calculated as in a regular full cohort analysis.

Case-control studies are best known for their role in etiologic research on relations between determinants and rare outcomes. However, case-control studies also may be fruitfully employed in descriptive research, such as in diagnostic and prognostic studies. In Chapter 9, the case-control method is explained in much more detail.

Experimental or Observational Studies

The world is full of data, most of which are waiting to be studied. Indeed, most published clinical epidemiologic research is based on data that were collected from available sources, like data in patient records of clinical files, or from data that were collected in groups of subjects for the purpose of research. To take the paradigmatic cohort study again, investigators typically start with a goal to relate a particular determinant to an outcome, as for example in a study on the breast cancer risk among women using long-term estrogen-progestin treatment. They start by collecting data on hormone use

FIGURE 7.1 Advertisement for the drug diethylstilbestrol (DES).

plus relevant confounders, and then follow the population over time to relate baseline drug information to future occurrences of breast cancer.

Every so often, a cohort study is started from a particular research aim, but with time the data offer many other opportunities to address questions that were not on the mind of the investigator when the research was initiated. This makes cohorts highly valuable assets to investigators. The limitations only rest in the type of population studied and the extent of determinant and outcome (and, if applicable, confounder or modifier) information collected.

Sometimes the investigator will not rely on the mere recording of determinant data that occur "naturally," but may wish to manipulate exposure to certain determinants or allocate patients purposely to a particular exposure, such as a drug, with the principal goal of learning about the effects of this exposure. This is called *experimentation*, and the investigator thus conducts an experiment. The difference between a physician treating patients with a particular drug and an investigator allocating a patient to a particular drug is in the *intention*. The intention of the physician is simply to improve the condition of the patient, while the investigator wants to learn about the effect of the drug, quantify the extent of improvement, and document any safety risks. Experiments in clinical epidemiology are called *trials*.

The best known and most widely used type of trial is the *randomized trial* where patients are allocated to different treatment modalities by a random process. A randomized trial obviously differs from the deliberate prescription of drugs to patients in clinical care. However, when an investigator decides to study a new series of arthritis patients, to specifically determine the functional benefit of knee replacement surgery where he measures functional status before and after the operation, he is also engaged in a trial. Studies are either experimental or non-experimental. The term *non-experimental*, while logical, is not commonly used. Rather, non-experimental studies in epidemiology are called *observational*. The contrast between experimental and observational is somewhat peculiar because it seems to imply that in experiments no observations are made.

Taxonomy of Epidemiological Data Collection

Like many young scientific disciplines, epidemiology suffers from a confusing and inconsistent terminology. Many epidemiologists use the same wording to describe different studies or use different words for the same research approach. Particularly problematic is the naming of studies by words that seem to have a qualitative implication. As indicated in this chapter, by itself the word observational is a clean term that applies to any form of empirical research. Too often the adverb observational is used to suggest a limitation of the research.

The word *descriptive* has a similar history of misuse. In several textbooks, a distinction between analytical and descriptive research is made, where descriptive studies are supposed to not provide definitive answers. We use the term *descriptive* as contrasted with *causal* to indicate whether the determinant-outcome relation under study is meant to explain causality or is only meant to describe the strength of the association.

All research is analytical by nature. In our view, epidemiological studies should be classified according to three dimensions: (1) time, including the time (zero or >0) between measurement of the determinant and the outcome as well as the prospective or retrospective nature of the data collection; (2) census or sampling; and (3) experimental or non-experimental. We recommend that you use all of these elements in the nomenclature in texts describing the nature of data collection. This removes the need to rely on vague, suggestive, and non-informative jargon such as *retrospective study, prospective study, survey, follow-up study,* and the like. Note that a prospective study could refer as well to a cohort study, a case-control study, or to a randomized trial. Also, the meaning of the term *longitudinal* is unclear. All studies, except diagnostic studies, address longitudinal associations.

TABLE 7.1   Taxonomy of epidemiological data collection

Type of clinical epidemiological study	Time: Time between measurement determinant and outcome	Time: data collection prospective or retrospective	Census or sampling	Observational or experimental
Cohort study	> 0	Can be both	Census	Observational*
Dynamic population study**	> 0	Can be both	Census	Observational
Case-control study	> 0 (usually)	Can be both	Sampling	Observational
Cross-sectional study	0	Can be both	Can be both	Observational
Randomized trial	> 0	Prospective	Census	Experimental

*If a cohort study is experimental, it is called a trial.

**Because the term *dynamic population study* is hardly ever applied in the literature, we use the term *cohort study* throughout the book to indicate both studies involving dynamic populations and cohorts.

Thus, the characteristics of the main approaches to data collection in clinical epidemiology can be summarized as follows (Table 7.1):

- A *cohort study* has a time dimension greater than zero; analyses are based on a census of all subjects in the study population and the data collection can be conducted prospectively or retrospectively. The study can be observational or experimental, but if it is observational it is usually named a *randomized trial*.

- A *dynamic population study* has a time dimension greater than zero; analyses are based on a census of all subjects in the study population for the time they are a member of the population and the data collection can be conducted prospectively or retrospectively. Such studies are typically observational. Because the term *dynamic population* study is hardly ever applied in the literature, we use the term *cohort study* throughout the book to indicate both studies involving dynamic populations and cohorts.

- A *case-control study* typically has a time dimension greater than zero (albeit that cross-sectional case-control studies are sometimes performed); analyses are based on sampling of subjects from the study population and the data collection can be conducted prospectively or retrospectively. Case-control studies are observational (although theoretically they could be experimental if performed within a randomized trial).

- A *cross-sectional study* can be a cohort study or a case-control study and has a time dimension of zero; analyses can be based on a census or on sampling of the study population. The data collection can be conducted prospectively or retrospectively. In principle, cross-sectional studies are observational.

- *A randomized trial* is a cohort study, is an experiment, and has a time dimension greater than zero; the analyses are based on a census of all subjects from the study population and the data collection can only be conducted prospectively.

8

Cohort and Cross-Sectional Studies

The classic epidemiological approach is to collect data on a defined population (a cohort) and relate determinant distributions at baseline to the occurrence of disease during follow-up. This research approach has led to our understanding such diverse cause and disease relationships as: the lifetime risk of coronary heart disease by cholesterol levels at selected ages in the Framingham Heart Study [Lloyd-Jones et al., 2003], the relationship between physical activity and risk of prostate cancer in the Health Professionals Follow-up Study [Giovannucci et al., 2005], the relationship between smoking and lung cancer during 50 years of observation in the British Doctor's Study [Doll et al., 2004], the relationship between caloric restriction during the Dutch famine 1944–1955 and future breast cancer in the DOM cohort [Elias et al., 2004], the relationship between apolipoprotein E (Apo-E) and Alzheimers disease in the Rotterdam Study [Hofman et al., 1997], and the relationship between radiation and leukemia in atomic bomb survivors in Hiroshima [Pierce et al., 1996].

The essential characteristic of a cohort study is that data are collected from a defined group of people, which forms the cohort. Cohort membership is defined by being selected for inclusion according to certain characteristics. For example, in the Rotterdam Study, 7983 subjects aged 55 years and over who agreed to participate after invitation of all inhabitants in a particular neighborhood of Rotterdam formed the Rotterdam Study cohort [Hofman et al., 1991].

The typical design of data collection in a cohort study is by starting to collect data at the time of the inception of the cohort. The starting point of a cohort, at T zero, is called the *baseline*. Sometimes, like in the Framingham Study, data collection is subsequently repeated at certain time intervals but for other cohorts only single baseline data are collected. After the baseline collection, a cohort is generally followed over time and disease occurrences among the members are collected. The term *cohort study* was used for the first time in research in the 1930s.

Some of the best-known cohort studies start from a population of presumed healthy individuals, but cohort studies can equally well be conducted starting with groups of patients. For example, one etiologic study followed a cohort of premature neonates for chronic cerebral damage and related behavioral problems [Rademaker et al., 2004]. This same cohort was also used to study the prognostic meaning of neonatal cerebral imaging by ultrasound compared to magnetic resonance imaging (MRI) scanning [Rademaker et al., 2005]. Prognostic cohort studies are obviously conducted on cohorts of patients. In diagnostic studies, the cohort typically consists of subjects suspected of the disease of interest in whom the value of diagnostic testing is studied.

Timing of the Association Relative to the Timing of Data Collection

Most cohort studies are planned in advance and data are collected prospectively. However, this is not a necessary condition. Sometimes, a cohort is defined retrospectively and historic data are used that are already available, such as in the studies on the Hiroshima atomic bomb survivors. This study's cohort comprised all those who survived the bomb attack and investigators used the limited available baseline data, notably age, sex, and degree of nuclear exposure, to relate the exposure to subsequent cancer occurrence. This cohort study had both a retrospective and a prospective component in the data collection. In a rather unusual approach, Vandenbroucke [1985] conducted a fully retrospective cohort study to investigate survival and life expectancy at age 25 years and older in 1282 European noblemen who had been members of the Knighthood Order of the Golden Fleece between its founding in 1430 and the early 1960s.

In these examples, the timing of data collection took place in whole or in part in the past. This infers that the associations examined in a cohort study are always prospective, whatever the timing of data collection. Etiological research aims to learn about causes of disease. Several criteria for causal associations have been proposed, but at the very least the cause is assumed to precede the consequence (i.e., the disease). Therefore, the (causal) determinant always precedes the outcome no matter what order the data have been collected. All etiological research is inherently prospective, yet the data may be collected before, during, or after the determinant-outcome relation has materialized. Even when data are collected prospectively, they will probably not be collected for all members of the cohort at the same time. Baseline data collection may take time to be completed and during that time subsequent participants enter the cohort. This type of cohort is built up obliquely.

When the time between collection of determinant and outcome data is zero, the cohort study is *cross-sectional*. For example, in the study on Alzheimer's disease and Apo-E genotype, Apo-E genetic polymorphisms were determined at the same time that cognitive examinations were performed to assess the presence of dementia. Data collection in this cohort was cross-sectional for this particular research question. However, even though data collection was cross-sectional, the conclusion was that the Apo-E ε4 genotype, in the presence of atherosclerosis, increased the patients' risk of dementia. The determinant-outcome relation was interpreted prospectively. The tenable assumption was that the genetic variant had been present long before dementia developed and would not change due to the occurrence of the disease.

In the design and analysis of cohort studies, it is important to be aware of differences in the timing of data collection and the true time relationship between the determinant and outcome. In etiological research, it is necessary to be confident that, while data may be collected in a different order, the resulting association(s) indeed may be interpreted causally. For example, in a study on dietary habits and risk of heart disease, the collection of dietary data after symptomatic coronary disease has occurred may be problematic because patients may change their diet after becoming aware of the disease. Consequently, the observed associations may be confounded.

Another problem is that when outcome data on a cohort are not recorded continuously and prospectively but rather after a longer time interval, some subjects with the outcome may be missed. As long as the chance of being missed is random, this is no real threat to validity. However, it may be likely that the chance of being detected and recorded as someone who developed the outcome is somehow related to the determinant of interest. This may apply equally to causal and descriptive studies. In a prognostic study, the prognostic meaning of a patient characteristic may be overestimated when patients with the characteristic are more likely to be followed more closely. In a diagnostic study, only certain patients may be referred for diagnostic work-up, making it more likely that the outcome is eventually diagnosed. For example, in a study on exercise testing in the diagnosis of coronary disease, only those with abnormal test results will be referred for invasive imaging using coronary angiography. If not all patients undergo the same reference test, some may be missed leading to false negatives and an overestimation of the diagnostic value of the test.

Causal and Descriptive Cohort Studies

The origins of cohort studies lie in studies initiated to address causal associations. Much of the methodology and strategies for data analyses for cohort studies have been developed with a view to causal explanation. The cohort approach is also a highly effective data collection design for descriptive research. Either diagnostic or prognostic research questions can be effectively addressed using a cohort study. Clearly, for a diagnostic study where the prevalence of the diagnosis of interest in relation to a set of diagnostic indicators is studied, the time between the occurrence of the outcome and the determinants is zero. Typically, therefore, determinant and outcome information is collected simultaneously, thus making a diagnostic study a cross-sectional cohort study (see below). However, frequently the optimal approach to research on prognosis is through a cohort study (with time exceeding zero). One or multiple prognostic factors are collected at baseline and the cohort is followed up to record the occurrence of events. For example, in a prognostic study, levels of circulating carcinoembryonic antigen (CEA) were measured in a cohort of patients with a primary colon tumor resection who were followed up for mortality to determine the prognostic value of CEA after treatment for the malignancy [Stelzner et al., 2005] (Textbox 8.1).

The difference in data collection in causal and descriptive cohort studies follows from the difference in objectives between causal and descriptive studies. In etiological research, determinant information and data on confounders are collected. By nature of the aim to obtain valid estimates of the causal association between determinant and outcome, confounder data need to be complete and of high quality.

If confounders are measured poorly or not measured at all, the results of the analyses may show an association that is quantitatively or qualitatively incorrect. In descriptive research there is no need to worry about confounders. Rather, the variables considered as determinants should be as complete as is necessary for the results of the research to be relevant and in agreement with the research question.

For example, in the study on the prognosis after primary tumor resection in patients presenting with unresectable synchronous metastases from colorectal carcinoma, six independent variables with a relationship to survival were found: performance status, ASA-class, CEA level, metastatic load, extent of primary tumor, and chemotherapy. Whether this includes information on all potential prognostic indicators that a reader may find useful for his or her patients depends on two factors: (1) whether the final six variables agree with the set of variables available to a clinician who wants to use the research for his or her patients; and (2) in the case where a favorite variable of the reader of the research is not included in the six predictors, whether this particular variable has been included in the research at all.

Suppose, for example, that a particular clinic routinely measures lactate dehydrogenase (LDH) in serum to set the prognosis in these patients. The research is clinically relevant if LDH was indeed included but was eventually shown to have no added value over the other six variables. According to the same principles, the mode of data collection will vary in cohort studies aiming to explain causality or aiming toward prediction. In the first goal,

TEXTBOX 8.1 Survival in patients with stage IV colorectal cancer

BACKGROUND: The prognostic impact of primary tumor resection in patients presenting with unresectable synchronous metastases from colorectal carcinoma (CRC) is not well established. In the present study, we analyzed fifteen factors to define the value of primary tumor resection with regard to prognosis.

PATIENTS AND METHODS: We identified 186 consecutive patients with proven stage IV CRC from the years 1995 to 2001. Variables were tested for their relationship to survival in univariate analyses with the Kaplan-Meier method and the log rank test. Factors that showed a significant impact were included in a Cox proportional hazards model. The tests were repeated for 107 patients who had no symptoms from their primary tumor. RESULTS: Overall there were six independent variables with a relationship to survival: performance status, ASA-class, CEA level, metastatic load, extent of primary tumor, and chemotherapy. In the asymptomatic patients we investigated 13 factors, 3 of which proved to be independent predictors of survival: performance status, CEA level, and chemotherapy. Resection of primary tumor was only predictive of survival if in-hospital mortality was excluded.

CONCLUSION: Resection of the tumor, if possible, is doubtless the best option for stage IV CRC patients with severe symptoms caused by their primary tumor. In asymptomatic patients, chemotherapy is preferable to surgery.

Source: Stelzner S, Hellmich G, Koch R, Ludwig K. Department of General and Abdominal Surgery, Dresden-Friedrichstadt General Hospital, Teaching Hospital of the Technical University Dresden, Dresden, Germany. J Surg Oncol 2005; 89:211–217.

the determinant (and confounder information) must be collected as accurately as possible. In the second goal, the data on determinants are collected according to general clinical standards because that is the way the results will eventually be applied. For either type of cohort study, outcome data should be collected as accurately as possible.

For diagnostic and prognostic studies, timing the association relative to the timing of data collection has some specific features. For prognostic studies, the same principles apply as for etiological studies. Whatever the timing of data collection, the association is always prospective. For a variable to be prognostic with regards to a given outcome, the prognostic factor needs to be observed before the outcome has occurred. In diagnostic studies, by definition the determinant and outcome occur at the same time. Diagnostic studies are typically cross-sectional. In a cohort of patients suspected of a certain diagnosis, data on putative diagnostic indicators are collected at the same time that the outcome is determined by some reference test. Next, these cross-sectional determinants and outcome data are analyzed for the strength of their association. Here no prospective association is assumed.

There is one subtlety in data collection in some diagnostic studies. Suppose, for example, that the diagnostic value of mammography for detection of early breast cancer is being studied [Moss et al., 2005]. Data from mammography are collected and women are referred for further diagnostic workup. After mammography, it may take some time before outcome data are available in those women with abnormal mammographic findings. Once the diagnosis has been established in all those who are referred, it may take even longer before those breast cancers that were missed by the mammography become apparent. Consequently, this diagnostic study may include data collection on the cohort over a prolonged period of time. Still, the determinant-outcome relation in this study—as in any diagnostic study—has a time interval of zero.

A classical example of the problem of an inevitable incomplete follow-up in a cohort is the study of congenital malformations caused by medication use during pregnancy. When congenital malformations are recorded at birth, the presence (i.e., prevalence) rather than the incidence is determined. It is difficult to exclude that some pregnancies were terminated early and these may have been related to the drug exposure. If so, then the risk estimates are too low.

Experimental Cohort Studies

Cohort studies are generally assumed to be based on data that occur in real life, that is, without a particular interference by the investigator. Therefore, cohort studies are typically considered to be observational. However, a randomized trial is also a cohort study, given that a study population is defined by taking part in the trial and is subsequently followed over time. Yet, trials are experimental because the exposure, such as allocation to the drug, is not taken from real-life prescriptions but manipulated by the investigator through randomization with the goal of improving the possibility of the study to give unbiased estimates of the association between the drug and the outcome.

The experimental nature of trials requires prospective collection of the data. However, even though data are collected prospectively, the collection of outcome data needs to be complete to prevent selective recording of outcome events according to allocated treatment. In trials this rule is known as the *intention to treat* principle. The principle is, however, not different for the need for outcome assessment independent from the determinant as in any cohort study. A more extensive discussion of intervention research and trials is in Chapters 5 and 10.

There are good examples of cohorts that were first assembled for a trial but were continued after the randomized period as a plain cohort study. Here, the *exposure* is experimental during a period of the cohort study and non-experimental thereafter. Also, patients considered for the trial but eventually not randomized may be followed up alongside the randomized subgroup of the cohort. For example, all subjects screened for the Multiple Risk Factor Intervention Trial (MRFIT) were used to create one of the largest cohort studies on cardiovascular risk factors [Stamler et al., 1986].

Cross-Sectional Studies

Cross-sectional studies can best be viewed as cohort studies with a time interval between collection of determinant and outcome data of zero. In other words, the determinant and outcome information is collected simultaneously. An example is a study on the relationship between certain determinants and joint bleeds in hemophilia patients, where a history of bleeding is obtained at the same time as the possible risk factors for bleeding (e.g., compliance with treatment, dosage of treatment, and engagement in sports and other activities with trauma risk).

Another example is the analysis of risk of congenital malformations after exposure to antidepressant drugs during pregnancy, where all the data are collected from women at the time of delivery of their children, who may or not may have malformations. It is important to realize that while the data collection of determinants and outcome is organized at the same time, the association being studied is longitudinal. The assumption is that drug exposure precedes the occurrence of malformations. The consequence is that the investigators need to seek assurance that despite this difference between timing of data collection and the temporal sequence of the presumed cause and effect, no bias is introduced by nature of this difference. For example, suppose that women with malformed children have a better recollection of their drug use during pregnancy, this may induce an invalid, biased, association between the drug use and the congenital malformation. This problem is known as *recall bias*.

When a study is cross-sectional, it is not necessarily conducted at a single point in time. Even though data collection of determinants and outcome in an individual takes place simultaneously at a particular moment, different individuals participating in a study may be examined sequentially over a longer time period.

Ecological Studies

Ecological studies are cohort studies. The cohort is assembled from the aggregate experience of several populations, for example, those living in different geographic areas. In contrast to the usual approach in cohort studies, here data are collected from summary measures in populations rather than from individual members of populations. For example, a study on the proportion of alcohol intake from wine and the occurrence of coronary heart disease used the distribution of wine intake across countries and the country-specific rates of coronary heart disease to determine the possible cardioprotective effect of different levels of wine consumption. The data were from different populations but the inference was made for individuals within populations, suggesting that rather than alcohol *per se*, the cardioprotective effect of wine was particularly clear (Figure 8.1) [Criqui & Ringel, 1994]. The study was etiological and this implies that the effect from wine on heart disease risk should be adjusted for confounders. In particular, there seem to be several aspects of lifestyle, including dietary habits, which could confound the observed crude association.

A major problem in ecological studies is the very limited extent to which confounder information is generally available. Confounder data simply may not be available, as for example data on differences in fat intake in populations between countries with a different wine consumption, or when data are available on a population level the distribution within a country and its relationship to the distribution of wine intake within that country remains unknown. Even when two countries show similar overall levels of intake of say fat and wine, within the country the relationship between fat intake and wine consumption on an individual level may be different. Indeed, with regard to wine and heart disease risk, a more extensive analysis of a number

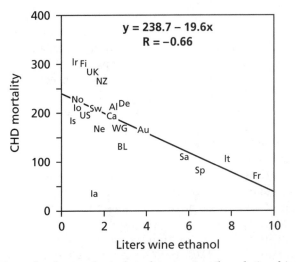

FIGURE 8.1 Example of an ecological study assessing the relationship between wine consumption and the coronary heart disease (CHD) mortality rate in men aged 44 to 64.

of cohort studies with ample adjustment for confounders showed that an initial ecological observation of a higher cardiovascular protection from wine compared to other alcoholic beverages could not be confirmed [Rimm et al., 1996]. This implies that it is the alcohol, rather than its form, that conveys protection. In clinical epidemiology, an example of an ecological comparison is that between different hospital infection rates in relationship to local policies regarding infection prevention. Even though the crude association suggests that infection rates are higher in those hospitals with a less extensive prevention program, this still may be confounded by, for example, differences in the type of surgery between hospitals. Because of inherent difficulties with handling of confounding, ecological studies generally do not provide strong evidence in favor or against causal associations.

Cohort Studies Using Routine Care Data

There are an endless number of subjects potentially eligible for inclusion in clinical epidemiological research among patients who are routinely seen in clinical care. The world is one big cohort. Routinely collected patient data offer an immense and underutilized resource of knowledge for diagnostic, prognostic, intervention and etiological research. Routine care data from patients who present with a particular symptom or sign that makes the physician suspect that they have a particular disease can be used for diagnostic research [Moons et al., 2004a]. Routine care data from patients diagnosed with a particular disease who were clinically followed over time can be used for prognostic research [Braitman & Davidoff, 1996; Concato, 2000]. Also, follow-up data from patients routinely treated for a particular disease with a particular treatment can be used for research on intended and unintended treatment effects [Concato et al., 2000; Ioannidis et al., 2001]. Obviously, routinely collected data must meet certain criteria to be used in clinical epidemiological research and their potential and problems need to be well understood for the research conclusions to be valid. There are various problems with routine care data drawn from patient files, which vary per type of research.

To facilitate research, patients must be coded in a specific and uniform way in the hospital or general practice files. For example, diagnostic research starts with a series (cohort) of patients who are selected on the presence of a particular symptom or sign. To select the proper patients from routine care data requires that they are classified uniformly according to their presented symptom or sign. Commonly, patients are (only) coded by the final diagnosis or disease, for example, using International Classification of Disease version 10 (ICD10) or International Classification of Primary Care (ICPC) codes.

However, when patients are selected on the basis of their final diagnosis as determined by a gold standard for inclusion in diagnostic research, this commonly leads to *selection bias*, which is also known as *verification*, *work-up*, or *referral bias* [Moons et al., 2004a; Ransohoff & Feinstein, 1978; Begg, 1987]. This bias occurs because in routine care patients are commonly selectively referred for eventual disease verification based on previous test results. For example, before patients suspected of coronary heart disease are submitted to coronary angiography on which the eventual diagnosis is based, they have undergone other, less invasive testing. Thus, the disease is ruled out in many subjects before ever reaching angiography. Consequently, if patients are selected for a diagnostic study using angiographically confirmed coronary disease as a criterion, they will not represent the full spectrum of patients suspected of coronary disease in real life. To achieve full representation, patients should be selected on the criterion, "suspicion of coronary disease requiring further diagnostic work-up." Standard and uniform coding of patients according to their main symptom or sign at presentation is unfortunately not very common, but is likely to increase with the increasing use of electronic patient records [Oostenbrink et al., 2003]. In contrast to diagnostic research, the classification in routine care of patients according to their final diagnosis does facilitate the selection of cohorts of patients with a particular disease to be included in prognostic research. Moreover, because administered treatments are commonly documented as well, routine care data in principle also provide for research on intended and unintended effects of treatments, although sometimes this may be prohibited by insurmountable problems of confounding by indication (see Chapter 6).

Another potential problem when using routine care data is the absence of a blinded outcome assessment. Clinical epidemiological research often requires that the presence or absence of the outcome under study is documented in each study subject without knowledge of (i.e., blinded for) the determinant(s) under study. Otherwise, knowledge of the determinant status may (partly) be used and included (or incorporated) in the assessment of the outcome. Consequently, the association between the determinant(s) and outcome will be biased; a phenomenon also known as *information, observer, assessment,* or *incorporation* bias [Pocock, 1984; Guyatt et al., 1993; Laupacis et al., 1997; Moons & Grobbee, 2002b].

Of course, in routine care the patient outcome recorded in files is commonly affected by knowledge of preceding or even after the initial patient information. Hence, in studies solely based on routine care data, a blinded outcome assessment is commonly lacking. While sometimes acceptable, a non-blinded outcome assessment in particular may pose validity problems when the assessment of the presence or absence of an outcome is sensitive to subjective (observer) interpretation, as for example in imaging tests. Suppose that the goal of a diagnostic study is to determine the value of routine chest radiographs to detect small lung tumors. Interpretation of minor abnormalities on the radiograph in routine care may be quite different if the observer has additional information that would make the presence of a malignancy more or less likely. Clearly, the unblinded outcome assessment is a non-issue for unequivocal outcomes such as mortality or for measurements providing objective results such as biochemical parameters (e.g., cholesterol level or leukocyte count) or automatically measured blood pressure levels.

Finally, the problem can be circumvented when the investigators use routine care data to select study subjects, but reassess the outcome by approaching individual patients, disregarding previously recorded patient information.

Missing Data

Probably one of the most general and difficult problems with the use of routine care data is that certain data are missing in the files. Missing data pose a problem in all types of medical research, no matter how strictly designed and protocolized. But this problem is accentuated in research based on routine care data, as there is commonly no strict case-record-form or data measurement protocol in daily practice.

In epidemiological research we distinguish three types of missing data [Rubin, 1976]. If subjects whose data are missing are a random subset of the complete sample of subjects, the missing data are called *missing completely at random (MCAR)*. Typical examples of MCAR are an accidentally dropped tube containing venous blood (thus blood parameters cannot be measured) or a questionnaire that is accidentally lost. The reason for the missing data is completely random. In other words, the probability that an observation is missing is not related to any other patient characteristic.

If the probability that an observation is missing depends on information that is not observed, like the value of the observation itself, the missing data are called *missing not at random (MNAR)*. For example, data on smoking habits may be more likely to be missing when subjects do not smoke.

When missing data occur in relationship to observed patient characteristics, subjects with missing data are a selective rather than a random subset of the total study population. This pattern of missing data is confusingly called *missing at random (MAR)*, where missing values are random conditional on other available patient information [Rubin, 1976]. Data that are missing at random are very common in routine care databases. For example, in a diagnostic study among children with neck stiffness, investigators quantified which combination of predictors from patient history and physical examination could predict the absence of bacterial meningitis (outcome), and which blood tests (e.g., C-reactive protein level) have added predictive value. Patients presenting with severe signs such as convulsions, which commonly occur among those with bacterial meningitis, often received additional (blood) testing before full completion of patient history and physical examination, which in turn were largely missing in the records. On the other hand, patients with very mild symptoms, who frequently had no bacterial meningitis, were more likely to have a completed history and physical but were less likely to have additional tests, because the physician already ruled out a serious disease. Missing data on particular tests was thus related to other observed test results and—although indirectly—to the outcome.

This mechanism of missing data is even more likely to occur in longitudinal studies based on routine care data. When following patients over time in routine care practice, loss to follow-up is a common problem and often is directly related to particular patient characteristics. Accordingly, outcomes may be only available for particular patients the selection of whom is related to certain determinants. Consider a study to compare the prognosis of patients with minimally versus more invasive cancer. Suppose that patients who were treated in a particular hospital during a certain period were followed up over time using data from patient records. Follow-up information for subsequent morbidity may be more complete for patients with initial invasive cancer, because these patients more regularly and during a longer time period visited the clinic as part of routine procedures. One can easily check whether data are MCAR [Van der Heijden et al., 2006]. If the subset of patients with and without missing values does not differ on the other (observed) patient characteristics, then the missing values were likely MCAR (although theoretically they might still be MNAR).

Typically, in epidemiological research, missing data are neither MCAR nor MNAR but MAR, although this cannot be tested but only assumed [Little & Rubin, 1987; Schafer, 1997; Vach, 1994; Schafer& Graham, 2002; Greenland & Finkle, 1995; Donders et al., 2006].

There are various methods to deal with missing values in clinical epidemiological research. The best method obviously is to conduct a more active follow-up of the patients for whom crucial information is (partly) missing, in order to obtain as much as possible of this information. For example, in the cancer study with the selective follow-up, the researchers could conduct a more active follow-up of all patients regardless of the baseline disease condition. Similarly, in the Utrecht Health Project, routine care data are supplemented with predetermined data collection [Grobbee et al., 2005]. The quality of the routine care data is further optimized by a dedicated training program of health care personnel with ample attention to assure complete and adequate coding.

If a more active follow-up does not suffice or is not feasible, however, researchers usually exclude all subjects with a missing value on any of the variables from the analysis. The so-called *complete* or *available* case analysis is the most common method currently found in (clinical) epidemiological studies. This is probably because most statistical packages implicitly exclude the subjects with a missing value on any of the variables analyzed. Simply excluding subjects with missing values always affects precision. But it is commonly not appreciated that—more seriously—it produces severely biased estimates of the associations investigated when data are not missing completely at random, as shown in the examples of the diagnosis of bacterial meningitis and prognosis of cancer patients presented earlier in this chapter. It is better to use other methods in the data analysis than a complete case analysis [Little, 1987; Schafer, 1997; Vach, 1994; Schafer & Graham, 2002; Donders et al., 2006; Rubin, 1987; Vach & Blettner, 1991].

There are a variety of alternative methods to cope with missing values in the analysis. Some of these are briefly discussed below. An illustrative example can be found in Textboxes 8.2 and 8.3.

1. *Maximum likelihood estimations.* This method (e.g., using the expectation-maximation [EM]-algorithm) is used for multilevel or repeated measurement analysis in studies where determinants or outcomes are documented more than once [Little & Rubin, 1987; Schafer, 1997; Vach, 1994; Schafer & Graham, 2002].

2. The *missing indicator method.* This method uses a dummy (0/1) variable as an indicator for missing data [Greenland & Finkle, 1995; Miettinen, 1985]. For example, if there are missing values on a particular variable, an indicator is defined with "1" if the variable value was missing and "0" otherwise. In the case of categorical variables, this is equal to treating the missing values as a separate result. For the variable, the missing values are commonly recoded as zero, although any value would suffice. The idea behind this method is that the association between the original (though recoded) variable and the outcome is always fitted in combination with the indicator variable. Accordingly, all subjects are used in the (multivariable) analysis, being the supposed advantage of the missing indicator method.

3. *Unconditional imputation.* Replacing or "filling in" the missing value of a particular variable with the mean or median of that variable as estimated from the other patients in whom that variable was observed. This replacement is more technically called *imputation of a missing value.* Because here the missing value is imputed by the overall variable mean or median irrespective (unconditional) of any other patient information, this method is also called the *overall or unconditional* (mean or median) *imputation* [Little & Rubin, 1987; Schafer, 1997; Vach, 1994; Schafer & Graham, 2002; Greenland & Finkle, 1995; Donders et al., 2006].

4. *Conditional imputation.* In this method, it is not the overall (unconditional) mean or median of a variable that is imputed for a missing value on that variable but rather a value based or conditional on as many as possible other patient characteristics. To do so, one commonly uses the data from all patients without missing values on the

variable, to develop a multivariable prediction model using regression analysis. In such a model, the variable with missing values is the dependent or outcome variable and all other patient characteristics are the independent or predictor variables. Subsequently, this imputation or prediction model is used in the patients with missing values on that variable to predict the most likely value conditional on his/her observed characteristics. After this, a complete data set has been established and standard software can be applied to estimate the association between the determinant(s) and outcome under study. We note that in the case of missing determinant values, the outcome variable must be included in the imputation model. Similarly, when outcome values are missing, all determinants under study should be included in the imputation model. This seems like a circular process. It has been shown, empirically, however, that imputation of outcome values that are MAR, using all observed information including the determinants under study, causes less bias in the associations between these same determinants and the outcome than, for example, unconditional imputation [Unnebrink & Windeler, 2001; Crawford et al., 1995; Rubin, 1996]. Similarly, imputation of missing determinant values using the outcome eventually results in less biased associations than imputations unconditional on the outcome [Moons et al., 2006]. This can simply be explained by appreciating that missing data on a determinant are commonly related to other determinants and directly or indirectly to the outcome, as was also shown in the earlier example of the diagnosis of bacterial meningitis and cancer. Conditional imputation can be done once (i.e., single imputation) or more than once (multiple imputation).

When missing data are MNAR, valuable information is lost from the data and there is no universal method of handling the missing data properly [Little & Rubin, 1987; Schafer, 1997; Vach, 1994; Schafer & Graham, 2002; Rubin, 1987]. When missing data are MCAR, the complete case analysis gives unbiased, although obviously less precise, results [Little & Rubin, 1987; Schafer, 1997; Vach, 1994; Schafer & Graham, 2002; Greenland & Finkle, 1995; Rubin, 1987; Moons et al., 2006]. However, the missing-indicator method and the unconditional mean imputation method still lead to biased results when data are MCAR [Greenland & Finkle, 1995; Donders et al., 2006]. In the case of MAR, which is most commonly encountered in research based on routine care data (as described earlier), a complete case analysis will result in biased associations between determinants and outcome due to selective missing data. Also, the indicator method and the unconditional mean imputation method then give biased results [Little & Rubin, 1987; Schafer, 1997; Vach, 1994; Schafer & Graham, 2002; Greenland & Finkle,

TEXTBOX 8.2 Example of a simulated diagnostic study with missing data

Consider a diagnostic study with only one continuous diagnostic test and a true disease status (present/absent).

We simulated 1000 samples of 500 subjects drawn from a theoretical population consisting of equal numbers of diseased and non-diseased subjects. The true regression coefficient in a logistic regression model linking the diagnostic test to the probability of disease was 1.0 (odds ratio = 2.7), with an intercept of 0. The diagnostic test was normally distributed with mean 0 and standard deviation 2. No other tests or subject characteristics were considered. In each sample, 80% of the non-diseased subjects was assigned a missing value on the test. The diseased subjects had no missing data. Accordingly, missing data were MAR as they were based on other observed variables; here the true disease status only. Overall about 40% of the data was missing. Using the procedure mice (for details about the software we refer to the literature [van Buuren, 1999]), ten multiple imputed data sets were created for each sample. Then the association between the test and the disease status plus standard error was estimated in each data set using a logistic regression model. Subsequently, all associations with standard errors were analyzed within each of the 10 multiply imputed data sets. The ten regression coefficients and standard errors were then combined using standard formulas [Rubin, 1987]. One extra data set was imputed and analyzed as a single imputed data set. Finally, the results were averaged over the 1000 simulations. For both the single and multiple imputation procedure, the estimate of the association was indeed unbiased. The single imputation procedure appears more precise because of the smaller standard error thus leading to smaller confidence intervals, but the 90% confidence interval does not contain the true parameter as often (only 63.6%) as it should, i.e. 90%. Multiple imputation leads to a larger standard error and wider confidence intervals, but the estimated standard errors are more correct and the confidence interval has the correct coverage (i.e., 90.3%). Hence, in contrast to single imputation, multiple imputation gives sound results both with respect to bias and precision.

Method	Regression coefficient	Standard error	Coverage of the 90% confidence intervals
Single imputation	0.98904	0.090186	63.6
Multiple imputation	0.98920	0.136962	90.3

Source: Author.

TEXTBOX 8.3 Illustration of the problems with the missing indicator method and the unconditional mean imputation, even when values are missing completely at random

Missing indicator method. We use the same example study as in Textbox 8.2, but consider a second continuous test, which is a proxy for the first test. This means that the second test is not directly related to the disease (OR = 1; regression coefficient = 0), but only via the first test. Fitting a logistic regression model to predict disease status using the first test only a positive regression coefficient is found (case 1). When only the second test is included, we also would find a positive association because of the indirect relation between disease status and the second test (case 2). Using both tests, only a positive association for the first test would be found, comparable to case 1, and a regression coefficient near 0 for the second test (case 3). Suppose there are missing values on the first test but not on the second test, and that these are MCAR, i.e. equal proportion in diseased and non-diseased subjects. We define a missing indicator variable as 1 if the result of the first test was missing and 0 otherwise. One can see that in a model to predict the true disease status using both tests plus missing indicator, the regression coefficient of the second test will not be 0 as it should be. For the subjects with no missing data indeed case 3 will apply. But for the subjects with a missing value on the first test, case 2—rather than case 3—suddenly applies as there are no observations for the first test. Hence the estimate for the regression coefficient of the second test is biased and will be somewhere between 0, the true estimate (case 3), and the value of case 2. Moreover, if the regression coefficient of the second test is biased, so is the regression coefficient of the first test due to the mutual adjustment in multivariable modelling. To illustrate this, we performed a second simulation study similar to that of Textbox 8.2. We again simulated 1000 samples of 500 subjects drawn from the same theoretical population, which now also included a proxy variable for the first test with a correlation of 0.75 with the first diagnostic test. For the first test 40% missing values were assigned completely at random, that is, 20% for the diseased and non-diseased. The table below shows that the regression coefficient of the diagnostic test is indeed heavily biased (as the true value is 1.0) and also of the proxy variable (as the true value is 0). Thus, although the indicator method has the appealing property that all available information and subjects are used in the analyses, the fact that it can lead to biased associations for the original variables is reason enough to discard this method even when missing data are MCAR, let alone when data are MAR.

Unconditional mean imputation. In the example study in Textbox 8.2 it may be obvious that the magnitude and significance of the association (regression coefficient) of the continuous test with the outcome is completely determined by the difference in overlap of the test result distributions between the diseased and non-diseased subjects. The less overlap, the higher and more

(continues)

TEXTBOX 8.3 Continued.

significant the regression coefficient. If the two distributions completely overlap, the regression coefficient will be 0. Consider the same simulation study as was used for the missing indicator method, with 40% missing values assigned completely at random (20% for the diseased and 20% for the non-diseased). Imputing or replacing these missing values by the overall mean of the test result as estimated from the remaining (observed) subjects—i.e., non-diseased and diseased subjects combined—will obviously increase the amount of overlap in the two test result distributions. Hence, the association between the test result and the outcome will dilute and the regression coefficient will be biased toward 0 and non-significance. This is illustrated in the lower part of this box. The regression coefficient is not 1 but 0.55. Like the indicator method, the overall mean imputation of missing values should also be discarded as it will lead to biased associations, even when missing data are MCAR.

Method	Diagnostic test Regression coefficient (standard error)	Proxy Regression coefficient (standard error)
Indicator method*	0.55 (0.14)	0.51 (0.08)
Overall mean	0.55 (0.14)	not applicable

*The logistic model included: $\ln[P(\text{Disease})/(1 - P(\text{Disease}))]$ = Intercept + b1 × Diagnostic test' + b2 × Proxy + b3 × Indicator, where the Indicator = 1 if the value for Diagnostic test was missing and 0 otherwise, and where Diagnostic test was set to 0 if its value was missing.

Source: Author.

1995; Donders et al., 2006; Moons et al., 2006]. Only more sophisticated techniques, like conditional single or multiple imputation and the maximum likelihood estimation method, give less biased or rather the most valid estimations of the study associations. Although single and multiple conditional imputations both yield unbiased results, the latter is preferred as it results in correctly estimated standard errors and confidence intervals; single imputation yields standard errors that are too small. All this is illustrated using simple simulation studies in Textboxes 8.2 and 8.3. Empirically, it has been shown that even in the presence of missing values in about half of the subjects, multiple conditional imputation still yields less biased results as compared to the commonly used complete case analysis [Moons et al., 2006]. The question arises, however, how many missing values one may accept and how many subjects can be imputed before multiple imputations will not suffice. There are yet no empirical studies showing an upper limit of missing values that can be imputed validly.

Apart from the above problems, routine care data comply with two essential characteristics of determinant data in descriptive (diagnostic and prognostic) research. First, routine care data are likely to match the range of variables that are of interest to the investigator. For example, if an investigator wants to study the diagnostic value of symptoms, signs, and results from diagnostic tests in setting a diagnosis of heart failure in general practice and the need for referral to secondary care, the patient files from primary care practices will likely provide those variables that a general practitioner will use when suspecting a patient of the disease. General practitioners may use electrocardiography but are unlikely to routinely have results from chest x-rays. Therefore, although chest x-rays may add diagnostic information, such data would not be relevant in view of the research question. Hence, the lack of this variable in the patient records is no problem. Second, routine data likely reflect a quality of data collection that is typical for the quality of the data in the application of the research findings in clinical practice. As an example, when the goal is to determine the diagnostic value of abdominal palpation for aortic aneurysms in patients suspected of this vascular problem, routine records with results from palpation performed by the average physician are likely to offer a better view on the diagnostic value of this test in the diagnostic work-up of these patients than when all patients were carefully examined by a highly skilled vascular surgeon.

To conclude, the extent to which patient data from routine care may effectively and validly be used to answer research questions depends on the type of research question and the type of research. For causal research, the availability and quality of confounder data needs to be carefully addressed and may often be shown to be inadequate. In descriptive research, it is important that the routine care data comprise all of the diagnostic or prognostic determinants to yield a relevant research result. For all types of research it is necessary that the patients can indeed be retrieved from the files based on uniform and unselective coding, that the outcome is assessed in each subject, and that missing data are properly dealt with.

Limitations of Cohort Studies

There are no intrinsic limitations of cohort studies. They offer a highly effective approach in epidemiology. However, there are situations in which cohort studies cannot be used and some research questions are difficult to address in a cohort study when the study is not experimental. Cohort studies in which data collection is prospective are generally time consuming and expensive. The time for a cohort study to be completed depends on the duration of follow-up, but for research on common causes of chronic disease this may require large numbers of subjects followed for considerable amounts of time. This makes a prospective approach less attractive when a quick answer is desired.

For the same reason, prospective cohort studies are expensive. They require the planned and systematic collection of data on the members on the cohort, which calls for an adequate infrastructure and personnel. Time and expenses may be less of a problem when data can be used that have already been recorded in the past, so data collection thus can be retrospective. However, rather than from practical limitations, retrospective data collection may suffer from incomplete or low-quality data because they were probably recorded without the current research question in mind. This may leave the investigator without important confounder data in etiological research or without a highly interesting prognostic indicator in prognostic research. It should be noted that sometimes confounding cannot be sufficiently removed even when extensive data on confounders are available. This may apply when the determinant of interest is too closely linked to a confounder, as for example, the indication for drug use that can hardly be separated from the drug use itself, or when the full range of confounders is unclear or difficult to measure. An example of the latter situation is given by the highly contradictory results of observational cohort studies and trials with regard to the putative cardioprotective effect of postmenopausal hormone replacement therapy. A range of well-designed prospective cohort studies supported the view that hormone replacement therapy reduced the risk of coronary heart disease. However, these study results were not substantiated when hormone replacement therapy was studied in randomized trials. Unmeasured confounders could account for this discrepancy, and the indication for treatment in observational studies may have played a role.

Finally, there remains discussion as to whether the randomized trials have included the same women that were included in the observational research [Van der Schouw & Grobbee, 2005]. It is important to realize that for a given population, the only difference between a randomized trial and an observational cohort study lies in the fact that in the randomized trial the determinant (e.g., drug use) is randomly allocated to the members of the cohort, whereas in the observational study the participants are *naturally* exposed to the determinant. In the latter setting, exposure to the determinant is either a characteristic of certain individuals or the individuals have chosen to be exposed or the exposure is applied by someone else, such as a physician prescribing a drug. Any reason for being exposed that in itself is associated with the outcome could act as a confounder and should therefore be taken into account. If this is not possible, then the cohort study will not yield valid results.

Worked-Out Example: The SMART Study

As a result of both aging and the impact of factors such as elevated choles-terol, diabetes, or high blood pressure, arteries may stiffen. Increased arte-rial stiffness amplifies the risk of future symptomatic cardiovascular events that these factors by themselves already confer. Whether arterial stiffening also increases the risk of reoccurrence of events in those who have already been diagnosed with manifest arterial disease is largely unknown.

At the University Medical Center Utrecht, a cohort is continuously being built up of patients referred with symptomatic cardiovascular disease, named the Second Manifestations of ARTerial disease (SMART) cohort. This is an example of a cohort study that can be conducted with patients who are referred to a hospital as part of routine care. In the SMART cohort, we prospectively examined whether stiffer arteries put patients with diagnosed cardiovascular disease at increased risk of re-occurrence of events and of cardiovascular mortality [Dijk et al., 2005] (Textbox 8.4).

TEXTBOX 8.4 Cohort study on the causal link between carotid stiffness and new vascular events in patients with manifest cardiovascular disease

AIMS: To study whether arterial stiffness is related to the risk of new vascu-lar events in patients with manifest arterial disease and to examine whether this relation varies between patients who differ with respect to baseline vascular risk, arterial stiffness, or systolic blood pressure (SPB). METHODS AND RESULTS: The study was performed in the first consecutive 2183 pa-tients with manifest arterial disease enrolled in the SMART study (Second Manifestations of ARTerial disease), a cohort study among patients with manifest arterial disease or cardiovascular risk factors. Common carotid distension (i.e., the change in carotid diameter in systole relative to diastole) was measured at baseline by ultrasonography. With the distension, several stiffness parameters were determined. In the entire cohort, none of the carotid artery stiffness parameters was related to the occurrence of vascular events. However, decreased stiffness was related to decreased vascular risk in subjects with low baseline SPB. The relation of carotid stiffness with vas-cular events did not differ between tertiles of baseline risk and carotid stiff-ness. CONCLUSION: Carotid artery stiffness is no independent risk factor for vascular events in patients with manifest arterial disease. However, in patients with low SBP, decreased carotid stiffness may indicate a decreased risk of vascular events.

Source: Dijk DJ, Algra A, van der Graaf Y, Grobbee DE, Bots ML on behalf of the SMART study group. Carotid stiffness and the risk of new vascular events in patients with manifest cardiovascular disease. The SMART study. Eur Heart J. 2005 Jun; 26 (12): 1213-20. Epub 2005 Apr 11.

Theoretical Design

The research question was, "Does arterial stiffness predict recurrent vascular events in patients with manifest vascular disease?" This leads to the etiological occurrence relation: incidence of vascular events as a function of arterial stiffness conditional on confounders. The domain is "patients referred to hospital, and diagnosed with cardiovascular disease." The operational definition of "recurrent vascular disease (the outcome) was vascular death, ischemic stroke, coronary ischemic disease, and the composite of these vascular events." Measurement of arterial stiffness was operationalized by measurement of distension of the left and right common carotid arteries. Measurement of several possible confounders and effect modifiers was operationalized using questionnaires, blood chemistry, and measurement of blood pressure.

Design of Data Collection

Data were collected from an ongoing (since September 1, 1996) prospective single-center cohort of patients aged 18 to 80 years with manifest arterial disease who were referred to the University Medical Center Utrecht. More then 6000 patients were enrolled during ten years. For the arterial stiffness substudy, data from patients included from September 1, 1996, until March 1, 2003, were used because during that time period, the necessary vascular measurements were obtained. At baseline, a general questionnaire on cardiovascular risk factors and previously diagnosed diseases was completed (Table 8.1).

At the screening visit, simple measurements such as blood pressure, height, and weight were done and venous blood samples were taken for analysis of blood chemistry. Common carotid intima-media thickness

TABLE 8.1 General characteristics of the study population ($n = 2183$)

Men (%)	75
Age (years)	59.7
Systolic blood pressure (SBP) (mm Hg)	141
Diastolic blood pressure (DBP) (mm Hg)	79
Mean arterial pressure (MAP) (mm Hg)	99
Triglycerides (mmol/L)	2.0
Total cholesterol (mmol/L)	5.5

Dijk DJ, Algra A, van der Graaf Y, Grobbee DE, Bots ML on behalf of the SMART Study Group. Carotid stiffness and the risk of new vascular events in patients with manifest cardiovascular disease. The SMART Study. Eur Heart J. 2005 Jun; 26(12):1213–20.

(CIMT) was measured at the left and right common carotid arteries with an ATL Ultramark 9 (Advanced Technology Laboratories, Bethel, WA, USA) equipped with a 10 MHz linear array transducer. Duplex scanning of the carotid arteries was performed for assessment of presence of internal carotid artery stenosis. Stiffness was assessed by measurement of distension of the left and right common carotid arteries. The distension of an artery is the change in diameter in systole relative to the diastolic diameter during the cardiac cycle. The displacement of the walls of the left and right common carotid artery was measured with a Wall Track System (Scanner 200, Pie Medical, Maastricht, The Netherlands) equipped with a 7.5 MHz linear transducer. To obtain information on baseline vascular risk, the previously developed SMART risk score was used. The SMART risk score is based on baseline data of pre-existing disease and risk factors. Patients receive points for gender, age, body mass index, smoking behavior, hyperlipidemia, hyperglycemia, hypertension, medication use, medical history, and prevalent vascular disease at baseline. Patients were biannually asked to fill in a questionnaire on hospitalizations and outpatient clinic visits in the preceding six months. Events of interest for this study were vascular death, ischemic stroke, coronary ischemic disease, and the composite of these vascular events. When a possible event was recorded by the participant, hospital discharge letters and results of relevant laboratory and radiology examinations were collected. With this information, all events were audited by three members of the SMART study Endpoint Committee comprising physicians from different departments.

Design of Data Analysis

The principal analysis was performed on the participants who were included from September 1, 1996, until March 1, 2003, excluding the 193 patients in whom stiffness measurements were missing due to equipment failure or logistical problems, and the measurements of 94 participants in whom the intra-individual variance between stiffness measurements was considered out of range, and of six patients in whom no follow-up information was available. Finally, the data of 2183 participants were used in the analysis.

Because the main interest was the causal relation between arterial stiffness and new cardiovascular events, age, mean arterial pressure, sex, pack-years smoked, and use of antihypertensive medication were considered as potential confounders. The modifying effect of baseline systolic blood pressure and baseline risk was investigated by calculating separate hazard ratios for tertiles of systolic blood pressure and baseline risk. First, the crude hazard ratio for arterial stiffness (per standard deviation increase in stiffness) was calculated with the Cox proportional hazard analysis (Model I in Table 8.2). Next, age was included in the model (Model II in the table) and, finally, an additional adjustment for potential confounders (notably mean arterial pressure, sex, pack-years smoked, and use of antihypertensive medication at baseline) was done (Model III in the table). To evaluate whether baseline risk (with the SMART score) and systolic blood pressure (SBP) were effect modifiers, interaction terms were included in the model and stratified analyses were performed in tertiles of baseline risk and SBP.

Implications and Relevance

The results of this study show that in patients with manifest arterial disease, increasing arterial stiffness, unadjusted, is associated with an increased risk of vascular events and vascular death. The relationship disappears after adjustment for age (Table 8.2). Thus, in this population as a whole, carotid stiffness is not an independent risk factor for the occurrence of vascular events. Stiffness probably reflects the (long-term) exposure to several of these risk

TABLE 8.2   Relationship between carotid stiffness and vascular events

Vascular event (no. of events)	Model	Hazard ratio (95% CI)
		Distension/SD[a]
All vascular events (192)	I	0.87 (0.75–1.01)
	II	0.97 (0.85–1.17)
	III	0.95 (0,79–1.13)
Vascular death (107)	I	0.74 (0.59–0.91)
	II	0.94 (0.75–1.18)
	III	0.86 (0.67–1.11)
Ischemic stroke (47)	I	1.14 (0.87–1.51)
	II	1.20 (0.89–1.61)
	III	1.20 (0.86–1.63)
Coronary ischemic event (117)	I	0.86 (0.71–1.05)
	II	0.99 (0.81–1.23)
	III	0.92 (0.73–1.16)

Key:

Model I: unadjusted
Model II: Model I additionally adjusted for age
Model III: Model II additionally adjusted for mean arterial pressure, sex, age^2, pack-years smoked, and use of antihypertensive medication at baseline

[a] In all models adjusted for end-diastolic diameter carotid arteries and mean arterial pressure.

Dijk DJ, Algra A, van der Graaf Y, Grobbee DE, Bots ML on behalf of the SMART Study Group. Carotid stiffness and the risk of new vascular events in patients with manifest cardiovascular disease. The SMART Study. Eur Heart J. 2005 Jun; 26(12):1213–20.

factors but does not increase the risk of these patients over and beyond the risk conferred by the risk factors. We did find that in patients with low SBP, patients with less stiff vessels had a lower vascular risk. Previous studies, largely in patients without diagnosed vascular disease and thus at a yet lesser developed stage of cardiovascular damage, mainly showed a direct relationship between arterial stiffness and subsequent disease, although the magnitude varied considerably. In our patient group, we found no relationship between arterial stiffness and vascular events.

As published data mainly reported on subjects with risk factors for vascular disease who generally can be considered to have a lower risk than the patients with manifest arterial disease in our study, the different reported relationship between arterial stiffness and vascular disease may be explained by an association between arterial stiffness and vascular events in low-risk patients only. However, the observation in studies on patients with end-stage renal disease who are known to be at high vascular risk, that arterial stiffness was associated with vascular events, does not agree with this explanation. Moreover, our finding that the association between arterial stiffness and vascular events is not modified by baseline risk does not support this hypothesis either.

9

Case-Control Studies

There is no doubt that of all the available approaches to data collection in epidemiology, case-control studies continue to attract the most controversy (see Textbox 9.1). On the one hand this is understandable, because an abundant number of poorly conducted case-control studies have been reported in the literature and most textbooks in epidemiology present famous examples of case-control studies that produced biased results. Indeed, the validity of case-control studies in general is often questioned, and some epidemiologists go as far as to place case-control studies at the low end of their hierarchy of study designs, just above the case-report or case-series. This is illustrated by the following statement drawn from the first edition of a textbook by of one of the founders of clinical epidemiology:

> If the best you can find is a case-control study, you must recognize that this is a weak design that often has led to erroneous conclusions [Sackett et al., 1985].

On the other hand, one cannot deny that since their introduction in clinical research in 1920, case-control studies have proven their potential value, notably in etiologic research, and in particular in identifying and quantifying risks of drugs. These include the association between aspirin use and Reye syndrome in children [Hurwitz et al., 1987] and of diethylstilboestrol (DES) use by pregnant women and the occurrence of clear-cell vaginal carcinoma in their daughters [Herbst et al., 1971]. The potential strength of case-control studies in medicine was emphasized by Kenneth Rothman in the first edition of his textbook:

> The sophisticated use and understanding of case-control studies is the most outstanding methodological development of modern epidemiology [Rothman, 1986].

TEXTBOX 9.1 Warhol's "Campbell Soup Can"

Many researchers conduct case-control studies where a group of patients with a certain disease is identified and compared with another group who does not have the disease. Selection of controls is often done as if quickly opening a "can" of non-cases, without an appreciation of the primary principal of case-control studies: controls should be representative of the population experience from which the cases emerge. In addition, there is a tendency to match controls to the cases according to a range of characteristics (notably, potential confounders). This often results in very atypical control subjects (those with many risk factors for the disease but who manage not to develop the disease), who share more similarities with "museum exhibits" than with existing individuals. Consequently, and unfortunately, too many case-control studies could be summarized by the famous Andy Warhol canvas "Campbell Soup Can."

Source: Author.

Although these rather opposing views on the value of case-control studies were expressed over 20 years ago, discussions regarding the validity of case-control studies continue. The reasons for the air of suspicion surrounding the results of case-control studies are difficult to fully elucidate but are no doubt related to both the complexity of their design and the prevailing misconception about their rationale and essence among both researchers performing them and the readers and reviewers of case-control study results. In addition, case-control studies are often applied in etiological research and because these studies are non-experimental by definition, confounding may bias the results and should be dealt with appropriately. Of course, appropriate coping with confounding holds equally true for non-experimental cohort studies.

The main problem with case-control studies is that too often they are presented as "quick and dirty" epidemiological studies involving some group of cases (those with the outcome or disease of interest) and a group (sometimes even several groups) of readily available human beings without that particular outcome (controls), often matched to the cases according to several (sometimes > 10) characteristics such as age, gender, and comorbidity. Then, the determinant of interest, typically a risk factor believed to be causally implicated in the disease, as well as potential confounders are measured in both cases and controls, producing an adjusted measure of association (usually an odds ratio) between the determinant and outcome. Too often, such studies are conducted and presented without appreciation of the principles of case-control studies, and they do not provide the reader with the rationale for the design of data collection chosen: Why choose a case-control study? Why these particular cases? Why this control group? Why is there (no) matching of cases and controls? This leaves the reader with the difficult task of judging the validity of these choices and therefore the results.

In this chapter, we first present the rationale and essence of case-control studies, provide a brief history of case-control studies in clinical research, and emphasize the methods available to identify cases and, in particular, to sample controls. Furthermore, several more recently developed types of case-control studies, including case-cohort and case-crossover studies, are reviewed critically. We argue that when the principles of case-control studies are appreciated, these studies can be of great value in both causal and descriptive clinical research.

Rationale and Essence of Case-Control Studies

Case-control studies are conducted for *efficiency* reasons. Under certain circumstances, it may be cumbersome or even impossible to study an entire cohort or dynamic population during a certain time period. Examples include: when the outcome of interest is very rare (for example, anaphylactic shock following the use of a certain drug); when the time between exposure to the determinant and the occurrence of the outcome is very long (for example, the use of DES by pregnant women and the occurrence of vaginal carcinoma in their daughters) or unknown; or when the measurement of the determinant(s) and other relevant variables (e.g., confounders) is time-consuming, patient-burdening, and/or expensive (e.g., when imaging techniques or DNA-material are involved). Instead of studying the *census* (that is all members of the cohort or dynamic population during the entire follow-up period) in detail, it is more efficient to study only those who develop the outcome of interest during the study period (the *cases*) and a *sample* of the population from where the cases emerge (the *controls*). The determinant(s) of interest and other relevant factors (typically the potential confounders in case of etiologic research but also possible modifiers when one is interested in assessing effect modification) are then measured in cases and controls only (Textbox 9.2).

In terms of the *design of data collection* (see Chapter 7), the essence of case-control studies is, therefore, *sampling* (as opposed to census). The strength of case-control studies is that they allow the researcher to quantify the occurrence relation of interest by studying cases and only a sample of the population where the cases stem from, while still producing the same estimates as would have been obtained from a cohort or dynamic population study (i.e., using a census approach). A valid result, however, can only be guaranteed when the controls are sampled correctly from the population experience from which the cases emerge.

TEXTBOX 9.2 Case-control studies: semantics

One of the problems surrounding case-control studies is the large number of terms applied to indicate the case-control method or to describe its subtypes. A non-exhaustive list includes:

Case-referent study	Case-cohort study
TROHOC study	Nested case-control study
Retrospective study	Case-crossover study
	Case-only study
	Case-specular study

The left row lists alternative terms for case-control studies that have been suggested over the years. Although the term *case-referent study* seems more appropriate, we propose to only use the term case-control study to ensure that both researchers and readers understand the underlying methodology. Especially terms such as TROHOC (the reverse of cohort study) and retrospective studies should be avoided [Schulz & Grimes, 2002], because they imply a "reverse" nature of the case-control approach (from disease to determinant instead of the other way around), while the direction of the occurrence relation in fact is similar as studies using a census approach: outcome as a function of the determinant. Moreover, case-control studies can be both retrospective and prospective. In the right row, several types of case-control studies are listed. These terms could be used, because they do indicate several methods that can be applied in case-control studies, as long as one realizes that these studies are in fact case-control studies in that they sample controls from the study base.

Source: Author.

Figure 9.1 illustrates the essence of a case-control study [Hoes, 1995b]. A population, being a cohort, dynamic population, or (less frequently) a cross-section of these, is identified. Although one can also imagine cross-sectional case-control studies (where the time-dimension is zero), let us assume that a population is followed for a certain time period and that the aim of the study is to quantify the association of a determinant (det) with the future occurrence of a particular disease (dis). The population followed over time is often referred to as the *study base* or the *source population*. It equals the population experience available to perform the study. Members of the population do not yet have the disease under study when the investigation starts. Part of the population members will have the determinant or exposure of interest (det+) and others will not (det−). In addition, other characteristics or co-variables, notably confounders when the aim is to study etiology, of the participants may be relevant.

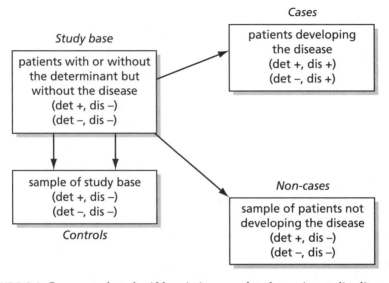

FIGURE 9.1 Case control study. Abbreviations are det, determinant; dis, disease.

In a *census* approach, such as in a cohort study, including a randomized trial, all members of the study population will be identified when they enter the study and all relevant characteristics, including the determinants and co-variables of interest, will be measured. Then, all members will be monitored over time to establish whether they do (dis+) or do not (dis–) develop the disease. At the end of the study, the incidence of the disease in those with and without the determinants can be compared, where the numerators are provided by the number of cases (cases in Figure 9.1), and the denominator either by the total number of participants with and without the determinant (when cumulative incidences are calculated) or by the number of person-years those with and without the determinants contribute to the study base (when incidence rates are calculated).

In a case-control and thus a *sampling* approach, the same study base as in the census approach is being followed over time to monitor the occurrence of the disease of interest. In contrast, however, the determinants and relevant co-variables are not measured in all members of the study base, but only in those developing the disease (the *cases*) and in a sample of the study base (*controls* or *referents*). The term *referents* is more appropriate because it clearly indicates that the sample members are referents from the study base from which the cases emerge, but we use the term *controls* because of its widespread use in the literature. By definition, the members of the control group do not have the disease of interest when they are selected as controls.

It should be emphasized, however, that the controls are not a sample of the *non-cases* (shown in Figure 9.1), because these non-cases represent those participants who do not develop the disease during the total follow-up period. In fact, some of the members of the control group could subsequently develop the disease. Therefore, in the likely event of changes in the population during the study period (often new people will enter and others leave the study base with or without having developed the outcome), it is wiser not to sample controls at one specific time during the study, but at several time points during the entire study experience, to ensure a proper representation of the study base from whom the cases develop. Below, the methods to validly sample controls from the study base will be outlined in more detail with the introduction of the "swimming-pool principle."

A Brief History of Case-Control Studies in Clinical Research

The case-control method was developed in the field of sociology. To our knowledge, the first case-control study in medicine was published in 1920 (Figure 9.2 and Table 9.3) [Broders], assessing the role of smoking in the development of epithelioma of the lip. Smoking habits of 537 patients with epithelioma of the lip were compared to 500 patients without epithelioma. Although tobacco use was similar in both groups (79% and 80%, respectively), the proportion of pipe smokers was much higher in the cases (78%) than in the controls (38%). In this first case-control study, neither additional characteristics of the control group nor information on the way controls were sampled were provided. In addition, no formal measure of association between pipe smoking and lip carcinoma was calculated and no discussion on possible confounding was included, let alone that the author adjusted for confounding in the analysis. These latter limitations are understandable, because it took an additional 30 years for the (exposure) odds ratio (the measure of association usually applied in case-control studies) to be introduced and eight more years before a method to adjust for confounding was first described. Nevertheless, a causal association between pipe smoking and epithelioma of the lip was later confirmed in other studies.

The year 1950 heralded an important period in the acceptance of the case-control method in clinical research. In that year, four case-control studies assessing the association between tobacco consumption and the risk of lung cancer were published. Despite methodological problems in several aspects, including the way the control group was sampled and misclassification of smoking history, these early studies clearly illustrated the potential of this study design.

SQUAMOUS-CELL EPITHELIOMA OF THE LIP

A STUDY OF FIVE HUNDRED AND THIRTY-SEVEN CASES *

A. C. BRODERS, M.D.
ROCHESTER, MINN.

Of all the malignant neoplasms with which man is afflicted, few cause more concern and inconvenience than that of epithelioma of the lip. In the past, pathologists have been content to classify cancer of the lip as cancer, without any distinction as to the degree of malignancy. It is a well established fact that some cancers of the lip are fatal to patients and others are not. There must be a reason for this. One theory is that some persons are resistant to cancer, and this seems to be borne out ·in a certain percentage of cases.

Undoubtedly, a large proportion of cancer cells are destroyed by the defense cells of the body; of these, the fibrous connective tissue cell is the most important, since it cuts off nourishment from the cancer cells.

The endothelial leukocyte and lymphocyte evidently also play an important rôle in the destruction of cancer cells, for practically always they may be seen in the neighborhood of a cancerous growth. Foreign body giant cells that are most probably formed from the endothelial leukocytes are not infrequently found lying adjacent to cancer cells.

The most important factor in squamous-cell epithelioma of the lip seems to be the degree of cellular activity. The cells of some epitheliomas of the lip show a marked tendency to differentiate, that is, to produce a growth similar to the normal; the pearly body is an example. The pearly body corresponds to the horny layer of the epidermis. In other squamous-cell epitheliomas there is no differentiation whatever. In the large majority of growths whose cells show no

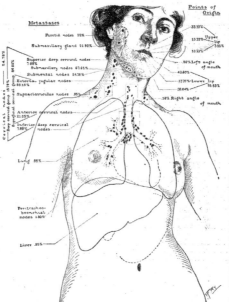

Fig. 1.—Percentages of points of origin of epithelioma of the lip, and percentages of location of metastasis.

tendency to differentiate, or at least very little, there are many mitotic figures.

In studying these epitheliomas, therefore, it occurred to me that they should be graded according to differentiation and mitosis, special stress being laid on the former. The grading was made on a basis of 1 to 4, and absolutely independent of the clinical history. If an epithelioma shows a marked tendency to differentiate, that is, if about three fourths of its structure is differentiated epithelium and one fourth undifferentiated epithelium, it is graded 1; if the differentiated and undifferentiated epithelium are about equal, it is graded 2; if the undifferentiated epithelium forms about three fourths and the differentiated about one fourth of the growth, it is graded 3; if there is no tendency of the cells to differentiate, it is graded 4. Of course the number of mitotic figures and the number of cells with single large deeply staining nucleoli (one-eyed cells) play an important part in the grading.

Some epitheliomas of the lip are very active and from the start show little or no tendency to differentiate; some grow more malignant with time, and others increase in malignancy and then retrogress. Unquestionably an epithelioma of a low grade of malignancy is made more malignant by irritation with chemicals such as hydrochloric or nitric acid, silver nitrate or arsenic paste.

Chronic ulcers of the lip, like chronic ulcers of the stomach, should be examined very closely for cancer, provided syphilis has been eliminated. MacCarty [1] has demonstrated early cancer in the epithelium at or near the edge of gastric ulcers; practically the same process is found in early cancer or ulcer of the lip. In the lip the cancer starts in the stratum germinativum of the epithelium at or near the border of the ulcer. Not all cancers of the lip are preceded by ulcers, but the majority are.

I shall present the facts in statistical form and make the deductions, not from one, but from various standpoints: (1) the duration and size of the lesion; (2) the

* From the Section on Surgical Pathology, Mayo Clinic.
* Presented before the Richmond Academy of Medicine and Surgery, Richmond ,Va., Nov. 25, 1919, and before the Roanoke Academy of Medicine, Roanoke, Va., Dec. 1, 1919.

1. MacCarty, W. C.: Pathology and Clinical Significance of Gastric Ulcer: From a Study of Material from Two Hundred and Sixteen Partial Gastrectomies for Ulcer, Ulcer and Carcinoma, and Carcinoma, Surg., Gynec. & Obst. **10**: 449-462, 1910.

FIGURE 9.2 The first report of a case-control study published in the medical literature in 1920.

Reprinted with permission from the American Medical Association. Broders AC. Squamous-cell epithelioma of the lip. A study of 537 cases. JAMA 1920;74:656–64.

In 1951, Cornfield gave a strong impulse to the further application of the case-control method by proving that, under the assumption that the outcome at interest is rare, the odds ratio resulting from a case-control study equals the incidence ratio that would result from a cohort study [Cornfield, 1951]. Another influential paper was published in 1959 where Mantel and Haenszel described a procedure to derive odds ratios from stratified data and thus enabled adjustment for potential confounding variables. Later, Miettinen [1976b] made several important contributions to the development of case-control studies, including landmark publications on how to appropriately sample controls from the study base in such a way that the resulting odds ratio always (also when the outcome is *not* rare) provides a valid estimate of the incidence density ratio that would be observed in a cohort study.

Over the last decades, the case-control method has been applied throughout the field of clinical medicine far beyond research on cancer etiology for which it was first developed. The method also provides important applications for the study of treatment efficacy and adverse effect of interventions. Especially for the latter, case-control studies have proven their enormous potential. Examples include studies on the risk of fatal asthma in recipients of beta-agonists, cancer of the vagina in daughters of mothers receiving DES during their pregnancy, and, more recently, deep venous thrombosis resulting from the use of third generation oral contraceptives. Thus far, the case-control method has not been widely applied in descriptive research, but its efficiency in both diagnostic and prognostic research is increasingly being recognized.

Theoretical Design

The occurrence relation and associated research question may take any form, depending on the objective of the case-control study. Usually, case-control studies are applied when the goal is to unravel causality and therefore the occurrence relation should include conditionality on extraneous factors (i.e., confounders).

More recently, the case-control method has been applied in descriptive research. The study presented in Textbox 9.3 illustrates the efficiency of the design in a prognostic case-control study that assessed the value of bone resorption markers in predicting the future occurrence of bone metastases in patients with resectable non-small-cell lung cancer [Papotti et al., 2006]. The ten expensive prognostic markers were measured only in cases and controls.

PURPOSE: Bone metastases (BM) in non-small-cell lung cancer (NSCLC) may be detected at diagnosis or during the course of the disease, and are associated with a worse prognosis. Currently, there are no predictive or diagnostic markers to identify high-risk patients for metastatic bone dissemination. PATIENTS AND METHODS: Thirty patients with resected NSCLC who subsequently developed BM were matched for clinicopathologic parameters to 30 control patients with resected NSCLC without any metastases and 26 patients with resected NSCLC and non-BM lesions. Primary tumors were investigated by immunohistochemistry for 10 markers involved in bone resorption or development of metastases. Differences among groups were estimated by chi2 test, whereas the prognostic impact of clinicopathologic parameters and marker expression was evaluated by univariate (Wilcoxon and Mantel-Cox tests) and multivariate (Cox proportional hazards regression model) analyses. RESULTS: The presence of bone sialoprotein (BSP) was strongly associated with bone dissemination ($P < .001$) and, independently, with worse outcome ($P = .02$, Mantel-Cox test), as defined by overall survival. To evaluate BSP protein expression in nonselected NSCLC, a series of 120 consecutive resected lung carcinomas were added to the study, and BSP prevalence reached 40%. No other markers showed a statistically significant difference among the three groups or demonstrated a prognostic impact, in terms of both overall survival and time interval to metastases. CONCLUSION: BSP protein expression in the primary resected NSCLC is strongly associated with BM progression and could be useful in identifying high-risk patients who could benefit from novel modalities of surveillance and preventive treatment.

TEXTBOX 9.3 A prognostic case-control study on bone sialoprotein and bone metastases in patients with non-small-cell lung cancer

Source: Papotti M, Kalebic T, Volante M, Chiusa L, Bacillo E, Cappia S, Lausi P, Novello S, Borasio P, Scagliotti GV. Bone sialoprotein is predictive of bone metastases in respectable non-small-cell lung cancer: a retrospective case-control study. J Clin Oncol 2006;24:4818–24.

Design of Data Collection

Sampling in Non-Experimental and (Usually) Longitudinal Studies

By definition, case-control studies take a sampling (not a census) approach and are non-experimental. Because most case-control studies address causality, they are longitudinal, that is, there is conceptual time between the presence of a determinant and occurrence of the outcome (t > 0). Typically, diagnostic case-control studies are cross-sectional, where the time axis equals zero.

It should be emphasized that case-control studies can be both prospective and retrospective. When all data on determinant(s), outcome, and other factors (confounders, modifiers) are already available when the researcher initiates the study, the case-control study is retrospective. Often, however, a case-control study is prospective, so the researcher develops a method to identify cases, starting "now" and ending when enough cases have been included and further samples a control group during the same time period. The common view that case-control studies are retrospective by definition is wrong.

Analogy of a Swimming Pool, Lifeguard Chair, and a Net

When designing a case-control study, it may be helpful to compare the study base from which both the cases and controls originate with a swimming pool. The researcher should then envision him- or herself sitting on a lifeguard chair, overlooking the water surface from a distance, while holding a net with a long handle (Figure 9.3).

In the swimming pool, a changing population is present where several swimmers have the determinant(s) of interest and the remaining swimmers

FIGURE 9.3 A swimming pool, a lifeguard chair, and a net.

Source: Aerial of swimming pool, © Carolina/ShutterStock, Inc.; Man using net, © Eyüp Alp Ermis/ShutterStock, Inc.; Lifeguard chair, © Brett Stoltz/ShutterStock, Inc.

do not. Importantly, as in an ordinary swimming pool, people can enter and leave the study, and possibly re-enter it. Such a dynamic population most closely resembles the source populations of many case-control studies, which may include inhabitants of a certain town or region, those enlisted with a primary care practice or a health maintenance organization, or the catchment population of a certain hospital (i.e., those living in the vicinity of a hospital, who would be referred to that hospital should they develop the disease of interest). New people may enter these populations when they are born, move to that particular area, and so on, and they may also leave this study base (swimming pool) for various reasons (e.g., when they die, move away from the area, or develop the outcome under study). The role of the researcher closely resembles that of the lifeguard sitting high up in a chair, overlooking the swimming pool. Typically, the lifeguard does not know exactly how many individuals are in the pool at a certain point in time, nor their characteristics, let alone their identities. In case-control terminology, the determinant and other relevant characteristics (e.g., confounders) are not measured in all individuals in the study base. The net is designed such that it will catch those fulfilling the criteria of the case disease of interest. Once a swimmer gets into trouble or—worse—is floating around in the pool (i.e., becomes a case), then the lifeguard springs into action and uses the net to capture the case. This happens each time a case occurs.

Consider a case-control study in the pool where the mission is to select a control series who are representative of the pool population. Because the controls in a case-control study should be representative of the study base from which the cases originate and the population of a swimming pool changes continuously, it is preferable to sample the controls at different points in time and not at one specific point in time. One possibility is to sample one (or a few, say three) control from the swimming pool each time a case is taken out of the pool. Then, the lifeguard who is still sitting in the chair, takes the net and *randomly* samples other swimmers (controls) from the pool. By definition, these controls are representatives of the swimming pool from which the cases emerge. Subsequently, the lifeguard (i.e., researcher) gets out of the chair and closely examines the cases and the randomly sampled controls (in case-control terminology, the researcher measures the determinant and other relevant characteristics). Alternatives for sampling controls each time a case is identified are available, such as sampling at random points in time.

The principles of identifying cases and sampling controls also apply to a case-control study that is being conducted within a cohort, that is, a particular swimming pool that is closed at some point in time and does not allow new individuals to enter. In contrast to the more typical dynamic source population outlined in previous paragraphs, the number of swimmers included in the pool (i.e., the size of the initial cohort) is generally known. Just as in other case-control studies, however, the researcher obtains information on determinant and other relevant characteristics in the cases and the sampled controls only. The methods available to validly sample controls within a cohort study as well as from a dynamic population is discussed later in this chapter.

Identification of Cases

As in any other type of study, the definition of the outcome is crucial. The challenge of the researcher lies in designing a "net" that is capable of capturing all members of the swimming pool (study base) that fulfill the case definition during the study period, while ignoring those not fulfilling the case criteria. In addition, a date at which the outcome occurred should be designated to each case to facilitate valid sampling of the control subjects.

Ideally, existing registries should be applied to identify all cases during a time period. Examples include cancer or death registries, hospital discharge diagnoses, or coded diagnoses in primary care of health maintenance organization databases. It should be emphasized that the number of false-positive and -negative diagnoses may be considerable and they clearly depend on the outcome; for example, death is much easier to diagnose than depression, benign prostatic hyperplasia, or sinusitis.

When valid registries of the case disease are not available, then ad-hoc registries may be necessary. For example, in a case-control study on the risk for sudden cardiac death of diuretics and other classes of blood pressure lowering drugs, we developed a method to detect cases of sudden cardiac death among all treated hypertensive patients in a well-defined geographical area [Hoes at al, 1995a]. During the 2.5-year study period, all doctors signing a death certificate received a very short questionnaire, including a question about the period between the onset of symptoms and the occurrence of death and the probability of a cardiac origin. Sudden cardiac death was defined as death occurring within one hour of symptom onset and in which a cardiac origin could not be excluded.

Although in theory, rigorous criteria to define the case disease should be applied, one should weigh the feasibility of these methods against the consequences of false-positive diagnoses and of missing cases (false-negatives). Misclassification of the outcome will dilute the association between the determinant and the outcome in case such misclassification occurs independently from the determinants studied. Usually, false-positive diagnosis (i.e., non-cases counted as cases) leads to a larger bias in case-control studies than non-recognition of cases; most of these false-negatives will not be sampled as controls because in most case-control studies the outcome is rare. Consequently, incompleteness of a registry does not necessarily reduce the validity of a study. Misclassification also could be differential and indeed depend on the presence of the determinant. In a case-control study on the risk for deep vein thrombosis among users of different types of oral contraceptives, such differential misclassification might occur when thrombosis is more often classified as such in women using particular oral contraceptives. The bias resulting from such misclassification may be considerable, but often its direction and magnitude are difficult to predict.

Prevalent or Incident Cases

By definition a cross-sectional case-control study, such as a diagnostic case-control study, will include prevalent cases only. In the vast majority of case-control studies, however, the time dimension is not zero and the study base (swimming pool) is followed over time, either prospectively or retrospectively. The goal of these case-control studies is to quantify the *incidence* of the outcome as a function of determinants(s) and it is logical to include incident cases. This is analogous to a cohort or dynamic population study in which the numerator of the incidence rates will include incident disease only.

Especially when the incidence of the outcome is very low, which is one of the main reasons to choose a case-control design, inclusion of an adequate number of incident cases may be extremely difficult. Under such circumstances, one might consider including prevalent cases, or to combine incident and prevalent cases. However, potential major drawbacks exist for using prevalent cases.

First and foremost, one should realize that the prevalence of disease reflects both the incidence and the duration of the disease. Assume that a case-control study aims to quantify the relationship between radiation because of an earlier cancer and the development of leukemia as a secondary malignancy. A researcher could decide to include prevalent cases of leukemia being treated at several clinics in the region. This will lead to the inclusion of patients who on average have a better prognosis (survivors) than if only incident cases were considered, because the former group includes more patients with a longer survival time. In case radiation causes leukemia with a relatively poor prognosis, a case-control study using prevalent cases may fail to show the increased risk.

Second, it is sometimes difficult to ensure that the determinant preceded the outcome and to exclude the possibility that the outcome changed the determinant when prevalent cases are used. The resulting bias obviously depends on the determinant of interest; for example, food intake poses many more potential problems here than gender or a genetic marker. In a case-control study on the association between coffee consumption and pancreatic cancer using prevalent cases, it may be difficult to rule out that (an early phase of) the disease changes coffee drinking habits.

However, when the determinant is unlikely to influence the duration of the case disease or survival and the "chicken or egg" (which came first?) dilemma plays no role, the inclusion of prevalent cases may further increase the efficiency of case-control studies. Moreover, a disease is often diagnosed (i.e., considered *incident*) quite some time after the first clinical symptoms occur, for example, in diabetes mellitus or rheumatoid arthritis. Consequently, under these circumstance *incident* cases may actually represent prevalent cases.

Vandenbroucke and co-workers [1982] examined the alleged protective effect of oral contraceptives on the development of rheumatoid arthritis. A case-control design was chosen because rheumatoid arthritis is relatively rare and they included prevalent cases because the incidence of the disease is extremely low. The findings of the study are summarized in Table 9.1.

In the discussion paragraph of their article, the authors provided a further rationale for including prevalent cases: "We opted for prevalent cases because an incident case of rheumatism is hard to define when sampling from a specialist outpatient clinic: most patients will already have been treated by their GPs and by other specialists before coming to a particular clinic." They further stated that, "In principle, prevalent cases can yield valid rate-ratio estimates, on condition that the survival of cases and controls is not affected differentially by the exposure of interest. It is unlikely that his condition would not be met in this investigation." In their rebuttal to criticism that women with rheumatoid arthritis would tend to avoid oral contraceptives and that this may have led to a spurious protective effect, the researchers emphasized that classification of exposure was based on oral contraceptive use *before* or at the first visit to their general practitioner for rheumatic complaints. Consequently, the possibility of reversed causality was minimized.

Not All Those Who Develop the Disease Need to Be Included as Cases

Because case-control studies are often done when the outcome is rare, it would be unwise not to include all members of the study base who fulfill all case criteria during the study period. There are, however, circumstances

TABLE 9.1 Use of oral contraception and risk of developing rheumatoid arthritis

	Never use	Ex-use	Current use	Ever use
Crude	1	0.26	0.46	0.36
		(0.16–0.42)*	(0.30–0.70)	(0.25–0.52)
Adjusted	1	0.40	0.45	0.42
		(0.22–0.72)	(0.28–0.75)	(0.27–0.65)

*95% confidence interval.

Vandenbroucke JP, Valkenburg HA, Boersma JW, Cats A, Festen JJ, Huber-Bruning O, Rasker J. Oral contraceptives and rheumatoid arthritis: further evidence for a preventive effect. Lancet 1982;320:1839–42. Used with permission.

under which only a *sample* of those with the case disease is included as a case. When the outcome is relatively common and there is enough statistical power, the cases may consist of a random sample of all those developing the outcome. An example of this approach is a study on the risk factors for hip fractures [Grisso et al., 1991]. A random sample of 174 female patients admitted with a first hip fracture to one of the 30 participating hospitals were included as cases.

In addition, a *stratified sample* of all subjects with the case disease may sometimes be obtained. This could be done, for example, to facilitate an adjustment of confounding (or assessment of effect modification) in causal case-control studies, when it is expected that one or more of the confounder or modifier categories may be too small to allow for proper assessment in the data analysis. Consider a case-control study on pet bird keeping as a causal factor in lung cancer. This relationship has been suggested to be caused by pollution of the domestic interior environment. In such a study, cigarette smoking is an important confounder, because bird keepers are known to smoke more often and smoking is the main cause of lung cancer (Figure 9.4).

Inclusion of all lung cancer patients diagnosed at two hospitals as the cases may result in very few cases who never smoked because of the very high prevalence of smoking among lung cancer patients, while the proportion of smokers among the controls will be much lower. Adjustment for confounding by smoking history would then be virtually impossible. One solution would be to decide to include all lung cancer patients who never smoked and a random sample (say 30%) of the lung cancer patients with a positive smoking history as cases. Importantly, this stratified sampling of

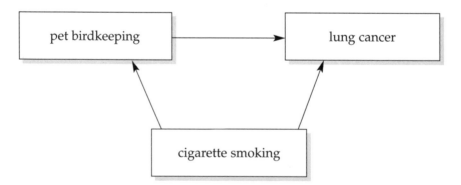

FIGURE 9.4 Confounding. Link between pet birdkeeping and lung cancer. Because pet bird keepers more often smoke cigarettes than those who do not keep birds (arrow to the left) and cigarette smoking strongly increases lung cancer risk (lower arrow to the right), cigarette smoking may confound the relationship between pet bird keeping and lung cancer.

the cases has important implications for the sampling of controls. In fact, the controls should be sampled analogously. This means that of all controls who were sampled from the study base, all controls with a negative smoking history and a sample (again 30%) of all non-smoking controls should be included as the control group.

Interestingly, one could also imagine sampling cases in strata according to the determinant of interest, although this may seem counterintuitive. Stratified sampling should be considered particularly when the number of cases in a certain category of the determinant is expected to be very small. Again, this implies a similar sampling strategy in the control patients. It is beyond the scope of this chapter to further elaborate on the specifics of stratified sampling of cases, because this approach is hardly ever used by researchers. More information can be found elsewhere [Weinberg & Wacholder, 1990; Weinberg & Sandley, 1991].

Sampling of Controls: The Study Base Principle

The strength of case-control studies lies in their capability to quantify the occurrence relation by studying in detail only those developing the outcome and a sample of the study base (which as explained earlier can be viewed as a swimming pool) from which the cases originate. This efficiency gain is only acceptable when the association between the determinant and outcome can be estimated validly and is not compromised by the selection of controls. To achieve this, adequate sampling of the controls is crucial. Only then will the resulting measure of association (typically the odds ratio) be similar to the measure of association (usually an incidence rate ratio) that would be obtained from a cohort study (i.e., using a census approach). Valid sampling from the study base means taking into account the study base (or swimming pool) principle, and implies that the controls should be a representative sample of the study base experience from whom the cases are drawn during the entire study period. To illustrate the methods that can be applied to provide for a valid sample of controls, we consider the two types of "swimming pools" that form the study base of virtually all case-control studies: dynamic populations and cohorts.

Control Sampling from a Dynamic Population

Most case-control studies are conducted in a dynamic population. These are characterized by their dynamic nature: people enter and leave the study base all the time. As mentioned in the first section of this chapter, examples of dynamic populations include inhabitants of a neighborhood, town, or region; those living in the catchment area of a hospital; and those enlisted with a health insurance company or primary care practice. Figure 9.5 shows an example of a dynamic population (albeit unrealistically small). In this population, which is followed for a one-year period, a case-control study is being performed. Assume that the study base represents the area around a hospital in which the cases (say everyone admitted with acute appendicitis) are identified. Inhabitants of that catchment area would typically be admitted to that particular hospital when they develop the case disease.

In total, 15 subjects are part of the study base for at least part of the study period. Subjects 1 and 3 are part of the study base when the study is initiated and remain there without developing the outcome of interest. In subject 2, the case disease is also not diagnosed during the study period, but she enters the study base approximately 1.5 months after initiation of the study, possibly because she moves into the catchment area of the hospital. Subject 4 is in the study base from the beginning and develops the case disease after six months. Subject 5 enters the study base three to four months into the study period and leaves it again before the eleventh month, possibly because he moves to another area and, if he is not followed to measure the outcome, is considered lost to follow-up. He is not diagnosed with appendicitis during the seven months of his membership of the study base. In

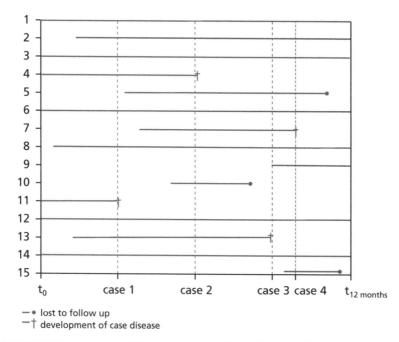

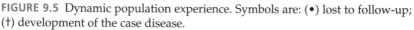

FIGURE 9.5 Dynamic population experience. Symbols are: (•) lost to follow-up; (†) development of the case disease.

total, four cases are identified during the 12-month study period and, one control subject will be sampled per case. Because of the dynamics of the population, representative samples of the study base cannot be obtained by sampling all controls in one point in time during the 12-month study period. For example, sampling at 12 months implies that subjects 5 and 10 can never be included as controls whereas they do contribute to the study base during a considerable period (and could even have become a case during that period). An attractive method to select controls who are representative for the study base from which the cases originate is to sample a control each time a case is identified. In this example, the first control is randomly sampled at three months, at which time the study base contains ten subjects. By definition, a control does not have acute appendicitis when he is selected as a control. The same approach is taken each time a case is identified (dotted vertical lines in Figure 9.5).

A control could develop the case disease later during the study period, although this is unlikely because the outcome in most case-control studies is rare. Importantly, however, control subjects who later become a case do not violate the study base principle at all. Such an individual was at the time of being sampled as a control representative of the study base in which the case occurred, while the case definition is fulfilled later during the study. Consequently, this subject should be included *both* as a case *and* a control. Similarly, a control subject could again be randomly sampled as a control later in the study, for example, when case 4 is diagnosed. Because both times this control is representative of the study base from whom the cases originate, this control should be included twice. Including an individual twice during the same study period does not necessarily mean that all characteristics are the same; exposure (e.g., being prescribed a certain drug) may have changed.

Sometimes it may be difficult to sample a control each time a case occurs. An alternative would be to assign each case a random date during the study period, and sample controls from the members of the study base on that particular day. In addition, one could sample controls after a well-defined time period, say after each month.

To assess whether control subjects are indeed part of the swimming pool, the researcher should primarily answer the following question:

> Would the control subject be identified as a case should he or she develop the outcome under study during the study period?

This rule of thumb can be applied for essentially all case-control studies.

The study on the risk of sudden cardiac death associated with diuretics and other antihypertensive drug classes among treated hypertensive patients (introduced earlier in *Identification of Cases*) may serve as an example of how to sample controls each time a case develops. The study base consisted of all inhabitants of Rotterdam who were treated pharmacologically for hypertension, which clearly bears all of the characteristics of a dynamic population. Each time a case of sudden cardiac death was identified, a random control was selected as follows: a general practitioner (GP) in Rotterdam was randomly selected using a designated computer program and this GP was visited at her or his surgery by one of the researchers. Then, using a computer file of all enlisted adult patients or the alphabetically-ordered paper files, the first patient with the same sex and within the same five-year age category was chosen, starting from the first name following the case's surname. If, according to the GP, that patient was using antihypertensive drugs for hypertension on the day the corresponding case had died, that patient was included as a case. Age and gender were chosen as matching variables in this study for reasons that will be provided later in this chapter. It should be emphasized that the sampling of controls benefited from the fact that in the Netherlands all inhabitants are enlisted with one general practice and that virtually all relevant clinical information, including drugs prescribed and GP and hospital diagnoses, are kept on file there. This system greatly facilitates control sampling in case-control studies.

Control Sampling from a Cohort: Case-Control Studies Nested within a Cohort

Figure 9.6 shows a very small cohort. Although the graphic suggests that all cohort members are included on the same day (t0), this is never the case; it may take years to recruit the anticipated number of patients for a cohort. Once a member is included in the cohort, his or her follow-up time is set at t0 and the subject is followed until a certain point in time and sometimes indefinitely. In contrast to a dynamic population, at a certain point in time the cohort is complete and no additional members are allowed in. Unlike most dynamic populations, the members of a cohort are known and at least some characteristics have been assessed. Nevertheless, it may be efficient to perform a case-control study within this cohort for a number of reasons, but particularly when the assessment of the determinant is time-consuming and expensive.

If the aim is to quantify the association between certain genetic polymorphisms and the occurrence of Alzheimer's disease, a case-control within a cohort may be very efficient. Such studies are often termed *nested case-control studies*, but other terms are applied, sometimes depending on the method applied to sample the controls. In this case-control study, three cases of Alzheimer's disease are diagnosed among the 15 cohort members during the 12-month follow-up period. Several methods to sample controls can be applied.

Analogous to sampling controls from a dynamic population, one could randomly select a control each time a case is diagnosed. At three months, the first control will be sampled from the 13 remaining in the cohort: 15

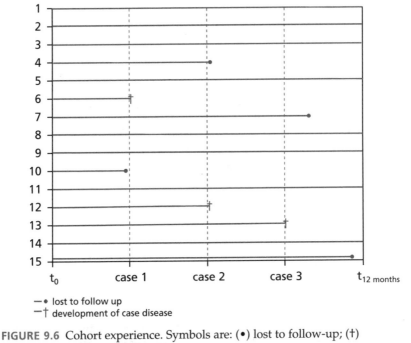

−• lost to follow up
−† development of case disease

FIGURE 9.6 Cohort experience. Symbols are: (•) lost to follow-up; (†) development of the case disease.

minus the first case and individual number 10, who was lost to follow-up. Similarly, the other methods presented earlier for dynamic populations can be applied. One could sample a control at a random date assigned each time a case is diagnosed or one may sample at regular time intervals, say every week or month. Again, the control who is sampled is representative of the study base by definition and sampling at multiple points in time during the study period will produce a valid sample. Such an approach may pose a logistical problem, however, because sampling frames including all members still in the cohort are needed each time a control is sampled randomly.

In many earlier case-control studies and sometimes even today, the controls are *sampled at the end* of the study period from the remainder of the cohort. This method excludes all cases as well as cohort members who are lost to follow-up. In our example, the three controls would be sampled from the eight subjects still in the cohort after the one-year follow-up period. In contrast to the sampling methods outlined in previous sections of this chapter, this method clearly violates the study base principle because the controls are not a representative sample from the population experience during the entire study period. Especially when many cohort members are lost to follow-up and many develop the case disease (i.e., the outcome is not rare), this method will lead to biased estimates of the determinant-outcome association. For that reason, sampling of controls at the end of the follow-up period from the remainder of the cohort is discouraged.

A much better alternative is to sample the control group *at the beginning* of the follow-up period (t0). Although intuitively sampling at one specific point in time seems to carry the danger of violating the study base principle, sampling at t0 is an important exception. A quick look at Figure 9.6 clearly shows that a random selection of the cohort (at t0) provides for a sample that is representative of the full cohort (e.g., gives full information on the determinant distribution), from which all future cases will develop during the study period. This type of nested case-control study is usually referred to as a *case-cohort study*. This term is rather confusing because it does not clearly indicate that, in essence, this study is a case-control study because sampling is involved, and not a cohort study. Because this method is increasingly being applied, a more elaborate discussion on case-cohort studies and their advantages and limitations is included in a separate paragraph in the next section.

Specific Types of Control Series

Sampling from the study base (whether a dynamic population or a cohort) is the optimal approach in case-control studies. However, sometimes this may be difficult to achieve, notably in dynamic population studies in which less is known about the members than in cohort studies [Grimes & Schulz, 2005]. To facilitate sampling of controls, specific groups of controls, such as those from the population at large (population controls), those in the hospital because of another disease (hospital controls), and those from the same neighborhood (neighborhood controls), are often used and advocated. Although it seems attractive for logistical reasons to take neighbors, family members, or people admitted with some other diseases as controls, this may compromise the validity of the sampling of controls (and thus of the study findings) when choices for a control group are made without appreciation of the study base principle. Unfortunately, the rationale of the choice of a control group is often not provided by researchers and the reader is confronted with a "can" or—even worse—several "cans" of controls (cf. Textbox 9.1), leaving it to the researcher to judge whether these controls are representative of the study base. The next paragraphs discuss several types of control series widely used in the literature.

Population Controls

In theory, population controls should be sampled when the cases included in the case-control study originate from the same population. This often is the case, notably when the domain of the occurrence relation is humanity, such as in etiological studies examining the links between smoking and lung cancer, and physical exercise and cardiovascular disease. In case-control studies, because case identification is commonly restricted in time or region, control sampling from the population at large ideally should be restricted in a similar manner. The main advantage of sampling population controls in this manner is that these are, by definition, representative of the study base.

In a case-control study addressing the putative causal relationship between alcohol intake and acute appendicitis (domain: all humans) in which cases are drawn from a large general hospital in a defined area during a one-year study period, the population at large represents the source of the cases. However, control sampling, ideally, should be restricted to inhabitants of that defined area (i.e., the catchment area population of that hospital) during that time period. As outlined above, this may be achieved by sampling from available population registries at multiple points in time during the study period. Again, posing the question, "Would the control subject be identified as a case should he or she develop the outcome under study during the study period" helps the researcher and reader to assess the validity of control selection.

Several methods other than sampling from population registries have been proposed to efficiently draw population controls. Random digital dialing, where a (usually computer-generated) random telephone number is dialed, is quite popular. Depending on the information required from the controls, computerization in such an approach could go as far as using the computer to pose the necessary, multiple choice questions and to store the respondent's answers. The advantages of this approach are self-evident. The relatively low response rate is a major disadvantage of this method, especially when a potential participant is being interviewed by a computer. In addition, not all men and women have a telephone, some only have a cellular telephone and many calls will remain unanswered. These phenomena are related to, for example, socioeconomic status, employment, and health status. If these factors are studied as (or related to) the determinant (or a confounder), the resulting non-differential non-response can lead to bias. Selective non-response may threaten any method applied to sample population controls, because the motivation of members of the population at large to be involved in clinical research is usually lower than for example hospital controls. In Textbox 9.4, an example of a case-control study using population controls is shown. Controls were sampled by means of random digital dialing [Fryzek et al., 2005]. Both cases and controls were interviewed to obtain the required information.

The following quotation from this study illustrates the selection process typical of population controls, although it should be emphasized that the response rate among controls (76%) was relatively high. Of all eligible cases, 92% participated.

TEXTBOX 9.4 A case-control study examining the association of body mass index with pancreatic cancer using population controls

---

Increased body mass index has emerged as a potential risk factor for pancreatic cancer. The authors examined whether the association between body mass index and pancreatic cancer was modified by gender, smoking, and diabetes in residents of southeastern Michigan, 1996–1999. A total of 231 patients with newly diagnosed adenocarcinoma of the exocrine pancreas were compared with 388 general population controls. In-person interviews were conducted to ascertain information on demographic and lifestyle factors. Unconditional logistic regression models estimated the association between body mass index and pancreatic cancer. Males' risk for pancreatic cancer significantly increased with increasing body mass index (p_{trend} = 0.048), while no relation was found for women (p_{trend} = 0.37). Among nonsmokers, those in the highest category of body mass index were 3.3 times (95% confidence interval: 1.2, 9.2) more likely to have pancreatic cancer compared with those with low body mass index. In contrast, no relation was found for smokers (p_{trend} = 0.94). While body mass index was not associated with pancreatic cancer risk among insulin users (p_{trend} = 0.11), a significant increase in risk was seen in non-insulin users (p_{trend} = 0.039). This well-designed, population-based study offered further evidence that increased body mass index is related to pancreatic cancer risk, especially for men and nonsmokers. In addition, body mass index may play a role in the etiology of pancreatic cancer even in the absence of diabetes.

Source: Fryzek JP, Schenk M, Kinnaid M, Greenson JK, Garabrant DH. The association of body mass index and pancreatic cancer in residents of southeastern Michigan, 1996–1999. Am J Epidemiol 2005;162:222-8.

Of the 597 general population controls eligible for the study, 19 could not be reached by phone, one died before being contacted, and 27 were not contacted because there was an overselection of controls under 45 years of age early in the study period. The remaining 550 people were invited to participate, and 420 (76 percent) agreed.

Hospital Controls

The study presented in the last paragraph also illustrates one of the advantages of using hospital controls in case-control studies: their willingness to participate. In general, the response rate in diseased and in particular in those being admitted to the hospital is higher than in the population at large. Moreover, selecting control subjects from the same hospital but with another illness than the case disease is efficient because the researcher is collecting similar data from the cases admitted to the same hospital anyway. From the very introduction of the case-control method, hospital controls have been widely applied, and their popularity continues to date.

Disadvantages of hospital controls are, however, considerable. In particular, the validity of the case-control study is at stake if the hospital controls are not a representative sample from the study base that produces the cases. One could think of many reasons why, in patients with another illness than the case disease, the distribution of relevant characteristics (notably the determinant of interest and possible confounders or effect modifiers) differs from the members of the study base. For example, smoking and other unhealthy habits, overweight, comorbidity, and medication use generally will be more common in those admitted to a hospital than in the "true" study base (i.e., the catchment area population of that hospital for the case disease). In addition, the catchment population varies with the disease studied. For example, acute appendicitis cases will originate from a much smaller area around the hospital than childhood leukemia cases in that same hospital. If, however, the distribution of the relevant characteristics in both catchment areas is similar, this has little influence on the validity of the study.

A common approach to prevent bias when taking hospital controls is the use of multiple control diseases. The rationale for such a "cocktail" of diseases is simple, if not somewhat naïve; should one control disease lead to bias (e.g., because the exposure to the determinant of interest in the control disease is higher than in true study base), this bias will be offset by other control diseases (of which some may have a lower exposure than the study base). Alternatively, control diseases known to be associated with the determinant of interest are often excluded or patients visiting the emergency room are taken as controls. The advantage of the latter control group is that the prevalence of comorbidity and unhealthy habits may be lower than in other hospital controls.

However, these methods all contribute to the complexity of using hospital controls. It is usually very difficult for the readers and the researchers alike to judge whether the essential prerequisite of a case-control study—namely, that the controls are a valid sample from the study base—is met. Too often, the researchers only mention the control disease(s) chosen without providing a rationale and fail to discuss the potential drawbacks of this choice. They then leave it up to the readers of their work to determine whether indeed the crucial characteristics of the hospital controls (the "opened cans" of control diseases) are similar to those of the study base (i.e., the catchment area population). We do not suggest a moratorium on hospital controls, despite some of the logistical problems sometimes encountered when sampling controls from catchment areas of hospitals. But there should be no doubt that the responsibility to prove the validity of the control sampling lies with the researcher and no one else. In their famous case-control study published more than half a century ago, Doll & Hill [1950] took up this responsibility and discussed the validity of their choice of hospital controls (Textbox 9.5).

Neighborhood Controls

Controls from the same neighborhood as the cases are often drawn as an alternative for population controls. Instead of taking a random sample of the population at large (or when hospital cases are used from the catchment population), the researcher samples one or more individuals from the same neighborhood as the corresponding case. Inclusion of neighborhood control is attractive for several reasons, but mostly because they, almost literally,

---

TEXTBOX 9.5 Example of a case-control study using hospital controls

An example of a case-control study using hospital controls is the famous paper on smoking and lung cancer by Doll and Hill. The following excerpt from the original paper highlights the way the control subjects were sampled:

"As well, however, as interviewing the notified patients with cancer of one of the specified sites, the almoners were required to make similar inquiries of a group of "non-cancer control" patients. These patients were not notified, but for each lung-carcinoma patient visited at a hospital, the almoners were instructed to interview a patient of the same sex, within the same five-year age group and in the same hospital at about the same time."

The 709 control patients had various medical conditions, including gastrointestinal and cardiovascular disease and respiratory disease other than cancer. The authors fully recognized the importance of ensuring that the control patients were not selected on their smoking habits and it is worth studying the additional data provided and reading their arguments to convince the reader that:

"There is no evidence of any special bias in favour of light smokers in the selection of the control series of patients. In other words, the group of patients interviewed forms, we believe, a satisfactory control series for the lung-carcinoma patients from the point of view of comparison of smoking habits."

This study, although performed more than half a century ago, can still serve to exemplify the potential advantage of hospital controls and the way researchers should argue the validity of their control group.

Source: Doll R, Hill AB. Smoking and carcinoma of the lung. BMJ 1950;ii:739-48.

seem to originate from the same study base as the case and often the researcher is already in the neighborhood collecting the necessary information from the cases. Another often mentioned advantage is the homogeneity of the neighborhood with regard to certain characteristics, including potential confounders such as socioeconomic status.

The latter, however, also should be viewed as a potential disadvantage. Cases and controls will be matched according to these characteristics. But matching in case-control studies (as discussed in more detail later in this chapter) carries important dangers, including the impossibility of studying these characteristics as determinants. It would be unwise, for example, to sample neighborhood controls in a case-control study quantifying the causal relationship of living near high voltage power lines and the occurrence of childhood cancer. Other disadvantages of neighborhood controls are the relatively low response and the time and costs involved, notably when the researcher needs to travel to the neighborhood to select a neighboring household.

In Textbox 9.6, an excerpt from the methods section of a case-control study performed to identify lifestyle and other risk factors for thyroid cancer describes the way neighborhood controls can be sampled and further illustrates the enormous efforts sometimes involved [Mack et al., 2002].

One could argue that the control selection in this study was independent from the risk factors studied (such as dietary habits) and that these controls may indeed represent a valid sample from the study base also producing the cases. It is unfortunate, however, that the authors did not discuss their choice of control group.

TEXTBOX 9.6 Example of neighborhood controls

A single neighborhood control was sought for each interviewed patient. Using a procedure defining a housing sequence on specified blocks in the neighborhood in which the patient lived at the time of her thyroid cancer diagnosis, we attempted to interview the first female matching the case on race and birth year (within five years). For each case, up to 80 housing units were visited and three return visits made before failure to obtain a matched control was conceded. We obtained matched controls for 296 of the 302 cases. For 263 patients, the first eligible control agreed to participate. Three controls were later found to be ineligible due to a prior thyroidectomy, and one control was younger than the matched case was at diagnosis. Questionnaires on 292 case-control pairs were available for analysis. The average interval between the case and matched control interview was 0.3 years.

Source: Mack WJ, Preston-Martin S, Bernstein L, Qian D. Lifestyle and other risk factors for thyroid cancer in Los Angeles County females. Ann Epidemiol 2002;12:395-401.

Other Types of Control Series: Family, Spouses, and Others

The attraction of using family members or spouses (or friends, colleagues, etc.) as control subjects is obvious: response rates will be very high and data collection will be relatively easy. Disadvantages of these control series, however, are that this method implies matching of cases and controls according to several known or unknown characteristics, such as socioeconomic status, age, family, environment, and/or lifestyle parameters. As will be explained later in this chapter, matching of cases and controls may lead to considerable bias. Clearly, the use of very specific groups of control series deviates from the principle that controls should be representative of the study base from which the cases emerge, and thus endangers the validity of control selection and consequently of the study findings. For example, it is not difficult to imagine that asking the case to choose a family member, friend, or colleague as a control (a frequent approach) can lead to considerable bias, because the distribution of important characteristics in the controls will be similar to the cases instead of being representative of the study base.

Multiple Control Series

In many case-control studies, multiple control series are included. From a theoretical point of view, this is difficult to understand. The control group serves to provide information on determinants(s) and other relevant characteristics of the study base from which the cases emerge during the study period and one such a valid sample is all that is required. So why use several groups?

In a study on the role of aspirin in the occurrence of Reye syndrome in children, no less than *four* different control groups were sampled: children admitted to the same hospital, children visiting the emergency room of the same hospital, children attending the same school as the corresponding case, and population controls identified by means of random digital dialing [Hurwitz et al., 1987]. The main reason for inclusion of several control groups is no doubt the uncertainty of the researchers about the appropriateness of control sampling. As such, multiple control groups can be considered a sign of weakness of the design of data collection. Nevertheless, under those circumstances where sampling from the study base is considered problematic and the validity of a control sample is not straightforward, similar results obtained in two different control groups can be reassuring. When, however, the findings differ according to the control group used in the analysis, interpretation of the study results becomes problematic. The researcher *retrospectively* must decide which of the control groups best meets the study base principle. Had this decision been made *before* the study was executed, inclusion of more than one control group would have become unnecessary.

In a case-control study on the risk factors for hip fractures, the findings resulting from the use of hospital controls (from orthopedic or surgical wards) were compared with those from community controls [Moritz et al., 1997]. As expected, the prevalence of many potential determinants was higher in the hospital controls while the corresponding odds ratios were lower, even after adjustment for potential confounders. The authors concluded that, "Community controls were quite similar to representative samples of community-dwelling elderly women, whereas hospital controls were somewhat sicker and more likely to be current smokers" and that ". . . community controls comprise the more appropriate control group in case-control studies of hip fracture in the elderly." We believe that this conclusion can be extended far beyond this particular disease.

Matching of Cases and Controls

There is continuing controversy regarding the benefits and disadvantages of matching cases and controls. Some epidemiologists strongly advise against matching according to one or more characteristics, while others advocate close matching of cases and their corresponding control(s).

In essence, matching of cases and controls should be viewed as an *efficiency* issue. Just as it may be more efficient to study a sample of controls instead of the census (i.e., to perform a case-control study), it may be more efficient to match cases and controls than take a larger, unmatched sample [Miettinen, 1985].

Consider an etiological study on the association between frequent sun exposure and the occurrence of melanoma and assume that gender is considered an important potential effect modifier of this relationship. Let us further assume that in order to efficiently estimate the association between frequent sun exposure and melanoma in both males and females, inclusion of five controls per case in each gender subdomain provides optimal statistical power. Power calculations for case-control studies are not included in our textbook, but it is generally acknowledged that a case-control ratio exceeding 4:5 does not add appreciable statistical power and is unlikely to offset the efforts required to obtain the necessary information in additional control subjects [Miettinen, 1985]. Presume that in the study base, a dynamic population of a well-defined region where 60% are female is followed during a five-year period. During the five-year study period, 100 cases (70 men and 30 women) of melanoma are diagnosed. A large, unmatched sample of 500 controls from the study base would include 300 women (60%) and 200 men. In the female subgroup, the case:control ratio would then be 1:10 (30/300), while the corresponding ratio among men would be 1:2.9 (70/200), thus implying excessive sampling of women from the study base. In contrast, the number of males is too small too provide optimal power. Matching cases and controls according to gender would maximize efficiency: for the 70 male and 30 female cases, respectively, 350 males and 150 females would be sampled from the study base. Thus, matching may be efficient when a large unmatched sample would generate small numbers of controls per case in subcategories of the matching variables (usually potential effect modifiers or confounders). This would make the assessment of effect modification of confounding inefficient or sometimes even impossible.

In another study, examining whether head trauma is a cause for Alzheimer's disease, an unmatched sample from the population at large would generate an inefficiently large number of controls in the younger age categories, because most cases will be octogenarians or even older. Then, matching according to age may be applied to increase the power of the study, to assess the role of age as a potential confounder or modifier.

Although matching of cases and controls can be helpful in determining the role of an effect modifier or confounder, matching is not the preferred means to deal with confounding in case-control studies. Unfortunately, however, this seems to be the predominant rationale for matching according to multiple potential confounders in many case-control studies. Often, researchers perceive matching of cases and controls a "similar" method to prevent confounding (i.e., to achieve comparability of natural history) as matching in cohort studies or randomization in randomized trials. But there is a crucial difference between these last two methods and matching in case-control studies.

Randomization in trials and matching of those with and without the *determinant* in cohort studies will create subgroups of individuals who are similar according to relevant co-variates (notably, of factors related to the outcome) except, of course, for the determinant (or exposure) of interest. Then, any difference in the future occurrence of the outcome is likely to be attributable to the determinant and not to confounding. Matching in case-control studies, however, will *not* lead to comparability of the distribution of confounders between those with and without the determinant. In contrast, matching will result in a similar distribution of potential confounders among those with (cases) and without (controls) the *disease*. This is counterintuitive, because cases and controls are expected to differ considerably according to all characteristics associated with the outcome (i.e., risk factors), including confounders. Consequently, the often-heard criticism of case-control studies, that "cases and controls differ too much," is unjustified; one should actually be surprised and question the validity of the data if cases had *similar* characteristics as control subjects (see also the worked-out example at the end of this chapter).

Consider a case-control study assessing the causal association between a novel marker of lipid metabolism [say the ratio of apolipoprotein (Apo) B:ApoA1] and myocardial infarction. Many potential confounders should be taken into account in this study, most notably those established cardiovascular risk factors known or anticipated to be related to the ApoB/A1 ratio. According to some, prevention of confounding in a case-control study warrants rigorous matching of a case with its corresponding control according to a large number of cardiovascular risk factors, including (apart from age and gender) other lipid parameters, blood pressure, glucose metabolism, smoking habits, family history of cardiovascular disease, etc. This will result in a control series consisting of subjects with a relatively unfavorable cardiovascular risk profile (comparable to the cases in the same study), but who managed *not* to develop myocardial infarction. Such patients belong in a museum, rather than in the control group of a case-control study. Moreover, lipid parameters (including the ApoB/A1 ratio) may well have become similar as a result of the matching procedure, because cardiovascular risk factors are known to cluster.

Although the matching of cases and controls should be taken into account in the design of data analyses (discussed later in this chapter), rigorous matching according to many potential confounding seriously complicates such an analytical approach. Other disadvantages of matching of cases and controls include the time and costs involved in identifying matched controls, notably when several matching factors are used, and the consequence that the matching factor cannot be studied as a determinant of the outcome. In addition, matching according to a factor that is not a confounder but is nevertheless associated with the determinant may even decrease efficiency [Miettinen, 1985; Rothman, 1986].

Because alternative methods to deal with confounding in case-control studies (i.e., multivariable regression techniques to adjust for confounding in the data analysis) are available, matching should be restricted to those case-control studies where a disproportionate case-control ratio in subcategories of an effect modifier or confounder is expected, as illustrated in the melanoma example presented earlier in this chapter. If applied, matching preferably should be restricted to one or two important factors. Typically, these include age and gender. Matching of controls according to all potential confounders with the aim to prevent confounding bias is irrational and should be discouraged. The statement included in the first book devoted entirely to case-control studies and published about 25 years ago still holds today: "Unless one has very good reason to match, one is undoubtedly better off avoiding the inclination" [Schlesselman, 1982].

Design of Data Analysis

As in any clinical epidemiological study, the design of data analysis depends on the theoretical design (notably, whether the study is descriptive or aimed at unraveling causality) and the design of data collection (for example, whether the study is nested within a cohort study or a dynamic population). We first explain the importance of the exposure odds ratio in case-control studies. Subsequently, a summary of the main methods to adjust for confounding in the data analysis is provided, because the vast majority of case-control studies are performed to quantify causal associations. For the analysis of diagnostic and prognostic case-control studies, we refer you to Chapters 3 and 4, respectively. Finally, the data-analytical consequences of matching cases and controls are discussed briefly.

The Odds Ratio Equals the Incidence Rate Ratio

Table 9.2 summarizes the major results of the first case-control study performed in the medical domain [Broders, 1920]. That study compared the smoking habits of 537 cases (with squamous epithelioma of the lip) with those of 500 control subjects (without epithelioma of the lip).

When asked about the analysis of this 2×2 table typical of case-control studies, those who have been exposed to a course in epidemiology or an epidemiology textbook will immediately calculate the odds ratio by taking the cross-product (ad/bc) and possibly also calculate a 95% confidence interval (CI). In this example, the odds ratio is $(421 \times 310)/(190 \times 116) = 5.9$ (95% CI 4.5–7.8). This odds ratio is then—correctly—interpreted as an approximation of the relative risk: in this example, the risk of squamous epithelioma of the lip in pipe smokers is six times the risk in those not smoking a pipe.

It should be noted that the odds ratio in fact is the *exposure* odds ratio, that is, the odds of exposure in the cases (a/c) divided by the odds of exposure in the controls (b/d). Moreover, the strength of the case-control method is that if indeed the controls are a valid sample of the study base from which the cases originate, the exposure odds ratio is by definition a valid estimate of the *incidence rate ratio* one would obtain from a cohort study; that is, if one would take a census approach. It can be shown this is true irrespective of the frequency of the outcome of interest, and, thus, any assumption about the rarity of the outcome is irrelevant.

Imagine a dynamic population, including in total N+N' participants during the entire study period. Note that, because this is a dynamic population, the time that a subject is part of the study base theoretically ranges from one second to the full study period. Assuming, for simplicity, that exposure in a subject is constant, N subjects are exposed to the determinant and N' are not (Table 9.3).

To calculate the association between the determinant and the outcome, incidence rates of the disease in those with and without the disease will be calculated. Taking an average follow-up time (t) of the members in the

TABLE 9.2 Case-control study linking smoking and epithelioma of the lip

	Patients with lip epithelioma	Patients without lip epithelioma
Pipe smoking	421 (a)	190 (b)
No pipe smoking	116 (c)	310 (d)
Total	537	500

Broders AC. Squamous-cell epithelioma of the lip. A study of 537 cases. JAMA 1920;74:656–64. Used with permission.

TABLE 9.3 Dynamic population

	Outcome	*No outcome*	
Determinant +	a	N-a	N
Determinant −	c	N'-c	N'
			N+N'

study base, the incidence rate, or incidence density of the outcome in those with the determinant, equals a $/(N \times t)$ while the incidence rate in the unexposed equals c $/(N' \times t)$.

The incidence rate ratio can be calculated as (a / $(N \times t)$) / (c / $(N' \times t)$) or $(a \times N' \times t)/(c \times N \times t)$ or $(a \times N')/(c \times N)$.

The major findings of a case-control study conducted within this dynamic population are summarized in Table 9.4.

In such a study, and in contrast to the cohort study shown in Table 9.3, the exact number (N + N') and specifics (notably exposure/non-exposure to the determinant) of the members of the study base are not known. The relevant characteristics are only measured in the cases (a + c) and in a sample from the study base (b + d). The numerator of the incidence rate of the outcome in those with and without the determinants is provided by a and c, respectively, and, thus the case series. The denominator is now provided by the controls. If indeed a valid sample from the study base is taken, b will represent an unknown proportion p of N (b = p $\times$ N and N = b/p) and d will represent an unknown proportion p' of N' (d = p' $\times$ N' and thus N' = d/p'). The incidence rate ratio (a $\times$ N')/(c $\times$ N) derived from the cohort study can then be rewritten as, [a $\times$ (d/p')]/[c $\times$ (b/p)]. Say, 10% of all members of the study base throughout the study period are sampled; then one will sample 10% of all exposed N, 10% of all unexposed N', 10% of all left-handed subjects, 10% of all subjects with blue eyes, etc. If indeed p = p', then the incidence rate ratio can be rewritten as (a $\times$ d)/(b $\times$ c). This equals the cross-product from a case-control study and is similar to the ratio of the exposure odds in the cases (a/c) and the controls (b/d). Consequently, if a valid sample from the study base is drawn, the (exposure) odds ratio obtained from a case-control study is exactly the same as the incidence rate ratio that would be obtained from a follow-up study in the same study base. Note that this is always true, irrespective of the frequency of the disease. Thus, there is no need for a "rare disease" assumption [Miettinen,

TABLE 9.4 Findings in a case-control study in a dynamic population

	Cases	*Sample from the study base*
Determinant +	a	b
Determinant −	c	d

1985; Rothman, 1986]. It follows from these calculations that a typical case-control study will only provide relative measures of the association between the determinant (odds ratios) and no absolute disease frequencies (incidence rates) in those with and without the determinant, *unless* the sampling fraction p is known. This sampling fraction is usually not known, with the important exception of case-control studies that are performed within cohort studies. If in the latter type of studies individuals are followed in detail, the fraction p will be known and incidence rates can be estimated. Case-cohort studies are examples of case-control studies with a known sampling fraction.

Adjustment for Confounding

Almost all available case-control studies deal with etiological research questions and because by definition no randomization of the determinant takes place in case-control studies, adjustment for confounding is crucial, just as for other non-experimental studies addressing causality.

Methods available to adjust for confounding are essentially similar for all types of clinical epidemiological studies. As a first step, a stratified analysis that estimates the odds ratio from 2×2 tables constructed separately for the categories of the confounder is useful. When, for example, gender is considered an important confounder, the odds ratio for both men and women will be calculated. Subsequently, a pooled estimate can be obtained using a Mantel-Haenszel approach or maximum likelihood methods, for example (see also Chapter 12). This gender-adjusted odds ratio can then be compared to the overall crude estimate. If these two estimates are the same, confounding by gender is a non-issue. When multiple confounders should be taken into account, stratified analyses become complicated and alternative methods such as multivariable regression analyses are usually applied. Currently, multivariable logistic regression is used in most case-control studies. For a more elaborate discussion on adjustment for confounding, we refer you to other textbooks [Rothman, 2002; Schlesselman, 1982].

Taking Matching of Cases and Controls into Account

Although we discourage matching of cases and controls, there may be a reason to match but it should be emphasized that matching of cases and controls has important repercussions for the design of data analysis. Through the matching procedure cases and controls are made more similar than when unmatched samples of the study base were to be taken. Consequently, this induced effect should be taken into account by performing *conditional* analyses, that is, analyses conditional on the matching factor(s).

In fact, failure to take this matching into account may bias the odds ratio. This phenomenon has been used to illustrate that matching of cases and controls can actually *induce* confounding, rather than facilitate its adjustment. Importantly, this bias can be prevented (unless too many matching factors are involved) by means of stratified analyses according to strata of the matching factor and *conditional* regression analyses.

Case-Cohort Studies

Recall that a case-cohort study is a case-control study nested within a cohort, in whom the controls are sampled at the beginning of the study period (t0). By definition these controls are free from the disease at t0 and are a representative sample of all members of the cohort. Note that, in contrast to sampling at multiple points in time during the study period (typically each time a case develops) from either a dynamic population or a cohort, in a case-cohort study the researcher samples from the members of the full cohort. In other words, a representative sample of persons, instead of person-years, is obtained as if the time that each cohort member is part of the study base is not taken into consideration. As a consequence, the odds ratio from a case-cohort study should be viewed as a valid estimate of the risk (or cumulative incidence) ratio and not of the rate (or incidence rate) ratio. Note that if the number of cohort members that develop the outcome is small (and this very often applies to case-control studies), the cumulative incidence ratio approximates the incidence risk ratio. In essence, therefore, both sampling of persons (from the members of the full cohort) and of person-time (from the total number of person-years all cohort members contribute to the study) is possible in a case-cohort study. If, as is relatively often the case, the sampling fraction (i.e., the proportion of all persons or person-years that is sampled) is known, one can even calculate *absolute* cumulative incidences or incidence rates for those with and without the determinant.

The case-cohort study is generally attributed to Prentice [1986] but Miettinen already introduced the method in 1982. Until recent years, however, the method often was not applied. This is partly attributable to the initial problems pertaining to the data analysis of case-cohort studies, including the difficulties in calculating confidence intervals [Schouten et al., 1993]. These problems have been solved. In the analyses of case-cohort studies (with a known sampling fraction), the full cohort is first more or less "reconstructed" by multiplying the sample of controls. Subsequently, absolute risks and rates can be estimated, but the inflation of the control sample needs to be taken into account when calculating the confidence limits. Several methods are available to analyze case-cohort data and adjust for confounding, including the Cox proportional hazards model.

The main advantage of the case-cohort approach is its efficiency, as for all case-control studies, but the fact that the controls can be identified in the beginning of the study further adds to its attractiveness. Furthermore, a single control group could be applied for multiple outcomes. In effect, several case-control studies can be performed using the same control group. An advantage compared to most other case-control studies is the possibility of calculating absolute risks or incidence rates (and risk or rate differences).

Case-cohort studies are less suited when many cohort members are lost to follow-up, when the outcome is very common and when the exposure changes over time. Moreover, the number of controls to be sampled in the beginning is difficult to predict, because the number of cases are unknown at t0, which may lead to some loss in efficiency. In addition, the data analysis is less straightforward than in most other types of case-control studies. The abstract of a case-cohort study is shown in Textbox 9.7 [Van der A et al., 2006].

TEXTBOX 9.7 A case-cohort study on the causal link between iron and the risk of coronary heart disease

Background—Epidemiological studies aimed at correlating coronary heart disease (CHD) with serum ferritin levels have thus far yielded inconsistent results. We hypothesized that a labile iron component associated with non–transferrin-bound iron (NTBI) that appears in individuals with overt or cryptic iron overload might be more suitable for establishing correlations with CHD.

Methods and Results—We investigated the relation of NTBI, serum iron, transferrin saturation, and serum ferritin with risk of CHD and acute myocardial infarction (AMI). The cohort used comprised a population-based sample of 11,471 postmenopausal women aged 49 to 70 years at enrollment in 1993 to 1997. During a median follow-up of 4.3 years (quartile limits Q1 to Q3: 3.3 to 5.4), 185 CHD events were identified, including 66 AMI events. We conducted a case-cohort study using all CHD cases and a random sample from the baseline cohort ($n = 1134$). A weighted Cox proportional hazards model was used to estimate hazard ratios for tertiles of iron variables in relation to CHD and AMI. Adjusted hazard ratios of women in the highest NTBI tertile (range 0.38 to 3.51) compared with the lowest (range –2.06 to –0.32) were 0.84 (95% confidence interval 0.61 to 1.16) for CHD and 0.47 (95% confidence interval 0.31 to 0.71) for AMI. The results were similar for serum iron, transferrin saturation, and serum ferritin.

Conclusions—Our results show no excess risk of CHD or AMI within the highest NTBI tertile compared with the lowest but rather seem to demonstrate a decreased risk. Additional studies are warranted to confirm our findings.

Source: Van der A DL, Marx JJ, Grobbee DE, Kamphuis MH, Georgiou NA, van Kats-Renaud JH, Breuer W, Cabantchik ZI, Roest M, Voorbij HA, Van der Schouw YT. Non-transferrin-bound iron and risk of coronary heart disease in postmenopausal women. Circulation 2006;113:1942–9.

The following paragraph from the study of Van der A et al. describes the rationale and methodology of this case-cohort study.

> The case-cohort design consists of a subcohort randomly sampled from the full cohort at the beginning of the study and a case sample that consists of all cases that are ascertained during follow-up. With this sampling strategy, the subcohort may include incident cases of CHD that will contribute person-time as controls until the moment they experience the event. We selected a random sample of [almost equal to] 10% ($n = 1134$) from the baseline cohort to serve as the subcohort. The advantage of this design is that it enables the performance of survival analyses without the need to collect expensive laboratory data for the entire cohort.

The complexity of the data analysis is illustrated in the next few lines from the same article:

> To assess the relationship between the iron variables (i.e., NTBI, serum iron, transferrin saturation, and serum ferritin) and heart disease, we used a Cox proportional hazards model with an estimation procedure adapted for case-cohort designs. We used the unweighted method by Prentice, which is incorporated in the macro ROBPHREG made by Barlow and Ichikawa. This macro is available at http://lib.stat.cmu.edu/general/robphreg [accessed July 3, 2007] and can be implemented in the SAS statistical software package version 8.2. It computes weighted estimates together with a robust standard error, from which we calculated 95% confidence intervals.

Case-Crossover Studies

The case-crossover study was introduced in 1991 by Maclure. A case-crossover study bears some resemblance to a crossover randomized trial. In the latter, each participant receives all (usually two) interventions and the order in which he or she receives the interventions in this experimental study is randomly allocated, with some time between the two interventions, allowing for the effect of the intervention to wear off. Assumptions underlying a crossover trial include the transient effect of each intervention and that the interventions do not exert an effect during the time period the participant receives the other intervention (i.e., there is no carry-over effect; see also Chapter 10).

In a case-crossover study, *all* participants are also considered to experience periods of exposure as well as periods of non-exposure to the determinant of interest. However, a case-crossover study is non-experimental and thus the order in which exposure or non-exposure occurs is anything but random. In fact, exposure or non-exposure may change multiple times in a participant during the study period. Importantly, the above-mentioned prerequisites for crossover trials also pertain to case-crossover studies: the exposure being transient and the lack of a carry-over effect.

A case-crossover study is a case-control study because a sampling instead of a census approach is taken. Instead of comparing cases with a sample from the study base, however, the exposure is compared in the risk period preceding the outcome and the usual exposure in the same case. The latter may be measured by calculating the average exposure over a certain time period or measuring exposure at a random point in time or specified period, for example, 48 hours, before the event. The type of transient determinants that have been evaluated in case-crossover designs include coffee drinking, physical exertion, alcohol intake, sexual activity, and cocaine consumption [Mittleman et al., 1993, Mittleman et al., 1999].

Let us consider the example of a study aimed to quantify the occurrence of myocardial infarction as a function of strenuous physical exertion [Willich et al., 1993]. In the article, both a typical case-control study and a case-crossover study are presented. Both designs are shown in Figure 9.7.

Time 0 indicates the occurrence of the outcome in a member of the study base. The determinant is defined as "being engaged in physical exertion one hour before a certain point in time," and for the cases this is the time of onset of non-fatal myocardial infarction. In their case-control analysis, Willich et al. compared the prevalence of strenuous physical exertion of cases in the risk period with the prevalence in age-, sex-, and neighborhood-matched population controls. The adjusted odds ratio resulting from this analysis was 2.1 (95% CI, 1.1–3.6). In their case-crossover analysis, the authors compared the exposure during the risk period of the cases with their usual frequency of strenuous exercise. The data were obtained by interviewing the participants. In the analyses, the observed odds of strenuous exercise (1:0 or 0:1) within the hour before the onset of myocardial infarction and the expected odds (x:y) that the case would have been engaged in ex-

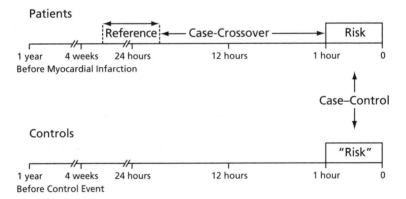

FIGURE 9.7 Comparison of a case-crossover and case-control study examining the link between myocardial infarction and exercise.

Reprinted with permission from Willich SN, Lewis M, Lowel H, Arntz HR, Schubert F, Schroder R. Physical exertion as a trigger of acute myocardial infarction. Triggers and mechanisms of myocardial infarction study group. N Engl J Med 1993;329:1684–90.

ercise, based on the usual exercise frequency, were calculated. The risk ratio was calculated as the ratio of the sums of y in patients who were exercising and the sum of x in patients who did not engage in exercise within one hour before symptom onset. The risk ratio resulting from this approach was similar to the case-control estimate: 2.1 (95% CI, 1.6–3.1).

The major strength of a case-crossover design is the within-person comparison, just as in crossover trials. The case and its matched control (who in fact is the same person) will be matched according to characteristics that are constant in a certain (usually short) time span (e.g., comorbidity, socioeconomic status, gender). Because of this matching, these characteristics can never be studied as a determinant of the outcome event, but a case-crossover study usually focuses on one transient exposure only. The most important threat to case-crossover studies is the possibility that the determinant exerts its effect way beyond the risk period defined. This "carry-over" effect cannot always be ruled out.

Case-Control Studies with No Controls

The case-crossover study is an example of a case-control study without control subjects; in other words, the cases are the only subjects included in the analysis. Under specific circumstances, several other designs that only include cases are in use. *Case-only studies* are particularly useful to assess gene-environmental interactions [Piegorsch et al., 1994; Khoury & Flandes, 1996]. In such a study, a 2×2 table is drawn comparing the single and combined exposure of the cases to the environmental and genetic determinant. Then, the case-only odds ratio (COS) is calculated as ad/bc. The COS allows the researcher to assess whether there is multiplicative interaction between the two determinants or a departure from multiplicative risk ratios. A major limitation of the design is the essential assumption of independence between the two factors in the population [Albert et al., 2001].

When the determinant under study is the distance from a potentially harmful source, such as a power line or magnetic field, a *case-specular study* may be a design option. In such studies, hypothetical controls are created by reflecting the residence of the case (or reflecting the power line), for example, by mirroring the image of the case residence, taking the middle of the street as the reference [Zaffanella et al., 1998].

Advantages and Limitations of Case-Control Studies

The strengths and limitations of case-control studies follow from the particularities of the design. In Table 9.5 the major advantages and disadvantages are summarized.

The main advantage of a case-control study is its efficiency. Information on the determinant (and other relevant characteristics, notably confounders

TABLE 9.5 Case-control studies: strengths and limitations

Strengths of case-control studies	Limitations of case-control studies
Efficiency (sampling instead of census) in case of	Less suited when determinant is rare
	Usually no absolute rates/risks
—rare disease	More prone to bias (?)
—multiple determinants/dosages	Often performed "quick and dirty"
—assessment determinants expensive	
—duration of exposure long or unknown	
are 4 circumstances when efficiency is crucial	

and effect modifiers) only need to be obtained in the cases and a sample of the study base from which the case originates. Thus, the costs of case-control studies are relatively low. Especially when the outcome is rare, when measurement of the relevant (co-)variates is expensive (i.e., for genetic markers), or multiple variables (including multiple exposure dosages) are involved, a sampling rather than a census approach becomes the preferred strategy in the design of data collection. Moreover, case-control studies provide ample opportunity to address the effect of determinant exposure duration on the occurrence of the outcome, for example in the assessment of drug risks.

Several limitations inherent to a case-control design exist, such as their inefficiency when the determinant is rare. Case-control studies are often considered to be more liable to bias than other designs, notably full cohort studies. When one realizes that a case-control study is just a more efficient way to conduct a follow-up study, the nonsense of this common myth becomes clear. Obviously, if sampling of controls depends on the determinant studied, if the cases and controls are asked retrospectively about exposure, or if confounding is not adequately addressed, bias (also termed selection bias, recall bias, and confounding bias, respectively) may occur in case-control studies. Bias, however, can be present in any other non-experimental study. It seems that the bad reputation of case-control studies has resulted from the "quick and dirty" manner (remember Andy Warhol's can of soup introduced in Textbox 9.1) in which many of them have been performed. Poor conduct of case-control studies clearly contributes to the air of suspicion often surrounding the results from case-control studies.

State-of-the-art case-control studies offer an extremely powerful epidemiological tool, notably in etiologic research. Provided that the underlying principles are appreciated, case-control studies will continue to play a prominent role in providing evidence for clinical practice, because of their application in both causal and descriptive clinical research.

Worked-Out Example

Anesthetic care in Westernized societies is of high quality and safety. Although very rare, accidents still occur that may have serious health consequences. The Netherlands Society for Anaesthesiology decided to estimate the incidence of serious morbidity and mortality during or following anesthesia and study possible causal factors related to procedures and organization with the goal of reducing risks further. Because of the rarity of the event, large numbers of anesthetic procedures were needed for the study. In view of the necessary detailed information to be obtained, a case-control study was conducted (Textbox 9.8) [Arbous et al., 2005].

TEXTBOX 9.8 Impact of anesthesia management characteristics on severe morbidity and mortality

Background: Quantitative estimates of how anesthesia management impacts perioperative morbidity and mortality are limited. The authors performed a study to identify risk factors related to anesthesia management for 24-h postoperative severe morbidity and mortality.

Methods: A case-control study was performed of all patients undergoing anesthesia (1995–1997). Cases were patients who either remained comatose or died during or within 24 h of undergoing anesthesia. Controls were patients who neither remained comatose nor died during or within 24 hours of undergoing anesthesia. Data were collected by means of a questionnaire, the anesthesia and recovery form. Odds ratios were calculated for risk factors, adjusted for confounders.

Results: The cohort comprised 869,483 patients; 807 cases and 883 controls were analyzed. The incidence of 24-h postoperative death was 8.8 (95% confidence interval, 8.2–9.5) per 10,000 anesthetics. The incidence of coma was 0.5 (95% confidence interval, 0.3–0.6). Anesthesia management factors that were statistically significantly associated with a decreased risk were: equipment check with protocol and checklist (odds ratio, 0.64), documentation of the equipment check (odds ratio, 0.61), a directly available anesthesiologist (odds ratio, 0.46), no change of anesthesiologist during anesthesia (odds ratio, 0.44), presence of a full-time working anesthetic nurse (odds ratio, 0.41), two persons present at emergence (odds ratio, 0.69), reversal of anesthesia (for muscle relaxants and the combination of muscle relaxants and opiates; odds ratios, 0.10 and 0.29, respectively), and postoperative pain medication as opposed to no pain medication, particularly if administered epidurally or intramuscularly as opposed to intravenously.

Conclusions: Mortality after surgery is substantial and an association was established between perioperative coma and death and anesthesia management factors like intraoperative presence of anesthesia personnel, administration of drugs intraoperatively and postoperatively, and characteristics of delivered intraoperative and postoperative anesthetic care.

Source: Arbous MS, Meursing AEE, van Kleef JW, de Lange JJ, Spoormans HHAJM, Touw P, Werner FM, Grobbee DE. Impact of anesthesia management characteristics on severe morbidity and mortality. Anesthesiology 2005;102:257–68.

Theoretical Design

The research question addressed was: *Which characteristics of anesthesia management are causally related to 24-hour postoperative severe morbidity and mortality?* This translates to the following occurrence relation: *[severe postoperative morbidity and mortality] as a function of [factors related to anesthesia management] conditional on [confounders].* The domain is *all patients undergoing anesthesia for surgery.* The operational definition of the outcome was *coma or death during or within 24 hours of undergoing anesthesia.* The determinant and confounders were operationalized by recording all relevant characteristics of anesthesia, hospital, and patients by means of a questionnaire and by scrutinizing anesthesia and recovery forms.

Design of Data Collection

The data collection was designed as a prospective case-control study. Cases were patients who either remained comatose or died during or within 24 hours of undergoing anesthesia from a cohort formed by all patients undergoing anesthesia (general, regional, or a combined technique) from January 1, 1995, to December 31, 1996, in three of the 12 provinces in the Netherlands. The number of anesthetics in the study area and study period was 869,483. Controls were obtained by taking a random patient from the remainder of the cohort immediately after a case was identified. Note that cases were in no way defined as *a priori* related to anesthesia management (the determinant of interest). Consequently, most of the cases were likely to have become comatose or have died because of other reasons, notably severity of the health condition for which surgery was needed or because of the risks associated with the surgery.

Design of Data Analysis

The principal analysis was performed on controls ($n = 883$) and all cases ($n = 807$) jointly. Crude rate ratios and 95% confidence intervals (CIs) of all preoperative, intraoperative, and postoperative factors for perioperative morbidity or mortality, estimated as odds ratios, were calculated by univariate logistic regression.

Because the main interest was in the causal relationship between anesthesia management and perioperative coma and death, anesthesia management-related preoperative, intraoperative, and postoperative risk factors were also considered to be potential determinants of the outcome. Patient-, surgery-, and hospital-related factors were treated as potential confounders of this relationship of interest. Potential determinants were considered in the analyses if, in the univariate analysis, two-sided P values were less than 0.25 or if the variable seemed relevant from a biological or anesthesia management point of view. To adjust risk estimates of the determinants for confounders, multivariable logistic regression was used. Patient-, surgery-, and hospital-related factors were considered as possible confounders if they were statistically significantly related to the determinant or were judged to be biologically relevant. While for the study as a whole, multiple possible causal determinants were considered, the per-analysis focus was on a single determinant-outcome relation. For each determinant that was significantly related to the outcome in the univariate analysis, a set of possible confounders were tested by multivariable logistic regression. Please note that a unique regression model was considered for each individual determinant at the time, because particular variables could act as a confounder for one determinant but not necessarily for others.

The importance of each potential confounder included in the model was verified by the likelihood ratio test and a comparison of the estimated odds ratio of the determinant from models containing and not containing the potential confounder. A significant likelihood ratio test with a change of the estimated odds ratio was taken as evidence that a biologically plausible factor was a confounder and, therefore, it was included in the model. Subsequently, for each adjusted determinant, interaction of biologically plausible combinations of the determinant and one or more confounders was tested by the likelihood ratio test. Adjusted risks for anesthesia management factors were calculated, controlling for confounders. Patients with more than 10% missing values were excluded. Missing data are a common problem in research using data that as a whole or in part are based on routine clinical records. If the proportion of missing data is not too large, the data may be imputed using various regression-based techniques. For the current study, data were analyzed both with and without imputation of variables showing up to 10% missing values. Results were virtually the same.

Implications and Relevance

The results of the study show that in spite of the high-quality level of current anesthetic practice, several characteristics of anesthesia management could be related to risk of mortality independent of confounding variables. These findings point to a causal role of these characteristics. During the review process of this manuscript, a rather common comment was made by several reviewers regarding the nature of the cases that was reiterated in letters sent to the journal in response to the study's publication [Robertson, 2006].

> When one looks at baseline characteristics of the study and control groups, there are, as the authors note, huge differences in the categories of urgent/emergent nature, time of day procedure performed, and ASA physical status. In fact, 40% of the study cases were rated ASA V—not expected to survive for 24 hours, with or without surgery (regardless of anesthetic

management). If we accept that a very large proportion of the study cases carry greater risk by virtue of their physical status and the emergent nature of the injury or disease process, and that urgent/emergent cases generally account for all the outside working hour cases, then differences in anesthetic management processes between the two groups appear more coincidentally associated than causative.

The point made by this author is illustrated in the baseline table from the original report from which a section is shown in Table 9.6 [Arbous et al., 2005].

The observation of marked differences in risk between cases and controls is correct but the inference is erroneous [Arbous et al., 2006]. Cases and controls should be inescapably different if cases are the ones who experience problems and controls are randomly sampled from the remainder of the cohort. In particular, they should be different in factors that reflect known mortality risks such as age, ASA physical status, or urgency of the

TABLE 9.6 Baseline characteristics of participants in the anaesthesia management study

Characteristic	Cases (n = 807)	Controls (n = 883)	Two-sided P value
Mean age, yr	64.4 (62.8–65.0)*	63.6 (62.1–65.2)*	0.53
Sex, % women	38.5	42.9	0.06
ASA physical status, %			< 0.01
I	2.2	30.6	
II	6.2	47.8	
III	21.8	19.9	
IV	30.3	1.5	
V	39.5	0.2	
Urgency of procedure, %			< 0.01
Elective	21.5	87.4	
Nonelective	15.1	10.5	
Urgent	63.4	2.0	
Time of procedure, %			< 0.01
During working hours (08:00–16:00 h)	50.7	96	
Outside working hours (<23:00 h)	32.3	3.4	
Outside working hours (>23:00 h)	17.1	0.6	
Duration of procedure, h	2.7 (2.5–2.9)*	1.5 (1.4–1.6)*	< 0.01

*95% confidence interval.

Arbous MS, Meursing AEE, van Kleef JW, de Lange JJ, Spoormans HHAJM, Touw P, Werner FM, Grobbee DE. Impact of anesthesia management characteristics on severe morbidity and mortality. Anesthesiology 2005;102:257–68 procedure. The question is whether these prognostic factors are also (re-lated to) characteristics of anesthetic management.

To address this question, extensive confounder information was col-lected, including those variables so dramatically different between cases and controls, and multivariate adjustments were made. Some reviewers would have rather seen controls who were closely matched to cases on as many risk factors as possible. However, this would violate the study base principle that controls in a case-control study should be representative of the population experience from which the cases originate and provide esti-mates of the background frequency of an exposure (such as anesthesia management-related factors) in individuals who are free from the outcome. While matching may sometimes be needed for reasons of statistical power, this procedure by itself does not exclude confounding, as explained earlier. Moreover, most individuals in the thus highly selected group of controls would be patients who should belong in a museum for surviving the anes-thesia and the operation.

10

Randomized Trials

Randomized trials are cohort studies in which allocation to the determinant is made by the investigator. Moreover, in randomized trials the allocation is made at random by some algorithm. Because the determinant is allocated on purpose with a view to learning about its effect on the outcome, randomized trials are experiments. The determinant that is allocated is typically a treatment such as a drug or another intervention intended to provide relief, cure, or prevention of disease.

Randomized trials have an important role in determining the efficacy and safety of treatments. A trial can be viewed as a measurement of the effect of a treatment. It should provide a precise and quantitative estimate of the benefits or risks that can be expected when given to patients with an indication for the treatment.

Randomized trials can be distinguished according to the phase of development of a treatment. This distinction most frequently is applied in drug trials. Phase I trials primarily aim to determine the pharmacologic and metabolic effects of the drug in humans and the more common side effects and are carried out after satisfactory findings in animal experiments. Study subjects usually are healthy volunteers who typically undergo dose escalating studies, first in single doses and later in multiple ones. In this phase also, the effects of the drug on physiological measures may be determined, for example, on the aggregation of platelets in studies of platelet inhibitors. Most often the number of participants in a phase I trial is no more than 100.

In phase II trials, the new treatment is studied for the first time in the type of patients for whom the treatment is intended. Emphasis is again on safety but also on (intermediate; see below) outcomes that broaden insight into the pathophysiological effects and possible benefits of the treatment. Drug studies often test several doses in order to find the optimal dose for a large-scale study. For example, a trial group sought to determine whether and at what dose recombinant activated factor VII can reduce hematoma growth after intracerebral hemorrhage (ICH) [Mayer et al., 2005]. The investigation randomized 399 patients with ICH within three hours of disease onset to either placebo or three different doses of the drug. Primary outcome was the percent change in volume of the hemorrhage from admission to 24 hours; clinical status was determined after three months as a secondary outcome.

In phase III trials, the treatments are brought to a "real-life" situation with outcomes that are considered to be clinically relevant in patients who are diagnosed with the indication for the treatment. Phase III trials are large (often 1000 or more patients) and hence costly. Much of the practical aspects of clinical trials discussed in this chapter pertain specifically to phase III trials.

Phase IV trials, also termed *post-marketing (surveillance) trials*, usually concentrate on the study of (rare) side effects after a treatment has been allowed access to the market. Sometimes such phase IV trials are conducted to assess possibly new, beneficial effects of registered drugs. Phase IV trials frequently are used for the promotion of the newly registered treatment, which is an understandable approach from the perspective of the industry but less attractive from a scientific point of view. There is currently ample discussion on how to best monitor the total (both beneficial and untoward) effects of a drug once it has entered the market. For example, conditional approvals are considered where the pharmaceutical industry is required to provide updated information on the effects of a drug during the first period of real-life use. This could include the continuation of specifically-designed randomized comparisons to quantify side effects. However, there are several other research approaches to address the study of side effects once a treatment has come to the market (see Chapter 6).

When designing the data collection and organizational aspects of a clinical trial, it is useful for the researcher to have conceptualized the structure of the written manuscript about the study. As the methodology of the design and conduct of trials was one of the first aspects to be well developed in clinical epidemiology, a guideline on what to report and how to do it has been issued already. This document, the Consolidated Standards of Reporting Trials (CONSORT), has been revised and adopted as an obligatory format by major medical journals [Moher et al., 2001b].

However, even before starting to think about the written report on the trial, the International Committee of Medical Journal Editors (ICMJE) currently requires all trials (including phase III trials) for the assessment of efficacy to be registered [De Angelis et al., 2005]. Registration must be done before the first patient is enrolled and the registry must be electronically searchable and accessible to the public at no charge. If no such registration was done, the manuscript on the results of the trial will not be acceptable for publication by the journals that adhere to the ICMJE statement, which include all major general medical journals. The rationale for a trial registry is the responsibility of investigators to present the design of the study and give an account of the results of the trial, irrespective of the nature of the findings. In the past, too often the design features of a trial were changed during the study or so-called negative trials were not published, leaving the international scientific community with mainly the positive trials, thus creating publication bias (see also Chapter 11 on meta-analysis).

"Regular", Parallel, Factorial, Crossover, and Cluster Trials

In a so-called *"regular"* randomized trial, two or sometimes more parallel treatments are directly compared between the patients who form the treatment groups. In a *parallel group* trial, the patient is the unit of randomization and there is no intent to switch the allocated treatment within a patient.

Sometimes, however, there are several treatment modalities to be compared for the same group of patients. In a *factorial design*, two treatment contrasts may be studied simultaneously, with the patients being randomized twice. A typical prerequisite is that there is no pharmacological interaction between the two treatment regimens. For example, in the Dutch TIA Trial [1991, 1993], the investigators simultaneously studied the effects of two different aspirin dosages (30 vs. 283 mg daily) and that of the beta-blocker atenolol (50 mg daily vs. matching placebo) on the occurrence of new vascular events in patients who had had a transient ischemic attack (TIA) or minor ischemic stroke. Patients were randomized twice. A factorial design has the advantage of efficiency. It basically gives the results of two trials for the price of one, because there is no need to increase the number of patients beyond that which would have been required for a single treatment comparison. A factorial design also may be favorable when it is difficult to recruit a sufficiently large number of patients with more or less rare diseases or conditions. Sometimes, an interaction between treatments is assumed to be likely rather than presumed absent. By nature of its design, the factorial study offers the opportunity to explicitly examine interaction. In the ADVANCE trial, two treatments of diabetic patients were compared to decide the optimal prevention of vascular events. Patients were first randomized to intensified versus usual glucose control, and next to the standard treatment of hypertension versus blood pressure reduction irrespective of blood pressure level, for example also in normotensive diabetic patients [Study Rationale and Design of ADVANCE, 2001]. Four groups resulted: intensive glucose control plus standard blood pressure treatment, intensive glucose control without standard blood pressure treatment, usual glucose control plus standard blood pressure treatment, and usual glucose control without

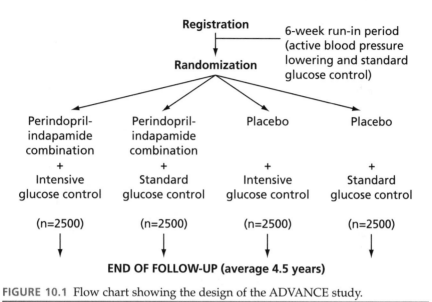

FIGURE 10.1 Flow chart showing the design of the ADVANCE study.

Used with permission from *Diabetologia*. Study rationale and design of ADVANCE: Action in diabetes and vascular disease–preterax and diamicron MR controlled evaluation. Diabetologia 2001;44:1118–20.

standard blood pressure treatment (Figure 10.1). The four groups allowed a comparison of the benefit of intensive glucose control and of non-standard blood pressure reduction but also of the effect of the two treatments combined versus usual care, which may well be more than the sum of either effect (indicating interaction).

In a trial with a *crossover design*, the primary comparison of treatment effects is within a single patient. To this purpose, one-half of the patients first receives treatment A and then treatment B with the possibility of a wash-out period between the two treatment periods. The other half of the patients is randomized to receive treatments in the reverse order (first B, then A). The number of treatment periods may be larger than two, for example, allowing the comparison of the schemes ABAB and BABA.

A major advantage of the crossover design is that it removes between-patient variability and hence offers a more efficient approach (fewer patients are needed) to measure a treatment effect than a conventional parallel group trial when the between-patient variability of the outcome is high relative to the within-patient variability. However, not all research questions can be validly addressed with a crossover design. First, the disease should return to its "baseline" level once treatment is removed and last sufficiently long to have two disease episodes with comparable severity. Second, there should be an outcome measure that can be obtained after a limited period of observation. Third, the effects of the treatment given during the first period should not carry over to the second period. If the first condition is not met, a so-called *period effect* will be present; if the third condition is not fulfilled a *carry-over* effect will occur. In an example of a crossover trial, the effects of azithromycin on forced expiratory volume in one second (FEV_1) was assessed in 41 children diagnosed with cystic fibrosis and reduced FEV_1 [Equi et al., 2002]. Half of the children first received azithromycin for six months, and subsequently had a washout of two months and then continued with six months of placebo. The other half received placebo first and then active treatment. In both treatment periods, there was a consistent difference between the effects of azithromycin and placebo on FEV_1; thus on the basis of this small trial, the investigators concluded that four to six months of treatment with azithromycin is justified in children with cystic fibrosis who do not respond to conventional treatment. Crossover trials are particularly suited for treatment effects that occur relatively quickly and are reversible after cessation in more or less stable chronic disease. Outcomes typically are intermediate end-points such as biochemical or physiological measurements. For details on the design and interpretation of crossover trials, the reader is referred to the book by Senn [1993].

Sometimes it is preferable or only possible to randomize *groups* of patients to different interventions. Take, for example, the study of a minimal intervention strategy aimed at assessment and modification of psychosocial prognostic factors in the treatment of low back pain in general practice [Jellema et al., 2005]. It would be very difficult to randomize the patients within the practice of a single general practitioner (GP), because the GP would have to switch back and forth between two treatment strategies: the new minimal intervention strategy and the usual care. It also could create dilemmas in the randomization. Moreover, it would be difficult to fully separate the strategies in patients that are in frequent contact with each other, and *contamination* (of the two strategies to be compared) may occur. Hence, randomization at the level of the practices of the GPs is the obvious solution and was chosen in what is termed a *cluster randomized trial* with 30 GPs randomized to the minimal intervention strategy and 32 to usual care. A total of 314 patients were enrolled, that is, about five patients per practice. Because data in a cluster, here a general practice, are related, the sample size calculated on the basis of individual patient data should be increased by a factor that depends on the degree of correlation of data within a cluster. Design and data-analytical features of cluster randomized trials need careful consideration and an extension of the CONSORT statement may be helpful in the issues faced by the researcher [Campbell et al., 2004].

In the remainder of this chapter, we follow global categories of items that need to be addressed in a report of a clinical trial. These guide us along

TABLE 10.1 Important items in reporting on randomized trials

Global Category	Items to be Addressed
Patients	Eligibility criteria
	Setting and location
Intervention	Details on the treatments
	Methods of random allocation
Outcome	Well-defined primary and secondary outcome measures
	Outcome assessment blinded?
Data analysis	Sample size: How calculated?
	Interim analyses?
	Methods for comparison of primary outcome between groups
	Absolute risks

Moher D, Schulz KF, Altman DG; CONSORT Group (Consolidated Standards of Reporting Trials). The CONSORT statement: revised recommendations for improving the quality of reports of parallel-group randomized trials. J Am Podiatr Med Assoc. 2001a;91:437–42.

the most important practical items in the preparation and conduct of trials (see Table 10.1).

Participants

Trials are both prognostic and etiological studies. Trials are conducted to measure the benefit and risks of treatment in particular groups of patients. The study population in a trial should reflect these future patients in relevant aspects, that is, it should reflect the domain. The first step, therefore, is to define clearly to which future patients the findings of the trial should apply: the domain. This immediately refers to the *generalizability* of the trial findings, sometimes also called the *external validity of the trial*. The more immediately the results of interventions need to be implemented in clinical practice, the more closely a trial population needs to resemble the population for whom the treatment is intended. Consequently, a phase I trial may well be conducted in healthy volunteers but a phase III trial, just before registration, should be performed in patients who are closely similar to the patients for whom the drug will be marketed. First and foremost, the domain of a phase III trial is defined by the presence of a treatment indication and the absence of known contraindications.

Domain characteristics are operationalized by specifying eligibility criteria. Typical selection criteria for a study population in a trial may relate to age, sex, clinical diagnosis, and comorbid conditions; exclusion criteria are often used to ensure patient safety. Eligibility criteria should be explicitly defined. The conventional distinction between inclusion and exclusion criteria is unnecessary [Moher et al., 2001b]. There are many additional characteristics of the population eventually included in a trial that may further restrict the domain and thus affect generalizability. Examples are the setting of the trial (country, health care system, primary vs. tertiary care), run-in periods of trial medication, and stage of the disease [Rothwell, 2005].

The CONSORT statement recommends using a diagram to delineate the flow of patients through the trial (Figure 10.2) [Moher et al., 2001b]. Its upper part describes the enrollment of patients into the trial and subsequent allocation to the trial treatments. In fact, this part still could be expanded with the stages that precede the actual randomization, for example, identi-

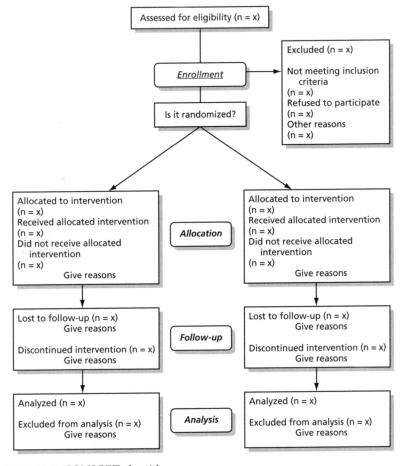

FIGURE 10.2 CONSORT algorithm.

Used with permission from *The Lancet*. Moher D, Schulz KF, Altman D for the CONSORT group. The CONSORT statement: revised recommendations for improving the quality of reports of parallel-group randomised trials 2001. *Lancet* 2001;357:1191–4.

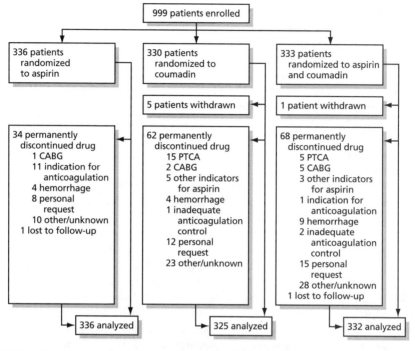

FIGURE 10.3 Patient algorithm for the ASPECT II study trial.

Used with permission from *The Lancet*. Van Es RF, Jonker JJ, Verheugt FW, Deckers JW, Grobbee DE. Antithrombotics in the secondary prevention of events in coronary thrombosis-2 (ASPECT-2) research group. Aspirin and coumadin after acute coronary syndromes (the ASPECT-2 study): a randomised controlled trial. *Lancet* 2002;360:109–13.

fication of affected patients in primary care, referral to secondary care (typically a hospital that participates in the trial), under care of a physician taking part in the trial, meeting the eligibility criteria, and giving informed consent [Rothwell, 2005]. Figure 10.3 shows the patient flow in the ASPECT-2 trial [Van Es et al., 2002].

Treatment Allocation and Randomization

In Chapter 5, emphasis was placed on the three comparability issues that govern the design of a clinical trial: natural history (or prognosis), extraneous effects, and observer effects. In the design of data collection in trials, comparability of external effects and comparability of observer effects go hand in hand. Comparability of extraneous effects is achieved by the use of placebo treatment and comparability of observer effects by blinding. It is inherent to the nature of placebo treatment, even if intended to just remove extraneous effects, that a patient is not informed on the precise treatment that is being given and, consequently, the patient will be blinded simultaneously and observer effects originating from the patient are removed at the same time.

Randomization is used to create two or more groups with equal prognosis. There are many methods to perform randomization, one of the simplest being the toss of a coin. Although acceptable from a statistical perspective, this technique is vulnerable with regard to its actual performance, because doctors may have an implicit or explicit preference for one of the treatments that are being randomized.

So, if the patient had "bad luck" and did not draw the doctor's favorite treatment, why not flip the coin once more? Perhaps you may be "luckier" next time. Such very familiar human behavior, however, would completely distort the process of creating two groups with equal prognoses. Hence, the randomization process should be designed such that the randomizing doctor has no influence on the outcome of the randomization once the patient and doctor agree to participate in the trial. Opaque, sealed, numbered envelopes may seem to be a reasonable alternative; however, envelopes may be manipulated as well. Sir Richard Peto, a well-known trialist from Oxford, warned that such envelopes may sometimes be unsealed before the next patient is entered [Peto, 1999]. That information could influence the decision to ask a next potential candidate to participate, again harming the aim of balanced prognosis. These problems may be circumvented by centralized randomization. This can be done by means of a telephone call with a central trial office that determines the treatment allocation in exchange for a basic set of data on the patient. If randomization does not need to be done acutely, faxes or e-mails may be used for communication as well. In trials examining acute diseases, 24-hour access should be available, a possibility that can be provided with Internet-based computer programs. When trials use blinded drug treatments, numbered boxes with trial medication may be shipped in advance to the participating hospitals; the boxes contain the study treatments in a random order. Then whenever a patient agrees to participate, the next box of trial medication can be used.

The simplest approach to randomization is to have one computer list generated with random numbers from which a random allocation scheme for a trial is made. In small trials, however, this still may lead to imbalance in important prognostic factors. This may be solved by stratified randomization, that is, randomization within groups with a more or less homogeneous prognosis, for example, separately for young and old patients. To make stratified randomization practical, the number of stratification factors should not be too large, say no more than three or four.

In multicenter clinical trials, the hospital is often chosen as one of the factors for stratified randomization. This prevents small numbers of patients in a particular hospital from all receiving, by chance, the same treatment. For small trials, it may be important to have about equal numbers of patients in the treatment groups. This can be realized by means of random permuted blocks in the strata. Within each block of say six patients in a two-treatment trial, both treatments are allocated three times; the random order differs per block. To prevent that at the end of a block, here after five patients, the next treatment is known (as in an open trial), block size should not be made public or, even better, its size should vary. With the help of computer programs, the prognosis and number of patients across the randomized groups may be more thoroughly balanced by a so-called *minimization procedure*. Basically, with minimization the probability of the next treatment depends on the number of patients with a specific treatment already randomized into a certain risk stratum. Assume for example that in a certain risk stratum ten patients already were allocated to treatment A and eight to treatment B. Then for the next patient the probability of treatment B could be increased to, say, 60%, rather than the standard 50%, to re-achieve balance in the number of patients in the treatment arms.

Informed Consent

An essential part of the randomization process is the step that precedes the actual randomization: the discussion with the patient or his family on participation in the trial. Ideally, this discussion is done by a physician who is not the treating physician in order to avoid a conflict of interest between care and science within the mind of a single doctor. The potential benefits and harms of the study treatments need to be explained as well as all practicalities on the trial, including the fact that the patient will be randomized. All information also should be given in a patient information document. In trials with non-acute treatments, the patient may ask for some time to decide on participation, and only after written informed consent has been obtained will the patient be randomized.

Blinding

The need to blind patients and doctors for the actual treatment given depends on the type of research question (pragmatic or explanatory; see Chapter 5) and the type of outcome event (hard or soft) that is taken as the primary one of the trial. If the trial has an explanatory nature, there should be full comparability of external effects and all extraneous effects need to be eliminated: a placebo is required, which implies that treatment needs to be given in a blinded fashion. If, however, a pragmatic design is preferred, the need for blinding depends on the type of outcome event. If an objective measure is chosen, like death, blinding is not mandatory. If quality of life is the primary outcome, blinding is definitely needed because of the subjective nature of this outcome. In an open trial, outcome assessment still can be done blinded by an independent assessor who does not know which study treatment has been given. For example, records on potential outcome events may be sent to a central trial office where all information on treatment allocation is removed. The blinded outcome data are then classified by members of an adjudication committee [Algra & van Gijn, 1994].

Placebos should be made such that they cannot be distinguished from the active treatment. They should be similar in appearance and, in the event of oral administration, taste the same. Even with the use of capsules that are meant to be swallowed at once, one should be careful as de-blinding has been reported because patients first bit the capsule and then tasted its content! Even with the most careful preparation of placebos, the effects or side effects of the treatment may give the allocation code away. For example, the effect on the need to urinate of a diuretic drug may be so obvious that this cannot be concealed from the patient.

When the allocation and blinding of trial treatment is finally organized, it is also important to monitor to what extent the allocated treatments are actually used. In the eventual publication, that information may be given in the trial flowchart as discussed above, for example, by the number of patients allocated to surgery who actually went on the operation and reversely the number of patients who were allocated to receive medical treatment but still underwent surgery. In drug trials, compliance with study treatment may be monitored by pill counts, defined as the count of tablets remaining in the blisters that were distributed during the previous contact with the patient. Of course, such a system is not perfect but it may guide in the detection of overt non-compliance. Registration of compliance may be viewed as less important in pragmatic trials because non-adherence with a treatment is part of "real life." If unequivocal measurement of compliance is deemed necessary, one may consider measuring plasma levels of the study drugs or levels of its metabolites in urine, or even add a more easily measured tracer to the study medication.

Outcome

The choice for a particular outcome, its definition, and measurement completely depend on the goal of the trial. If, for example, the researcher wants an answer that has immediate relevance for clinical practice another outcome may be chosen than if the primary aim is to show that an intervention exerts the anticipated pathophysiological effect. In phase II trials, the emphasis is on safety and pathophysiology. In the example of recombinant activated factor VII, the primary outcome was the percent change in volume of the hemorrhage from admission to 24 hours, which is important for a "proof of concept" but less relevant from the perspective of a patient. In phase III clinical trials with a primary explanatory design, pathophysiology driven or clinical outcomes may be chosen, whereas in pragmatic trials, investigators tend to concentrate particularly on those outcomes that are most relevant for patients.

Sometimes investigators disagree on what they deem is important for patients. For example, a recent debate addressed the question whether in stroke prevention studies one should take only strokes as outcome [Albers, 2000] or use all vascular events because of the atherosclerotic nature of cerebrovascular disease [Algra, 2000]. The latter outcome is a so-called *composite outcome* because it consists of several contributing outcomes (in this example death due to vascular diseases, nonfatal stroke, and nonfatal myocardial infarction) and the composite outcome is reached as soon as one of the contributing outcomes has occurred.

Phase II and initial phase III trials often use intermediate (or surrogate) outcomes, that is, outcomes that on the basis of pathophysiological reasoning will proceed to the occurrence of the clinically relevant outcome event. The validity of an intermediate outcome as a proxy for the real outcome relies heavily on the extent to which the intermediate outcome truly reflects the risk of the true outcome of interest. For example, ventricular arrhythmias were chosen as an intermediate outcome for sudden death in patients with cardiac disease. In the early assessment of the effects of anti-arrhythmic drugs, the reduction of the number of ventricular premature complexes at a 24-hour electrocardiogram from baseline to follow-up was used. With this outcome, several anti-arrhythmic drugs proved to be promising. However, these promising effects were completely negated in a phase III trial that used the final outcome of sudden death [The CAST Investigators, 1989]. The anti-arrhythmic drugs proved to be dangerous! Clearly, one should always be careful in extrapolating findings from trials with an intermediate outcome to the outcome of interest.

Still, a major advantage of the use of an intermediate outcome is that it may lead to results sooner because these outcomes occur more frequently or are continuous rather than dichotomous variables. Moreover, an intermediate outcome may effectively be used to establish the effect of a treatment by a presumed pathophysiological pathway and thus may demonstrate the primary mode of action. Sometimes the consequence of the intermediate outcome on disease is assumed to be so clear that the measure itself suffices as an indicator of treatment effect, as for example for blood pressure lowering drugs; although the clinically relevant outcome in trials on antihypertensive drugs would be the incidence of cardiovascular events, phase III trials typically use blood pressure level as the (intermediate) outcome. A well-established example of a proxy measure that is generally accepted as a continuous measure of atherosclerotic vascular disease is the thickness of the combined intima and media of the carotid arteries (Figure 10.4) [Bots et al., 1997]. When continuous outcome measures are used, such as carotid

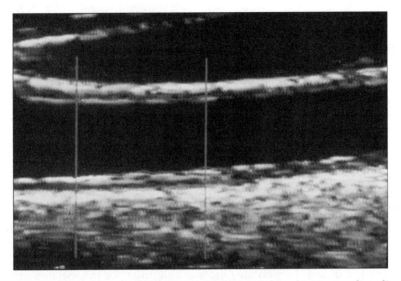

FIGURE 10.4 Measurement of the thickness of the combined intima and media of the carotid arteries.

wall thickness or blood pressure, it is possible to increase precision by taking the mean of multiple measurements, thus reducing measurement error.

Design of Data Analysis

When a trial is still on the drawing board, one should already be thinking about the design of data analysis. It is very helpful to "think 2 × 2" and to envision what the main 2 × 2 table of the trial would look like. But one can only do so after having thought about the precise treatments that are being compared and the definition of the primary outcome. Below, we will do the exercise of calculating the outcome of a hypothetical trial.

For example, suppose mortality is studied in 1000 patients with new treatment A and 1000 patients with standard treatment B. Assume that from an observational study it is known that 15% of the patients with standard treatment died after a follow-up of two years, and also that treatment A is supposed to reduce that percentage to 13%. Table 10.2 summarizes the data. The absolute risk difference between the two groups would be 15 − 13 = 2%; the precision of that estimate is described by its 95% confidence interval (CI; see Chapter 12 for details) that ranges from −1% (the old treatment is 1% better than the new one) to +5% (the new treatment is 5% better than the old one). The ratio of the two risks, the risk ratio, is 13/15 = 0.87 with a 95% CI from 0.70 to 1.08. Note that the absolute risk difference could be presented

TABLE 10.2 Data from a hypothetical trial

	Treatment A	Treatment B
Death	130	150
Survivor	870	850
At risk	1000	1000
Risk (%)	13	15
Risk difference (%)	2.0	reference
95% CI RD	−1.0 to 5.0	—
Risk ratio	0.87	reference
95% CI RR	0.70 to 1.08	—

Abbreviation key:
CI—confidence interval
RD—risk difference
RR—risk ratio

differently as the number needed to treat to prevent one death. The latter is the reciprocal of the absolute risk difference: $1/0.02 = 50$.

The data in the above example are not sufficiently precise to infer that new treatment A is better than old treatment B; the trial was too small. Thus, before one embarks on a trial, a *sample size calculation* needs to be done. With a fairly simple formula one can calculate the number needed. Advanced methods for calculating the power of a study and the required sample size may seem attractive, but the numbers that follow from any calculation are highly dependent upon the assumptions that are being made. By definition the researcher is uncertain and subjective about the size of the expected treatment effect. Here, not only the plausible size but also the relevance of the estimate matters.

A parameter that one needs to estimate or assume is the percentage of outcome events in the patients who receive standard treatment (denoted as p_0), which is 15% in the above sample. This is also called the *background rate*. The expected percentage in the treated group (p_1) would be 13%. The sample size per treatment group needed would then be:

$$f(\alpha,\beta) * [p_0 * (100 - p_0) + p_1 * (100 - p_1)] / (p_1 - p_0)^2$$

where $f(\alpha,\beta)$ is a statistical constant. It depends on the type I error (α) and the type II error (β) that one accepts. The type I error is the probability that one incorrectly would infer that there is a difference between the two treatments when there is no such difference. The type II error is the probability that one incorrectly concludes that there is no difference between the two treatments when in fact there is a difference. Conventional values for α and β are 0.05 and 0.20, respectively. With these values $f(\alpha,\beta)$ is equal to 7.9. In our example, we now calculate that 4750 patients are required for each treatment group.

With the anticipated values of p_1 and p_0 the 95% CI would then range from 0.78 to 0.96. The CI no longer contains the neutral value of 1 (no difference) for the risk ratio and the data now are sufficiently precise to conclude that the new treatment is better. The sample size can be further refined by estimating the percentage of patients that will drop out in a trial and the percentage of patients that will cross over from one arm in the trial to the other.

Before the analyses of a trial can start, several steps need to be taken first. Again, the CONSORT flow diagram (Figure 10.2) can be used as a guide. The lower panels of Figure 10.2 describes the numbers of patients who were lost to follow-up, those who discontinued the intervention, and finally the numbers of patients included in and excluded from the data analyses. Inclusion of these numbers allows the reader to judge whether the authors have done an intention-to-treat analysis (see also Chapter 5). In the intention-to-treat analysis, *all* patients who were randomized should be analyzed irrespective of the fact whether they really received that treatment, only part of it, or not at all. Thus, the intention of a treatment strategy in a realistic clinical situation is evaluated.

Take for example a trial comparing the effects of coronary angioplasty and coronary artery bypass surgery in patients with angina pectoris and narrowed coronaries [RITA Trial Participants, 1993]. After randomization, the procedures could not be performed instantaneously and some primary outcome events (death or myocardial infarction) occurred before revascularization was done. Still, in an intention-to-treat analysis these events should be counted in the treatment arm the patient was allocated to, an approach in agreement with real-life clinical practice. The alternative of an intention-to-treat analysis is the *on-treatment* or *per-protocol analysis*. This is typically done in the setting of an explanatory trial where only those patients who, in retrospect, fulfilled all eligibility criteria and also received the allocated trial treatment will be in the analysis. The resulting effect size will likely be higher than in real life.

However, a problem in per-protocol analyses is that non-compliance with the allocated treatment is generally not random and the resulting selection may induce prognostic imbalances between groups. In other words, the beneficial effect of the randomization process (achievement of comparability of prognosis) is, at least partly, counteracted. As a rule, an on-treatment analysis cannot be interpreted without knowledge of the intention-to-treat results. Often it is possible to perform both types of analyses. For example, in the Dutch TIA Trial [1991], the primary analysis was on an intention-to-treat basis: all 3131 patients randomized to either low- or medium-dose aspirin were analyzed, and the resulting hazards ratio for the primary outcome of vascular death, myocardial infarction, or stroke was 0.95. In the on-treatment analysis, the 23 patients who in retrospect appeared to have been enrolled inappropriately (14 had a brain tumor, four an intracerebral hemorrhage, and five other diseases) were excluded from the analysis [The

Dutch TIA Trial Study Group, 1991]. Moreover, patients contributed only to the survival analyses for the time that they were on trial medication and the 28 days after discontinuation of such medication to allow for a washout effect. That analysis resulted in a hazards ratio of 0.92. The larger effect in the on-treatment analysis supports the view that the treatment in the indicated patients is indeed effective, because one would assume that with a better indication and a higher compliance a greater benefit results.

To be able to conduct an intention-to-treat analysis, it is of paramount importance to obtain a follow-up that is as complete as possible. Without complete follow-up, the comparability between the randomized treatment groups may be compromised. Therefore, the extent to which follow-up is complete is often viewed as a quality marker of a trial. To minimize loss-to-follow-up, it is very helpful to ask the trial patient to provide the address and telephone number of a contact person, for example, a brother, sister, or a neighbor, as long as this person lives at another address than the patient. This will help to trace the patient if contact is lost.

Another important step that needs to be taken before a reliable analysis can be done is quality control of the data. If done properly, this was already an ongoing process during the trial on the basis of feedback that was provided by the central trial office. For all forms that are sent to the office, a check needs to be done on the completeness and actual values of the data. For example, a value of 510 mm Hg for systolic blood pressure should not be accepted automatically, because it most likely was a reporting error for a value of 150 mm Hg. Missing and (potential) erroneous values may be resolved by sending queries from the central trial office to the local investigators. This entire process can be speeded up considerably when electronic data forms are being used with built-in error checks and checks for consistency.

By means of interim analyses, an external Data Monitoring Committee (DMC) may evaluate whether such large benefits or harms already are present in an early phase of the trial, where it is no longer ethically justifiable to continue with the study. For this purpose, so-called *stopping rules* have been developed that assist the DMC in deciding to recommend early termination of the trial. Monitoring also may be done more frequently by means of sequential analysis techniques.

Interim analyses force the investigators to periodically generate a report on their data, and this definitely stimulates the collection of good quality data early on. There are also downsides to a too rigorous obedience to stopping rules and several trials have been terminated too early. A randomized controlled trial that is stopped prematurely because of a striking benefit or a strong untoward effect is most probably suffering from a random "high." At premature stopping, the conclusions often will be either too optimistic or too pessimistic. In the early phases of an investigation, the intermediate results show wider fluctuations around the hypothetical "truth" than in the later phases because of small numbers and thus lack of precision. Subjective arguments involved in the stopping of a trial may be limited by a so-called *triple blind design*, where the data monitoring and safety committee receives the intermediate results but is not told which data are from the experimental group and which are from the placebo group.

The next step is to generate the baseline table, which in most published papers will be the well-known Table 1. This table describes the baseline characteristics of the patients according to the allocated treatment. Use of the table for its readers is twofold: to assess whether randomization achieved comparability of prognosis between the treatment groups and to describe the patients who were enrolled in the trial to the reader. The latter allows the readers to decide on the domain of the trial results, which is typically defined by the presence of an indication and absence of a contraindication for the treatment, but other restrictions may apply. The description of the patients by means of the baseline table will give a good notion of the domain and thereby of the generalizability of the trial findings. However, for this purpose, one also should keep in mind the process by which the patients were actually recruited into the trial and which selections were made along the way [Rothwell, 2005].

In large trials, there hardly ever is important prognostic incomparability between the treatment groups, because of the large numbers. However, in small trials and/or inadequate randomization procedures (described earlier in this chapter) imbalance may occur that still may be repaired in the analyses by means of the calculation of adjusted effect estimates using regression analysis (see Chapter 12 for more details). Sometimes, investigators provide *P*-values to judge the difference in baseline characteristics of a randomized trial. This is a strange approach because in case of adequate randomization, any difference is the result of the play of chance by definition and *P*-values have no meaning. Rather, qualified judgment of the size of the differences and the extent to which this may have led to differences in prognosis and the size of the treatment effect is needed to decide whether the crude results can be interpreted validly.

A second major table describes the occurrence of outcome events in relationship to allocated treatment with measures of the size and precision of the treatment effects. Often the table contains both data on the primary outcome event as well as on the secondary events. It is important to realize that a hierarchy among the outcome events may need to be taken into account. For example, in a cardiovascular outcome trial, it may be quite misleading to only analyze the occurrence of non-fatal myocardial infarction, because a favorable trend for this outcome may be offset by an increase in fatal events. Hence, non-fatal outcomes never should be analyzed in isolation.

Often a trial protocol specifies that the treatment effects will also be determined in specific *subgroups* of patients, for example, in men and women. It is very important to keep in mind that such subgroups are likely to be too small to estimate the treatment effect with sufficient precision. After all, the size of the trial was determined for the main outcome in the entire study and not for the subgroups. This being said, nevertheless it may be worthwhile to study treatment effects in a limited number of subgroups.

Note that studying effects of treatment according to subgroups with a certain characteristic, such as age or gender, implies an analysis of the modification of treatment effects by these characteristics (see Chapter 2 for a discussion of modification). Be aware of the risks of so-called "fishing expeditions" if one pursues such analyses on the basis of curiosity. One certainly might "catch a fish" but such a fish is not suited for consumption. Take for example the Dutch TIA Trial discussed earlier in this chapter. In an analysis by month according to the start of their trial medication, it appeared that the 207 starters in August experienced a tremendous benefit with the 30 mg dose of aspirin in comparison to those on the dose of 283 mg; the hazard ratio was 0.38 (95% CI 0.16–0.89) whereas when all participants were included in the analysis, there was no difference. This finding clearly is implausible and the "fish" should be thrown back immediately (and not have been caught in the first place). Note that this example is a variant on the famous example on the effects of aspirin according to birth sign in the ISIS-2 trial as discussed in Chapter 2 [ISIS-2, 1988]. Again, sensible judgment, biological plausibility, or definition of subgroups in advance (thus in the protocol, before data are available) may help to prevent spurious results.

Meta-Analyses

The decision of whether to apply findings from research in clinical practice is rarely based on a single study. Trust that a research finding is correct grows after its replication in similar studies in several populations. Moreover, the results of a single study are often not sufficiently precise and leave room for doubt about the exact magnitude of the association between determinant(s) and outcome, for example, the effect of a treatment. This is particularly important when a careful balance between the magnitude of the expected benefits and the possible risks of an intervention is required. Under these circumstances, evidence that a treatment works may be valid but imprecise or still too general. What works in a high-risk patient may be counterproductive in a low-risk patient because the balance between benefits and risks probably differ. Here, the purpose of meta-analysis is to summarize findings from several relevant studies and improve the precision of the estimate of the treatment effect, thereby increasing confidence in the true effect of a treatment.

Meta-analysis is a method of locating, appraising, and summarizing similar studies; assessing similar determinants and comparable outcomes in similar populations; and synthesizing their results into a single quantitative estimate of the occurrence relation. The magnitude of the "average" association between determinant and outcome can be used in decisions in clinical practice or health care policy. Meta-analysis may reduce or resolve uncertainty when individual studies provide conflicting results, which often leads to disagreement in traditional (narrative) reviews.

Traditional reviews typically only offer a qualitative assessment; for example, a treatment seems to work and appears to be safe or not. In addition to providing a quantitative estimate across studies, meta-analyses use a transparent approach to the retrieval of all relevant evidence; employ explicit methods aimed at reducing bias; and apply a formal, commonly statistical, procedure for synthesizing the evidence. Unless individual patient data from the studies selected for inclusion are available, a meta-analysis treats the summary result of each study (e.g., the number of events and the number of patients randomized by treatment group) as a unit of information.

Meta-analysis originated in psychological research and was introduced in medicine around 1980. With the rapid adoption of evidence-based medicine and the increasing emphasis on the use of quantitative evidence in patient management, meta-analyses have become popular. Today, meta-analysis is an indispensable part of medicine in general and clinical epidemiological research in particular.

This chapter introduces the design and methods of meta-analysis aimed at summarizing the results from randomized trials on treatment effects. Meta-analysis of etiologic, diagnostic, and prognostic studies is increasingly common but is beyond the present scope.

Rationale

Meta-analysis helps to answer questions like: What is the best treatment for this patient? How large is the expected effect? and How sure are we about the magnitude of this effect? Definite answers are rarely provided by the results of a single study and often become obscured when several studies have produced seemingly discordant results. Traditionally, decisions about the preferred treatment of a disease have largely relied on expert opinion and narrative reviews in medical textbooks. These usually rely heavily on a selected part of the evidence, which frequently stem from only the largest studies, studies with clearly positive results (in particular, those reporting *P*-values less than 0.05), or—even worse—only in studies yielding results that support the expert's personal opinion. Clearly, such studies are not necessarily the most valid. Moreover, due to the rapid accumulation of evidence from clinical research, expert opinion and medical textbooks are quickly out of date.

Access to up-to-date evidence on treatment effects is needed for informed decisions about patient management and health policy. For instance, several authors have shown convincingly that medical textbooks lag behind medical journals in presenting the evidence for important treatments in cardiology [Antman et al., 1992; Lau et al., 1992]. Often, investigators perform a meta-analysis before starting a new study. In this way, they learn from previous trials which questions remain unanswered, what pitfalls exist in the design and conduct of the anticipated research, and which common errors must be avoided. Meta-analyses may provide valuable assistance in deciding on the best and most relevant research questions and in improving the design of new clinical studies. In addition, the results of meta-analyses are increasingly being incorporated in clinical guidelines.

An example of the value of meta-analysis is given by research on the putative benefits of minimally invasive coronary artery bypass surgery. Minimally invasive coronary bypass surgery is a type of surgery on the beating heart that uses a number of technologies and procedures, but without the need for a heart-lung machine. After this procedure's introduction, the results of the first randomized trial were published in 1995 [Vural et al., 1995] and four years later the initial results of a second randomized trial were published [Angelini et al., 2002]. Subsequently, 12 trials were published up to January 2003, 12 trials were published between January 1 and December 31, 2003, while another ten were published in the first four months of 2004 [Van der Heijden et al., 2004]. Meta-analysis is extremely helpful in summarizing the evidence provided by studies done in this field. In particular, it may support timely decisions about the need of more evidence and prevent the conduct of additional trials when precise effect estimates are available.

Principles

The concepts and methods of research on effects of treatment have been discussed in detail in Chapters 5, 6, and 10. The direction and size of the estimate of a treatment effect observed in a trial, commonly expressed as a ratio of, or a difference between, two measures of occurrence, indicates the strength of effect of an index treatment relative to that of a reference treatment. The validity of the estimate of the treatment effect depends on the quality of the study. In research on treatment effects, this rests in particular on the use of randomization to achieve comparability with regard to the initial prognostic status, and (if necessary) the use of blinding to achieve comparability of extraneous effects and comparability of observer effects. In addition, the validity of the observed treatment effect depends on completeness of follow-up data and whether the data were analyzed correctly.

The precision of the estimate of the treatment effect from a study is reflected in the confidence interval of the effect estimate. This denotes the probabilistic boundaries for the true effect of treatment. That is, if a study was repeated again and again, the 95% confidence interval would contain the true effect in 95% of the repetitions. The width of the confidence interval is determined by the number of the outcome events during the period of observation, which in turn depends on the sample size and the incidence of the outcome of interest or risk of event at baseline) in the trial population. In general, a large study with many events yields a result with a narrow confidence interval. Inconsistent results of multiple randomized trials lead to uncertainty regarding the effect of a treatment. Discrepant results, such as a different magnitude or even a different direction of the effect, may be reported from different trials. In addition, some trials may be inconclusive, for example, when the point estimate of effect clearly deviates from unity (i.e., a risk ratio of 1 or a risk difference of 0) while its confidence interval includes unity. Such uncertainty about the estimate of treatment effect can be overcome by combining the results of trials through meta-analysis.

It should be emphasized, however, that apart from a lack of precision, other reasons may explain differences in results between studies.

Diversity in the way trials are conducted and in the type of study populations may also lead to different trial results. To maintain validity when different studies are combined in a meta-analysis, aggregation of data is usually restricted to trials considered combinable with respect to patients, treatments, end-points, and measures of effect. To assure adequate selection of trials, their design needs to be systematically reviewed and grouped according to their resemblance. Discrepant results also may reflect some problem in the study design or data analysis that may have biased the findings in some trials. Because the results of meta-analysis cannot be trusted when flawed trials are included, it is important to make explicit efforts to limit such bias. Hence, the study design needs to be critically appraised, with regard to the randomization and concealment of treatment allocation, blinding of particular assessments, deviation from the allocation scheme, contamination of treatment contrast [e.g., unequal provision of care (apart from the allocated treatment) due to extraneous factors], and incompleteness of follow-up data, as well as the statistical analysis.

Small trials may particularly suffer from a lack of statistical power. In meta-analysis, the statistical power is enhanced by aggregation of data through statistical pooling of summary effect estimates from original trial publications into a single effect estimate. Many methods for statistical pooling exist, and their appropriateness depends on underlying assumptions and on practical considerations. Unfortunately, quite often the possibilities for pooling are restricted by poor reporting of effect estimates in individual studies.

Adherence to a few fundamental design principles of meta-analyses can prevent misleading results and conclusions. These should be elaborated in a protocol that can be used as a reference in conducting the meta-analysis and for writing the methods section of the report. Guidelines and manuals for writing a protocol for meta-analyses are available [Higgins, 2006; Khan et al., 2003] (Textbox 11.1). For all clinical epidemiological studies, the design of meta-analyses involves:

1. The theoretical design and research question, including the specification of the determinant-outcome relation;
2. The design of data collection, comprising the retrieval of publications, the selection and critical appraisal of trials, and the data extraction;
3. The design of data analysis and the reporting of the results.

TEXTBOX 11.1 Internet resources for writing a protocol for meta-analyses (accessed July 6, 2007)

---

http://www.cochrane.org/resources/handbook/hbook.htm from the Cochrane Collaboration

http://www.york.ac.uk/inst/crd/report4.htm from the Center for Reviews and Dissemination, University of York, UK

Source: Author.

Theoretical Design and Research Question

As in any research, a meta-analysis should start with a clear, relevant, and unambiguous research question. The design of the occurrence relation includes three sections: the determinant (typically, compared treatments), the outcome of interest, and the domain. All need to be explicitly defined to frame the search and selection strategy for eligible trial publications. By using unambiguous definitions of these elements, the scope and objective of the study are narrowed. This directly impacts on the applicability of the results of a meta-analysis.

For example, there are similarities between the following questions: "What is the effect of intermittent lumbar traction on the severity of pain in patients with low back pain and sciatica?" and, "What is the effect of spinal traction on the recovery of patients with back pain?" [Clarke et al., 2006]. However, these questions do have a completely different scope that will result in different criteria for selection of trials and subsequently different estimates of treatment effect and applicability of the findings. Due to its more detailed wording, the former may provide a more informative summary of evidence for patient management, while the more general wording of its domain, determinant, and outcome in the latter may serve public health policy. Although it is not the primary objective of meta-analysis to formulate recommendations for patient management, but rather to quantitatively summarize the evidence on a particular mode of treatment, they are often used in the development of clinical guidelines.

Just as in the design of any epidemiological study, it is necessary to carefully decide on the domain, that is, the type of patients or subjects to whom the results of the meta-analysis are going to apply. Definition of the domain guides the selection of study populations to be considered and thus assists in obtaining relevant summaries of evidence from published trials.

Design of Data Collection

The challenge in the retrieval and selection of publications is to identify all relevant and valid evidence from previous research. The rapid growth of electronic publication and improved accessibility to electronic bibliographic databases and availability of complete journal contents on the Internet has facilitated the retrieval and filtering of pertinent evidence, in particular those of trial publications. To comprehensively locate all available evidence, however, skills in the design of search strategies are required. With proper library and information technology skills, information retrieval will be less time-consuming and searches will be more comprehensive.

Bibliographic Databases

For a comprehensive search, several medically oriented electronic bibliographic databases are available. These include: PubMed (National Library of Medicine and National Institutes of Health) [Dickersin et al., 1985; Gallagher et al., 1990]; EMBASE (Elsevier, Inc.) [Haynes et al., 2005; Wong et al., 2006a], Web of Science (Thompson Scientific), PsycINFO (American Psychological Association) [Watson & Richardson, 1999a; Watson & Richardson, 1999b]; CINAHL (Cumulative Index to Nursing and Allied Health Literature, EBSCO Industries) [Wong et al., 2006b]; LILACS (Literatura Americana e do Caribe em Ciências da Saúde) [Clark, 2002]; and Cochrane Database of Randomized Trials (Wiley Interscience). A listing of bibliographic databases is available at the following URL: http://www.york.ac.uk/inst/crd/revs2 .htm (accessed July 8, 2007). The coverage of subject matter and the list of scientific journals included in these databases are different, and the highest yield is likely to depend on the topic that is studied [Watson & Richardson, 1999a; Suarez-Almazor et al., 2000; Minozzi et al., 2000; McDonald et al., 1999].

Search Filters

Search filters are command syntax strings in the database language for retrieving relevant records. Most electronic bibliographic databases provide indexing services and search facilities, which make it easy to create and use search filters. For every research question, a reproducible subject-search filter must be made. There is no standard for building a subject-specific search filter, and they need to be customized for each database. The art of building a subject-specific search filter comes down to reducing the numbers needed to read to find a single pertinent record for an original trial publication [Bachmann et al., 2002].

Building a Search Filter

Building a subject-specific search filter starts with breaking down the defined research question into parts: the patients (part of the domain), treatments (determinants), and end-points (outcomes). Candidate terms and relevant synonyms should be listed for each part of the question. To accomplish this, medical dictionaries, medical textbooks, but also the thesaurus and the index of bibliographic databases can be used. After selecting the search terms for the domain, these terms are usually combined with the Boolean operator *OR*. The same is done with the selected search terms for the determinant and for the outcome. These three separate search queries are then combined by the Boolean operator *AND*. Depending on the focus of the research question, *limits* such as age categories or publication date can be used to restrict the number of retrieved records to more manageable proportions. However, this is not recommended in the context of meta-analysis because it will easily lead to exclusion of relevant records of publications. Moreover, language restrictions should be avoided in the context of meta-analyses, as the aim is to retrieve all relevant evidence on, for example, treatment effects, which may come from publications in languages other than English.

Thesaurus and Index

The thesaurus and index of bibliographic databases may assist the identification and selection of candidate search terms for the domain, determinant, and outcome. A *thesaurus* is a systematic list, or database, of hierarchically arranged related standardized subject headings, the so-called *controlled vocabulary*. The hierarchy of a thesaurus, that is, the more specific narrower terms are arranged beneath more general broader terms, provides a context to topical search keywords. Standardized subject headings are available and may be helpful when exploring and identifying relevant candidate retrieval terms for well-defined and generally accepted medical concepts. In general, about ten standardized subject headings are assigned to each record contained by electronic bibliographic databases, that is, the tagging of articles.

One should be aware of the drawbacks in using the thesaurus database in the exploration and identification of relevant candidate retrieval terms. First, while searching with subject terms in the thesaurus database, for example, in the PubMed MeSH (Medical Subject Headings; NIH and NLM) database, the so-called *term explosion* function by which a default automatically includes all hierarchical lower subject heading terms in the search, dramatically increases the number of retrieved records. This increase in number of retrieved records invariably includes many non-relevant records, which always reduces the retrieval efficiency by an increase of the number needed to read. Second, it takes time before a term is included in the thesaurus as a standardized subject heading. Research that is published before its appropriate medical subject heading is added to the thesaurus will be indexed under different headings. Therefore, studies that opened a specific research field will not be found under the appropriate subject heading that is added to the thesaurus at a later stage. Third, indexing of records is static, which means that subject terms attached to older records are not updated when the thesaurus is changed. So, records indexed according to the previous version of the thesaurus may not be retrieved when newer standardized subject headings are used in a search filter. Fourth, one should be aware of the time lag between the publication date and tagging date. Thus, the most recent pertinent records will always be missed when searching with only standardized subject headings. Finally, a thesaurus grows over time, and so it is subject to change. This means that the context of and relationship between subject heading terms is subject to change, which may result in misspecification of retrieval terms and, consequently, omission of pertinent records.

An *index* is a detailed list, or database, of alphabetically arranged search keywords, which for example, is found under the PubMed Preview/Index tab. The index of a bibliographic database contains search keywords from different indexed fields of records, for example, author, title, abstract, keywords, publication type, or author affiliation. An index is not subject to the obvious drawbacks of a thesaurus, which include time lags for standardized tagging, term misspecification, and explosion of attached lower terms. Using index databases facilitates exploration and identification of relevant candidate retrieval terms because the frequency of occurrence of words per field is usually listed. Authors of original publications will use terms and synonyms relating to the patients (domain), treatments, and outcomes in both the title and (often more than once) the abstract. One should make use of this and explore relevant candidate search terms and synonyms, in particular in the title and abstract fields, to retrieve pertinent records.

A drawback of this approach may be that one should always include several different synonyms for the same concepts and take into account differences in U.K. and U.S. spelling. But when a search string is designed properly, the efficiency of the search increases, notably the number of records retrieved decreases while the number of pertinent records increases (i.e., the number needed to read decreases). Using the thesaurus database may help to identify candidate search terms that can be explored for their relevance in the title and abstract fields with the index.

In building a search filter, one should always avoid the pitfalls of so-called *automatic term mapping*, where search terms without a field specification are automatically translated to, for example, MeSH terms. Whether this happens (at least in PubMed) can be checked under the Details tab. For example, when in PubMed, "blind" without field specification is used to identify trials with blind outcome assessment; this word is translated to the MeSH term *visually impaired*. This leads to misspecification of the context and results of the retrieved records, leading to a large number of irrelevant records and hence to a dramatic increase of the numbers needed to read. Therefore, we advise that the researcher always use a field specification, in particular, the title and abstract fields (tiab in PubMed syntax). Under the PubMed Index/Preview tab, the frequency of tagged search terms can be explored for each field, and this will automatically provide the adequate syntax for the fields of the search terms.

Clinical Queries

PubMed includes so-called *Clinical Queries* that can be found in the blue side bar at the PubMed home page. The therapy query, using the Boolean operator *AND*, can be combined with the constructed subject-specific search filter in order to retain records about treatment effects, while reducing the search yield to more manageable numbers of records.

Several other methods filters for different bibliographic databases are available [Wong et al., 2006a; Watson et al., 1999b; Wong et al., 2006b; Zhang et al., 2006]. Some of these have been tested intensively [Shojania & Bero, 2001; Wilczynski et al., 1994; Wilczynski & Haynes, 2002; Wilczynski et al., 2005; Montori et al., 2005; Jadad & McQuay, 1993] but none are perfect, and often certain relevant articles will be missed. The added value of methods filters, in terms of accuracy of their yield, however, may depend on the medical field or research question of interest [Sampson et al., 2006a]. For PubMed clinical queries, a broad (i.e., sensitive or inclusive) or a narrow (i.e., specific or restrictive) prespecified search methods filter is available. While a broad methods search filter is more comprehensive, the number needed to read will always be higher. With a narrow methods filter, the number of records retrieved will be smaller, but the likelihood of excluding pertinent records is higher. Therefore, it is advised not to use narrow methods filters in the context of meta-analyses.

Complementary Searches

Publications are not always properly included or indexed in electronic bibliographic databases. Sometimes, pertinent studies identified by other means turn out to be included in electronic bibliographic databases but are inappropriately indexed, for example, because of changes in the thesaurus. Therefore, searching for *lateral references* always remains necessary to supplement initial retrieval of relevant publications and to optimize your search filter.

Additional relevant publications can be found by screening the reference lists of available systematic reviews, meta-analyses, expert reviews, and editorials on your topic, for publications not retrieved by your search filter. Web of Science, the bibliographic database of the Institute of Scientific Information (ISI), facilitates such cross-reference searching by links to publications cited in the identified paper but also links to publications citing the identified paper. PubMed facilitates such cross-reference searching by a link to so-called *related articles*. It is advisable to use cross-reference searching for all pertinent records selected with your initial search, and use the Boolean operator *OR* to combine them all. To avoid duplication of work, records already retrieved by the initial search filter can be excluded by combining the collection *related articles* and the initial search filter by the Boolean operator *NOT*. Then, the remainder of the related articles is screened for relevant additional records.

When cross-reference searching yields additional relevant publications, these should be scrutinized for new relevant search terms for domain, determinants, and outcomes in the title and abstract. These should always be added to update the initial subject-specific search filter. Again, the Boolean operator *NOT* should be used to exclude the records already retrieved by the initial search filter (plus the combined related articles). Then the remaining records are screened for other additional relevant records and new search terms. Thus, building a subject-specific search filter becomes a systematic iterative process. Still, the total number of original studies published on a topic of a particular meta-analysis always remains unknown. Therefore, it may be useful to write to experts, researchers, and authors, including a list of the retrieved trial publications, and ask them to add studies not yet on the list.

Most electronic bibliographic databases only include citations of studies published as full text articles. To retrieve studies without full publication it is useful to write to researchers, authors, and experts for preliminary reports, and search in Web of Science or on the Internet (e.g., Web sites of conferences and professional societies) for abstracts of meetings and conference proceedings. The recently initiated registry for clinical trials [De Angelis et al., 2004; Couser et al., 2005] promises a better view on all studies conducted, some of which may never be published in full (Textbox 11.2). Some authors have suggested that journal hand searching, which is a manual page-by-page examination of contents of relevant journals, may reveal additional relevant publications [Jefferson & Jefferson, 1996; McDonald et al., 2002; Hopewell et al., 2002, Sampson et al., 2006b]. In addition, Internet search engines, in particular, Google-Scholar (http://scholar.google.com/; accessed July 8, 2007), may prove useful in the retrieval of citations [Eysenbach et al., 2001] and, in particular, full-text articles that somehow have not made it to other databases.

Screening and Selection

Aggregation of data in a meta-analysis is restricted to trials judged to be combinable with respect to patients, treatments, and end-points. If the trials differ considerably in these aspects, it may not be appropriate to combine

TEXTBOX 11.2 Internet resources for trial registries (accessed July 7, 2007)

http://www.clinicaltrials.gov from the U.S. National Library of Medicine

http://www.controlled-trials.com from the International Standard Randomised Controlled Trial Number registry, Bio Med Central

http://www.update-software.com/national from the the National (UK) Research Register, Department of Health

http://eudract.emea.europa.eu from the European Clinical Trials Database, EudraCT

Source: Author.

the results. Hence, trials are selected and grouped according to similarity of study design.

Titles and abstracts of all records should be screened using prespecified and explicit selection criteria that relate to the combinability of studies. These include:

- Domain: types of patients, for example, disease or health problem, specific subgroups, and setting (e.g., general practice or hospital).
- Treatments: for example, characteristics of treatment, type of comparator (placebo, active, add-on).
- Outcomes: for example, type of end-points, scales, dimensions and follow-up time.
- Design of data collection and analysis and reporting of data: for example, randomization, concealment of treatment allocation, blinded end-point assessment, reporting of absolute risks.

Based on the results of the selection process, combinable studies can be identified or grouped for separate or stratified analysis. In our experience, any physician familiar with the subject but untrained in library information can handle the scanning of titles at a pace of about 250 per hour, provided that abstracts are read only when the title does not provide sufficient information. For this, it is convenient and advisable to store titles and abstracts of all retrieved electronic records in a citation management software program (Textbox 11.3). When doubts remain about the appropriateness of selection of a particular study after reading the abstract, the full publication must be scrutinized.

Avoiding Bias

Retrieval and selection of original studies should be based on a comprehensive search and explicit selection criteria. Relevant publications are eas-

TEXTBOX 11.3 Internet resources for bibliographic and citation management software programs

Endnote (Thomson ResearchSoft, Thomson Scientific):
http://www.endnote.com

Reference manager (Thomson ResearchSoft Thomson Scientific):
http://www.refman.com

Pro-cite (Thomson ResearchSoft, Thomson Scientific):
http://www.procite.com

Refworks (Bethesda, MD, USA): http://www.refworks.com

Connotea (Nature Publishing Group): http://www.connotea.org

*All URLS accessed July 7, 2007

Source: Author.

ily missed with an incomprehensive or even flawed retrieval and selection procedure. Selection must be based on criteria related to the study design rather than on results of a particular study or its purported appropriateness and relevance. Holes in a methods filter as well as searching in a limited number of bibliographic databases may lead to serious omissions. When a search is not comprehensive or selection is flawed, this may lead to biased results of meta-analysis, which is known as *retrieval and reviewer bias*.

To prevent reviewer bias, the selection of material should preferably be based on consensus of at least two independent researchers [Moher et al., 1999; Jadad et al. 1996; Edwards et al., 2002]. Still, any comprehensive strategy for the retrieval and selection of relevant original studies can be frustrated by flaws in reporting of individual trials [Sutton et al., 2002].

Trials with positive and significant results are more likely to be reported and are published faster, particularly when they are published in English (i.e., *publication bias*) [Juni et al., 2002; Sterne et al., 2002]. Furthermore, such positive trials are cited more often (i.e., *citation bias*), which makes them easier to locate, so only a comprehensive search can prevent such retrieval bias [Ravnskov, 1992]. Multiple reporting of a single trial, for example, reporting of initial and final results, different follow-up times or end-points in subsequent publications, and preferential reporting of positive results, are difficult to disclose (i.e., *dissemination bias*). There is no complete remedy against these types of bias in reporting and dissemination of trials.

Omission of pertinent studies and inclusion of multiple publications may change the results of a meta-analysis dramatically [Stern & Simes, 1997; Simes, 1987]. For example, from around 2000 eligible titles that were retrieved in a meta-analysis assessing the effect of off-pump coronary surgery, only 66 publications remained after exclusion of publications of non-randomized trials and randomized trials with another treatment comparison or another end-point. After assessing the 66 reports, seven conference abstracts of trials not fully published were excluded. There were 17 duplicate publications relating to three trials, leaving 42 full trial publications for further analysis [Van der Heijden et al., 2004].

Critical Appraisal

Randomized trials are the cornerstone for evaluation of treatment effects. They frequently offer the best possibility for valid and precise effect estimations, but many aspects of their design and conduct require careful handling for their results to be valid. Hence, critical appraisal of all elements of study design is an important part of meta-analysis. Critical appraisal concentrates on aspects of study design that impact the validity of the study, notably randomization techniques and concealment of treatment allocation, blinded end-point assessment, adherence to the allocation scheme, contamination of treatment contrast, post-randomization attrition, and statistical techniques applied. This requires information regarding inclusion and exclusion criteria, treatment regimens, and mode of administration, the type of end-points, their measurement scale, and the duration of follow-up and time points of follow-up assessments. Each aspect of the study design needs to be documented on a predesigned critical appraisal checklist to decide whether the publication provides sufficient information and, if so, whether the applied methods were adequate and bias is considered likely or not. Based on this critical appraisal, studies can be grouped by the type and number of design flaws as well as by the level of omitted information. Accordingly, decisions about which studies are combinable in a pooled or a stratified analysis can be taken.

Although the requirements for reporting the methods of clinical trials are well-defined and have been generally accepted [Chalmers et al., 1987a, 1987b; Moher et al., 2005; Plint et al., 2006], for many studies, information on important design features cannot be found in the published report. For example, only 11 of 42 trials comparing coronary bypass surgery with or without a cardiopulmonary bypass pump that are reported as a "randomized trial" provided information on the methods of randomization and concealment of treatment allocation in establishing outcomes, while only 14 reported on blinding of treatment or standardized post-surgical care and 30 stated the conversion of treatment [Van der Heijden et al., 2004]. The unavailability of this information hampers a complete and critical appraisal of studies and raises questions about the validity of their results.

Blinding during critical appraisal for the journal source, the authors, and their affiliation, and the study results by editing copies of the articles requires ample time and resources. Therefore, it only should be considered when reviewer bias is considered an important threat to the validity of the meta-analysis [Jadad et al., 1996; Verhagen et al., 1998]. To avoid errors in the assessment of trials, critical appraisal should be standardized using a checklist that is preferably completed independently by two reviewers as they read the selected publications. In the event of disagreement between these two reviewers, the eventual data analyzed can be based on a consensus meeting or a third reviewer may provide a decisive assessment.

Studies that are the same with respect to the outcome, including scales used and follow-up times, can be pooled by conventional statistical procedures. Similarity can be judged by the information that is derived during data extraction. Data extraction entails documentation of relevant data for each study on a standardized data registry form, and should include the number of patients randomized per group and their baseline characteristics, notably relevant prognostic markers. The follow-up data to be recorded for each treatment group should, for each outcome and follow-up time, include the point estimates and variance and the number of patients analyzed, with accrued person-time at risk. Using these data, trials can be grouped by outcome, follow-up time, or even risk status at baseline. Accordingly, this gives a further quantitative basis for decisions about which studies are combinable in the pooled or a stratified analysis. Unfortunately, necessary quantitative details of follow-up data are frequently omitted, and inadequate or incomplete reporting of distribution of outcome parameters for trials precludes them from statistical pooling in a meta-analysis. For example, only four of 42 trials comparing coronary bypass surgery with or without a cardiopulmonary bypass pump reported data that allowed calculating a composite end-point for death, stroke, and myocardial infarction [Van der Heijden et al., 2004].

Design of Data Analysis

The ultimate goal of meta-analysis, while maintaining validity, is to obtain a more precise estimate of treatment effect. The confidence interval of the combined estimate of effect should be narrow relative to the confidence interval of the individual studies included. Thus, a meta-analysis increases the statistical power. But sophisticated statistical procedures cannot compensate for inclusion of flawed data. There is an analogy between individual studies included in a meta-analysis and the analysis of subgroups in single trials. Subgroup analyses are suspected of producing spurious results due to their limited statistical power. The best estimate of effect for a particular subgroup in general will be the overall effect of the total population. The principle of this so-called *Stein's paradox* is the "shrinkage" of individual data points toward the grand mean. The extent of the shrinkage of an observed value depends on the precision of the observed value. Based on the principle of shrinkage, combined analysis of studies included in a meta-analysis will improve statistical power of the estimate of effect and reduce chance findings. The principle of shrinkage also is used in a so-called *cumulative meta-analysis*, where in a Bayesian approach information from a new trial is incorporated in the full knowledge provided by prior trials. For example, thrombolytic treatment (streptokinase) was shown to provide a clinically important and statistically significant benefit in terms of survival for patients with an acute myocardial infarction, long before it became widely accepted as being effective. Similarly, corticosteroids were shown to speed fetal lung maturity long before they became widely accepted as being effective [Antman et al., 1992; Lau et al., 1992; Lau & Chalmers, 1995; Berkey et al., 1996; Whitehead, 1997].

Measures of Effects

In trials, effects are often expressed as a relative measure of occurrence, such as a risk ratio, an odds ratio, or a hazards ratio. Alternatively, differences in risks or hazards can be used. The decision about which measure of an effect to use in a meta-analysis must be carefully considered and depends on the purpose for which the analysis is done. Occurrence measures differ primarily in the way the denominator is chosen. For a risk, the denominator is the number of randomized patients, for an odds the number of patients without events, and for a hazard the person-time "at risk" for the event of interest. For example, the total person-time at risk for myocardial infarction is the time from randomization until first infarction, death, or end of the follow-up period (whichever comes first) summed for all patients assigned to a particular treatment. Death or end of follow-up is often denoted as censoring of follow-up for infarction.

Person-Time At Risk

For acute conditions, events cluster within a relatively short time period. A fixed duration of follow-up that is the same for all patients can be chosen long enough to cover the outcome of the acute condition concerned (e.g., in otitis media research) and risks are usually appropriate measures of occurrence. For a chronic condition (e.g., chronic heart failure, rheumatoid arthritis), however, events do not cluster in time, so the follow-up can never be long enough to observe all eventual outcomes of the condition concerned. Trials of chronic conditions vary considerably in duration of follow-up chosen. Usually, the duration of follow-up also differs within a particular trial. This occurs when a so-called *common stopping date* is used, that is, because patients are never all included on the same day. For chronic conditions, therefore, the hazard is usually the most appropriate measure of occurrence.

Unfortunately, the term *hazard* is rarely used in clinical trial reports in medical journals, where hazards are usually denoted by terms such as rate, incidence, incidence rate, or (how confusing!) risk. In meta-analyses, extracting hazard data is important because differences in follow-up times are a source of heterogeneity and competing risks give rise to biased estimates. (This is explained below.) Regrettably, few reports on chronic disease trials report hazards, or mean durations of follow-up "at risk" by treatment, which allow calculation of hazards. Only occasionally will all sufficient data be given that do allow calculation of hazards. This is illustrated with the Kaplan-Meier plot from the SOLVD-trial (Figure 11.1), where the effect of the angiotensin converting enzyme (ACE)-inhibitor enalapril on mortality and hospitalization was assessed in patients with chronic heart failure with an ejection fraction below 35% [The SOLVD Investigators, 1991]. From the data beneath the Kaplan-Meier plot, the person-time at risk of an event is calculated for both groups: for placebo = $\Sigma(1159 \times 6 + 125 \times 3 + ...) = 42,624$ months (mean 33.2) and for enalapril = $\Sigma(1195 \times 6 + 90 \times 3 + ...) = 44,943$ months (mean 35.0). The results of this trial are summarized in Table 11.1. The event-rate for enalapril is 12.1 per 100 patient-years (452/44,943) with a mean duration of follow-up until death or end of trial participation of 35.0 months. The event-rate for placebo is 14.4 per 100 patient-years (510/42,624) with a mean duration of follow-up until death or end of trial participation of 33.2 months. Thus, the hazard ratio is 0.84 (12.1/14.4), and the relative risk reduction is 16% (1 − 0.84).

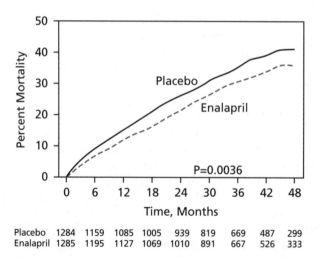

Placebo	1284	1159	1085	1005	939	819	669	487	299
Enalapril	1285	1195	1127	1069	1010	891	667	526	333

FIGURE 11.1 Kaplan-Meier plot of mortality curves from the randomized placebo-controlled trial on the effect of enalapril in patients with chronic heart failure and ejection fractions less than or equal to 0.35. The numbers of patients alive in each group at the end of each period are shown at the bottom of the graphic. $P = 0.0036$ for the comparison of survival between groups by the log-rank test.

Used with permission from *The New England Journal of Medicine*. The SOLVD Investigators. Effect of enalapril on survival in patients with reduced left ventricular ejection fractions and congestive heart failure. N Engl J Med 1991;325:293–302.

TABLE 11.1 Summary of the results for the randomized placebo-controlled trial on the effect of enalapril (an angiotensin-converting-enzyme inhibitor) in patients with chronic heart failure and ejection fractions less than or equal to 0.35

These summary data are based on the figures below the Kaplan-Meier plot (see Figure 11.1).

Treatment	Number of patients	Number of events	Mean rime of follow-up (months)	Person time at Risk (months)	Hazard per 100 patient years	Risk	Odds
Enapril	1285	452	35.0	44943	12.1	0.352	0.543
Placebo	1284	510	33.2	42624	14.4	0.397	0.659

The hazard ratio is 0.84 (12.1/14.4 or a relative risk reduction of 16%), the risk ratio is 0.89 (0.352/0.397 or a relative risk reduction of 11%), and the odds ratio is 0.82 (0.543/0.659 or a relative risk reduction of 18%). Another useful way of expressing the effect of enalapril is the mean additional survival time: 1.8 months (= 35.0 – 33.2).

It should be noted that the vertical axis of a Kaplan-Meier curve gives the event-free survival, that is, the probability of an event (or no event) assuming that there was no censoring. This is correct as long as the only reason for censoring is variability in duration of follow-up. Usually censoring is related to other (competing) events, for example, myocardial infarction, and then a Kaplan-Meier curve (and rates or risks derived from it) becomes meaningless.

Hazards Instead of Risks and Odds Ratios

As hazards are usually not given in published reports and can often not be calculated based on the data given, most meta-analyses are based on odds or risks as these can always be abstracted. Although different effect measures are useful, relative measures of occurrence have rather convenient mathematical properties. For this reason, most meta-analyses consider relative effect measures.

For chronic conditions, the hazard ratio would be the relative measure of choice also because the "risk reductions" reported for individual trials are in fact hazard reductions when these were obtained using either the log-rank test or Cox-regression. These methods relate the hazard in the index group to the hazard in the control group, assuming that their ratio is constant over time. While these methods do not make any assumptions about how the hazards behave over time, the additional implicit assumption (that the hazards are constant over time) is often appropriate for chronic disease trials with a limited duration of follow-up. This additional assumption, however, is a useful one when combining results of chronic disease trials by meta-analysis.

Another important reason for not using a risk or odds-based measure of an effect when meta-analyzing chronic disease trials with variable durations of follow-up is that it depends on the duration of follow-up, even when the hazards are constant over time. This is illustrated in Table 11.2 using simulated data for seven trials (A–F) with different follow-up times (each involving 1000 randomized patients) and constant hazards for treatment and placebo, 14 and 20 per 100 patient-years, respectively (hazard ratio = 0.70). From the odds-ratio, risk-ratio, and risk differences calculated for these trials, it follows that the variability of follow-up durations between trials is an unnecessary and also unhelpful source of variability of effect estimates between the trials considered.

Finally, the use of risk- or odds-based measures of effect may lead to spurious conclusions about effects on competing events, such as cause-specific death. In Table 11.3, simulated data are given for a trial of a chronic condition, assuming constant hazards of cardiovascular (CV) and non-CV death. Note that the hazards for treatment and placebo can be obtained by using the number of events given for each cause of death in each treatment group as the numerator, and the mean follow-up time multiplied by the number of patients in each treatment group as the denominator, for example, the all cause mortality hazard is 14 per 100 person-years for active treatment: $686/(2000 \times 2.45)$ and 20 per 100 person-years for placebo treatment, $904/(2000 \times 2.26)$. The benefit of active treatment, of course, should be expressed as the hazard ratio for all cause mortality, which is 0.7, thus, a 30% relative risk reduction following active treatment. Note that the treatment has an effect only on cardiovascular death (hazard ratio = 0.4); the

TABLE 11.2   Simulated data for seven trials (A–F) with different follow-up times (each 1000 patients randomized) and constant hazards for treatment and placebo, respectively 14 and 20 per 100 patient-years (hazard ratio = 0.70), showing biased effect estimates when calculated as odds ratio, risk ratio and risk difference, which clearly depend on the follow-up rime

Trials	Follow-up (Years)	Treatment Number of events	Placebo Number of events	Odds Ratio	Risk Ratio	Risk Difference
A	1	131	181	0.68	0.72	−0.05
B	2	244	330	0.66	0.74	−0.09
C	3	343	452	0.63	0.76	−0.11
D	5	503	632	0.59	0.80	−0.13
E	10	753	865	0.48	0.87	−0.11
F	30	985	998	0.16	0.99	−0.01

TABLE 11.3 Simulated data for a placebo-controlled trial for patients with a chronic condition, randomized to two treatment groups, each of 2000 patients, assuming constant hazards of cardiovascular and non-cardiovascular death, showing spurious findings of an adverse treatment effect for non-cardiovascular death when risk ratios or odds ratios are applied

	Active	Hazards per 100 person-years	Placebo	Hazards per 100 person-years	Hazard ratio	Risk ratio	Odds ratio
Number of patients	2000		2000				
Mean follow-up (years)	2.45		2.26				
Death (total N)	686	14	904	20	0.7	0.76	0.63
Cardiovascular death (n)	196	4	452	10	0.4	0.43	0.37
Non-cardiovascular death (n)	490	10	452	10	1.0	1.08	1.11

hazards of non-cardiovascular death are the same in each treatment group (hazard ratio = 1.0). Using odds ratio or risk ratio, however, would lead to spurious findings of an adverse treatment effect for non-cardiovascular death: the risk ratio for non-cardiovascular death would be 1.08 (or [490/2000]/[452/2000]) while the odds ratio would be 1.11 (or [490/1510]/[452/1548]).

Weighing

Small sample studies are more subject to the play of chance than large sample studies and in general their effect estimate is less precise. A straightforward arithmetic average of the effect estimates reported for the individual studies will provide an inappropriate summary effect estimate, because the difference in information contributed by the various trials included is not considered. Adding up the individual 2 × 2 tables of all studies in one summary 2 × 2 table gives a fairly adequate summary result of the combined trials, but still may not weigh the information in each trial correctly. Therefore, in meta-analyses, a weighted average effect estimate across trial results is calculated, where the weights express the amount of information contributed by the study. In this way, larger trials have more impact on the pooled effect estimate. There are several procedures for weighing individual studies but all give larger trials with a smaller standard error of the effect estimate more weight than smaller trials [DerSimonian & Laird, 1986]. The sample size of each trail (i.e., the Mantel-Haenszel method) or the inverse variance of the effect estimate of each trail (i.e., the inverse variance method) is most often used as weights. Then, the effect estimate of each trial is multiplied by its weight and the results are summed. The total is then divided by the sum of the weights.

Table 11.4 is an example of a meta-analysis and includes the formulas used for weighing and calculating the average effect estimate across trial results, using the inverse variance method for which the effect estimate of each trial is weighted relative to its variance. It should be noted that a simple Excel software spreadsheet may satisfy for these calculations. For risk differences, particularly when baseline risk is low for one of the treatment groups of an individual trial, the inverse variance weighting is reported to produce biased summary effect estimates [Sweeting et al., 2004]. With the inverse variance weighting method, individual trials reporting no events for one or both treatment groups are omitted from the meta-analysis. Under those circumstances, the Mantel-Haenszel method should be used.

Heterogeneity

Effect estimates may vary in magnitude and direction across trials. Heterogeneity is defined as the variability in effect size estimates that exceed those expected from random variation (or sampling error) alone. There are essentially two models for statistical pooling that differ in the way they handle variability across summary effect estimates of trials. First, the fixed-effects model assumes that variability across effect estimates of trials is entirely due to random variation. This means that with infinite sample sizes all trials would provide an identical "typical" effect estimate. Second, the random-effects model assumes a random distribution of treatment effects across trials, so the homogeneity assumption underlying the fixed-effects model does not apply. Due to this additional source of variation, the confidence interval obtained for the summary effect estimate with a random-effects model is, in general, wider than for the fixed-effects model. Conventionally, the random-effects model is used when one of the available statistical tests indicates marked heterogeneity across the effect estimates of individual trials. Statistical tests for heterogeneity, such as the (Peto or Cochrane) chi-square test, evaluate whether the underlying true treatment effect is constant across studies or whether the observed variability of treatment effect across studies is more than just random error [Berry, 1998]. However, there are subtle problems in handling heterogeneity. First, the absence of significance for a test for heterogeneity is no proof of homogeneity. Statistical tests for heterogeneity are subject to the play of chance and their results depend largely on the number of trials included. When the number of trials is limited, they commonly lack statistical power. An alternative test statistic, the I^2, does not depend on the number of studies included [Higgins & Thompson, 2002].

TABLE 11.4 Example of the calculations for a meta-analysis using weights according to the inverse variance method; the pooled risk ratio is 0.67, with a confidence interval ranging from 0.57 to 0.80

	ACE		Placebo		Risk ratio	Natural logarithm of the RR	Standard error RR	95% confidence interval		Weight	Weight*ln(RR)	chi	chi-square
	Events	Subjects	Events	Subjects				Lower limit	Upper limit				
Hope [Lonn, 2004]	156	4645	226	4652	0.69	0.369170	0.102004	0.57	0.84	96.10959	−35.4810793	0.256037	0.065555
Part 2 [MacMahon, 2000]	7	308	4	309	1.76	0.562857	0.621590	0.52	5.94	2.58165	1.456767465	1.541446	2.376055
Quiet [Pitt, 2001]	1	878	1	872	0.99	0.006860	1.413405	0.06	15.85	0.500572	−0.00343251	0.274821	0.075526
Scat [Teo, 2000]	2	229	9	231	0.22	1.495380	0.776154	0.05	1.03	1.659984	−2.4823103	−1.41736	2.008916
Prevent [Tulenko, 1999]	5	417	5	408	0.98	0.021820	0.628610	0.29	3.35	2.530679	−0.055217	0.594121	0.352980
Systeur [Staessen, 1997]	49	2398	80	2297	0.59	0.533240	0.179041	0.41	0.83	31.1956	−16.6346649	−0.77048	0.593637
									total	134.5846	−53.1999366		5.472670
									weighted mean	−0.39529			0.360952

Summary RR 0.67
Lower limit 95%CI of RR 0.57
Upper limit 95%CI of RR 0.80

Risk ratio (RR)*	= (events treated/total treated)/(events control/total control)
Natural logarithm RR	= Ln (RR)
Standard error RR*	= Square root of (1/events treated −1/subjects treated +1 / events control −1/subjects control)
Lower limit 95%CI	= Exponent of (Ln (RR) − 1,96 * Standard error RR)
Upper limit 95%CI	= Exponent of (Ln (RR) + 1,96 * Standard error RR)
Weight	= 1/square of Standard error RR
Weight*Log(RR)	= Weight * Ln (RR)
Chi	= (Ln (RR) − weighted mean)/Standard error RR
Chi-square	= Square of Chi
Σ weights	= Sum of weights
Σ Weight*Log(RR)	= Sum of (Weight * Ln (RR))
Weighted mean	= Σ Weight*Log(RR)/Σ weights
Summary RR	= Exponent of (weighted mean)
Lower limit 95%CI Summary RR	= Exponent of (weighted mean − 1,96*square root(1/ Sum of weights))
Upper limit 95%CI Summary RR	= Exponent of (weighted mean + 1,96*square root(1/ Sum of weights))
Σ Chi-squares	= Sum of Chi-squares

* For odds ratio based meta-analyses, the risk ratio is replaced by the odds ratio, which is calculated by (events treated/no events treated)/(events control/no events control) and the standard error of the RR is replaced by the standard error of the OR which is calculated by the square root of (1/events treated +1/subjects treated +1/events control +1/subjects control).

Used with permission from *Statistics in Medicine*. Sweeting MJ, Sutton AJ, Lambert PC. What to add to nothing? Use and avoidance of continuity corrections in meta-analysis of sparse data. *Stat Med* 2004;23:1351–75.

Second, when heterogeneity is observed across individual trials, one may question whether trials can be combined in the first place. Using a statistical method, such as a random-effects model, to then combine the individual studies may be a disquieting solution, as it hides a possible underlying relevant and true source of heterogeneity that is, however, not detected using the available characteristics of the studies.

Therefore, when effect estimates across trials appear heterogeneous, the robustness of the random-effects model for possible different sources of heterogeneity should be explored. For instance, it could be biologically unlikely for the treatment effect to be the same across different patient subgroups. In particular, the risk status at baseline may have an impact on (i.e., modifies) the treatment effect [Arends et al., 2000]. Other reasons for heterogeneity could relate to specific aspects of study design, for example, type of treatment comparison (e.g., a placebo, an active treatment, no treatment, or add-on treatment), concealment of treatment allocation, and blinding of outcome assessment.

Fitting a Model to the Data

Meta-analysts tend to force their data to fit a preconceived model, such as a model that assumes the odds ratio to be constant across levels of absolute risk. It should be emphasized that this may result in inappropriate estimates of effect, in particular when the heterogeneity test is not statistically significant. A powerful way to examine which model fits the data best is to first plot the absolute occurrence measures for index treatment and control treatment in a so-called *L'Abbé plot* [L'Abbé et al., 1987]. Such a plot can be used to explore the degree of heterogeneity between trials and to identify the effect model that seems to best describe the relationship, if any. It should be noted that this method can be used only when it is possible to obtain the absolute occurrence measures for each treatment arm for each trial considered, expressed in such a manner that these can be compared. For chronic disease trials, this is usually the hazard. Risks and odds can be compared only when the duration of follow-up over which these measures are taken is always the same.

Various effect models that the data can suggest are shown in Figure 11.2. The gray line represents the traditional fixed-effects model for the hazard ratio, where the ratio of the absolute occurrence measures of the index and control treatment is constant. The black line represents a fixed-effects model for the hazard difference, where the difference of the absolute occurrence measures of the index and control treatment is constant. The dotted line represents a model that assumes a linear relationship between the hazard in the intervention and the hazard in the control group, where the absolute occurrence measure of the index treatment is proportional to absolute occurrence measures of the control treatment plus a constant. The latter is particularly plausible biologically because it allows for the possibility that a treatment is

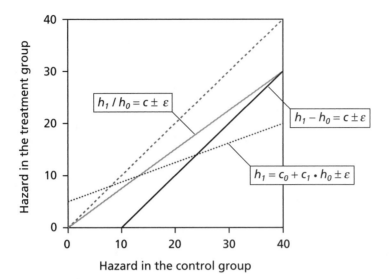

FIGURE 11.2 L'Abbé plot. Symbols are: (gray line) a fixed-effects model assuming a constant ratio between the absolute occurrence measures (hazards) for the treatment and control groups; (black line) a fixed-effects model assuming a constant difference between the absolute occurrence measures (hazards) for the treatment and control groups; (dotted line) a model that assumes a linear relationship between the hazards in the treatment group and the control group, with a hazard of the index treatment that is proportional to the hazard in the control treatment plus a constant. Above the dotted black line, the treatment is harmful; below the dotted line the treatment is beneficial.

harmful in individuals at low risk (represented by a small hazard in the control group) and beneficial at high risk (represented by a big hazard in the control group). Traditional weighted-averaging will work for the green and the black models, using inverse variances as weights. The red model requires weighted linear regression or a Bayesian approach [Van Houwelingen et al., 2002]. As an alternative to the L'Abbé plot, it has been proposed to plot for each trial the effect measure chosen on the vertical axis against the occurrence measure for index and control treatment combined [Arends et al., 2000]. This method, however, does not suggest directly which models will fit the data most closely.

Meta-Regression

Staessen et al. [2001] plotted treatment effects expressed as the difference between treatment and control groups in mean on-treatment blood pressure levels against treatment effect on outcome, expressed as odds ratios (Figure 11.3). These so-called *meta-regression* methods may help to explore possible sources of heterogeneity across trials. More often, meta-regression is

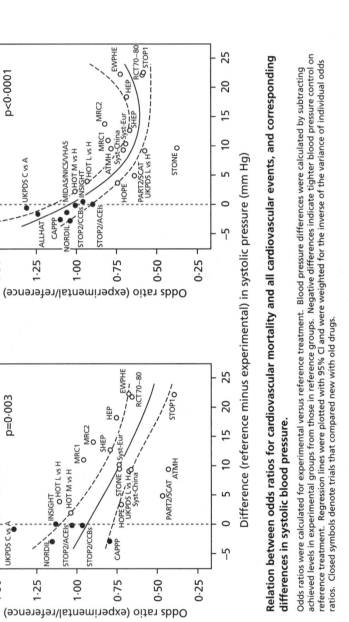

Relation between odds ratios for cardiovascular mortality and all cardiovascular events, and corresponding differences in systolic blood pressure.

Odds ratios were calculated for experimental versus reference treatment. Blood pressure differences were calculated by subtracting achieved levels in experimental groups from those in reference groups. Negative differences indicate tighter blood pressure control on reference treatment. Regression lines were plotted with 95% CI and were weighted for the inverse of the variance of individual odds ratios. Closed symbols denote trials that compared new with old drugs.

FIGURE 11.3 Example of a meta-regression analysis [Staessen, 2001]. On the horizontal axis the difference in systolic blood pressure (mm Hg) is depicted. The vertical axis shows the odds ratio for cardiovascular mortality (left panel) and cardiovascular events (right panel) of the trials considered.

Used with permission from *The Lancet*. Staessen JA, Whang J., Thijs L. Cardiovascular protection and blood pressure reduction: a meta-analysis. *Lancet* 2001; 358:1305–1315.

performed on the basis of potential bias of individual studies, that is, type of flaw in the study design [Sterne et al., 2002; Bjelakovic et al., 2007] or on the basis of specific characteristics of the trial populations, that is, average baseline data for individual trial populations, which are handled as if they were individual baseline observations.

Meta-regression with covariates on patient level and study level may show modification of the summary effect estimate. However, the use of such "mean" co-variates reduces power and can even lead to bias [Thompson & Higgins, 2002; Berlin et al., 2002; Lambert et al., 2002]. Meta-regression, however, must be distinguished from meta-analyses for subgroups. For the latter, the goal is to stratify individual trials according to specific characteristics of the trial populations, such as a meta-analysis that considers treatment effects for men and women separately. Like any subgroup analysis, these approaches to analyzing treatment effects in subgroups should be based on sound reasoning and preferably a plausible biomedical mechanism. However, because effect estimates for exactly the same subgroups are rarely reported for all trials considered, a subgroup meta-analysis is hardly ever seen. In such a stratified analysis, Berger et al. [2006] showed that aspirin therapy reduced the risk of cardiovascular events in both men and women due to its reduction of the risk of ischemic stroke in women and myocardial infarction in men. This difference in cardioprotection observed between the sexes, however, might have been attributable to other phenomena, such as gender differences in the baseline risk, that is, the risk in the control groups in the included trials. Moreover, men also might differ from women with respect to other cardiovascular risk factors, such as age and prevalence of a history of myocardial infarction and diabetes.

Individual Patient Data Meta-Analyses

Meta-analyses based on pooled raw trial data, also called *individual patient-data (IPD)* meta-analyses, are considered to be a more reliable alternative to meta-regression and meta-analysis for subgroups [Clarke & Stewart, 2001; Oxman et al., 1995; Stewart & Tierney, 2002]. For this, two approaches can be used. First, pooled raw data of individual trials can be merged in one database, and subsequently the data are modeled directly, for example, by means of regression techniques, including treatment-covariate interaction terms. Depending on the modification of the treatment effect, that is, statistical significance of the treatment-covariate interaction, summary effect estimates for stratified subgroups are reported. For example, Rovers et al. [2006] performed an IPD meta-analysis of six randomized trials on the efficacy of antibiotics in children with acute otitis media. Otorrhea, age (cut-off at two years of age), and bilateral acute otitis media were shown to modify the effect of antibiotics. The authors showed that children younger than two years of age with bilateral acute otitis media, and children in whom acute otitis media was accompanied by otorrhea benefited most from antibiotics in terms of pain, fever, or both at three to seven days. Second, a so-called two-stage method can be used, where summary results are derived by re-analyzing the raw data of individual trials separately, which subsequently are meta-analyzed using conventional techniques. For both approaches, stratification for included studies, where a dummy variable for study is included in the model, is often used to adjust for possible residual confounding, in particular when statistically significant heterogeneity for the effect estimates of individual studies is considered. Although many IPD meta-analyses have been published, most still emphasize the main treatment effect instead of the treatment effects for subgroups; while examining treatment effects for subgroups is one of the main strengths of IPD meta-analyses. Moreover, for those reporting on treatment effects in subgroups, the two-stage approach appears to be used more often; few use the statistically more efficient direct modeling approach [Koopman et al., 2007].

Reporting Results from a Meta-Analysis

The report of any meta-analysis should be explicit about the study design and account for explicit and repeatable methods of retrieval, selection, critical appraisal, data extraction, and data analysis. Clear numerical tabulation and graphical presentation of data should precede transparent decisions and comments on the completeness and combinability of evidence. Apparent results of the data-analysis and unambiguous conclusions on the effects of treatment should be separated from value judgments. Guidelines for reporting of meta-analyses can be found in the Quality of Reporting of Meta-Analyses (QUORUM) statement (available at http://www.consort-statement.org/complements .htm. Accessed July 9, 2007) [Clarke, 2000].

Flowchart

A report of any meta-analysis should explicitly account for the strategy of publication retrieval and selection and its results. The search filter syntax per bibliographic source with the subsequent number of retrieved publications, the number and reasons for exclusion of publications, the final number of publications included, and the number of trials concerned should be reported preferably in a flowchart (Figure 11.4).

Funnel Plot

A funnel plot is a scatter plot of the treatment effect from individual studies against their sample size or variance of effect measure. Its proponents suggest that it can be used to explore the presence of publication and retrieval bias. It is believed that effect estimates from small studies scatter more

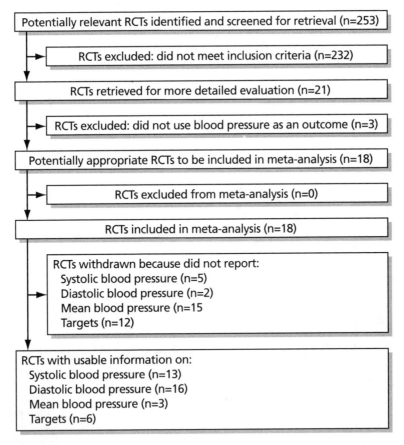

FIGURE 11.4 Example of a flow diagram representing the search and selection of trials.

Used with permission from the *British Medical Journal*. Cappuccio FP, Kerry SM, Forbes L, Donald A. Blood pressure control by home monitoring: meta-analysis of randomised trials. BMJ 2004;329:145.

widely than from larger studies because the precision of treatment effect increases when the sample size increases. Conventionally, a skewed (asymmetrical) funnel plot is considered to indicate bias in publication, retrieval, and selection of trials [Sterne et al., 2000]. For example, if smaller trials with a beneficial treatment effect are more prone to be published and are more likely to be retrieved and selected than smaller studies with no or even a harmful effect of treatment, asymmetry will occur (Figure 11.5).

Many other reasons for funnel plot asymmetry have been suggested, but a rigorous simulation study exploring the impact of several explanations on the impact of funnel plot asymmetry is lacking. Hence, the relevance of

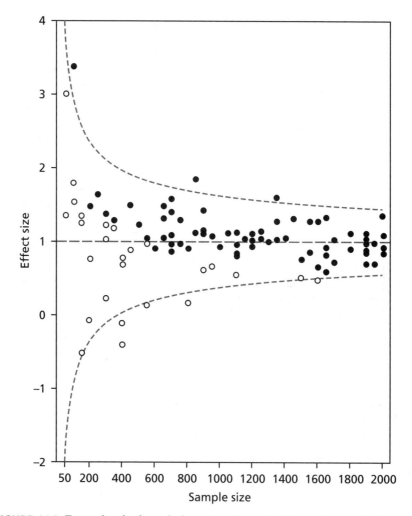

FIGURE 11.5 Example of a funnel plot using theoretical data. The vertical axis shows the effect size (estimate of effects divided by its variance) of the trials considered, and the horizontal axis represents their sample size. Symbols are: (•) trials identified from a literature search; (○) trials that were performed but not published or not detected in a literature search. The funnel plot indicates retrieval or publication bias where almost all of the smaller trials showing a beneficial effect were included in the meta-analysis, while those with a negative effect were unlikely to be published or retrieved.

Used with permission from the *Journal of Clinical Epidemiology*. Sterne JA, Gavaghan D, Egger M. Publication and related bias in meta-analysis: power of statistical tests and prevalence in the literature. J Clin Epidemiol 2000;53:1119–29.

funnel plots for evaluating completeness of the studies included in a meta-analysis remains questionable.

Tables

The results of the critical appraisal and data extraction should be reported in tables. These tables should account for the validity of trials and their combinability. Notably, this includes the relevant characteristics of the participating patients, the compared treatments, and reported end-points. The occurrence measures per treatment group should be tabulated with the effect estimate and its confidence interval for each trial. Examples are Tables 11.5 and 11.6.

Forrest Plot

The results from the data analysis are preferably displayed as a Forrest plot including the pooled effect estimate, its confidence interval, and the heterogeneity of treatment effect of the trials (Figure 11.6). The treatment effect estimate of each trial is represented by a black square with a size that is proportional to the weight attached to the trial, while the horizontal line represents the confidence interval.

The 95% confidence intervals would contain the true underlying effect in 95% of the occasions if the study was repeated again and again. The solid vertical line corresponds to no effect of treatment. If the confidence intervals cross this solid line, the difference in the effect of experimental and control treatment is not significant at the conventional level ($P > 0.05$). The diamond represents the combined treatment effect. The horizontal width of the diamond represents its confidence interval.

The dashed line is plotted vertically through the combined treatment effect. When all confidence intervals cross this plotted line, the trials are rather homogeneous. Ratio (e.g., risk ratio or hazard ratios) measures of effect are typically plotted on a logarithmic scale. The most important reason for using a logarithmic scale is that a ratio and its reciprocal, for example 0.5 and 2.0, have the same magnitude but opposite directions and are equidistant from 1. Thus, the confidence intervals are then plotted symmetrically around the point estimate.

Data Analysis Software

There are many computer programs and software for meta-analyses, which usually include various methods of data analysis and allow different output in tables and graphs. A list of computer programs for meta-analysis is given in Textbox 11.4.

TABLE 11.5 Example of table for reporting results of critical appraisal of the methodology of individual studies from a meta-analysis of trials comparing off-pump and on-pump coronary bypass surgery (ordered by the number of items satisfied)

Trial ID	Concealed treatment allocation	Standardized post-surgical care	Blinding of outcome assessment	Intention to treat analysis	Contamination	Attrition
				Critical Appraisal Items		
Zamvar	●	●	●	●	●	●
Ascione	●	●	●	●	●	●
Puskas	●	●	●	●	●	●
Octopus	●	○	●	●	●	●
Lee	○	●	●	○	●	●
Gulielmos	●	●	○	●	●	●
Parolari	●	●	○	●	●	●
Gulielmos	○	○	○	●	●	●
Diegeler	○	●	○	●	●	●
Matata	○	○	○	●	●	●
Velissaris	○	○	○	●	●	●
Tang	○	○	○	●	●	●
Guler	○	○	○	●	○	●
Al-Ruzzeh	○	○	○	●	○	●
Vural	○	●	○	●	○	●
Baker	○	●	○	◐	●	◐
Wandschneider	○	○	○	◐	●	●
Czerny	○	○	○	◐	●	●
Malheiros	○	○	○	○	●	●
Penttilä	○	●	○	○	○	○

Krejca	o	o	o	o	o	o
Wildhirt	o	o	o	o	o	o
Czerny	o	o	o	∞	o	o
Covino	o	∞	o	o	o	o

Meaning of item ratings:

Contamination: • ≤ 10% cross-over ∞ > 10% cross-over

All other items: • = bias unlikely (yes, adequate design or method)
∞ = bias likely (no, inadequate design or method)
o = unclear (insufficient information available)

Used with permission from the *Journal of Clinical Epidemiology*. Sterne JA, Gavaghan D, Egger M. Publication and related bias in meta-analysis: power of statistical tests and prevalence in the literature. J Clin Epidemiol 2000;53:1119–29.

TABLE 11.6 Example of table for reporting results of data extraction from a meta-analysis of on the effect of lipid lowering treatment [Briel, 2004]

First author or study	Intervention	Follow-up (years)	Coronary heart disease* (%)	Mean age (years)	Men (%)	Diabetes* (%)	Hypertension* (%)	Baseline cholesterol (mmol/L) (%)†	Randomization (treatment/control)	Nonfatal/fatal stroke (treatment/control)	Nonfatal/Fatal myocardial infarction (treatment/control)
Pravastatin multinational study	Pravastatin	0.5	75	55	77	0	48	6.8 (18)	530/532	0/3	0/8
Sacks	Pravastatin	5	100	59	86	15	43	5.4 (20)	2081/2078	54/78	159/211
Bertrand	Pravastatin	0.5	100	58	84	7	31	5.9 (18)	347/348	1/0	5/4
Bradford	Lovastatin	0.9	33	56	59	1	40	6.7 (24)	6582/1663	10/1	63/20
4S	Simvastatin	5.4	100	58	82	5	26	6.8 (26)	2221/2223	56/78	464/491
Athyros	Atorvastatin	3	100	59	79	20	43	6.6 (32)	800/800	9/17	41/89
Blankenhorn	Lovastatin	2	100	58	91	0	46	6.0 (31)	123/124	0/3	4/5
Heart protection study	Simvastatin	5	65	64	75	25	31	5.9 (24)	10,269/10,267	444/585	944/1281
Holdaas	Fluvastatin	5.1	11	50	66	19	75	6.5 (14)	1050/1052	74/63‡	82/120

*Percentage of subjects per trial with the established diagnosis.
†Relative reduction of total cholesterol levels in the treatment group.
‡Includes transient ischemic attacks.

Used with permission from the *American Journal of Medicine*. Briel M, Studer M, Glass TR, Bucher HC. Effects of statins on stroke prevention in patients with and without coronary heart disease: a meta-analysis of randomised controlled trials. Am J Med 2004;117:596–606.

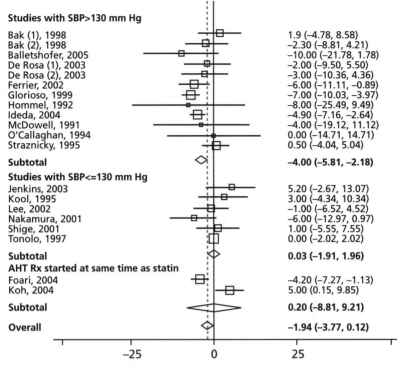

Studies with SBP>130 mm Hg

Bak (1), 1998	1.9 (–4.78, 8.58)
Bak (2), 1998	–2.30 (–8.81, 4.21)
Balletshofer, 2005	–10.00 (–21.78, 1.78)
De Rosa (1), 2003	–2.00 (–9.50, 5.50)
De Rosa (2), 2003	–3.00 (–10.36, 4.36)
Ferrier, 2002	–6.00 (–11.11, –0.89)
Glorioso, 1999	–7.00 (–10.03, –3.97)
Hommel, 1992	–8.00 (–25.49, 9.49)
Ideda, 2004	–4.90 (–7.16, –2.64)
McDowell, 1991	–4.00 (–19.12, 11.12)
O'Callaghan, 1994	0.00 (–14.71, 14.71)
Straznicky, 1995	0.50 (–4.04, 5.04)
Subtotal	**–4.00 (–5.81, –2.18)**

Studies with SBP<=130 mm Hg

Jenkins, 2003	5.20 (–2.67, 13.07)
Kool, 1995	3.00 (–4.34, 10.34)
Lee, 2002	–1.00 (–6.52, 4.52)
Nakamura, 2001	–6.00 (–12.97, 0.97)
Shige, 2001	1.00 (–5.55, 7.55)
Tonolo, 1997	0.00 (–2.02, 2.02)
Subtotal	**0.03 (–1.91, 1.96)**

AHT Rx started at same time as statin

Foari, 2004	–4.20 (–7.27, –1.13)
Koh, 2004	5.00 (0.15, 9.85)
Subtotal	**0.20 (–8.81, 9.21)**
Overall	**–1.94 (–3.77, 0.12)**

−25 0 25

Intervention effect

FIGURE 11.6 Example of a Forrest plot from a meta-analysis examining the relationship between use of statins and change in blood pressure level. Mean differences and 95% CIs in systolic blood pressure (SBP) achieved in patients who took statins compared with those who took placebo or other control treatment are shown. Separate evaluations were made for studies in which the baseline SBP was >130 or ≤ 130 mm Hg. Symbols are: (□) treatment effect estimate of each trial, with a size proportional to its weight; (—) CI of the treatment effect estimate of each trial (the treatment effect with 95% CI is also displayed on the right of the plot); (|) no effect of treatment; (⦙) combined treatment effect; (◇) width of the diamonds represents the CI of the combined treatment effect.

Used with permission from *Hypertension.* Strazzullo P, Kerry SM, Barbato A, Versiero M, D'Elia L, Cappuccio FP. Do statins reduce blood pressure? A meta-analysis of randomised, controlled trials. Hypertension 2007;49:792–8.

TEXTBOX 11.4 Internet resources for computer software and programs for meta-analysis (accessed July 7, 2007)

---

http://www.cc.ims.net: Cochrane Review Manager (RevMan), Information Management Systems (IMS).

http://www.meta-analysis.com: Comprehensive meta-analysis, Biostat.

Meta-Analyst software is available on request; send email to: joseph.lau@es.nemc.org

http://www.mix-for-meta-analysis.info: Mix (**M**eta analysis with **I**nteractive e**X**planation), Kanagawa, Japan

http://www.spc.univ-lyon1.fr/easyma.dos: EasyMA, Department of Clinical Pharmacology, Lyon, France

http://www.statsdirect.com: StatsDirect Ltd., Cheshire, England, UK

http://www.stata.com: STATA Data Analysis and Statistical Software, College Station, Texas

http://www.metawinsoft.com: MetaWin, Sinauer Associates, Inc. Sunderland, MA, USA

Source: An overview of internet resources is kept by A. Sutton, Department of Health Sciences, Leicester University, UK. Available at: *http://www.hs.le.ac.uk/epidemio/personal/ajs22/meta/* Accessed on July 7, 2007.

Inferences from Meta-Analyses

The decision for whether to apply the findings from research in clinical practice is rarely based on a single study, and meta-analyses have an increasing influence in daily practice. Therefore, conclusions from meta-analysis should not only concern the magnitude, direction, and precision of the summary effect estimate. The consistency of effect across trials should be related to potential sources of bias, while sources of heterogeneity between studies should be described and possibly explained. Meta-analyses summarize the evidence from available original trials. Meta-analyses, with the exception of some IPD meta-analyses, are not designed to provide specific guidance for practice on selecting patients for particular treatments. Their utility for such guidance may not be as good as the utility of the original data [Moses et al., 2002]. In addition, many subjective decisions are made when performing a meta-analysis. It is therefore important that value judgments are separated from repeatable methods and transparent decisions.

Meta-analyses have been criticized because they may not yield clear answers to relevant questions. The results and conclusions of many meta-analyses are considered confusing, and are unable to provide specific guidance for practice in selecting patients for certain interventions. Still, it is important that trial results are put in the appropriate scientific and clinical context and meta-analyses help the researchers and readers to do so. Without incorporating appropriate contextual information and results of other sources of evidence, there may be problems of implementation and dissemination of the results of meta-analysis.

Therefore, based on a transparent meta-analysis, the following inferences may be helpful in arriving at valid clinical recommendations:

- *Strong evidence*: A solid summary effect of clinically relevant magnitude, without apparent heterogeneity across a large number of exclusively high-quality trials, that is, the direction and size of effect is consistent across trials. Clinical recommendation: Treatment should be considered in all patients; effects in subgroups could still be of interest.
- *Moderate evidence*: A summary effect of clinically relevant magnitude, without apparent heterogeneity across multiple high- to moderate-quality trials, that is, the direction and size of effect is consistent across trials. Clinical recommendation: Treatment may be considered for all patients, but different subgroups effects could be of interest. Clinical consensus may be helpful.
- *Weak evidence*: A summary effect with statistical significance of clinically relevant magnitude, that is, the direction of effect is consistent across trials of moderate to low quality. Exploration for sources of heterogeneity across trials at patient level (i.e., subgroups) or study level (i.e., bias) appears justified. Clinical recommendation: Treatment may be taken into account for most patients, and different subgroup effects may be of interest. Clinical consensus could be helpful.
- *Inconsistent evidence*: The magnitude and direction of effect varies across moderate to low quality trials. Exploration for sources of heterogeneity across trials at patient level (i.e., subgroups) or study level (i.e., bias) appears justified. Clinical recommendation: Treatment may be taken into account for most patients, but clinical consensus will be helpful.
- *Little or no evidence*: Limited number of trials of low quality. Clinical consensus is needed; research is warranted.

Evidently, these inferences all pertain to *beneficial* effects of an intervention. If, for example, a meta-analysis reveals strong evidence that an intervention has *no effect* or is even *harmful*, then the ensuing clinical recommendations will be equally strong but clearly opposite. In this case, treatment should *not* be considered.

The so-called *stainless steel law* of research on treatment effects states that trials with a more rigorous design show less evidence favoring the effect of the treatment evaluated than earlier trials, if only by regression toward the mean. The same may hold true for meta-analysis: the more fastidious its design, the less marked its outcome. Because original trials may be insufficient in number or their design may be flawed, clear evidence may not exist and uncertainty remains. However, a well-designed and executed meta-analysis effectively maps the sources of uncertainty. Although meta-analysis includes an explicit approach to the critical appraisal of a study design, it is not a formal method of criticizing existing research. Still, meta-analysis can be extremely helpful when establishing the research agenda, thereby directing the design of new studies.

12

Clinical Epidemiological Data Analysis

The critically essential stages of designing clinical epidemiologic research are over when the occurrence relation and the mode of data collection have been established. Design of data analysis is important because it will determine the utility of the result and should maintain the relevance and validity achieved so far. Yet, in general, there are only a few appropriate and feasible ways to analyze the data of a given study. Ideally, the design of data analysis follows naturally from the type of data collected and the nature of the occurrence relation. Similar to the design of the occurrence relation and design of data collection, the design of data analysis in diagnostic, etiologic, prognostic, and intervention research each have their particular characteristics.

This chapter deals with elementary techniques used in data analysis. Often these techniques are sufficient to answer the research question. For more extensive information on data analysis, the reader must consult textbooks that are specifically dedicated to data analysis [Altman, 1991; Kleinbaum & Kupper, 1982] or the referred literature in the chapters on diagnostic, etiologic, prognostic, and intervention research. To provide some detail on the analysis of descriptive research, Chapter 3 (Diagnostic Research) has a more extensive data analysis section.

A typical data analysis begins with a description of the population by providing key characteristics in the first, so-called *baseline*, table. Its format depends on the type of research that is performed. In a randomized clinical trial, the baseline table summarizes the frequencies and levels of important prognostic variables in the randomized groups. This table is important because the reviewers and readers of the eventual publication learn about the study population and can judge the quality of the randomization. In etiologic research, the frequencies and levels of relevant characteristics (in particular potential confounders) will be summarized by categories of the determinant (in case of a cohort study) or the outcome (in case of a case-control study), while in diagnostic and prognostic research, predictors according to disease or outcome will be shown. In the first step of data analysis, the data are reduced by giving summary estimates (mean, range, standard deviation, frequencies). Next, association measures are calculated with corresponding 95% confidence levels. In etiologic research, the crude association measure will generally be adjusted by one or more confounding variables.

Before we deal with the data-analytical steps that are performed in nearly every clinical epidemiological study, we focus attention on how to calculate prevalence and incidence measures. Next, we cover the concept of variability in research and the way uncertainty is reflected in the description of the data. Finally, adjustment for confounding with several techniques like stratified analysis (Mantel-Haenszel), linear, logistic, and Cox regression is explained.

Measures of Disease Frequency: Incidence and Prevalence

Measurement is a central issue in epidemiology. The simplest way to measure the occurrence of disease in a population is by giving the *prevalence* (P). The prevalence estimates the presence of a disease in a given population by means of a proportion. For example, the prevalence of obesity in U.S. adults participating in a particular study is 40%. This proportion is calculated by dividing the number of subjects with a particular feature by the total number of subjects in the study. Prevalence applies only to a particular point in time and can change when time passes. To appreciate the estimate, we have to be informed about its precision. If we repeat the study, will the estimate have the same value? The 95% confidence interval of prevalence (or another yes/no characteristic) is calculated with the formula:

$$95\% \text{CI P} = P \pm 1.96\sqrt{\left[P(1-P)/N\right]} \tag{Eq. 1}$$

where CI is the confidence interval, P is probability, and N is the total number of study participants.

This formula can be used for all estimates that have a binomial distribution (yes/no) and that are based on large numbers. A disadvantage of this method is that it does not perform well when zeros or small numbers are involved and other methods have to be used which are less easy to understand but perform much better irrespective of the numbers involved [Altman et al., 2000b]. Altman and co-workers recommended a method for which the first three quantities have to be calculated (Textbox 12.1):

$$A = 2r + z^2; B = z\sqrt{(z^2 + 4rq)}; C = 2(n + z^2)$$

TEXTBOX 12.1 Calculating the prevalence (and confidence interval) of metabolic syndrome in 1000 patients with coronary ischemia

In a study population of 1000 patients with coronary ischemia the proportion (prevalence) of patients with the metabolic syndrome is 40% (400 patients). The 95% CI can be calculated with the traditional method with formula (1): 95% CI = 40% $\pm$ 1.96$\sqrt{[40*60/1000]}$ = 37% – 43%. In comparable populations the prevalence of diabetes will be found in the range between 37% and 43%. With the method proposed by Altman the following calculations need to be done: P = 400/1000 = 0.40 and q = 600/1000 = 0.60 and r = 400 [Altman, et al 2000b].

$A = (2*400)+ 1.96^2 = 803.84$

$B = 1.96\sqrt{(1.96^2 +4*400*0.6)} = 60.8)$

$C = 2(1000 + 1.96^2) = 2007.68$

The 95% CI of the 40% = (A – B)/C to (A + B)/C

(803.84 – 60.8)/2007.68 to (803.84 + 60.8)/2007.68

0.37 to 0.43

37% to 43%

Source: Data from Altman D, Machin D, Bryant TN, Gardner MJ. Statistics with Confidence. 2nd edition. BMJ Books, 2000b.

where r is the number of participants that has the feature, q is the proportion that does not have it, n is the total number of participants, and z (usually) is 1.96. The confidence interval for the population prevalence P is now calculated by:

(A – B)/C to (A + B)/C

Software such as Confidence Interval Analysis (CIA) [Altman et al., 2000b] dedicated to the estimation of confidence intervals is available and easy to use.

To estimate the *incidence,* two measures are common: *cumulative incidence* and *incidence rate*. The cumulative incidence is the number of subjects developing the disease during a particular time period divided by the number of subjects followed for the time period. The incidence rate estimates the occurrence of disease per unit of time. The incidence rate is also called *force of morbidity*. The cumulative incidence is a proportion, binomially distributed, and the 95% CI can be calculated with equation 1 or the alternative method as explained in the earlier calculations.

To calculate the 95% CI for the incidence rate, we need other tools. The incidence rate is the number of cases occurring per unit of follow-up time

TEXTBOX 12.2 Calculation of the incidence rate of myocardial infraction

In a population with a mean follow-up of 2.3 years cumulating in 9300 person-years of follow-up, 35 patients experience a myocardial infarction.

IR = I/PY = 35/9300person-years = 37.6/10,000 person years. In the confidence limits table for variables that have a Poisson distribution, we find that the lower border of the incidence rate (95% CI) is 24.379 and the upper border is 48.677. These are absolute numbers and have to be expressed per 10,000 person years:

24.379/9300 person-years to 48.677/9300 person years =
26.2/10,000 person years to 52.3/10,000 person years

Source: Author created with data available at: *http:/www.dok.wa.gov/data/guidelines/confintguide .htm* Accessed July 17, 2007.

and can be expressed as the number of cases (I) per 1000 (or 10,000) person-years (PY). For the prevalence and the cumulative incidence, the number of cases cannot become larger than the denominator, but in the formula of the incidence rate (IR = I/PY), the denominator has no fixed relationship with the numerator. Confidence intervals for this type of distribution can be calculated by assuming that the incidence rate has a Poisson distribution (Textbox 12.2) [Altman, 1991]. The 95% CI of incidence rates can be easily read from a table that can be found in most statistics textbooks or on the Internet (Health Data, Washington State Department of Health. Available at http://www.doh.wa.gov/Data/Guidelines/ConfIntguide.htm. Accessed July 10, 2007).

Data-Analytical Strategies in Clinical Epidemiology Research

Baseline Table

In the methods section of an article, the researchers meticulously describe the study population so the readers can get acquainted with this population and judge the domain to which the results of the study pertain. In the first part of the results section, the authors describe the key characteristics in the baseline table. In the example in Textbox 12.3, a baseline table is given from a study in which investigators examined the relationship between the presence of the metabolic syndrome in patients with symptomatic vascular disease and the extent of atherosclerosis [Olijhoek et al., 2004].

The baseline table provides an overview of the most important characteristics of the study population. In this example, the relationship between

TEXTBOX 12.3 Baseline characteristics of the study population from a study in which the relationship between metabolic syndrome and the extent of vascular disease is determined

	Metabolic syndrome		
	No (n = 576)	Yes (n = 469)	P-*value*
Male gender	84	74	< 0.001
Age (years)	59 ± 10	60 ± 10	0.4
Body mass index (kg/m^2)[1]	25 ± 3	28 ± 4	< 0.001
Smoking[a]	82	81	0.8
History of other vascular disease[b]	16	21	0.02
Total cholesterol (mmol/l)[2]	5.2 (4.5–5.9)	5.6 (4.8–6.2)	< 0.001
Homocysteine (μmol/l)[1]	14 ± 6	15 ± 7	0.2
Serum creatinine (μmol/l)[1]	93 ± 37	95 ± 46	0.4
Creatinine clearance (Cockcroft) ml/min[1]	76 ± 19	79 ± 22	0.01
Diabetes mellitus[c]	7	33	< 0.001
Glucose lowering agents	4	18	< 0.001
Anti-hypertensive drugs	25	45	< 0.001
Lipid lowering agents	38	38	0.4
Components of metabolic syndrome			
Waist circumference (cm)[1]	92 ± 9	10 ± 10	< 0.001
Blood pressure systolic (mm Hg)[1]	134 ± 21	143 ± 20	< 0.001
Blood pressure diastolic (mm Hg)[1]	78 ± 11	81 ± 10	< 0.001
HDL-cholesterol (mmol/l)[2]	1.21 (1.04–1.42)	0.96 (0.83–1.11)	< 0.001
Triglycerides (mmol/l)[2]	1.33 (1.05–1.65)	2.12 (1.72–2.78)	< 0.001
Fasting serum glucose (mmol/l)[2]	5.6 (5.2–5.9)	6.2 (5.6–7.2)	< 0.001

All data in percentages, or as indicated: [1]mean ± standard deviation or [2]median with interquartiles range.
HDL: high-density lipoprotein.
[a]Still smoking, recently stopped smoking, or previously smoking.
[b]History of vascular disease other than qualifying diagnosis.
[c]Fasting serum glucose ≥ 7.0mmol/l or self-reported diabetes.

Source: Olijhoek JK, van der Graaf Y, Banga JD, Algra A, Rabelink TJ, Visseren FL. The SMART Study Group. The metabolic syndrome is associated with advanced vascular damage in patients with coronary heart disease, stroke, peripheral arterial disease or abdominal aortic aneurysm. *Eur Heart J* 2004;25:342–8.

the metabolic syndrome and the extent of vascular disease was the subject of research. For patients with and without the metabolic syndrome, the relevant characteristics are summarized in the first table of the report [Olijhoek et al., 2004].

For each characteristic, either the mean (with standard deviation) or frequency is given. Variability is a key concept in clinical research. People differ in their characteristics and their responses to tests and treatment, so there are many sources of variability. To reduce the amount of available information, the data need to be summarized. A continuous variable (e.g., age, blood pressure) is summarized by a central measure (the mean) and a measure of variability (the standard deviation), or a median with an interquartile range. The mean is informative if the variable is normally (Gaussian) distributed.

The *standard deviation (SD)* characterizes the distribution of the variable and can be calculated by taking the square root of the variance. The mean ± 2 SD includes 95% of the observations. Normality can be checked by making a distribution plot. Normality also can be formally tested in most software packages but, in general, eyeballing it will be sufficient. If variables have a skewed distribution, the median will be a more relevant summary measure than the mean and in that event, the distribution is characterized by giving the interquartile ranges, i.e., the range from the 25th (P_{25}) to the 75th (P_{75}) percentile. Interquartile values are typically more useful than the full range as the extremes of a distribution may comprise erroneous or unlikely data (Figure 12.1).

Categorical variables are summarized by giving their frequencies. For example, 70% of the population is male. Data of this type with only two possibilities have a *binomial distribution* and are very common in medical research. If sample sizes are large enough, the binomial distribution approaches the *normal distribution* with the same mean and standard deviation.

Variability is not only present between subjects but also between studies. The variability of the sample is expressed by the *standard error (SE)* and can be calculated by dividing the population standard deviation by the square root of the number of observations.

In research, inferences on populations are made from samples. We cannot include all patients with a myocardial infarction in our study; instead we want to generalize the findings from our sample to all patients with myocardial infarction. So, we sample and estimate. The way we sample determines to what extent we may generalize. Generally, the results from a sample are valid for the study population from whom the sample was drawn and may be generalized to other patients or populations that are similar to the domain that is represented by the study population.

Extrapolations of inference on one population to other populations are not "hard science" but a matter of knowledge and reasoning and, consequently, are subjective. Variability of the sample mean is expressed with the

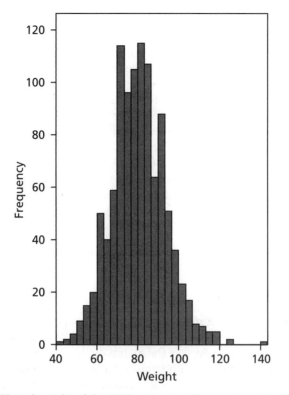

FIGURE 12.1 Plot of weight of the 1045 patients with symptomatic atherosclerosis: mean 80.25 k; SD 13.0; SEM (standard error of the mean) 0.40; median 80.0 k; interquartile range 17; P_{25} is 72 k and P_{75} is 89 k; range 42–143 k.

Used with permission from the *European Heart Journal*. Olijhoek JK, van der Graaf Y, Banga JD, Algra A, Rabelink TJ, Visseren FL; the SMART Study Group. The metabolic syndrome is associated with advanced vascular damage in patients with coronary heart disease, stroke, peripheral arterial disease or abdominal aortic aneurysm. Eur Heart J 2004;25:342–8.

95% CI of that mean that can be calculated from the SE. If the mean weight in the example above is 80.25 kilograms and the SE of the mean is 0.40, the upper and lower limits of the 95% CI can be calculated as 80.25 – (1.96 * 0.40) and to 80.25 + (1.96 * 0.40), respectively. This infers that the real population mean will be somewhere between 79.5 and 81.0 kilograms.

The 95% confidence interval (or the precision of a study result) indicates the reproducibility of measurements and reflects the range of values estimates can have when studies are repeated. The 95% confidence interval comprises the range of levels a parameter can have if the study is repeated 100 times, where the estimate will be between the boundaries of the 95% CI in 95 out of the 100 studies. A confidence interval for an estimated mean extends either side of the mean by a multiple of the standard error. The 95% CI is the range of values from mean −1.96 SE to mean + 1.96 SE. SEs can also be used to test the statistical significance of a difference between groups.

A common statistical test for continuous variables is the *unpaired* t-*test*, for example, to estimate the significance of a difference in age between patients with and without the metabolic syndrome. When a continuous variable is compared before and after the intervention, a paired *t*-test is done. Paired and unpaired *t*-tests assume normal distributions. In the event that normality is very unlikely, non-parametric variants of the paired and unpaired *t*-tests have to be chosen, such as the Mann-Whitney U-test. To compare categorical variables, cross-tables with corresponding chi-square analyses are chosen. In general, however, epidemiologists prefer an estimation of a particular parameter and description of its precision with a 95% CI instead of performing tests. We return to this issue later in this chapter.

Relationship between Determinant and Outcome

Continuous Outcome

In many studies, the outcome is a continuous variable such as blood pressure or body weight. In the above mentioned example in which the relationship between the presence of the metabolic syndrome and the extent of vascular disease in patients with symptomatic atherosclerosis was investigated, the extent of vascular damage was measured by ultrasound scanning of the carotid artery intima media thickness (IMT), the percentage of patients with a decreased ankle-brachial blood pressure index and the percentage of patients with albuminuria. As a first step in the comparison of the IMT of the patients with and without the metabolic syndrome, the mean IMT and its standard deviation and standard error are calculated for both groups. The mean IMT in patients with the metabolic syndrome was 0.98 mm and in patients without the syndrome 0.92 mm (Table 12.1).

The standard deviation gives an impression of the underlying distribution in the two groups. The mean ± 2 SD covers 95% of the observations in that population. The mean ± 1.96 SE reflects the variability of the population mean, as shown in the SPSS® (SPSS, Inc., Chicago, IL) output in Table 12.2.

TABLE 12.1 IMT data (MM) for metabolic syndrome

Metabolic syndrome	N	Mean	Standard deviation	Standard error of the mean
No	576	.9159	.33258	.01386
Yes	469	.9754	.34362	.01587
Total	1045	.9426	.33871	.01048

TABLE 12.2 Independent samples test: IMT in patients with and without metabolic syndrome

	Levene's test for equality of variances		t-test for equality of means					95% confidence interval of the difference	
	F	Significance	t	df	Significance (2-tailed)	Mean difference	Standard error difference	Lower	Upper
Mean IMT (mm)									
Equal variances assumed	4.242	0.040	2.831	1043	0.005	0.05944	0.02100	0.01824	0.10063
Equal variances not assumed			2.821	986,901	0.005	0.05944	0.02107	0.01810	0.10078

The *t*-test for unpaired samples estimates the likelihood that the means are really different from each other rather than arising from chance. From the SPSS output in Table 12.2, we can read that there are two possible answers. The first line gives the results if we assume the variance to be equal and the second line if variances are not assumed to be equal. Whatever we assume here, although the variances are equal in this situation, the conclusion is that the IMTs are different and that the mean difference of 0.059 mm is statistically significantly different from zero.

If we need to adjust our result for confounding variables (e.g., age and sex), there are several possibilities. We can adjust the mean IMT in both groups for age and sex with a general linear model procedure (available from PlanetMath, Inc., Blacksburg, VA. http://planetmath.org/encyclopedia/ GeneralLinearModel.html. Accessed July 10, 2007). It will provide us with adjusted mean IMTs in both groups that cannot be explained by differences in age and sex between the patients with and without the metabolic syndrome (Table 12.3).

If we want to quantify the differences between the two groups (with and without metabolic syndrome), we can also perform a linear regression in which we define IMT as a dependent variable and the metabolic syndrome as a yes/no (1/0) independent variable (available at http://planetmath.org/ encyclopedia/RegressionModel.html. Accessed July 10, 2007).

The regression coefficient of metabolic syndrome is 0.059 (Table 12.4), which means that in patients with the metabolic syndrome the mean IMT is 0.059 mm thicker. Exactly the same number is obtained when subtracting the mean IMT in patients with and without the metabolic syndrome. Using the same approach, we can now adjust for the confounders like gender and sex and directly obtain an adjusted difference (Table 12.5).

The regression coefficient changed after adjusting for age and gender from 0.059 to 0.061. This means that in patients with the metabolic syndrome, the mean IMT is 0.061 mm thicker when differences in age and gender are taken into account. The section on linear regression later in this chapter explains the principles of this type of analysis.

TABLE 12.3   IMT (mm) according to metabolic syndrome, taking gender and age into account as possible confounders, using a general linear model procedure

Metabolic syndrome	Mean	SE	95% Confidence interval Lower boundary	Upper boundary
No	0.915[a]	0.013	0.890	0.941
Yes	0.976[a]	0.014	0.948	1.005

[a]Covariates appearing in the model are evaluated at the following values: gender = 1.21, age = 59.66; SE = standard error.

TABLE 12.4 Relationship between metabolic syndrome and IMT, using linear regression analysis

	Unstandardized coefficients[a]		Standardized coefficients[a]			95% confidence interval for B	
Model	B	SE	Beta	t	Sig.	Lower boundary	Upper boundary
1 Constant	0.916	0.014		65.118	0.000	0.888	0.944
Metabolic syndrome	0.059	0.021	0.087	2.831	0.005	0.018	0.101

[a]Dependent variable: mean IMT (mm); SE = standard error; sig = significance.

TABLE 12.5 Relationship between metabolic syndrome and IMT, taking confounding by age and gender into account, using linear regression

	Unstandardized coefficients[a]		Standardized coefficients[a]			95% confidence interval for B	
Model	B	SE	Beta	t	Sig.	Lower boundary	Upper boundary
1 Constant	0.290	0.064		4.526	0.000	0.164	0.416
Metabolic syndrome	0.061	0.020	0.090	3.114	0.002	0.023	0.099
Gender	-0.089	0.024	-0.106	-3.693	0.000	-0.136	-0.042
Age	0.012	0.001	0.367	12.838	0.000	0.010	0.014

[a]Dependent variable: mean IMT (mm); SE = standard error; sig = significance.

Discrete Outcome

In medicine, often the outcome of interest is a simple yes/no event or continuous data are categorized in a structure that permits a yes/no outcome. Instead of calculating the difference in blood pressure levels between two treatment groups, we can compare the percentage of patients above or below a particular cut-off level. The study design dictates the data-analysis "recipe." In a longitudinal study, such as a cohort study, absolute risks and relative risks can be calculated, while in most case-control studies the odds ratios should be calculated.

Relative risks can be easily calculated with a hand-held calculator. The simplest layout for data obtained in a cohort study is summarized in Table 12.6, if we assume there is no differential follow-up time.

The absolute risk (cumulative incidence) for disease in the people with the determinant is $R_+ = a/(a + b)$, while the absolute risk in people without the determinant is $R_- = c/(c + d)$.

From these absolute risks, the *relative risk (RR)* can be calculated by dividing both absolute risks:

$$RR = \frac{a/(a + b)}{c/(c + d)}$$

The formula for the standard error is given below and the 95% CI of the relative risk is calculated from Equation 2:

$$SE_{lnRR} = \sqrt{b/a(a + b) + d/c(c + d)}$$

$$95\% \text{ CI RR} = e^{lnRR \pm 1.96\sqrt{[b/a(a+b)+d/c(c+d)]}} \qquad \text{(Eq. 2)}$$

An example of a cohort study examining the association between previous myocardial infarction and future vascular events including calculation of the relative risk with confidence interval in shown in Textbox 12.4.

The sampling in a typical case-control study conducted in a dynamic population of unknown size permits no direct calculation of absolute risks (see Chapter 9). Instead, the odds ratio can be calculated. The odds ratio is the ratio of exposure/non-exposure in cases and controls and provides a good estimate of the relative risk (Table 12.7).

TABLE 12.6   Data layout in a cohort study

Determinant	Disease during Follow-up	
	Yes	No
Present	a	b
Not present	c	d

TEXTBOX 12.4 Example of a cohort study on prior myocardial infarction and future vascular events

In a cohort study (N = 3288) in which patients with vascular disease are included 218 patients experienced a vascular event within three years. In the table, the occurrence of the event according to a history of previous myocardial infarction (MI) is summarized.

Previous MI	Event within 3 years		Total
	Yes	No	
Present	95	763	858
Not present	123	2307	2430

The cumulative incidence in three years in patients with a previous MI is 95/858 = 11%, the cumulative incidence in patients without previous MI is 123/2430 is 5%. The relative risk (RR) is the ratio of both risks ($R_{previousMI}$ = 95/858 divided by $R_{nopreviousMI}$ = 123/2430) = 2.1874. The

$SE_{lnRR} = \sqrt{[763/95(95+763)+2307/123(123+2307)]}$ is 0.13 and the

95% CI RR = $e^{ln2.2 \pm 1.96 \sqrt{[763/95(95+763)+2307/123(123+2307)]}} = e^{0.78845 \pm 0.25607} =$

e 1.7 – 2.8. The relative risk in the underlying population will be between 1.7 – 2.8. Patients with symptomatic vascular disease and a previous MI have 2.19 times the risk compared with patients with symptomatic disease without previous MI.

Source: Author.

TABLE 12.7 Data layout in a case control study

Determinant	Cases	Controls
Present	a	b
Not present	c	d

The odds ratio for being exposed versus non-exposed is a/c in the cases and b/d in the controls (Textbox 12.4). The odds ratio (OR) is the ratio of the two odds

$$OR = \frac{a/c}{b/d} = ad/bc$$

The formulas for the standard error of the odds ratio and the 95% CI (Equation 3) are given below. Note that a logarithmic transformation is needed just like when calculating the SE of the relative risk.

$$SE_{lnOR} = \sqrt{[1/a + 1/b + 1/c + 1/d]}$$

$$95\% \text{ CI}_{OR} = e^{lnOR \pm 1.96\sqrt{[1/a+1/b+1/c+1/d]}}$$

(Eq. 3)

An example of a case-control study assessing the relationship between the use of oral contraceptives and the occurrence of peripheral arterial disease, including calculations of the odds ratio with confidence interval, is shown in Textbox 12.5.

Probability Values or 95% Confidence Intervals

Epidemiologists generally prefer to estimate the magnitude of a difference in a variable between populations, and a measure of the precision of this estimate to mere significance testing. This view contrasts with that of those who are in favor of *hypothesis testing*. In hypothesis testing, the researcher ascertains whether the observed difference could have occurred purely by chance. This probability is given by the *P*-value. Hypothesis testing starts

---

TEXTBOX 12.5 Example of a case-control study on oral contraceptives and peripheral arterial disease

---

The following data are taken from a study that investigated the relationship between oral contraceptive use and the occurrence of peripheral arterial disease [Van den Bosch, et al, 2003]. Of the women with peripheral arterial disease (n = 39), 18 (46%) used oral contraceptives, while of the 170 women without peripheral arterial disease only 45 (26%) used oral contraceptives. The layout of the data table is as follows:

Oral contraceptive use	Peripheral arterial disease		
	Yes	No	
Yes	18	45	
No	21	125	OR = 2.4

The odds ratio for having peripheral arterial disease is

$(18*125)/(21*45) = 2.4$. The $SE_{ln2.4} = \sqrt{[1/18 + 1/45 + 1/21 + 1/125]}$

$95\% \text{ CI}_{OR} = e^{ln2.4 \pm 1.96\sqrt{[1/18 + 1/45 + 1/21 + 1/125]}} = 1.17 - 4.90$. The odds ratio of 2.4 means that women who use oral contraceptives have 2.4 times the risk to develop peripheral arterial disease compared to women who do not use oral contraceptives. If we repeat the study 100 times, the odds ratio will have a value of between 1.17 and 4.90 in 95 out of 100 studies.

Source: Adapted from Van den Bosch MA, Kemmeren JM, Tanis BC, Mali WP, Helmerhorst FM, Rosendaal FR, Algra A, van der Graaf Y. The RATIO Study: oral contraceptives and the risk of peripheral arterial disease in young women. *J Thromb Haemost* 2003;1: 439–444.

from the assumption that the observed difference is not a real difference but produced by chance; this is called the *null hypothesis*. Subsequently, one calculates the probability of the observed difference being due to chance. If the P-value is lower than the predetermined 0.05, the inference is that the observed difference is real and is not explained by chance and the null hypothesis is thus rejected.

Authors of current epidemiological and statistical studies favor the use of confidence intervals rather than P-values [Gardner & Altman, 1987; Goodman, 1999]. Many journals (but in our view still too few) discourage the use of P-values [Lang et al., 1998]. The P-value tells us only whether there is a statistically significant difference or not and provides little information about the size of the difference. For the same clinically relevant difference and standard deviation, the P-value can be very low if the populations are large or high if the populations are small. Similarly, a difference can be highly statistically significant but clinically irrelevant if the size of the study is large. The 95% CIs present a range of values that tell us about the size of difference in outcomes between two groups and allows us to make our own conclusions about the relevance and utility of the study result. Confidence intervals retain information on the scale of the measurement itself.

Adjustment for Confounding

Assessment of confounding to detect the presence and effect of possible extraneous determinants is critical to obtain valid results in etiologic studies. The process of assessment and the responsibility of the researcher to remove confounding before arriving at conclusions regarding causality are described in Chapter 2. In this section, a simple method to deal with confounding in the analysis phase is introduced. However, in real life, the situation is often much more complicated than in the examples provided in this chapter. Generally, several confounders must be taken into account that can only be handled with modeling techniques, so the use of statistical software is necessary. The Mantel-Haenszel procedure (explained in this section) can be used without a computer and can provide a great deal of insight into the process of adjustment for confounding.

Stratified Analysis

One way to address confounding is to do a stratified analysis, where the data are analyzed in strata of the confounding variable. Consequently, in each stratum, the effect of the confounder is removed and the determinant-outcome relationship is estimated conditional on the confounder. The effect estimates for the relationship between determinant and outcome are calculated in each stratum. Next, the investigator compares the magnitude of the strata-specific estimates before they are pooled in one summary estimate. Strata-specific estimates can only be pooled when they are more or less comparable and have the same direction and magnitude. If not, effect modification is likely to be present and the calculation of a single overall summary estimate may be of limited use. The relationship has to be expressed for each stratum of the effect modifier. Note that in that situation, confounding may still need to be removed from each stratum.

To estimate the degree of confounding, the crude effect estimate is calculated and compared with the pooled estimate adjusted for the confounding variable. The pooled estimate according to Mantel-Haenszel method is calculated with the following formula:

$$OR_{MH} = \Sigma \, (a_i d_i / N_i) / \Sigma \, (b_i c_i / N_i) \hspace{2cm} \text{(Eq. 4)}$$

In Textbox 12.6 the Mantel-Haenszel procedure is applied in the same case-control study on oral contraceptives and peripheral arterial disease risk presented earlier, to adjust for the confounder age.

Typically, the presence and extent of confounding is best detected by comparing crude to adjusted estimates of the relation (Textbox 12.6). There are other ways to adjust for confounding. Health statistics make use of so-called *direct or indirect standardization techniques* to control for differences in, for example, the age distribution, but in clinical epidemiology, direct and indirect standardization techniques are hardly ever used. A good description of the technique can be found in the work of Hennekes and Buring [1987].

Regression Analysis

In the event of one or two confounding variables and sufficient data, the Mantel-Haenszel technique is suitable for adjustment for confounding. If there are more confounders involved, the data quickly will not be of sufficient size to perform a stratified analysis. To overcome this problem, a regression technique such as linear regression, logistic regression, and Cox regression can be used (available at http://planetmath.org/encyclopedia/Probit.html. Accessed July 10, 2007). The occurrence relation and the type of the outcome variable largely determine the choice of the technique. If the outcome is measured on a continuous scale (blood pressure, weight, etc.), then linear regression analysis will be the first choice. If the outcome is dichotomous (yes/no), then logistic regression is chosen, while if time-to-event is the outcome (survival), a Cox model will be used to estimate the effect measure.

Linear Regression

Techniques for fitting lines to data and checking how well the line describes the data are called *linear regression methods*. With linear regression, we can examine the relationship between a change in the value of one variable (X) and the corresponding change in the outcome variable (Y).

TEXTBOX 12.6 Adjustment for the Confounder Age, using the Mantel-Haenszel approach in a case-control study on oral contraceptive use and the Occurrence of Peripheral Arterial Disease

Mantel-Haenszel odds ratio for peripheral arterial disease (PAD) in relation to oral contraceptive use in women [Van den Bosch, et al, 2003].

Age (years)	Oral contraceptive use	PAD patients	Control subjects	
< 40	Yes	25	249	
	No	7	223	$OR_{<40} = 3.0$
40–44	Yes	18	45	
	No	21	125	$OR_{40-44} = 2.4$
> 45	Yes	35	54	
	No	36	220	$OR_{>45} = 3.9$
All	Yes	78	348	
	No	64	568	$OR_{crude} = 2.0$

The odds ratios in the different age strata for age are 3.0, 2.4, and 3.9 respectively. The age-adjusted odds ratio (3.2) is quite different from the crude (2.0) odds ratio. This implies that age confounds the relationship between oral contraceptive use and the occurrence of peripheral arterial disease.

$$OR_{MH} = \frac{(25 \times 223)/504 + (18 \times 125)/209 + (35 \times 220)/345}{(7 \times 249)/504 + (21 \times 45)/209 + (36 \times 54)/345} = 3.2$$

Source: Adapted from Van den Bosch MA, Kemmeren JM, Tanis BC, Mali WP, Helmerhorst FM, Rosendaal FR, Algra A, van der Graaf Y. The RATIO Study: oral contraceptives and the risk of peripheral arterial disease in young women. J Thromb Haemost 2003;1: 439-444.

The simple linear regression model assumes that the relationship between outcome and determinant can be summarized as a straight line. The line itself is represented by two numbers, the intercept (where the line crosses the y axis) and the slope. The values of intercept and slope are estimated from the data.

Outcome (Y) = intercept + $\beta_1 X_1$ (Eq. 5)

In the observed relationship between IMT and age (Textbox 12.7), several confounders that are different between subjects with different ages and also have a relationship with IMT can play a role, for example, differences in sex. With regression analysis we can control for confounding in an easy way by including the confounder in the regression model. Assuming that we have enough data, we can extend Equation 5 with several confounders.

Outcome (Y) = intercept + $\beta_1 X_1 + \beta_2 X_2 + \beta_3 X_3 + ...$ (Eq. 6)

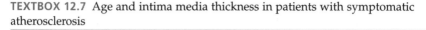

TEXTBOX 12.7 Age and intima media thickness in patients with symptomatic atherosclerosis

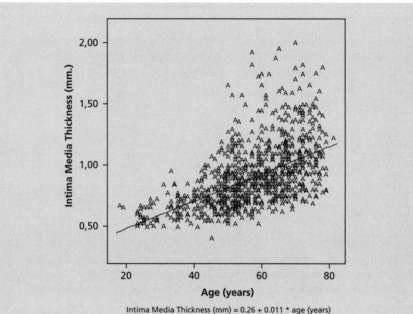

Intima Media Thickness (mm) = 0.26 + 0.011 * age (years)
$R^2 = 0.29$

In 1000 patients with symptomatic atherosclerosis the relation between intima media thickness (IMT) of the carotid artery and age (in years) is investigated. The intercept is 0.26 and the coefficient of age is 0.01. The interpretation of the coefficient is that with each year increase in age the mean IMT increases 0.01 mm. The R^2 is a measure for the variation in Y (IMT) that is explained by X (age). The precision of the coefficient is expressed with the 95% CI. The lower limit of the 95% CI (0.010) means that if we repeat this study generally the coefficient for age will not be below 0.010 (in 95 out of 100 studies).

Coefficients[a]

Model		Unstandardized coefficients		Standardized coefficients			95% confidence interval for B	
		B	SE	Beta	t	Sig.	Lower boundary	Upper boundary
1	Constant	0.260	0.034		7.700	0.000	0.193	0.326
	Age (years)	0.011	0.001	0.542	19.458	0.000	0.010	0.012

[a]Dependent variable: intima media thickness (mm); SE = standard error; sig = significance.

Source: Author.

We have extended our analysis by including sex in the regression model. In this example, the coefficient of age does not materially change, which means that sex is not a confounder in the relationship between IMT and age (Table 12.8).

The first step in fitting a regression line is always inspection of the data. Just plot Y and X; the shape of the plot may suggest whether or not a straight-line equation is appropriate. Rather than linear, the most likely line may be log-linear. In that case, log transformation of the variables can be a solution. A plot also gives insight in outlying data points. Generally, it is not desirable that one or two outliers determine the fitted regression line and after carefully examining the possible reasons for the deviant data points, removal of the outliers will be preferred. An impression of the variability of the outcome can be obtained by looking at the confidence interval curves of the fitted line.

When reporting results, the author should give the reader enough information and report the regression equation, the variances of the coefficients, and the residual variance of the regression model.

In the relationship IMT and age, we deal with two continuous variables and the coefficient is the unit change of Y when X_1 changes with one unit. In the event of a dichotomous variable, the coefficient represents the difference in Y in the two categories of the variable. For example, if we are interested in the relationship between IMT and gender, we can estimate the regression coefficient for sex (Table 12.9). The coefficient is −0.096 for sex, meaning that the mean IMT in women is 0.096 mm smaller than the mean IMT value in males. This value is exactly the same as when the mean of the IMT value for males and females would have been simply subtracted. The advantage of calculating this mean by regression modeling is that the model can be expanded by adding confounders and an adjusted mean will result. Note that the value may become different from simple subtraction once other variables have been added to the regression model to make adjustments for confounding.

Logistic Regression

Linear regression is indicated when the outcome parameter of interest is continuous. The dependent variable can either be continuous or dichotomous. When the outcome is discrete (often diseased/non-diseased), then logistic regression analysis is suitable. Logistic regression is very popular because in medicine the outcome variable of interest is often the presence or absence of disease or can be transformed into a "yes" or "no" variable. A regression model in this situation should not predict Y for a subject with a particular set of characteristics but should predict the proportion of subjects with the outcome for any combination of characteristics. The difference between linear regression and logistic regression is that instead of predicting

TABLE 12.8 Relationship between age and IMT in patients with atherosclerosis, adjusting for sex

Model		Unstandardized coefficients[a]		Standardized coefficients[a]	t	Sig.	95% confidence interval for B	
		B	SE	Beta			Lower boundary	Upper boundary
1	Constant	0.247	0.034		7.269	0.000	0.180	0.313
	Age (years)	0.011	0.001	0.528	18.730	0.000	0.010	0.012
	Sex	0.044	0.016	0.078	2.766	0.006	0.013	0.074

[a]Dependent variable: intima media thickness (mm); SE = standard error; sig = significance.

TABLE 12.9 Relationship between Sex and IMT

Model		Unstandardized coefficients[a]		Standardized coefficients[a]	t	Sig.	95% confidence interval for B	
		B	SE	Beta			Lower boundary	Upper boundary
1	Constant	0.836	0.015		55.831	0.000	0.806	0.865
	Sex	0.096	0.018	0.172	5.255	0.000	0.060	0.132

[a]Dependent variable: intima media thickness (mm); SE = standard error; sig = significance.

the value of the dependent variable, a transformation of the dependent variable is predicted. The transformation used is the *logit* transformation. The formula of the logistic model is:

$$\ln [Y/(1 - Y)] = b_0 + b_1 X_1 \qquad \text{(Eq. 7)}$$

where Y is the proportion of subjects with the outcome, the probability of disease, $(1 - Y)$ is the probability that they do not have the disease, $\ln [Y/(1-Y)]$ is the logit or odds of disease, b_0 is the intercept, and X_1 is one of the independent variables (or exposure or covariate).

From the regression model, we can directly obtain the odds ratio because the coefficient (b_1) in the regression model is the natural logarithm of the odds ratio. This is a major reason for the popularity of the logistic regression model. Computer packages not only give the coefficients but also the odds ratios and corresponding confidence limits. The 95% CI in the output in Textbox 12.8 shows that 1 is not included in the interval meaning that the relationship between smoking and the presence of cardiovascular disease is significant on the 5% level. Odds ratios are generally expressed in literature by giving its value and corresponding 95% confidence limits, for example, OR is 1.9 (95% CI 1.5–2.3). In the example in Textbox 12.8, the independent variable is entered as a discrete variable (yes/no) but also variables with more categories or even continuous variables are possible.

In the example in Table 12.10, smoking has three categories—present smoker, former smoker, never smoker—and the non-smoker is chosen as reference category. The outcome is coronary disease.

Some computer packages (e.g., the SPSS statistical software program) create so-called *dummies* when variables have more categories. In others, the user has to define the dummies before the variables can be included in the model. If a variable has three categories, two new variables are needed to translate that variable into a yes/no variable. If categorical variables are entered without recoding in dummies in the model, the model will consider the covariate as if it was a continuous variable. Now the regression coefficient applies to a unit change, which would be senseless, for example, in non-smoking (0), former smoker (1), and present smoker (2). Creating dummies is simple. Two new variables can be defined as smoking1 and smoking2, where smoking1 is 0 except when the subject is a former smoker and smoking2 is 0 except when the subject is a present smoker. The following possibilities appear:

- Smoking1 (dummy former smoker) = 0; Smoking2 (dummy present smoker) = 0 (the subject is non-smoker)
- Smoking1 (dummy former smoker) = 1; Smoking2 (dummy present smoker) = 0 (the subject is a former smoker)
- Smoking1 (dummy former smoker) = 0; Smoking2 (dummy present smoker) = 1 (the subject is a present smoker)

TEXTBOX 12.8 Smoking link with cardiac disease, logistic regression analysis

In a cross-sectional study of 3000 subjects, we estimated with logistic regression analysis the relationship between smoking and the presence of coronary disease.

Variables in the equation

		B	SE	Wald	df	Sig.	Exp (B)	95% CI for exp (B) Lower	Upper
Step	Smoking	0.641	0.105	37.641	1	0.000	1.899	1.547	2.330
	Constant	−1.550	0.095	267.521	1	0.000	0.212		

Variable(s) entered on step 1: smoking.

The regression equation for the model with one variable (smoking) is:

Logit (coronary disease) = −1.150 + 0.641 (smoking)

With this equation we can calculate the odds of coronary disease for smoker and for non-smokers:

For smokers: logit (coronary disease) = −1.150 + 0.641

For non-smokers: logit (coronary disease) = −1.150

$\text{Logit}_{(\text{smokers})} - \text{logit}_{(\text{non-smokers})} = 0.641$

$\text{Odds ratio}_{(\text{smokers})} = e^{0.641} = 1.89$

Source: Author.

Many dependent variables are continuous and generally it is not preferable to categorize a variable that is measured on a continuous scale because information will be lost. In a logistic model, the dependent variable is dichotomous, and the independent variables can be continuous or categorical. For example, if we determine the association between weight (in kilograms) and coronary disease (yes/no), the output is shown in Table 12.11.

The coefficient of weight is 0.008 and the odds ratio (Exp B) is 1.008. This means that for each kilogram increase in weight, the risk for coronary ischemia increases by 0.8%. Often age is treated as a continuous variable as well. In Table 12.12, the risk increases by 3.8% each year of increase in age (in years).

The absolute probability (or risk) of the outcome for each subject can be directly calculated from the logistic model by substituting the coefficients for each determinant in the following formula (Textbox 12.9):

$$P = \frac{1}{1 + e^{-(\beta_0 + \beta_1 X_1 + \beta_2 X_2 + \ldots)}}$$

TABLE 12.10 Smoking (in three categories) and coronary artery disease

									95.0% CI for exp (B)	
		B	SE	Wald	df	Sig.	Exp (B)		Lower	Upper
Step 1[a]	Smoking			72.118	2	0.000				
	Former smoker	0.332	0.122	7.365	1	0.007	1.394		1.097	1.772
	Present smoker	0.861	0.110	61.021	1	0.000	2.366		1.906	2.936
	Constant	-1.550	0.095	267.521	1	0.000	0.212			

[a]Variables entered on step 1: smoking

For former smokers: logit (coronary disease) = -1.150 + 0.332

For present smokers: logit (coronary disease) = -1.150 + 0.861

For non-smokers: logit (coronary disease) = -1.150

$\text{Logit}_{(former smokers)} - \text{Logit}_{(non-smokers)} = 0.332$

$\text{Logit}_{(present smokers)} - \text{Logit}_{(non-smokers)} = 0.861$

$\text{Odds ratio}_{(former smokers)} = e^{0.332} = 1.39$

$\text{Odds ratio}_{(present smokers)} = e^{0.861} = 2.36$

TABLE 12.11 Weight and the risk of coronary disease

		B	SE	Wald	df	Sig.	Exp (B)	95.0% CI for exp (B) Lower	Upper
Step 1[a]	Weight	0.008	0.003	08.554	1	0.003	1.008	1.003	1.013
	Constant	−1.676	0.223	56.317	1	0.000	0.187		

[a]Variable(s) entered on step 1: weight.

TABLE 12.12 Age and the risk of coronary disease

		B	SE	Wald	df	Sig.	Exp (B)	95.0% CI for exp (B) Lower	Upper
Step 1[a]	Age	0.037	0.003	116.355	1	0.000	1.038	1.031	1.045
	Constant	−3.199	0.209	234.707	1	0.000	0.041		

[a]Variable(s) entered on step 1: age.

TEXTBOX 12.9 Age, gender, and cardiac ischemia

With logistic regression, the relationship between the risk of cardiac ischemia and age and gender was examined. With each year increase in age the risk of the outcome increases 1.036 times, while males have 2.38 times the risk of women (output below). For each patient the absolute risk in the observed follow-up time for the presence of myocardial infarction can be calculated with the above-mentioned formula.

Variables in the equation

		B	SE	Wald	df	Sig.	Exp (B)	95% CI for exp (B) Lower	Upper
Step 1[a]	age	0.035	0.004	100.899	1	0.000	1.036	1.029	1.043
	sex	0.868	0.101	73.396	1	0.000	2.383	1.954	2.907
	Constant	−3.739	0.225	275.748	1	0.000	0.024		

[a]Variable(s) entered on step 1: age.

The coefficients are given in the printed output. β_0 is the intercept, β_1 is the age coefficient, and β_2 is the coefficient for gender for a 60-year-old male. The risk of cardiac ischemia in the observed follow-up time is:

$$P = \frac{1}{1 + e^{-(-3.739 + 60 \cdot 0.035 + 0.868)}} = 31.6\%$$

Source: Author.

Cox Regression

In many studies, not only the event but also the time-to-event is of interest. This event may or may not have occurred during the observation period. If an event did occur, it will have occurred at different intervals for each subject. For these type of data, linear and logistic regression techniques are not sufficient because it is not possible to include the time-to-event in the model [Steenland et al., 1986]. Generally, these type of data are referred to as *survival data*, but apart from death as an outcome, all kinds of yes/no events (e.g., disease progression, discharge from hospital, the occurrence of an adverse event, or incidence of disease) can be analyzed with survival techniques. If only one independent variable is investigated, then the Kaplan-Meier method of estimating a survival distribution can be used. If more variables have to be included in the analysis, then the Cox proportional hazards regression model is needed.

A *time-to-event* analysis supposes a well-defined starting point. This point, often referred to as T_0, may be (chronologically) different for all participants and is precisely defined by the researcher. Often it is the date of the baseline screening in a cohort study or the day of randomization in a clinical trial. Some participants will subsequently experience the event of interest and others will not. The survival function S_t describes the proportion of subjects (S) who survive beyond time (t). If death is not the outcome, the survival curve describes the proportion of subjects free from the defined outcome at t.

Censoring is a typical phenomenon that pertains to survival analysis. Subjects who do not experience the outcome during the follow-up period are censored at the end of the study period. Subjects who do not remain in the follow-up beyond a certain point of time and are lost to follow-up (e.g., because they move to another part of the country) are also censored. Censoring should be uninformative. This means that for all subjects, the risk to be censored is independent of the risk for the event. If subjects who are going to die are more likely to be lost, censoring is not uninformative and the results of survival analysis will be biased. In the example in Figure 12.2, the event-free survival is plotted for patients with symptomatic atherosclerosis. Here, the event is defined as the occurrence of non-fatal myocardial infarction, non-fatal stroke, or cardiovascular death. From Figure 12.2, we can see that, for example, after three years the event-free survival S is 95%. The 95% CI of this proportion can be calculated from the output [SE 4.6%; 95% CI = S ± (1.96 * SE)]. If we want to investigate whether the risk of the outcome in this example is determined by sex, we make two survival plots.

In males, the five-year event-free survival is 83.7%, while in females it is 92.1% (exact estimates can be read from the output). If we want to test if event-free survival is different between the two groups, we use the log-rank

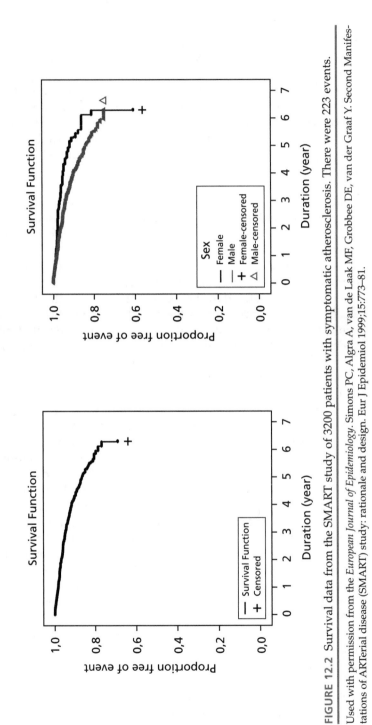

FIGURE 12.2 Survival data from the SMART study of 3200 patients with symptomatic atherosclerosis. There were 223 events.

Used with permission from the *European Journal of Epidemiology*. Simons PC, Algra A, van de Laak MF, Grobbee DE, van der Graaf Y. Second Manifestations of ARTerial disease (SMART) study: rationale and design. Eur J Epidemiol 1999;15:773–81.

test. With this test, we compare the survival distributions of males and females. In this example, the P-value of the log-rank test was 0.0001.

Often we are interested in the simultaneous and independent effects of different variables on the survival function, for example, when we want to adjust one variable for another (Table 12.13). The most common approach for this type of analysis is the Cox proportional hazard analysis. In the Cox model it is assumed that the independent variables are related to survival time by a multiplicative effect on the hazard function. If we want to simultaneously analyze the effect of age and sex on the event free outcome in the above-mentioned example, the Cox model assumes that the hazard function of a subject has the following expression:

$$h_0(t) \times e^{\beta_1 X_1 + \beta_2 X_2} \tag{Eq. 8}$$

where $h_0(t)$ is the underlying hazard; this is the proportion of subjects who fail at time t among those who have not failed previously; β_1 and β_2 are the unknown regression coefficients (for age and sex, respectively) that can be estimated from the data. The hazard functions for the different subjects would have the following form if we assume a female below 60 as the reference:

Female below age 60	$h_0(t)$
Female over age 60	$h_0(t) \times e^{\beta_2}$
Male below age 60	$h_0(t) \times e^{\beta_1}$
Male over age 60	$h_0(t) \times e^{\beta_1 + \beta_2}$

These hazard functions are proportional to each other, and it is not necessary to know the underlying hazard $h_0(t)$ in order to compare the four groups. From the Cox model, coefficients and their standard errors can be estimated and several computer packages generate the hazard ratios (HR), a type of relative risk, as well.

In the computer output in Table 12.13, the results of a Cox regression are shown. An event was defined as a non-fatal myocardial infarction, a non-fatal stroke, or cardiovascular death. Data were collected in a cohort of patients with elevated risk for cardiovascular disease. In this analysis, gender

TABLE 12.13 Sex, age, and the risk of cardiovascular events; results from Cox regression

	B	SE	Wald	df	Sig.	Exp (B)	95.0% CI for exp (B) Lower	Upper
Sex	0.572	0.169	11.502	1	0.001	1.772	1.273	2.466
Age > 60	1.043	0.144	52.768	1	0.000	2.839	2.142	3.762

and age are investigated as determinants of the outcome. Females below age 60 are considered as the reference group. A female above age 60 has a hazard ratio of 2.8 (β_2, coefficient of age). This hazard ratio can be interpreted as a relative risk meaning that, compared to women younger than 60 years of age, women older than 60 years have 2.8 times the risk for a cardiovascular event. A male below age 60 (β_1, coefficient of gender) has 1.7 times the risk compared to a female below age 60. A male older than age 60 has the coefficient of sex and age ($e^{0.572 + 1.043}$) leading to a hazard ratio of 5.0.

Frequentists and Bayesians

Frequentist analysis is the most common statistical approach [Bland & Altman, 1998]. Classical statistical data analysis rests on P-values and hypothesis testing, which is rooted in the work of Fisher, Neyman, Pearson, and others in the early 19th century, building upon randomized experiments and random sampling where random error provides the reference and hypothetical infinite replications of the experiment offer a distribution against which the observed data needs to be judged. The inference is a verdict. Either the hypothesis (e.g., a new drug is better than a placebo) is true, for example, sufficiently certain in view of the data, or it is not. In general, we are more interested in the *probability* of superiority of a particular treatment given the outcome of our experiment. Very likely, we will build our research upon previous findings or plausible mechanisms, and, as a consequence, there will be expectations about the results the research will yield even before the data are available. When a difference is observed, it may not be statistically significant but yet very plausible and in agreement with findings in other research and therefore confirming our expectations. The observed difference is credible, and, despite the lack of statistical significance that may reflect the small sample or large variance, we believe it to be true.

One area in which the importance of plausibility (or prior beliefs) is particularly important in judging the meaning of subsequent findings is in diagnosis. What is the risk for deep venous thrombosis given a positive D-dimer test? In the worked-out example at the end of Chapter 3 the multivariable process of diagnosis and updating the (posterior) probability is described. The result of a clinical trial should be valued in a similar way. Clinicians have prior beliefs about the benefits of treatment and these prior beliefs should influence the posterior probabilities. This way of reasoning is called *Bayesian*, named after the mathematician and Presbyterian minister, Thomas Bayes (1702–1761; Figure 12.3) and predominantly known from the Bayes theorem published in 1764. In a Bayesian statistical approach, prior beliefs are made explicit (Textbox 12.10)

It is not only the results of a particular study but also the already available knowledge (for example summarized in meta-analyses) that determines the credibility or superiority of a particular treatment strategy. Importantly,

The Reverend Thomas Bayes, F.R.S. —
1701?–1761
Who is this gentleman? When and where was he born?

The first correct (or most plausible) answer received in the Bulletin Editorial office in Montreal will win a prize!

This challenge was made in *The IMS Bulletin*, Vol. **17**, No. 1, January/February 1988, page 49. The photograph is reproduced, with permission, from the page facing December of the *Springer Statistics Calendar 1981* by Stephen M. Stigler (pub. Springer-Verlag, New York, 1980). It is noted there that "the date of his birth is not known: Bayes's posterior is better known than his prior. This is the only known portrait of him; it is taken from the 1936 History of Life Insurance (by Terence O'Donnell, American Conservation Co., Chicago). As no source is given, the authenticity of even this portrait is open to question". The original source of this photograph still remains unknown. The photo appears on page 335 with the caption "Rev. T. Bayes: Improver of the Columnar Method developed by Barrett. [There is a photo of George Barrett (1752-1821) on the facing page 334: "Mathematical genius and originator of Commutation Tables: Ignored by the august Royal Society in its *Transactions* because he had never gone to school." – See also comments by Stephen M. Stigler on page 278.]

The most plausible answer received in the Bulletin Editorial office is from Professor David R. Bellhouse, University of Western Ontario, London, Ontario, Canada. A prize is on its way to Professor Bellhouse, who wrote:

FIGURE 12.3 British mathematician, Reverend Thomas Bayes, whose solution to "inverse probability" was published posthumously.

TEXTBOX 12.10 Probability

Statistics as a discipline remains sharply divided even on the fundamental definition of "probability."

The frequentist's definition sees probability as the long-run expected frequency of occurrence. $P(A) = n/N$, where n is the number of times event A occurs in N opportunities. The Bayesian view of probability is related to degree of belief. It is a measure of the plausibility of an event given incomplete knowledge.

Thus a frequentist believes that a population mean is real, but unknown, and unknowable, and can only be *estimated* from the data. Knowing the distribution for the sample mean, he constructs a *confidence* interval, *centered at* the sample mean.

Here it gets tricky. Either the true mean is in the interval or it is not. So the frequentist can't say there's a 95% probability[1] that the true mean is in this interval, because it's either already in, or it's not. And that's because to a frequentist the true mean, being a single fixed value, doesn't have a distribution. The *sample mean* does. Thus the frequentist must use circumlocutions like "95% of similar intervals would contain the true mean, if each interval were constructed from a *different* random sample like this one." Graphically this is illustrated below:

Bayesians have an altogether different worldview. They say that only the data are real. The population mean is an abstraction, and as such some values are more believable than others based on the data and their prior beliefs. (Sometimes the prior belief is very non-informative, however.) The Bayesian constructs a *credible* interval, *centered near* the sample mean, but tempered by "prior" beliefs concerning the mean.

Now the Bayesian can say what the frequentist cannot: "There is a 95% probability[2] that this interval contains the mean."

Taken from: Charles Annis, P.E., Available at http://www.statisticalengineering .com/frequentists_and_bayesians.htm. Accessed July 7, 2007.

TEXTBOX 12.10 Continued

1 "Probability" = long-run fraction having this characteristic.

2 "Probability" = degree of believability.

3 A frequentist is a person whose long-run ambition is to be wrong 5% of the time.

4 A Bayesian is one who, vaguely expecting a horse, and catching a glimpse of a donkey, strongly believes he has seen a mule.

Source: Courtesy of Statistical Engineering. Available at: *www.statisticalengineering.com/ frequentists_and_bayesians.htm.* Accessed July 17, 2007.

as elegantly argued by Greenland [2006], frequentist as well as Bayesian techniques are based on models and assumptions that are subjective. Without a model and assumptions, any set of data is meaningless.

The Bayesian approach, however, makes the subjective and arbitrary elements shared by all statistical methods explicit. Bayesian analysis requires that prior beliefs are explicitly specified. This could be done using empirical evidence available before the next study is conducted, or insights into mechanisms that make the presence of an association likely, or any other belief or knowledge obtained without the data generated by the new study. It has been argued that Bayesian statistical techniques are difficult, but they are not necessarily more complicated than frequentist techniques. Rather, current Bayesian statistical software packages tend to concentrate on exact methods that require heavy computation. Interestingly, in frequentist analyses, we are well used to accepting approximate methods because they generally are sufficiently robust in view of the type of data used in epidemiological research. Most current statistical computer packages are implicitly based on the frequentist's way of thinking about hypothesis testing, *P*-values, and confidence intervals. However, even with standard frequentist software, it is possible to approximate Bayesian analyses and incorporate prior distributions of the data, for example, by inverse variance weighting of the prior information with the frequentist estimate [Greenland, 2006]. The advantages of the Bayesian approach are so important and so natural to medical reasoning that in the near future the frequentist's way of analyses in clinical epidemiology is likely to largely be replaced by Bayesian techniques [Brophy & Joseph, 1995]. To achieve this end, however, both the understanding of Bayesian concepts and analyses and the accessibility of Bayesian statistics in data-analytic software packages need to be improved.

References

Ahlbom A, Alfredsson L. Interaction: a word with two meanings creates confusion. *Eur J Epidemiol* 2005;20:563–4.

Albers GW. Choice of endpoints in antiplatelet trials: which outcomes are most relevant to stroke patients? *Neurology* 2000;54:1022–8.

Albert PS, Ratnasinghe D, Tangrea J, Wacholder S. Limitations of the case-only design for identifying gene-environment interactions. *Am J Epidemiol* 2001;154:687–93.

Algra A, van Gijn J. Is clopidogrel superior to aspirin in secondary prevention of vascular disease? *Curr Control Trials Cardiovasc Med* 2000;1:143–5.

Algra A, van Gijn J. Science unblinded [letter]. *Lancet* 1994;343:1040.

Altman DG. *Practical Statistics for Medical Research*. New York: Chapman & Hall/CRC; 1991.

Altman DG, Andersen PK. Bootstrap investigation of the stability of a Cox regression model. *Stat Med* 1989;8:771–83.

Altman D, Machin D, Bryant TN, Gardner MJ. *Statistics with Confidence*, 2nd ed. London: BMJ Books; 2000b.

Altman DG, Royston P. What do we mean by validating a prognostic model? *Stat Med* 2000a;19:453–73.

Andersohn F, Suissa S, Garbe E. Use of first- and second-generation cyclooxygenase-2-selective nonsteroidal antiinflammatory drugs and risk of acute myocardial infarction. *Circulation* 2006; 25;113:1950–7.

Angelini GD, Taylor FC, Reeves BC, Ascione R. Early and midterm outcome after off-pump and on-pump surgery in Beating Heart against Cardioplegic Arrest Studies (BHACAS 1 and 2): a pooled analysis of two randomised controlled trials. *Lancet* 2002;359:1194–9.

Antman EM, Lau J, Kupelnick B, Mosteller F, Chalmers TC. A comparison of results of meta-analyses of randomised control trials and recommendations of clinical experts. Treatments for myocardial infarction. *JAMA* 1992;268:240–8.

Apgar V. A proposal for a new method of evaluation of the newborn infant. *Curr Res Anesth Analg* 1953;32:260–7.

Arbous MS, Meursing AEE, van Kleef JW, de Lange JJ, Spoormans HHAJM, Touw P, Werner FM, Grobbee DE. Impact of anesthesia management characteristics on severe morbidity and mortality. *Anesthesiology* 2005;102:257–68.

Arbous MS, Meursing AE, van Kleef JW, Grobbee DE. Impact of anesthesia management characteristics on severe morbidity and mortality: are we convinced? (letter). *Anesthesiology* 2006;104:205–6.

Arends LR, Hoes AW, Lubsen J, Grobbee DE, Stijnen T. Baseline risk as predictor of treatment benefit: three clinical meta-re-analyses. *Stat Med* 2000;19:3497–518.

Bachmann LM, Coray R, Estermann P, Ter Riet G. Identifying diagnostic studies in MEDLINE: reducing the number needed to read. *J Am Med Inform Assoc* 2002;9:653–8.

Bak AA, Grobbee DE. The effect on serum cholesterol levels of coffee brewed by filtering or boiling. *N Engl J Med* 1989;321:1432–7.

Bayes T. An essay towards solving a problem in the doctrine of chances. *Philos Trans R Soc Lond* 1764;53:370–418.

Begg CB. Biases in the assessment of diagnostic tests. *Stat Med* 1987;6:411–23.

Begg CB, Metz CE. Consensus diagnoses and "gold standards." *Med Decis Making* 1990;10:29–30.

Berger JS, Roncaglioni MC, Avanzini F, Pangrazzi I, Tognoni G, Brown DL. Aspirin for the primary prevention of cardiovascular events in women and men: a sex-specific meta-analysis of randomised controlled trials. *JAMA* 2006;295:306–13.

Berkey CS, Mosteller F, Lau J, Antman EM. Uncertainty of the time of first significance in random effects cumulative meta-analysis. *Control Clin Trials* 1996; 17:357–71.

Berlin JA, Santanna J, Schmid CH, Szczech LA, Feldman HI. Individual patient-versus group-level data meta-regressions for the investigation of treatment effect modifiers: ecological bias rears its ugly head. *Stat Med* 2002;21:371–87.

Berry SM. Understanding and testing for heterogeneity across 2×2 tables: application to meta-analysis. *Stat Med* 1998;17:2353–69.

Biesheuvel CJ, Grobbee DE, Moons KG. Distraction from randomization in diagnostic research. *Ann Epidemiol* 2006;16:540–4.

Biesheuvel CJ, Vergouwe Y, Steyerberg EW, Grobbee DE, Moons KG. Polytomous logistic regression analysis should be applied more often in diagnostic research. *J Clin Epidemiol* 2007. (In press)

Bjelakovic G, Nikolova D, Gluud LL, Simonetti RG, Gluud C. Mortality in randomised trials of antioxidant supplements for primary and secondary prevention: systematic review and meta-analysis. *JAMA* 2007;297:842–57.

Bland JM, Altman DG. Statistics notes: regression towards the mean. *BMJ* 1994; 308:1499.

Bland JM, Altman DG. Statistics notes: Bayesians and frequentists. *BMJ* 1998; 317:1151–60.

Bleeker SE, Moll HA, Steyerberg EW, Donders AR, Derksen-Lubsen G, Grobbee DE, Moons KGM. External validation is necessary in prediction research: a clinical example. *J Clin Epidemiol* 2003;56:826–32.

Boersma E, Simoons ML. Reperfusion strategies in acute myocardial infarction. *Eur Heart J* 1997;18:1703–11.

Bombardier C, Laine L, Reicin A, Shapiro D, Burgos-Vargas R, Davis B, Day R, Ferraz MB, Hawkey CJ, Hochberg MC, Kvien TK, Schnitzer TJ; VIGOR Study Group. Comparison of upper gastrointestinal toxicity of rofecoxib and naproxen in patients with rheumatoid arthritis. VIGOR Study Group. *N Engl J Med* 2000;343:1520–8.

Bossuyt PM, Reitsma JB, Bruns DE, Gatsonis CA, Glasziou PP, Irwig LM, Moher D, Rennie D, de Vet HC, Lijmer JG. The STARD statement for reporting studies of diagnostic accuracy: explanation and elaboration. *Clin Chem* 2003;49:7–18.

Bossuyt PM, Reitsma JB, Bruns DE, Gatsonis CA, Glasziou PP, Irwig LM, Lijmer JG, Moher D, Rennie D, de Vet HC. Towards complete and accurate reporting of studies of diagnostic accuracy: the STARD initiative. Standards for Reporting of Diagnostic Accuracy. *Clin Chem* 2003;49:1–6.

Bossuyt PPM, Lijmer JG, Mol BW. Randomised comparisons of medical tests: sometimes invalid, not always efficient. *Lancet* 2000;356:1844–7.

Bots ML, Hoes AW, Koudstaal PJ, Hofman A, Grobbee DE. Common carotid intima-media thickness and risk of stroke and myocardial infarction: the Rotterdam Study. *Circulation* 1997;96:1432–7.

Braitman LE, Davidoff F. Predicting clinical states in individual patients. *Ann Intern Med* 1996;125:406–12.

Bresalier RS, Sandler RS, Quan H, Bolognese JA, Oxenius B, Horgan K, Lines C, Riddell R, Morton D, Lanas A, Konstam MA, Baron JA; Adenomatous Polyp Prevention on Vioxx (APPROVe) Trial Investigators. Cardiovascular events associated with rofecoxib in a colorectal adenoma chemoprevention trial. *N Engl J Med* 2005;352:1092–102.

Briel M, Studer M, Glass TR, Bucher HC. Effects of statins on stroke prevention in patients with and without coronary heart disease: a meta-analysis of randomised controlled trials. *Am J Med* 2004;117:596–606.

Broders AC. Squamous-cell epithelioma of the lip. A study of 537 cases. *JAMA* 1920; 74:656–64.

Brookhart MA, Wang PS, Solomon DH, Schneeweiss S. Evaluating short-term drug effects using a physician-specific prescribing preference as an instrumental variable. *Epidemiology* 2006;17:268–75.

Brophy JM, Joseph L. Placing trials in context using Bayesian analysis. GUSTO revisited by Reverend Bayes. *JAMA* 1995;273:871–5.

Burger H, de Laet CE, Weel AE, Hofman A, Pols HA. Added value of bone mineral density in hip fracture risk scores. *Bone* 1999;25:369–74.

Burton A, Altman DG. Missing covariate data within cancer prognostic studies: a review of current reporting and proposed guidelines. *Br J Cancer* 2004;91:4–8.

Campbell M, Machin D. *Medical Statistics. A Commonsense Approach.* Chichester: John Wiley and Sons, 1990.

Campbell MK, Elbourne DR, Altman DG, for the CONSORT Group. CONSORT statement: extension to cluster randomised trials. *BMJ* 2004;328:702–8.

Cappuccio FP, Kerry SM, Forbes L, Donald A. Blood pressure control by home monitoring: meta-analysis of randomised trials. *BMJ* 2004;329:145. Erratum in *BMJ* 2004;329:499.

Cardiac Arrhythmia Suppression Trial (CAST) Investigators. Preliminary report: effect of encainide and flecainide on mortality in a randomized trial of arrhythmia suppression after myocardial infarction. *N Engl J Med* 1989;321:406–12.

Casey BM, McIntire DD, Leveno KJ. The continuing value of the Apgar score for the assessment of newborn infants. *N Engl J Med* 2001;344:467–71.

Chalmers TC, Levin H, Sacks HS, Reitman D, Berrier J, Nagalingam R. Meta-analysis of clinical trials as a scientific discipline. I: Control of bias and comparison with large co-operative trials. *Stat Med* 1987a;6:315–28.

Chalmers TC, Berrier J, Sacks HS, Levin H, Reitman D, Nagalingam R. Meta-analysis of clinical trials as a scientific discipline. II: Replicate variability and comparison of studies that agree and disagree. *Stat Med* 1987b;6:733–44.

Christensen E. Prognostic models including the Child-Pugh, MELD and Mayo risk scores—where are we and where should we go? *J Hepatol* 2004;41:344–50.

Clark OA, Castro AA. Searching the Literatura Latino Americana e do Caribe em Ciencias da Saude (LILACS) database improves systematic reviews. *Int J Epidemiol* 2002;31:112–4.

Clarke J, van Tulder M, Blomberg S, de Vet H, van der Heijden G, Bronfort G. Traction for low back pain with or without sciatica: an updated systematic review within the framework of the Cochrane collaboration. *Spine* 2006;31:1591–9.

Clarke M. The QUORUM statement. *Lancet* 2000;355:756–7.

Clarke MJ, Stewart LA. Obtaining individual patient data from randomised controlled trials. In: Egger M, Smith GD, Altman DG, eds. *Systematic Reviews in Health Care: Meta-Analysis in Context*, 2nd ed. London: BMJ Publishing Group, 2001.

Concato J. Challenges in prognostic analysis. *Cancer* 2001;91(Suppl 8):1607–14.

Concato J, Feinstein AR, Holford TR. The risk of determining risk with multivariable models. *Ann Intern Med* 1993;118:201–10.

Concato J, Peduzzi P, Holford TR, Feinstein AR. Importance of events per independent variable in proportional hazards analysis. I. Background, goals, and general strategy. *J Clin Epidemiol* 1995;48:1495–501.

Concato J, Shah N, Horwitz RI. Randomized, controlled trials, observational studies, and the hierarchy of research designs. *N Engl J Med* 2000;342:1887–92.

Copas JB. Regression, prediction and shrinkage. *J R Stat Soc B* 1983;45:311–54.

Cornfield JA. A method of estimating comparative rates from clinical data. Applications to cancer of the lung, breast and cervix. *J Natl Cancer Inst* 1951;11:1269–1275.

Costantino JP, Gail MH, Pee D, Anderson S, Redmond CK, Benichou J, Wieand HS. Validation studies for models projecting the risk of invasive and total breast cancer incidence. *J Natl Cancer Inst* 1999;91:1541–8.

Couser W, Drueke T, Halloran P, Kasiske B, Klahr S, Morris P. Trial registry policy. *Nephrol Dial Transplant* 2005;20:691.

Cowling BJ, Muller MP, Wong IO, Ho LM, Lo SV, Tsang T, Lam TH, Louie M, Leung GM. Clinical prognostic rules for severe acute respiratory syndrome in low- and high-resource settings. *Arch Intern Med* 2006; 166:1505–11.

Crawford SL, Tennstedt SL, McKinlay KB. A comparison of analytic methods for non-random missingness of outcome data. *J Clin Epidemiol* 1995;48:209–19.

Cremer OL, Moons KG, van Dijk GW, van Balen P, Kalkman CJ. Prognosis following severe head injury: development and validation of a model for prediction of death, disability, and functional recovery. *J Trauma* 2006;61:1484–91.

Criqui MH, Ringel BL. Does diet or alcohol explain the French paradox? *Lancet* 1994;344:1719–23.

De Angelis C, Drazen JM, Frizelle FA, Haug C, Hoey J, Horton R, Kotzin S, Laine C, Marusic A, Overbeke AJ, Schroeder TV, Sox HC, Van der Weyden MB; International Committee of Medical Journal Editors. Clinical trial registration: a statement from the International Committee of Medical Journal Editors. *Ann Intern Med* 2004;141:477–8.

De Angelis CD, Drazen JM, Frizelle FA, Haug C, Hoey J, Horton R, Kotzin S, Laine C, Marusic A, Overbeke AJ, Schroeder TV, Sox HC, Van der Weyden MB; International Committee of Medical Journal Editors. Is this clinical trial fully registered?—A statement from the International Committee of Medical Journal Editors. *N Engl J Med* 2005;352:2436–8.

Denys D, Burger H, van Megen H, de Geus F, Westenberg H. A score for predicting response to pharmacotherapy in obsessive-compulsive disorder. *Int Clin Psychopharmacol* 2003;18:315–22.

DerSimonian R, Laird N. Meta-analysis in clinical trials. *Control Clin Trials* 1986;7: 177–88.

Detrano R, Janosi A, Lyons KP, Marcondes G, Abbassi N, Froelicher VF. Factors affecting sensitivity and specificity of a diagnostic test: the exercise thallium scintigram. *Am J Med* 1988;84:699–710.

Diamond GA. Off Bayes: effect of verification bias on posterior probabilities calculated using Bayes' theorem. *Med Decis Making* 1992;12:22–31.

Dickersin K, Hewitt P, Mutch L, Chalmers I, Chalmers TC. Perusing the literature: comparison of MEDLINE searching with a perinatal trials database. *Control Clin Trials* 1985;6:306–17.

Dijk JM, Algra A, van der Graaf Y, Grobbee DE, Bots ML: SMART study group. Carotid stiffness and the risk of new vascular events in patients with manifest cardiovascular disease. The SMART study. *Eur Heart J.* 2005;26:1213–20.

Doll R, Hill AB. Smoking and carcinoma of the lung. *BMJ* 1950;ii:739–48.

Doll R, Peto R, Boreham J, Sutherland I. Mortality in relation to smoking: 50 years' observations on male British doctors. *BMJ* 2004;328:1519.

Donders AR, Heijden van der GJ, Stijnen T, Moons KG. A gentle introduction to imputation of missing values. *J Clin Epidemiol* 2006;59:1087–91.

Doran MF, Crowson CS, Pond GR, O'Fallon WM, Gabriel SE. Predictors of infection in rheumatoid arthritis. *Arthritis Rheum* 2002;46:2294–300.

Dupont WD, Plummer WD Jr. Power and sample size calculations for studies involving linear regression. *Control Clin Trials* 1998;19:589–601.

Dutch TIA Trial Study Group. A comparison of two doses of aspirin (30 mg vs. 283 mg a day) in patients after a transient ischemic attack or minor ischemic stroke. *N Engl J Med* 1991;325:1261–6.

Dutch TIA Trial Study Group. Trial of secondary prevention with atenolol after transient ischemic attack or nondisabling ischemic stroke. *Stroke* 1993;24:543–8.

Edwards P, Clarke M, DiGuiseppi C, Pratap S, Roberts I, Wentz R. Identification of randomised controlled trials in systematic reviews: accuracy and reliability of screening records. *Stat Med* 2002;21:1635–40.

Efron B, Tibshirani R. *An Introduction to the Bootstrap. Monographs on Statistics and Applied Probability.* New York: Chapman & Hall, 1993.

Elias SG, Peeters PH, Grobbee DE, van Noord PA. Breast cancer risk after caloric restriction during the 1944–1945 Dutch famine. *J Natl Cancer Inst* 2004;96: 539–46.

El-Metwally A, Salminen JJ, Auvinen A, Kautiainen H, Mikkelsson M. Lower limb pain in a preadolescent population: prognosis and risk factors for chronicity—a prospective 1- and 4-year follow-up study. *Pediatrics* 2005;116:673–81.

Elwood P. Shattuck lecture. *N Engl J Med* 1988;318:1549–56.

Equi A, Balfour-Lynn IM, Bush A, Rosenthal M. Long term azithromycin in children with cystic fibrosis: a randomised, placebo-controlled crossover trial. *Lancet* 2002; 360:978–84.

Erkens JA, Klungel OH, Herings RM, Stolk RP, Spoelstra JA, Grobbee DE, Leufkens HG. Use of fluorquinolones is associated with a reduced risk of coronary heart disease in diabetes mellitus type 2 patients. *Eur Heart J* 2002;23:1575–9.

Eysenbach G, Tuische J, Diepgen TL. Evaluation of the usefulness of Internet searches to identify unpublished clinical trials for systematic reviews. *Med Inform Internet Med* 2001;26:203–18.

Fang MC, Go AS, Hylek EM, Chang Y, Henault LE, Jensvold NG, Singer DE. Age and the risk of warfarin-associated hemorrhage: the anticoagulation and risk factors in atrial fibrillation study. *J Am Geriatr Soc* 2006;54:1231–6.

Feenstra J, Lubsen J, Grobbee DE, Stricker BH. Heart failure treatments: issues of safety versus issues of quality of life. *Drug Saf* 1999;20:1–7.

Feinstein AR. "Clinical Judgment" revisited: the distraction of quantitative models. *Ann Intern Med* 1994;120:799–805.

Ferry SA, Holm SE, Stenlund H, Lundholm R, Monsen TJ. The natural course of uncomplicated lower urinary tract infection in women illustrated by a randomized placebo controlled study. *Scand J Infect Dis* 2004;36:296–301.

Fields HL, Price DD. Toward a neurobiology of placebo analgesia. In: Harrington A, ed. *The Placebo Effect: An Interdisciplinary Exploration.* Cambridge, MA: Harvard University Press, 1997.

Fijten GH, Starmans R, Muris JW, Schouten HJ, Blijham GH, Knottnerus JA. Predictive value of signs and symptoms for colorectal cancer in patients with rectal bleeding in general practice. *Fam Pract* 1995;12:279–86.

Fisher RA. *The Design of Experiments.* Edinburgh: Oliver & Boyd, 1935.

Fisher RA. Theory of statistical estimation. *Proc Camb Philol Soc* 1925;22:700–25.

Fryback D, Thornbury J. The efficacy of diagnostic imaging. *Med Decis Making* 1991; 11:88–94.

Fryzek JP, Schenk M, Kinnaid M, Greenson JK, Garabrant DH. The association of body mass index and pancreatic cancer in residents of southeastern Michigan, 1996–1999. *Am J Epidemiol* 2005;162:222–8.

Galea MH, Blamey RW, Elston CE, Ellis IO. The Nottingham Prognostic Index in primary breast cancer. *Breast Cancer Res Treat* 1992;22:207–19.

Gallagher KE, Hulbert LA, Sullivan CP. Full-text and bibliographic database searching in the health sciences: an exploratory study comparing CCML and MEDLINE. *Med Ref Serv Q* 1990;9:17–25.

Galton F. Regression towards mediocrity in hereditary stature. *J Anthr Inst* 1886; 15:246–63.

Garbe E, Suissa S. Hormone replacement therapy and acute coronary outcomes: methodological issues between randomized and observational studies. *Hum Reprod* 2004;19:8–13.

Garcia-Closas M, Malats N, Silverman D, Dosemeci M, Kogevinas M, Hein DW, Tardon A, Serra C, Carrato A, Garcia-Closas R, Lloreta J, Castano-Vinyals G, Yeager M, Welch R, Chanock S, Chatterjee N, Wacholder S, Samanic C, Tora M, Fernandez F, Real FX, Rothman N. NAT2 slow acetylation, GSTM1 null genotype, and risk of bladder cancer: results from the Spanish Bladder Cancer Study and meta-analyses. *Lancet* 2005;366:649–59.

Garcia Rodriguez LA, Jick H. Risk of gyneacomastia associated with cimetidine, omeprazole, and other antiulcer drugs. *BMJ* 1994;308:508–6.

Gardner MJ, Altman DG. Using confidence intervals. [Letter] *Lancet* 1987;1:746.

Giovannucci EL, Liu Y, Leitzmann MF, Stampfer MJ, Willett WC. A prospective study of physical activity and incident and fatal prostate cancer. *Arch Intern Med* 2005;165:1005–10.

Goodman SN. Toward evidence-based medical statistics. 1: The *P*-value fallacy. *Ann Intern Med* 1999;130:995–1004.

Govaert TM, Dinant GJ, Aretz K, Masurel N, Sprenger MJ, Knottnerus JA. Adverse reactions to influenza vaccine in elderly people: randomised double blind placebo controlled trial. *BMJ* 1993;307:988–90.

Graham DJ, Campen D, Hui R, Spence M, Cheetham C, Levy G, Shoor S, Ray WA. Risk of acute myocardial infarction and sudden cardiac death in patients treated with cyclo-oxygenase 2 selective and non-selective non-steroidal anti-inflammatory drugs: nested-case-control study. *Lancet* 2005;365:475–81.

Greenland S. Bayesian perspectives for epidemiological research: I. Foundations and basic methods. *Int J Epidemiol* 2006;35:765–76.

Greenland S, Finkle WD. A critical look at methods for handling missing covariates in epidemiologic regression analyses. *Am J Epidemiol* 1995;142:1255–64.

Grimes DA, Schulz KF. Compared to what? Findings controls for case-control studies. *Lancet* 2005;365:1429–33.

Grisso JA, Kelsey JL, Strom BL, Chiu GY, Maislin G, O'Brien LA, Hoffman S, Kaplan F. Risk factors for falls as a cause of hip fracture in women. The Northeast Hip Fracture Study Group. *N Engl J Med* 1991;324:1326–31.

Grobbee DE, Hoes AW, Verheij TJ, Schrijvers AJ, van Ameijden EJ, Numans ME. The Utrecht Health Project: optimization of routine healthcare data for research. *Eur J Epidemiol* 2005;20:285–7.

Grobbee DE, Hoes AW. Confounding and indication for treatment in evaluation of drug treatment for hypertension. *BMJ* 1997; 315:1151–4.

Grobbee DE, Miettinen OS. Clinical epidemiology: introduction to the discipline. *Neth J Med* 1995;47:2–5.

Grobbee DE, Rimm EB, Giovannucci E, Colditz G, Stampfer M, Willett W. Coffee, caffeine, and cardiovascular disease in men. *N Engl J Med* 1990;323:1026–32.

Grobbee DE. Epidemiology in the right direction: the importance of descriptive research. *Eur J Epidemiol* 2004;19:741–4.

Grundy SM, Balady GJ, Criqui MH, Fletcher G, Greenland P, Hiratzka LF, Houston-Miller N, Kris-Etherton P, Krumholz HM, LaRosa J, Ockene IS, Pearson TA, Reed J, Washington R, Smith SC Jr. Primary prevention of coronary heart disease: guidance from Framingham: a statement for healthcare professionals from the AHA Task Force on Risk Reduction. American Heart Association. *Circulation* 1998;97:1876–87.

Guyatt GH, Sackett DL, Cook DJ. Users' guides to the medical literature. II. How to use an article about therapy or prevention. A. Are the results of the study valid? Evidence-Based Medicine Working Group. *JAMA* 1993;270:2598–601.

Hahn RA. The Nocebo Phenomenon: scope and foundations. In: Harrington A, ed. *The Placebo Effect: An Interdisciplinary Exploration.* Cambridge, MA: Harvard University Press, 1997.

Hak E, Buskens E, van Essen GA, de Bakker DH, Grobbee DE, Tacken MA, van Hout BA, Verheij TJ. Clinical effectiveness of influenza vaccination in persons younger than 65 years with high-risk medical conditions: the PRISMA study. *Arch Intern Med* 2005;165:1921–2.

Hak E, Wei F, Grobbee D, Nichol K. A nested case-control study of influenza vaccination was a cost-effective alternative to a full cohort analysis. *J Clin Epidemiol* 2004;57:875–80.

Hak E, Verheij TJ, Grobbee DE, Nichol KL, Hoes AW. Confounding by indication in non-experimental evaluation of vaccine effectiveness: the example of prevention of influenza complications. *J Epidemiol Community Health* 2002;56: 951–5.

Hanley JA, McNeil BJ. A method of comparing the areas under receiver operating characteristic curves derived from the same cases. *Radiology* 1983;148:839–43.

Hanley JA, McNeil BJ. The meaning and use of the area under a receiver operating characteristic (ROC) curve. *Radiology* 1982;143:29–36.

Harrell FE, Califf RM, Pryor DB, Lee KL, Rosati RA. Evaluating the yield of medical tests. *JAMA* 1982;247:2543–6.

Harrell FE, Lee KL, Mark DB. Multivariable prognostic models: issues in developing models, evaluating assumptions and adequacy, and measuring and reducing errors. *Stat Med* 1996;15:361–87.

Harrell FE, Margolis PA, Gove S, et al. Development of a clinical prediction model for an ordinal outcome. *Stat Med* 1998;17:909–44.

Harrell FE. *Regression Modeling Strategies*. New York: Springer-Verlag, 2001.

Hayden JA, Cote P, Bombardier C. Evaluation of the quality of prognosis studies in systematic reviews. *Ann Intern Med* 2006;144:427–37.

Haynes RB, Kastner M, Wilczynski NL. Developing optimal search strategies for detecting clinically sound and relevant causation studies in EMBASE. *BMC Med Inform Decis Mak* 2005;5:8.

Heckbert SR, Weiss NS, Koepsell TD, Lemaitre RN, Smith NL, Siscovick DS, Lin D, Psaty BM. Duration of estrogen replacement therapy in relation to the risk of incident myocardial infarction in postmenopausal women. *Arch Intern Med* 1997; 157:1330–6.

Hennekens CH, Buring JE. *Epidemiology in Medicine*. Boston: Little, Brown, 1987.

Hennekens CH, Drolette ME, Jesse MJ, Davies JE, Hutchison GB. Coffee drinking and death due to coronary heart disease. *N Engl J Med* 1976;294:633–6.

Herbst AL, Ulfelder H, Poskanzer DC. Adenocarcinoma of the vagina. Association of maternal stilbestrol therapy with tumor appearance in young women. *N Engl J Med* 1971;284:878–81.

Higgins JP, Thompson SG. Quantifying heterogeneity in a meta-analysis. *Stat Med* 2002;21:1539–58.

Higgins JPT GSe. *Cochrane Handbook for Systematic Reviews of Interventions 4.2.6* (updated September 2006), Issue 4 ed. Chichester, UK: John Wiley & Sons, 2006.

Hilden J, Habbema JDF. Prognosis in medicine: an analysis of its meaning and roles. *Theor Med* 1987;8:349–65.

Hill AB. The clinical trial. *Br Med Bull* 1951;7:278–82.

Hill AB. The environment and disease: association or causation? *Proc R Soc Med* 1965;58:295–300.

Hlatky MA, Pryor DB, Harrell FE, Califf RM, Mark DB, Rosati RA. Factors affecting sensitivity and specificity of exercise electrocardiography. Multivariable analysis. *Am J Med* 1984;77:64–71.

Hobbs FD, Davis RC, Roalfe AK, Hare R, Davies MK, Kenkre JE. Reliability of N-terminal pro-brain natriuretic peptide assay in diagnosis of heart failure: cohort study in representative and high risk community populations. *BMJ* 2002;324:1498.

Hoehler FK, Mantel N, Gehan E, Kahana E, Alter M. Medical registers as historical controls: analysis of an open clinical trial of inosiplex in subacute sclerosing panencephalitis. *Stat Med* 1984;3:225–37.

Hoes AW. Case-control studies. *Neth J Med* 1995b;47:36–42.

Hoes AW, Grobbee DE, Lubsen J, Man in 't Veld AJ, van der Does E, Hofman A. Diuretics, beta-blockers, and the risk for sudden cardiac death in hypertensive patients. *Ann Intern Med* 1995a;123:481–7.

Hofman A, Ott A, Breteler MM, Bots ML, Slooter AJ, van Harskamp F, van Duijn CN, Van Broeckhoven C, Grobbee DE. Atherosclerosis, apolipoprotein E, and prevalence of dementia and Alzheimer's disease in the Rotterdam Study. *Lancet* 1997; 349:151–4.

Hofman A, Grobbee DE, de Jong PT, van den Ouweland FA. Determinants of disease and disability in the elderly: the Rotterdam Elderly Study. *Eur J Epidemiol* 1991; 7:403–22.

Hopewell S, Clarke M, Lusher A, Lefebvre C, Westby M. A comparison of hand-searching versus MEDLINE searching to identify reports of randomised controlled trials. *Stat Med* 2002;21:1625–34.

Hosmer D, Lemeshow S. *Applied Logistic Regression.* New York: John Wiley & Sons, 1989.

Hróbjartsson A. The uncontrollable placebo effect. *Eur J Clin Pharmacol* 1996;50: 345–8.

Hung RJ, Boffetta P, Canzian F, Moullan N, Szeszenia-Dabrowska N, Zaridze D, Lissowska J, Rudnai P, Fabianova E, Mates D, Foretova L, Janout V, Bencko V, Chabrier A, Landi S, Gemignani F, Hall J, Brennan P. Sequence variants in cell cycle control pathway, x-ray exposure, and lung cancer risk: a multicenter case-control study in Central Europe. *Cancer Res* 2006;66:8280–6.

Hurwitz ES, Barrett MJ, Bregman D, Gunn WJ, Pinsky P, Schonberger LB, Drage JS, Kaslow RA, Burlington DB, Quinnan GV, La Montagne JR, Fairweather WR, Dayton D, Dowdle WR. Public Health Service study of Reye's syndrome and medications. Report of the main study. *JAMA* 1987;257:1905–11. Erratum in *JAMA* 1987;257:3366.

Iglesias del Sol A, Moons KGM, Hollander M, Hofman A, Koudstaal PJ, Grobbee DE, Breteler MM, Witteman JC, Bots ML. Is carotid intima-media thickness useful in cardiovascular disease risk assessment? The Rotterdam Study. *Stroke* 2001;32:1532–8.

Ingenito EP, Evans RB, Loring SH, Kaczka DW, Rodenhouse JD, Body SC, Sugarbaker DJ, Mentzer SJ, DeCamp MM, Reilly JJ Jr. Relation between preoperative inspiratory lung resistance and the outcome of lung-volume-reduction surgery for emphysema. *N Engl J Med* 1998;338:1181–5.

Institute for International Health, Univeristy of Sydney, NSW, Australia. Study rationale and design of ADVANCE: action in diabetes and vascular disease—preterax and diamicron MR controlled evaluation. *Diabetologia* 2001;44:1118–20.

International Neonatal Network. The CRIB (clinical risk index for babies) score: a tool for assessing initial neonatal risk and comparing performance of neonatal intensive care units. *Lancet* 1993; 324:193–8.

Ioannidis JP, Haidich AB, Pappa M, Pantazis N, Kokori SI, Tektonidou MG, Contopoulos-Ioannidis DG, Lau J. Comparison of evidence of treatment effects in randomized and nonrandomized studies. *JAMA* 2001;286:821–30.

ISIS-2 (Second International Study of Infarct Survival) Collaborative Group. Randomised trial of intravenous streptokinase, oral aspirin, both, or neither among 17,187 cases of suspected acute myocardial infarction: *Lancet* 1988;2:349–60.

Jadad AR, McQuay HJ. A high-yield strategy to identify randomised controlled trials for systematic reviews. *Online J Curr Clin Trials* 1993;33:3973.

Jadad AR, Moore RA, Carroll D, Jenkinson C, Reynolds DJ, Gavaghan DJ, McQuay HJ. Assessing the quality of reports of randomised clinical trials: is blinding necessary? *Control Clin Trials* 1996;17:1–12.

Janssen KJM, Moons KGM, Kalkman CJ, Grobbee DE, Vergouwe Y. Updating clinical prediction models: simple recalibration methods improve performance in new patients. *J Clin Epidemiol* 2007 (In press).

Jefferson T, Jefferson V. The quest for trials on the efficacy of human vaccines. Results of the handsearch of vaccine. *Vaccine* 1996;14:461–4.

Jellema P, van der Windt DA, van der Horst HE, Twisk JW, Stalman WA, Bouter LM. Should treatment of (sub)acute low back pain be aimed at psychosocial prognostic factors? Cluster randomised clinical trial in general practice. *BMJ* 2005; 331:84.

Jick H, Vessey MP. Case-control studies of drug induced illness. *Am J Epidemiol* 1978;107:1–7

Jick H, Miettinen OS, Neff RK, Shapiro S, Heinonen OP, Slone D. Coffee and myocardial infarction. *N Engl J Med* 1973;289:63–7.

Joensuu H, Lehtimaki T, Holli K, Elomaa L, Turpeenniemi-Hujanen T, Kataja V, Anttila A, Lundin M, Isola J, Lundin J. Risk for distant recurrence of breast cancer detected by mammography screening or other methods. *JAMA* 2004; 292:1064–73.

Jones CE, Dijken PR, Huttenlocher PR, Jabborn JT, Maxwell KN. Inosiplex (isoprinosine) therapy in subacute sclerosing panencephalitis (sspe): a multicentre non-randomised study in 98 patients. *Lancet* 1982;i:1034–7.

Juni P, Holenstein F, Sterne J, Bartlett C, Egger M. Direction and impact of language bias in meta-analyses of controlled trials: empirical study. *Int J Epidemiol* 2002;31:115–23.

Justice AC, Covinsky KE, Berlin JA. Assessing the generalizability of prognostic information. *Ann Intern Med* 1999;130:515–24.

Kalkman CJ, Visser K, Moen J, Bonsel GJ, Grobbee DE, Moons KG. Preoperative prediction of severe postoperative pain. *Pain* 2003;105:415–23.

Kalow W, Staron N. On distribution and inheritance of atypical forms of human serum cholinesterase, as indicated by dibucaine number. *Can J Biochem* 1957; 35:1306–17.

Kannel WB, McGee D, Gordon T. A general cardiovascular risk profile: the Framingham Study. *Am J Cardiol* 1976;38:46–51.

Kemmeren JM, Algra A, Meijers JCM, Tans G, Bouma BN, Curvers J, Rosing J, Grobbee DE. Effect of second- and third-generation oral contraceptives on the protein C system in the absence or presence of the factor V-Leiden mutation: a randomized trial. *Blood* 2004;103:927–33.

Khan KS, Kunz R, Kleijnen J, Antes G. *Systematic Reviews to Support Evidence-Based Medicine: How to Review and Apply Findings of Healthcare Research*. Oxford: Royal Society of Medicine Press, 2003

Khoury MJ, Flandes WD. Nontraditional epidemiological approaches in the analysis of gene-environment interaction. Case-control studies with no controls! *Am J Epidemiol* 1996;144:207–13.

Kiemeney LA, Verbeek AL, van Houwelingen JC. Prognostic assessment from studies with non-randomized treatment assignment. *J Clin Epidemiol* 1994;47:241–7.

Kleinbaum DG, Kupper LL, Morgenstern H. *Epidemiologic Research. Principles and Quantitative Methods*. New York: Van Nostrand Reinhold Company Inc., 1982.

Kleinrath T, Gassner C, Lackner P, Turnher M, Ramoner R. Interleukin-4 promoter polymorphisms: a genetic prognostic factor for survival in metastatic renal cell carcinoma. *J Clin Oncol* 2007;25:845–51.

Knaus WA, Wagner DP, Draper EA, et al. The APACHE III prognostic system. Risk prediction of hospital mortality for critically ill hospitalized adults. *Chest* 1991;100:1619–36.

Knottnerus JA. Between iatrotropic stimulus and interiatric referral: the domain of primary care research. *J Clin Epidemiol* 2002a;55:1201–6.

Knottnerus JA. *The Evidence Base of Clinical Diagnosis. How to Do Diagnostic Research* (Evidence Based) (Taschenbuch). London: BMJ Publishing Group, 2002b.

Koefoed BG, Gulløv AL, Petersen P. The Second Copenhagen Atrial Fibrillation, Aspirin and Anticoagulant Trial (AFASAK 2): methods and design. *J Thromb Thrombolys* 1995;2:125–30.

Koopman L, Van der Heijden GJMG, Glaziou PP, Grobbee DE, Rovers MM. A systematic review of analytical methods used to study subgroups in (individual patient data) meta-analyses. *J Clin Epidemiol* 2007 (In press).

L'Abbe KA, Detsky AS, O'Rourke K. Meta-analysis in clinical research. *Ann Intern Med* 1987;107:224–33.

Lambert PC, Sutton AJ, Abrams KR, Jones DR. A comparison of summary patient-level covariates in meta-regression with individual patient data meta-analysis. *J Clin Epidemiol* 2002;55:86–94.

Lang JM, Rothman KJ, Cann CI. That confounded P-value. *Epidemiology* 1998;9:7–8.

LaRosa JC, He J, Vupputuri S. Effect of statins on risk of coronary disease: a meta-analysis of randomized controlled trials. *JAMA* 1999;282:2340–6.

Lau J, Antman EM, Jimenez-Silva J, Kupelnick B, Mosteller F, Chalmers TC. Cumulative meta-analysis of therapeutic trials for myocardial infarction. *N Engl J Med* 1992;327:248–54.

Lau J, Chalmers TC. The rational use of therapeutic drugs in the 21st century. Important lessons from cumulative meta-analyses of randomised control trials. *Int J Technol Assess Health Care* 1995;11:509–22.

Laupacis A, Sekar N, Stiell IG. Clinical prediction rules. A review and suggested modifications of methodological standards. *JAMA* 1997;277:488–94.

Le Gall JR, Lemeshow S, Saulnier F. A new Simplified Acute Physiology Score (SAPS II) based on a European/North American multicenter study. *JAMA* 1993;270:2957–63.

Lensing AW, Prandoni P, Brandjes D, Huisman PM, Vigo M, Tomasella G, Krekt J, Ten Cate WJ, Huisman MV, Butler HR. Detection of deep-vein thrombosis by real-time B-mode ultrasonography. *N Engl J Med* 1989;320:342–5.

Leserman J, Petitto JM, Golden RN, Gaynes BN, Gu H, Perkins DO, Silva SG, Folds JD, Evans DL. Impact of stressful life events, depression, social support, coping, and cortisol on progression to AIDS. *Am J Psychiatry* 2000;157:1221–8.

Leslie WD, Tsang JF, Caetano PA, Lix LM. Effectiveness of bone density measurement for predicting osteoporotic fractures in clinical practice. *J Clin Endocrinol Metab* 2007;92:77–81.

Lidegaard Ø, Edström B, Kreiner S. Oral contraceptives and venous thromboembolism: a five-year national case-control study. *Contraception* 2002;65:187–96.

Lijmer JG, Mol BW, Heisterkamp S, Bonsel GJ, Prins MH, van der Meulen JH, Bossuyt PM. Empirical evidence of design-related bias in studies of diagnostic tests. *JAMA* 1999;282:1061–6.

Little RA, Rubin DB. *Statistical Analysis with Missing Data*. New York: Wiley, 1987.

Lloyd-Jones DM, Wilson PW, Larson MG, Leip E, Beiser A, D'Agostino RB, Cleeman JI, Levy D. Lifetime risk of coronary heart disease by cholesterol levels at selected ages. *Arch Intern Med* 2003;163:1966–72.

Lonn E, Shaikholeslami R, Yi Q, Bosch J, Sullivan B, Tanser P, Magi A, Yusuf S. Effects of ramipril on left ventricular mass and function in cardiovascular patients with controlled blood pressure and with preserved left ventricular ejection fraction: a substudy of the Heart Outcomes Prevention Evaluation (HOPE) trial. *J Am Coll Cardiol* 2004;43:2200–6.

Lord SJ, Irwig L, Simes RJ. When is measuring sensitivity and specificity sufficient to evaluate a diagnostic test, and when do we need randomized trials? *Ann Intern Med* 2006;144:850–5.

Loy CT, Irwig L. Accuracy of diagnostic tests read with and without clinical information: a systematic review. *JAMA* 2004;292:1602–9.

Mack WJ, Preston-Martin S, Bernstein L, Qian D. Lifestyle and other risk factors for thyroid cancer in Los Angeles County females. *Ann Epidemiol* 2002;12:395–401.

Maclure M. The case-crossover design: a method for studying transient effects on the risk of acute events. *Am J Epidemiol* 1991;133:144–53.

MacMahon S, Sharpe N, Gamble G, Clague A, Mhurchu CN, Clark T, Hart H, Scott J, White H. Randomised, placebo-controlled trial of the angiotensin-converting enzyme inhibitor, ramipril, in patients with coronary or other occlusive arterial disease. PART-2 Collaborative Research Group. Prevention of atherosclerosis with ramipril. *J Am Coll Cardiol* 2000;36:438–43.

MacMahon B, Yen S, Trichopoulos D, Warren K, Nardi G. Coffee and cancer of the pancreas. *N Engl J Med* 1981;304:630–3.

Mantel N, Haenszel W. Statistical aspects of the analysis of data from retrospective studies of disease. *J Natl Cancer Inst* 1959;22:719–48.

Marsoni S, Valsecchi MG. Prognostic factors analysis in clinical oncology: handle with care. *Ann Oncol* 1991;2:245–7.

Martens EP, Pestman WR, de Boer A, Belitser SV, Klungel OH. Instrumental variables: application and limitations. *Epidemiology* 2006;17:260–7.

Mayer SA, Brun NC, Begtrup K, Broderick J, Davis S, Diringer MN, Skolnick BE, Steiner T; Recombinant Activated Factor VII Intracerebral Hemorrhage Trial Investigators. Recombinant activated factor VII for acute intracerebral hemorrhage. *N Engl J Med* 2005;352:777–85.

McClellan M, McNeill BJ, Newhouse JP. Does more intensive treatment of acute my-ocardial infarction in the elderly reduce mortality? Analysis using instrumental variables. *JAMA* 1994;272:859–66.

McColl KE, Murray LS, Gillen D, Walker A, Wirz A, Fletcher J, Mowat C, Henry E, Kelman A, Dickson A. Randomised trial of endoscopy with testing for Heli-cobacter pylori compared with non-invasive *H pylori* testing alone in the man-agement of dyspepsia. *BMJ* 2002;324:999–1002.

McDonald S, Lefebvre C, Antes G, Galandi D, Gotzsche P, Hammarquist C, Haugh M, Jensen KL, Kleijnen J, Loep M, Pistotti V, Ruther A. The contribution of hand-searching European general health care journals to the Cochrane Controlled Trials Register. *Eval Health Prof* 2002;25:65–75.

McDonald S, Taylor L, Adams C. Searching the right database. A comparison of four databases for psychiatry journals. *Health Libr Rev* 1999;16:151–6.

Medical Research Council. Streptomycin treatment of pulmonary tuberculosis. *BMJ* 1948;2:769–82.

Mennen LI, de Maat MP, Meijer G, Zock P, Grobbee DE, Kok FJ, Kluft C, Schouten EG. Postprandial response of activated factor VII in elderly women depends on the R353Q polymorphism. *Am J Clin Nutr* 1999;70:435–8.

Miettinen OS. Epidemiology: quo vadis? *Eur J Epidemiol* 2004;19:713–8.

Miettinen OS. The clinical trial as a paradigm for epidemiologic research. *J Clin Epi-demiol* 1989;42:491–6.

Miettinen OS. *Theoretical Epidemiology: Principles of Occurrence Research in Medicine.* New York: John Wiley and Sons, 1985.

Miettinen OS. The need for randomization in the study of intended effects. *Stat Med* 1983;2:267–71.

Miettinen OS. Design options in epidemiology research. An update. *Scand J Work En-viron Health* 1982;8(Suppl 1):7–14.

Miettinen OS. Stratification by a multivariate confounder score. *Am J Epidemiol* 1976a;104:609–20.

Minozzi S, Pistotti V, Forni M. Searching for rehabilitation articles on MEDLINE and EMBASE. An example with cross-over design. *Arch Phys Med Rehabil.* 2000;81:720–722.

Mittleman MA, Maclure M, Tofler GH, Sherwood JB, Goldberg RJ, Muller JE, for The Determinants of Myocardial Infarction Onset Study Investigators. Triggering of acute myocardial infarction by heavy physical exertion. Protection against trig-gering by regular exertion. *N Engl J Med* 1993;329:1677–83.

Mittleman MA, Mintzer D, Maclure M, Tofler GH, Sherwood JB, Muller JE. Trigger-ing of myocardial infarction by cocaine. *Circulation* 1999;99:2737–41.

Moher D, Schulz KF, Altman D. The CONSORT statement: revised recommenda-tions for improving the quality of reports of parallel-group randomised trials 2001. *Explore (NY)* 2005;1:40–5.

Moher D, Schulz KF, Altman DG; CONSORT Group (Consolidated Standards of Re-porting Trials). The CONSORT statement: revised recommendations for im-proving the quality of reports of parallel-group randomized trials. *J Am Podiatr Med Assoc* 2001a;91:437–42.

Moher D, Schulz KF, Altman DG, Lepage L. The CONSORT statement: revised rec-ommendations for improving the quality of reports of parallel-group random-ised trials. *Lancet* 2001b;357:1191–4.

Moher D, Cook DJ, Jadad AR, Tugwell P, Moher M, Jones A, Pham B, Klassen TP. Assessing the quality of reports of randomised trials: implications for the conduct of meta-analyses. *Health Technol Assess* 1999;3:98.

Montori VM, Wilczynski NL, Morgan D, Haynes RB. Optimal search strategies for retrieving systematic reviews from Medline: analytical survey. *BMJ* 2005;330:68. Comment in *BMJ* 2005;330:1162–3.

Moons KG, Biesheuvel CJ, Grobbee DE. Test research versus diagnostic research. *Clin Chem* 2004a;59:213–5.

Moons KG, Bots ML, Salonen JT, Elwood PC, Freire de Concalves A, Nikitin Y, Sivenius J, Inzitari D, Benetou V, Tuomilehto J, Koudstaal PJ, Grobbee DE. Prediction of stroke in the general population in Europe (EUROSTROKE): is there a role for fibrinogen and electrocardiography? *J Epidemiol Community Health* 2002c;56(Suppl 1):i30–6.

Moons KG, Donders ART, Steyerberg EW, Harrell FE. Penalized maximum likelihood estimation to directly adjust diagnostic and prognostic prediction models for overoptimism: a clinical example. *J Clin Epidemiol* 2004b;57:1262–70.

Moons KG, Donders ART, Stijnen T, Harrell FE Jr. Using the outcome variable to impute missing values of predictor variables: a self-fulfilling prophecy? *J Clin Epidemiol* 2006;59:1092–101.

Moons KG, Grobbee DE. Clinical epidemiology: an introduction. In: Vaccaro AR, ed. *Orthopedic Knowledge Update: 8*. Rosemont, IL: American Academy of Orthopedic Surgeons, 2005.

Moons KGM, Grobbee DE. Diagnostic studies as multivariable prediction research. *J Epidemiol Comm Health* 2002a;56:337–8.

Moons KG, Grobbee DE. When should we remain blind and when should our eyes remain open in diagnostic research? *J Clin Epidemiol* 2002b;55:633–6.

Moons KG, Harrell FE. Sensitivity and specificity should be deemphasized in diagnostic accuracy studies. *Acad Radiol* 2003;10:670–2.

Moons KG, van Es GA, Deckers JW, Habbema JD, Grobbee DE. Limitations of sensitivity, specificity, likelihood ratio, and Bayes' theorem in assessing diagnostic probabilities: a clinical example. *Epidemiology* 1997;8:12–7.

Moons KG, van Es GA, Michel BC, Buller HR, Habbema JD, Grobbee DE. Redundancy of single diagnostic test evaluation. *Epidemiology* 1999;10:276–81.

Moritz DJ, Kelsey JL, Grisso JA. Hospital controls versus community controls: differences in inferences regarding risk factors for hip fracture. *Am J Epidemiol* 1997;145:653–60.

Moses LE, Mosteller F, Buehler JH. Comparing results of large clinical trials to those of meta-analyses. *Stat Med* 2002;21:793–800.

Moss S, Thomas I, Evans A, Thomas B, Johns L; Trial Management Group. Randomised controlled trial of mammographic screening in women from age 40: results of screening in the first 10 years. *Br J Cancer* 2005;92:949–54.

Neaton JD, Grimm RH Jr, Cutler JA. Recruitment of participants for the multiple risk factor intervention trial (MRFIT). *Control Clin Trials* 1987;8(Suppl 4):41S–53S.

O'Leary D, Costello F. Personality and outcome in depression: an 18-month prospective follow-up study. *J Affect Disord* 2001;63:67–78.

Olijhoek JK, van der Graaf Y, Banga JD, Algra A, Rabelink TJ, Visseren FL; the SMART Study Group. The metabolic syndrome is associated with advanced vascular damage in patients with coronary heart disease, stroke, peripheral arterial disease or abdominal aortic aneurysm. *Eur Heart J* 2004;25:342–8.

Oostenbrink R, Moons KGM, Bleeker SE, Moll HA, Grobbee DE. Diagnostic research on routine care data: prospects and problems. *J Clin Epidemiol* 2003;56:501–6.

Oostenbrink R, Moons KG, Derksen-Lubsen G, Grobbee DE, Moll HA. Early prediction of neurological sequelae or death after bacterial meningitis. *Acta Paediatr* 2002a;91:391–8.

Oostenbrink R, Moons KG, Donders AR, Grobbee DE, Moll HA. Prediction of bacterial meningitis in children with meningeal signs: reduction of lumbar punctures. *Acta Paediatr* 2001;90:611–7.

Ottervanger JP, Paalman HJA, Boxma GL, Stricker BHCh. Transmural myocardial infarction with sumatriptan. *Lancet* 1993;341:861–2.

Oudega R, Hoes AW, Moons KG. The Wells rule does not adequately rule out deep venous thrombosis in primary care patients. *Ann Intern Med* 2005a;143:100–7.

Oudega R, Moons KGM, Hoes AW. A simple diagnostic rule to exclude deep vein thrombosis in primary care. *Thromb Haemost* 2005b;94:200–5.

Oxman AD, Clarke MJ, Stewart LA. From science to practice; meta-analyses using individual patient data are needed. *JAMA* 1995;274:845–6.

Papotti M, Kalebic T, Volante M, Chiusa L, Bacillo E, Cappia S, Lausi P, Novello S, Borasio P, Scagliotti GV. Bone saloprotein is predictive of bone metastases in resectable non-small-cell lung cancer: a retrospective case-control study. *J Clin Oncol.* 2006;24:4818–24.

Patino LR, Selten JP, Van Engeland H, Duyx JH, Kahn RS, Burger H. Migration, family dysfunction and psychotic symptoms in children and adolescents. *Br J Psychiatry* 2005;186:442–3.

Peduzzi P, Concato J, Feinstein AR, Holford TR. Importance of events per independent variable in proportional hazards regression analysis. II. Accuracy and precision of regression estimates. *J Clin Epidemiol* 1995;48:1503–10.

Peduzzi P, Concato J, Kemper E, Holford TR, Feinstein AR. A simulation study of the number of events per variable in logistic regression analysis. *J Clin Epidemiol* 1996;49:1373–9.

Peto R. Failure of randomisation by "sealed" envelope. *Lancet* 1999;354:73.

Piegorsch WW, Weinberg CR, Taylor JA. Non-hierarchical logistic models and case-only designs for assessing susceptibility in population-based case-control studies. *Stat Med* 1994;13:153–62.

Pierce DA, Shimizu Y, Preston DL, Vaeth M, Mabuchi K. Studies of the mortality of atomic bomb survivors. Report 12, Part I. Cancer: 1950–1990. *Radiat Res* 1996; 146:1–27.

Pitt B, O'Neill B, Feldman R, Ferrari R, Schwartz L, Mudra H, Bass T, Pepine C, Texter M, Haber H, Uprichard A, Cashin-Hemphill L, Lees RS; QUIET Study Group. The QUinapril Ischemic Event Trial (QUIET): evaluation of chronic ACE inhibitor therapy in patients with ischemic heart disease and preserved left ventricular function. *Am J Cardiol* 2001;87:1058–63.

Plint AC, Moher D, Morrison A, Schulz K, Altman DG, Hill C, Gabouri I. Does the CONSORT checklist improve the quality of reports of randomised controlled trials? A systematic review. *Med J Aust* 2006;185:263–7.

Pocock SJ. *Clinical Trials: A Practical Approach.* New York: John Wiley & Sons, 1984.

Prandoni P, Villalta S, Bagatella P, Rossi L, Marchiori A, Piccioli A, Bernardi E, Girolani B, Simioni P, Girolami A. The clinical course of deep-vein thrombosis. Prospective long-term follow-up of 528 symptomatic patients. *Haematologica* 1997;82:423–8.

Prentice RL. A case-cohort design for epidemiologic cohort studies and disease prevention trials. *Biometrika* 1986;73:1–11

Psaty BM, Heckbert SR, Koepsell TD, Siscovick DS, Raghunathan TE, Weiss NS, Rosendaal FR, Lemaitre RN, Smith NL, Wahl PW, et al. The risk of myocardial infarction associated with antihypertensive drug therapies. *JAMA* 1995;274: 620–5.

Rademaker KJ, Lam JN, Van Haastert IC, Uiterwaal CS, Lieftink AF, Groenendaal F, Grobbee DE, de Vries LS. Larger corpus callosum size with better motor performance in prematurely born children. *Semin Perinatol* 2004;28:279–87.

Rademaker KJ, Uiterwaal CS, Beek FJ, van Haastert IC, Lieftink AF, Groenendaal F, Grobbee DE, de Vries LS. Neonatal cranial ultrasound versus MRI and neurodevelopmental outcome at school age in preterm born children. *Arch Dis Child Fetal Neonatal Ed* 2005;90:F489–93.

Randolph AG, Guyatt GH, Calvin JE, Doig DVM, Richardson WS. Understanding articles describing clinical prediction tools. *Crit Care Med* 1998;26:1603–12.

Ransohoff DF, Feinstein AR. Problems of spectrum and bias in evaluating the efficacy of diagnostic tests. *N Engl J Med* 1978;299:926–30.

Rasanen P, Roine E, Sintonen H, Semberg-Konttinen V, Ryynanen OP, Roine R. Use of quality-adjusted life years for the estimation of effectiveness of health care: a systematic literature review. *Int J Technol Assess Health Care* 2006;22:235–41.

Ravnskov U. Frequency of citation and outcome of cholesterol lowering trials. *BMJ* 1992;305:717.

Rawlins MD, Thompson JW. Pathogenesis of adverse drug reactions. In: Davies DM, ed. *Textbook of Adverse Drug Reactions*. Oxford: Oxford University Press, 1977.

Reilly BM, Evans AT. Translating clinical research into clinical practice: impact of using prediction rules to make decisions. *Ann Intern Med* 2006;144:201–9.

Riegelman R. *Studying a Study and Testing a Test*. Boston: Little, Brown, 1990.

Rietveld RP, ter Riet G, Bindels PJ, Sloos JH, van Weert HC. Predicting bacterial cause in infectious conjunctivitis: cohort study on informativeness of combinations of signs and symptoms. *BMJ* 2004;329:206–10.

Riley RD, Abrams KR, Sutton AJ, Lambert PC, Jones DR, Heney D, Burchill SA. Reporting of prognostic markers: current problems and development of guidelines for evidence-based practice in the future. *Br J Cancer* 2003;88:1191–8.

Rimm EB, Klatsky A, Grobbee D, Stampfer MJ. Review of moderate alcohol consumption and reduced risk of coronary heart disease: is the effect due to beer, wine, or spirits. *BMJ* 1996;312:731–6.

RITA Trial Participants. Coronary angioplasty versus coronary artery bypass surgery: the Randomized Intervention Treatment of Angina (RITA) trial. *Lancet* 1993;341:573–80.

Robertson BC. Lies, damn lies, and statistics (letter). *Anesthesiology* 2006;104:202.

Roest M, van der Schouw YT, de Valk B, Marx JJ, Tempelman MJ, de Groot PG, Sixma JJ, Banga JD. Heterozygosity for a hereditary hemochromatosis gene is associated with cardiovascular death in women. *Circulation* 1999;100:1268–73.

Roland M, Torgerson DJ. Understanding controlled trials: what are pragmatic trials? *BMJ* 1998;316:285.

Rosenbaum PR, Rubin DB. Reducing bias in observational studies using subclassification on the propensity score. *J Am Stat Assoc* 1984;79:516–24.

Rothman KJ, Greenland S. Causation and causal inference in epidemiology. *Am J Public Health* 2005;95(Suppl 1):S144–50.

Rothman KJ. *Epidemiology. An Introduction*. New York: Oxford University Press, 2002.

Rothman KJ. *Modern Epidemiology*. Boston, Little & Brown, 1986.

Rothwell PM. External validity of randomised controlled trials: "to whom do the results of this trial apply?" *Lancet* 2005;365:82–93.

Roukema J, Loenhout van RB, Steyerberg EW, Moons KGM, Bleeker SE, Moll HA. Polytomous logistic regression did not outperform dichotomous logistic regression in diagnosing children with fever without apparent source. *J Clin Epidemiol* 2007 (In press).

Rovers MM, Glasziou P, Appelman CL, Burke P, McCormick DP, Damoiseaux RA, Little P, Le Saux N, Hoes AW. Predictors of a prolonged course in children with acute otitis media: an individual patient data meta-analysis. *Pediatrics* 2007;119: 579–85.

Rovers MM, Glasziou P, Appelman CL, Burke P, McCormick DP, Damoiseaux RA, Gaboury I, Little P, Hoes AW. Antibiotics for acute otitis media: a meta-analysis with individual patient data. *Lancet* 2006;368:1429–35.

Royston P, Altman DG, Sauerbrei W. Dichotomizing continuous predictors in multiple regression: a bad idea. *Stat Med* 2006;25:127–41.

Rubin DB. Estimating causal effects from large data sets using propensity scores. *Ann Intern Med* 1997;127:757–63.

Rubin DB. Multiple imputation after 18+ years. *J Am Stat Assoc* 1996;91:473–489.

Rubin DB. *Multiple Imputation for Non Response in Surveys*. New York: Wiley, 1987.

Rubin DB. Inferences and missing data. *Biometrika* 1976;63:581–590.

Rudakis T, Thomas M, Gaskin Z, Venkateswarlu K, Chandra KS, Ginjupalli S, Gunturi S, Natrajan S, Ponnuswamy VK, Ponnuswamy KN. Sequences associated with human iris pigmentation. *Genetics* 2003;165:2071–83.

Rutjes AW, Reitsma JB, Vandenbroucke JP, Glas AS, Bossuyt PM. Case-control and two-gate designs in diagnostic accuracy studies. *Clin Chem* 2005;51:1335–41.

Rutten FH, Cramer MJ, Grobbee DE, Sachs AP, Kirkels JH, Lammers JW, Hoes AW. Unrecognized heart failure in elderly patients with stable chronic obstructive pulmonary disease. *Eur Heart J* 2005a;26:1887–94.

Rutten FH. *Heart failure in COPD*. Thesis, Utrecht University, 2005c.

Rutten FH, Moons KG, Cramer MJ, Grobbee DE, Zuithoff NP, Lammers JW, Hoes AW. Recognising heart failure in elderly patients with stable chronic obstructive pulmonary disease in primary care: cross sectional diagnostic study. *BMJ* 2005b; 331:1379.

Rutten FH, Moons KGM, Hoes AW. Improving the quality and clinical relevance of diagnostic studies. *BMJ* 2006;332:1129–30.

Ryan CM, Schoenfeld DA, Thorpe WP, Sheridan RL, Cassem EH, Tompkins RG. Objective estimates of the probability of death from burn injuries. *N Engl J Med* 1998;338:362–6.

Sackett DL, Haynes RB, Tugwell P. *Clinical: Epidemiology: A Basic Science for Clinical Medicine*. Boston, Toronto: Little, Brown, 1985.

Sampson M, Barrowman NJ, Moher D, Clifford TJ, Platt RW, Morrison A, Klassen TP, Zang L. Can electronic search engines optimize screening of search results in systematic reviews: an empirical study. *BMC Med Res Methodol* 2006a;6:7.

Sampson M, Zhang L, Morrison A, Barrowman NJ, Clifford TJ, Platt RW, Klassen TP, Moher D. An alternative to the hand searching gold standard: validating methodological search filters using relative recall. *BMC Med Res Methodol* 2006b;6:33.

Sargeant JK, Bruce ML, Florio LP, Weissmann MM. Factors associated with 1-year outcome of major depression in the community. *Arch Gen Psychiatry* 1990;47: 519–26.

Schafer JL. *Analysis of Incomplete Multivariate Data*. London: Chapman & Hill, 1997.

Schafer JL, Graham JW. Missing data: our view of the state of the art. *Psychol Methods* 2002;7:147–177.

Schlesselman JJ. *Case Control Studies. Design Conduct, Analysis*. New York, Oxford: Oxford University Press, 1982.

Schouten EG, Dekker JM, Kok FJ, LeCessie S, van Houwelingen HC, Pool J, Vandenbroucke JP. Risk ratio and rate ratio estimation in case-cohort designs: hypertension and cardiovascular mortality. *Stat Med* 1993;12:1733–45.

Schulz KF, Grimes DA. Case-control studies: research in reverse. *Lancet* 2002;359: 431–4.

Schwartz D, Lellouch J. Explanatory and pragmatic attitudes in therapeutic trials. *J Chron Dis* 1967;20:637–48.

Selby JV, Smith DH, Johnson ES, Raebel MA, Friedman GD, McFarland BH. Kaiser Permanente Medical Care Program. In: Strom BL, ed. *Pharmacoepidemiology*, 4th ed. Chichester: John Wiley & Sons, 2005.

Senn SJ. *Cross-Over Trials in Clinical Research*. Chichester: John Wiley, 1993.

Shojania KG, Bero LA. Taking advantage of the explosion of systematic reviews: an efficient MEDLINE search strategy. *Eff Clin Pract* 2001;4:157–62.

Sierksma A, van der Gaag MS, Kluft C, Hendriks HF: Moderate alcohol consumption reduces plasma C-reactive protein and fibrinogen levels: a randomized, diet-controlled intervention study. *Eur J Clin Nutr* 2002;56:1130–6.

Silverman W. The schizophrenic career of a monster drug. *Pediatrics* 2002;110:404–6.

Simel DL, Samsa GP, Matchar DB. Likelihood ratios with confidence: sample size estimation for diagnostic test studies. *J Clin Epidemiol* 1991;44:763–70.

Simes RJ. Confronting publication bias: a cohort design for meta-analysis. *Stat Med* 1987;6:11–29.

Simon R, Altman DG. Statistical aspects of prognostic factor studies in oncology. *Br J Cancer* 1994;69:979–85.

Simons PC, Algra A, van de Laak MF, Grobbee DE, van der Graaf Y. Second Manifestations of ARTerial disease (SMART) study: rationale and design. *Eur J Epidemiol* 1999;15:773–81.

Snow J. *On the Mode of Communication of Cholera*, 2nd ed. London: John Churchill, 1855.

SOLVD Investigators. Effect of enalapril on survival in patients with reduced left ventricular ejection fractions and congestive heart failure. *N Engl J Med* 1991; 325:293–302.

Spijker J, de Graaf R, Ormel J, Nolen WA, Grobbee DE, Burger H. The persistence of depression score. *Acta Psychiatr Scand* 2006;114:411–6.

Staessen JA, Fagard R, Thijs L, Celis H, Arabidze GG, Birkenhager WH, Bulpitt CJ, de Leeuw PW, Dollery CT, Fletcher AE, Forette F, Leonetti G, Nachev C, O'Brien ET, Rosenfeld J, Rodicio JL, Tuomilehto J, Zanchetti A. Randomised double-blind comparison of placebo and active treatment for older patients with isolated systolic hypertension. The Systolic Hypertension in Europe (Syst-Eur) Trial Investigators. *Lancet* 1997;350:757–64.

Staessen JA, Wang JG, Thijs L. Cardiovascular protection and blood pressure reduction: a meta-analysis. *Lancet* 2001;358:1305–15.

Stamler J, Wentworth D, Neaton JD. Is relationship between serum cholesterol and risk of premature death from coronary heart disease continuous and graded? Findings in 356,222 primary screenees of the Multiple Risk Factor Intervention Trial (MRFIT). *JAMA* 1986;256:2823–8.

Starr JR, McKnight B. Assessing interaction in case-control studies: type I errors when using both additive and multiplicative scales. *Epidemiology* 2004;15:422–7.

Steenland K, Beaumont J, Hornung R. The use of regression analyses in a cohort mortality study of welders. *J Chronic Dis* 1986;39:287–94.

Stelzner S, Hellmich G, Koch R, Ludwig K. Factors predicting survival in stage IV colorectal carcinoma patients after palliative treatment: a multivariate analysis. *J Surg Oncol* 2005;89:211–7.

Stern JM, Simes RJ. Publication bias: evidence of delayed publication in a cohort study of clinical research projects. *BMJ* 1997;315:640–5.

Sterne JA, Gavaghan D, Egger M. Publication and related bias in meta-analysis: power of statistical tests and prevalence in the literature. *J Clin Epidemiol* 2000; 53:1119–29.

Sterne JA, Juni P, Schulz KF, Altman DG, Bartlett C, Egger M. Statistical methods for assessing the influence of study characteristics on treatment effects in "meta-epidemiological" research. *Stat Med* 2002;21:1513–24.

Stewart LA, Tierney JF. To IPD or not to IPD? Advantages and disadvantages of systematic reviews using individual patient data. *Eval Health Prof* 2002;25:76–97.

Steyerberg EW, Bleeker SE, Moll HA, Grobbee DE, Moons KGM. Internal and external validation of predictive models: a simulation study of bias and precision in small samples. *J Clin Epidemiol* 2003;56:441–7.

Steyerberg EW, Borsboom GJ, van Houwelingen HC, Eijkemans MJ, Habbema JD. Validation and updating of predictive logistic regression models: a study on sample size and shrinkage. *Stat Med* 2004;23:2567–86.

Steyerberg EW, Eijkemans MJ, Harrell FE, Habbema JD. Prognostic modelling with logistic regression analysis: a comparison of selection and estimation methods in small data sets. *Stat Med* 2000;19:1059–79.

Steyerberg EW, Eijkemans MJC, Habbema JDF. Application of shrinkage techniques in logistic regression analysis: a case study. *Stat Neerl* 2001a;55:76–88.

Steyerberg EW, Harrell FE Jr., Borsboom GJ, Eijkemans MJ, Vergouwe Y, Habbema JD. Internal validation of predictive models: efficiency of some procedures for logistic regression analysis. *J Clin Epidemiol* 2001b;54:774–81.

Steyerberg EW, Neville BA, Koppert LB, Lemmens VE, Tilanus HW, Coebergh JW, Weeks JC, Earle CC. Surgical mortality in patients with esophageal cancer: development and validation of a simple risk score. *J Clin Oncol* 2006;24:4277–84.

Stiell I, Wells G, Laupacis A, Brison R, Verbeek R, Vandenheen K, Naylor CD. Multicentre trial to introduce the Ottawa ankle rules for use of radiography in acute ankle injuries. Multicentre Ankle Rule Study Group. *BMJ* 1995;311:594–7.

Straus SM, Bleumink GS, Dielman JP, van der Lei J, 't Jong GW, Kinma JH, Sturkenboom MC, Stricker BH. Antipsychotics and the risk of sudden cardiac death. *Arch Intern Med* 2004;164:1293–7. Erratum in: *Arch Intern Med* 2004;164:1839.

Strazzullo P, Kerry SM, Barbato A, Versiero M, D'Elia L, Cappuccio FP. Do statins reduce blood pressure? A meta-analysis of randomised, controlled trials. *Hypertension* 2007;49:792–8.

Strom BL, ed. *Pharmacoepidemiology*, 4th ed. Chicester: John Wiley, 2005.

Suarez-Almazor ME, Belseck E, Homik J, Dorgan M, Ramos-Remus C. Identifying clinical trials in the medical literature with electronic databases: MEDLINE alone is not enough. *Control Clin Trials* 2000;21:476–87.

Sullivan JL. Iron and the sex difference in heart disease risk. *Lancet* 1981;1:1293–4.

Sun GW, Shook TL, Kay GL. Inappropriate use of bivariable analysis to screen risk factors for use in multivariable analysis. *J Clin Epidemiol* 1996;49:907–16.

Sutton AJ, Abrams KR, Jones DR. Generalized synthesis of evidence and the threat of dissemination bias. The example of electronic fetal heart rate monitoring (EFM). *J Clin Epidemiol* 2002;55:1013–24.

Swartzman LC, Burkell J. Expectations and the placebo effect in clinical drug trials: why we should not turn a blind eye to unblinding, and other cautionary notes. *Clin Pharmacol Ther* 1998;64:1–7.

Sweeting MJ, Sutton AJ, Lambert PC. What to add to nothing? Use and avoidance of continuity corrections in meta-analysis of sparse data. *Stat Med* 2004;23:1351–75.

Swets JA. Measuring the accuracy of diagnostic systems. *Science* 1988;240:1285–93.

Taubes G. Epidemiology faces its limits. *Science* 1995;269:164–9.

ten Have M, Oldehinkel A, Vollebergh W, Ormel J. Does neuroticism explain variations in care service use for mental health problems in the general population? Results from the Netherlands Mental Health Survey and Incidence Study (NEMESIS). *Soc Psychiatry Psychiatr Epidemiol* 2005;40:425–31.

Teo KK, Burton JR, Buller CE, Plante S, Catellier D, Tymchak W, Dzavik V, Taylor D, Yokoyama S, Monague TJ. Long-term effects of cholesterol lowering and angiotensin-converting enzyme inhibition on coronary atherosclerosis: the Simvastatin/Enalapril Coronary Atherosclerosis Trial (SCAT). *Circulation* 2000;102:1748–54.

Thompson JF, Man M, Johnson KJ, Wood LS, Lira ME, Lloyd DB, Banerjee P, Milos PM, Myrand SP, Paulauskis J, Milad MA, Sasiela WJ. An association study of 43 SNPs in 16 candidate genes with atorvastatin response. *Pharmacogenomics J* 2005;5:352–8.

Thompson SG, Higgins JP. How should meta-regression analyses be undertaken and interpreted? *Stat Med* 2002;21:1559–73.

Tu JV. Advantages and disadvantages of using artificial neural networks versus logistic regression for predicting medical outcomes. *J Clin Epidemiol* 1996;49:1225–31.

Tulenko TN, Brown J, Laury-Kleintop L, Khan M, Walter MF, Mason RP. Atheroprotection with amlodipine: cells to lesions and the PREVENT trial. Prospective Randomised Evaluation of the Vascular Effects of Norvasc trial. *J Cardiovasc Pharmacol* 1999;33(Suppl 2):S17–22.

Unnebrink K, Windeler J. Intention-to-treat: methods for dealing with missing values in clinical trials of progressively deteriorating diseases. *Stat Med* 2001;20:3931–46.

Vach W. *Logistic Regression with Missing Values in the Covariates*. New York: Springer, 1994.

Vach W, Blettner M. Biased estimates of the odds ratio in case-control studies due to the use of ad hoc methods of correcting for missing values for confounding variables. *Am J Epidemiol* 1991;134:895–907.

Van Berkum FN, Birkenhager JC, Grobbee DE, Stijnen T, Pols HA. Erasmus University Medical Center, Rotterdam, The Netherlands.

van Buuren S, Oudshoorn K. Flexible multivariate imputation by mice. Technical report. Leiden, The Netherlands: TNO prevention and Health, 1999. Available at http://web.intern.nl.net/users/S.vanBuuren/mi/html/mice.htm. Accessed July 30, 2007.

Van de Bosch J, Moons KGM, Bonsel GJ, Kalkman CJ. Does measurement of preoperative anxiety have added value in the prediction of postoperative nausea and vomiting? *Anesth Analg* 2005;100:1525–32.

Van de Brink RH, Ormel J, Tiemens BG, Os TW, Smit A, Jenner JA, Meer KV. Accuracy of general practitioner's prognosis of the 1-year course of depression and generalised anxiety. *Br J Psychiatry* 2001;179:18–22. Comment in *Br J Psychiatry* 2001;179:177–8.

Van de Garde EM, Hak E, Souverein PC, Hoes AW, van den Bosch JM, Leufkens HG. Statin treatment and reduced risk of pneumonia in patients with diabetes. *Thorax* 2006;61:957–61.

Van den Bosch MA, Kemmeren JM, Tanis BC, Mali WP, Helmerhorst FM, Rosendaal FR, Algra A, van der Graaf Y. The RATIO study: oral contraceptives and the risk of peripheral arterial disease in young women. *J Thromb Haemost* 2003;1: 439–44.

Van der A DL, Marx JJ, Grobbee DE, Kamphuis MH, Georgiou NA, van Kats-Renaud JH, Breuer W, Cabantchik ZI, Roest M, Voorbij HA, Van der Schouw YT. Nontransferrin-bound iron and risk of coronary heart disease in postmenopausal women. *Circulation* 2006;113:1942–9.

Van der Heijden G, Donders AR, Stijnen T, Moons KGM. Handling missing data in multivariate diagnostic accuracy research: a clinical example. *J Clin Epidemiol* 2006;59:1102–9.

Van der Heijden GJ, Nathoe HM, Jansen EW, Grobbee DE. Meta-analysis on the effect of off-pump coronary bypass surgery. *Eur J Cardiothorac Surg* 2004;26:81–4.

Van der Lei J, Duisterhout JS, Westerhoff HP, van der Does E, Cromme PV, Boon WM, van Bemmel JH. The introduction of computer-based patient records in the Netherlands. *Ann Intern Med* 1993;119:1036–41.

Van der Schouw YT, Grobbee DE. Menopausal complaints, oestrogens, and heart disease risk: an explanation for discrepant findings on the benefits of postmenopausal hormone therapy. *Eur Heart J* 2005;26:1358–61.

Van Dijk D, Jansen EW, Hijman R, Nierich AP, Diephuis JC, Moons KG, Lahpor JR, Borst C, Keizer AM, Nathoe HM, Grobbee DE, De Jaegere PP, Kalkman CJ; Octopus Study Group. Cognitive outcome after off-pump and on-pump coronary artery bypass graft surgery: a randomized trial. *JAMA* 2002;287:1405–12.

Van Es RF, Jonker JJ, Verheugt FW, Deckers JW, Grobbee DE; Antithrombotics in the Secondary Prevention of Events in Coronary Thrombosis-2 (ASPECT-2) Research Group. Aspirin and coumadin after acute coronary syndromes (the ASPECT-2 study): a randomised controlled trial. *Lancet* 2002;360:109–13.

Van Houwelingen JC. Shrinkage and penalized likelihood methods to improve diagnostic accuracy. *Stat Neerl* 2001;55:17–34.

Van Houwelingen HC, Arends LR, Stijnen T. Advanced methods in meta-analysis: multivariate approach and meta-regression. *Stat Med* 2002;21:589–624.

Van Houwelingen JC, Le Cessie S. Predictive value of statistical models. *Stat Med* 1990;9:1303–25.

Vandenbroucke JP. What is the best evidence for determining harms of medical treatment? *CMAJ* 2006;174:645–6.

Vandenbroucke JP. When are observational studies as credible as randomised trials? *Lancet* 2004;363:1728–31.

Vandenbroucke JP. Survival and expectation of life from the 1400s to the present. A study of the Knighthood Order of the Golden Fleece. *Am J Epidemiol* 1985; 122:1007–16.

Vandenbroucke JP, Valkenburg HA, Boersma JW, Cats A, Festen JJ, Huber-Bruning O, Rasker J. Oral contraceptives and rheumatoid arthritis: further evidence for a preventive effect. *Lancet* 1982;320:1839–42.

Vergouwe Y, Steyerberg EW, Eijkemans MJ, Habbema JD. Validity of prognostic models: when is a model clinically useful? *Semin Urol Oncol* 2002;20:96–107.

Verhagen AP, de Vet HC, de Bie RA, Kessels AG, Boers M, Knipschild PG. Balneotherapy and quality assessment: interobserver reliability of the Maastricht criteria list and the need for blinded quality assessment. *J Clin Epidemiol* 1998;51: 335–41.

Vural KM, Tasdemir O, Karagoz H, Emir M, Tarcan O, Bayazit K. Comparison of the early results of coronary artery bypass grafting with and without extracorporeal circulation. *Thorac Cardiovasc Surg* 1995;43:320–5.

Watson RJ, Richardson PH. Accessing the literature on outcome studies in group psychotherapy: the sensitivity and precision of MEDLINE and PsycINFO bibliographic database searching. *Br J Med Psychol* 1999a;72(Pt 1):127–34.

Watson RJ, Richardson PH. Identifying randomised controlled trials of cognitive therapy for depression: comparing the efficiency of EMBASE, MEDLINE and PsycINFO bibliographic databases. *Br J Med Psychol* 1999b;72(Pt 4):535–42.

Weijnen CF, Hendriks HA, Hoes AW, Verweij WM, Verheij TJ, de Wit NJ. New immunoassay for the detection of *Helicobacter pylori* infection compared with urease test, 13C breath test and histology: validation in the primary care setting. *J Microbiol Methods* 2001;46:235–40.

Weinberg C, Wacholder S. The design and analysis of case-control studies with biased sampling. *Biometrics* 1990;46:963–75.

Weinberg CR, Sandler DP. Randomized recruitment in case-control studies. *Am J Epidemiol* 1991;134:421–32.

Wells PS, Anderson DR, Bormanis J, Guy F, Mitchell M, Gray L, Clement C, Robinson KS, Lewandowski B. Value of assessment of pretest probability of deep-vein thrombosis in clinical management. *Lancet* 1997;350:1795–8.

Whang Y, Klein JG, Zhang Y, Sieuwerts AM, Look MP, Yang F, Talantov D, Timmermanns M, Meijer-van Gelder ME, Yu J, Jatkoe T, Berns EM, Atkins D, Foekens JA. Gene-expression profiles to predict distant metastasis of lymph-node-negative primary breast cancer. *Lancet* 2005;365:671–9.

Whitehead A. A prospectively planned cumulative meta-analysis applied to a series of concurrent clinical trials. *Stat Med* 1997;16:2901–13.

Whiting P, Rutjes AW, Reitsma JB, Glas AS, Bossuyt PM, Kleijnen J. Sources of variation and bias in studies of diagnostic accuracy: a systematic review. *Ann Intern Med* 2004;140:189–202.

Wilczynski NL, Haynes RB. Robustness of empirical search strategies for clinical content in MEDLINE. *Proc AMIA Symp* 2002;904–8.

Wilczynski NL, Morgan D, Haynes RB. An overview of the design and methods for retrieving high-quality studies for clinical care. *BMC Med Inform Decis Mak* 2005;5:20.

Wilczynski NL, Walker CJ, McKibbon KA, Haynes RB. Quantitative comparison of pre-explosions and subheadings with methodologic search terms in MEDLINE. *Proc Annu Symp Comput Appl Med Care* 1994;905–9.

Willich SN, Lewis M, Lowel H, Arntz HR, Schubert F, Schroder R. Physical exertion as a trigger of acute myocardial infarction. Triggers and Mechanisms of Myocardial Infarction Study Group. *N Engl J Med* 1993;329:1684–90.

Wong SS, Wilczynski NL, Haynes RB. Comparison of top-performing search strategies for detecting clinically sound treatment studies and systematic reviews in MEDLINE and EMBASE. *J Med Libr Assoc* 2006a;94:451–5.

Wong SS, Wilczynski NL, Haynes RB. Optimal CINAHL search strategies for identifying therapy studies and review articles. *J Nurs Scholarsh* 2006b;38:194–9.

Zaffanella LE, Savitz DA, Greenland S, Ebi KL. The residential case-specular method to study wire codes, magnetic fields, and disease. *Epidemiology* 1998;9:16–20.

Zhang L, Ajiferuke I, Sampson M. Optimizing search strategies to identify randomised controlled trials in MEDLINE. *BMC Med Res Methodol* 2006;6:23.

Index